THE FAITH

The Faith

A Symposium of Bible Doctrine

Edited by
Fredk. A. Tatford

40 Beansburn, Kilmarnock, Scotland

ISBN 0 946351 85 6

40 Beansburn, Kilmarnock, Scotland

Printed by Bell & Bain Ltd., Glasgow

FOREWORD

IN view of the number of textbooks and primers on Bible doctrine already in existence, it may be questioned whether there is any justification for adding to the list, but this symposium is not intended to supersede any of the standard works on dogmatic or systematic theology nor to act as a substitute for the more technical treatise needed by the theological student. Its object is rather to provide a simple restatement of Bible truths in language which can be understood by the ordinary reader, and all technical terms and textbook phraseology have, therefore, as far as possible, been avoided.

A symposium naturally differs from a book penned by one writer since a multiple authorship necessarily results in a variety of style and expression—and possibly even of literary and expositional standard. To some readers this may appear a disadvantage but, on the other hand, it may perhaps be argued that the combined witness of so many recognized teachers has a compensatory value.

No book on Bible doctrine can claim to be complete and this symposium is no exception. It will, however, be found to cover the principal doctrines of the Christian faith. A small measure of overlapping has been unavoidable in the case of some chapters but, in such instances, the chapters will be found to be complementary rather than repetitive.

We gratefully acknowledge the invaluable advice and counsel given by brethren who have been consulted on the subject of the book. Not only in Britain, but in America, India, Africa and the Antipodes, brethren have shown a keen interest in the matter. Thanks are particularly due to Dr. Rowland C. Edwards of Australia in this connection.

The whole of the manuscripts have been critically examined by Messrs. F. F. Bruce, G. C. D. Howley, E. W. Rogers and J. B. Watson, in addition to the editor, and the help rendered in this way has been of inestimable value. Despite his many other commitments Mr. J. B. Watson has maintained a close contact at all stages and much has been due to his wisdom and sound commonsense.

Although the contributors are fairly representative, the absence of some names will be regretted. It had been hoped to include contributions by other well-known brethren in Britain and America, but the many demands already made upon their time rendered it impracticable for them to help in this respect. This will explain the absence of papers by those who might otherwise have been expected to have been included as contributors in such a volume.

It is our sincere hope that this book will not only be profitable to older Christians but also be of special help to those who are younger in the faith, and that it will lead to a deeper study of the Scriptures on the part of all readers.

FREDK. A. TATFORD

PREFACE

ALMOST half a century has passed since this book was first published. The contributors have all been called home and perhaps are names which are not now known by many believers today. Why then reprint it? The material it contains and the purpose for which it was intended remain unaffected by the passage of time. It was deemed timely and needful when first published, and is even more appropriate as we cross the threshold of a new millennium, and increasing attacks on the foundational truths of the christian faith. The helpful subjects treated have proved of great benefit to many and our desire in making it available is that it will continue to upbuild and instruct believers of a later generation, and glorify the ONE who is central to all scripture.

September 1999

CONTENTS

CONTENTS

Page

CHAPTER I

The Right Use of Knowledge

KENNETH W. LUCKHURST

IS knowledge always a good thing? Many folk are beginning to have their doubts on this point, in view of the dangers in which increasing scientific knowledge is involving the world at large. The inhabitants of Hiroshima might well question the value of the American's knowledge of the atom. But what of the value of knowledge for those who actually possess it? Is it always a good thing for *them*?

This is one of the points on which the Bible seems to present opposite views. Solomon, for example, exclaims that 'wisdom is more precious than rubies,' and exhorts, 'therefore get wisdom, and with all thy getting, get understanding.' Yet he also declares that 'of making many books there is no end and much study is a weariness of the flesh.' Paul, too, prays that the Philippians 'may abound yet more and more in knowledge and in all judgment'; yet he warns the Corinthians that 'knowledge puffeth up,' and reminds them that God had said that He would 'destroy the wisdom of the wise and bring to nothing the understanding of the prudent.'

We must all have observed the opposite effects of knowledge, of spiritual matters just as much as of other things, in different individuals. There are those whose increasing knowledge seems only to make them clearer in their language, and more gracious, humble, and understanding in their attitude towards other people; and there are those, alas, whose great learning shuts them away in a world of their own, high above their fellows, and makes them crabbed, harsh in their judgment of those who differ from them and difficult to approach.

The same thing can be seen in history. For example, the great increase in the knowledge of Christian doctrine, which was so marked a feature of the movements which originated with St. Francis and St. Dominic, resulted on the one hand in the religious revolution of the Reformation, but on the other in the cruelty and spiritual slavery of the Inquisition and the Counter-Reformation.

I am reminded also of a lecture by G. K. Chesterton to which I once listened in my undergraduate days, in which he propounded (of course from the Roman Catholic point of view) the thesis that whenever in the course of history sections of the Christian church had burst out of what they felt was a spiritual prison, they had invariably ended up by shutting themselves inside a worse prison of their own building. There is an undoubted measure of truth in this view. Time and again the Holy Spirit has impressed some particular truth with great power upon a body of Christians, with dynamic and liberating results. But after a while the same truth, although still staunchly upheld, has seemed to lose its gracious effects, and has in the end become a cold dogma grimly hedging off one section of the Church from another.

It can be admitted that in many of these instances the position is complicated by an admixture of error with the truth. But the fact remains: both the Word of God and experience show that knowledge—knowledge of the truth—can sometimes be a curse instead of a blessing.

This is a point of the greatest importance for each of us as we turn to expositions, such as this book contains, of some of the greatest truths which God has revealed. What will the *effect* of them be on each of us as readers? Will our knowledge of these truths be something 'more precious than rubies' or a mere 'weariness of the flesh'; shall we 'adorn the doctrine' or will it 'puff us up'? The answer—the deciding factor—lies not in the truths, but in us.

As Andrew Murray said, referring to the tree of knowledge in Eden, 'The tempter of Paradise still moves about among men. Knowledge is still his great temptation. How many Christians there are who could confess that their knowledge of divine truth does little for them; it leaves them powerless against the world and sin. It is because they take to themselves God's truth in the power of human wisdom and human thought and wait not for the Spirit of truth to lead them into it. . . . Jesus said, "If any man will come after Me, let him deny himself and follow Me." There is nothing that more needs denying than our own wisdom, the energy of the fleshly mind as it exerts itself in the things of God.' (*The Spirit of Christ*).

The reason for this absolute necessity to wait upon God for *His* instruction arises from the nature of divine truth and the manner in which God has revealed it. In the first place His truth is essentially *personal*. God did not make a single complete revelation (although there is one revelation which eclipses all the others). But He used a variety of agents as His mouthpieces (Hebrews 1. 1). The Bible, accordingly, in which God has caused these various revelations to be recorded, is different from any works of human learning. Although complete in itself, it is not a unified treatise co-ordinating all truth into a single, logical system. It is an inspired record of revelations made through many different men at many different times. Even individual Scriptural terms are differently coloured by the differing background and experience of the various writers. This is not to say that God's truth changes. No other truth is so fixed and sure. Nor is it vague and hazy. No other truth is so positive, definite and accurate, with an edge 'sharper than any two-edged sword.' But its impact is essentially personal, and its target is the individual heart and life. Thus, although the mind is an essential intermediary, the mind without the heart can never properly grasp it, and the heart, if it is to grasp God's truth at all, must by its very nature be submissive to the Author of that truth.

Perhaps we might compare the study of divine truth with that of anatomy as contrasted, say, with mechanical engineering. A handbook of the latter will contain drawings showing exactly what various types of machines are like. There may be thousands of such machines in existence conforming exactly to the drawings in the book. It is possible, therefore, to acquire a very good knowledge of them all simply from a careful and intelligent study of the book. But anatomy is different. A handbook of that subject may be true of all human bodies, yet the drawings which it contains will probably portray *no* human body *exactly*. The handbook, therefore, is a true, and indeed, indispensable guide to the study of the subject, but none of us would trust himself to a surgeon who had only learned his anatomy from a textbook and had not in addition spent many hours on the direct study of actual bodies under the personal instruction of a live demonstrator. And a handbook of divine truth such as this must be similarly used. Theology learned merely from this or any other human book is knowledge of the wrong, the dangerous type. This kind of subject must ultimately be learned direct from the Scriptures under the tuition of the Divine Instructor, and the purpose of the textbook—the highly valuable purpose—is to provide us with finger-posts which put us on the right track; just as Philip pointed the eunuch to Christ—and was sent a long way in order to do it—but the groundwork of his spiritual illumination was the study of the Book of Isaiah under the guidance of the Holy Spirit.

And secondly, because divine truth is personal, it is also *purposive*. God did not reveal it in order to satisfy our intellectual curiosity, and to use it in such a spirit is to abuse one of God's greatest gifts. He intends that every one of these truths should have an effect on us, and the chapters of this book contain, not just a collection of interesting facts, but, potentially, a changed life, and an increase in God's glory thereby, in the case of each reader. However familiar, therefore, we may be, intellectually, with these great teachings, may the perusal of this book be an occasion for us to submit ourselves again to the power which lies within them.

In the words of an old poem about the Bible:

Read not this book in any case
  But with a single eye:
Read not, but first desire God's grace
  To understand thereby.
Pray still in faith with this respect
  To fructify therein;
That knowledge may bring this effect,
  To mortify thy sin.
Then happy thou in all thy life
  Whatso to thee befalls;
Yea, doubly happy shalt thou be,
  When God to death thee calls.

Then it will be possible for each of us to say hereafter with regard to our study of this book, in the words of Ridley, 'of which study, although in time a great part did depart from me, yet the sweete smell thereof I trust I shall carry with me into heaven, for the profite thereof I think I have felt in all my lyfe tyme ever after.'

CHAPTER II

The Scriptures

F. F. BRUCE

THREE hundred years ago the Assembly of Divines at Westminster introduced their best-known summary of Christian doctrine, the *Westminster Shorter Catechism*, with the following three propositions: (1) 'Man's chief end is to glorify God, and to enjoy Him for ever'; (2) 'The Word of God, which is contained in the Scriptures of the Old and New Testaments, is the only rule to direct us how we may glorify and enjoy Him'; (3) 'The Scriptures principally teach what man is to believe concerning God, and what duty God requires of man.'

If it be true, as these three propositions declare, that the Bible is the only means by which we can know and achieve the true purpose of our being, then no special argument is needed to justify giving a statement of the Bible's authority a prominent place in a symposium on the Christian faith. For the Holy Spirit speaking through the Bible is acknowledged by us, in common with all heirs of the Protestant Reformation, as the supreme judge by whom all questions of doctrine are to be adjudicated, and as the only infallible rule of faith and practice.

It might have been expected *a priori* that if God wished to communicate a knowledge of His will and character to men He might have done so in a series of propositions. But in fact He has not done so. We may draw up statements of doctrine and confessions of faith, article by article in logical sequence, and base them firmly on the Bible; but the Bible itself does not take this form.

At first glance, the Bible is seen to fall into two parts of unequal length, known respectively by the not very illuminating names of the Old Testament and the New Testament. But if for the misleading word Testament we substitute the word Covenant,[1]

[1] Gk. *diathēkē* may mean either 'covenant' or 'testament.' In early Latin Christian literature it was represented by both *instrumentum* and *testamentum*, but the rendering that prevailed was *testamentum*, whence 'testament' became the regular equivalent of *diathēkē* in English.

and then think of the Bible as divided into the Books of the Old Covenant and the Books of the New Covenant, we shall come to a much closer realization of what the Bible is. It is, in fact, a record of God's revelation of Himself among men, culminating in the incarnation, death and exaltation of Jesus Christ His Son, and intimately bound up with the relations established by God with His covenant-people—the nation of Israel in earlier times, and the Christian community in the new age which was inaugurated by Christ. There is an organic unity between these two groups of people, in that Jesus (who is the very embodiment of God's revelation) is both Israel's Messiah and Head of the Christian Church, while His first followers represent both the last faithful remnant of the old covenant-people and the nucleus of the new covenant-people.

Professor A. M. Hunter, in his book *The Unity of the New Testament*, finds that this unity consists in the fact that the New Testament tells the story of God's salvation, in relation to the Bringer of salvation, the way of salvation, and the heirs of salvation. And this is equally true of the Bible as a whole. 'Holy Scripture containeth all things necessary for salvation,' runs the sixth of the Thirty-nine Articles. It does not contain all things necessary (say) for a knowledge of the physical universe (although it insists that the physical universe is itself the work of God and a witness to His everlasting power and divinity: cf. Rom. 1. 20); but then that was not the object for which the Biblical revelation was given. It was given to fallen humanity in order that we might come to know God as a just God and a Saviour. And God revealed Himself thus by personally intervening in the course of human history through mighty acts which declared His nature and His will, and which found their consummation in the accomplishment of the world's redemption through the crucifixion and resurrection of Christ.

The Bible therefore begins by telling of the preparation of the world for the emergence of a chosen people with whom God entered into an intimate covenant-relationship in order that they might know Him personally and communicate His knowledge to other nations. This nation (the Bible goes on to narrate) He redeemed for Himself in the mighty events of their deliverance from Egypt and their entry into Canaan, and in spite of their general unfaithfulness to the terms of His covenant He dealt with them in mercy and judgment, preparing the way for the advent on earth of His Son, Who on the human plane was to be born of that nation. To them also from time to time He sent His messengers, from Moses, their first lawgiver, through Samuel and all the prophets. These men interpreted to them the significance of God's mighty self-revealing acts, and taught them the knowledge of His will in further ways, interpreting from the divine angle the events of their own time and pointing forward also to the time when God would fulfil His promises to them by sending the Messiah-Saviour. In the words of the prophets, then, God revealed Himself as well as in His mighty acts; and it is worth noting that in the Hebrew Bible most of the historical books of the Old Testament are enumerated among the prophetical books equally with the books which directly record the words of the prophets. The history of Israel in the Old Testament is told from the prophetic viewpoint. History and prophecy alike are recorded with a forward-looking view. The prophets, who were the authors of histories and prophecies alike, composed both under the inspiration of God with a view to that day of fulfilment of which they were dimly aware when they predicted, as Peter puts it, 'the sufferings of Christ and the subsequent glory' (1 Peter 1. 11, R.S.V.).[1]

The Old Testament is indispensable for a proper understanding of the New, but it cannot be understood itself except in the light of the New. Emil Brunner has compared the Old Testament to the first half of a sentence and the New Testament to the second half; each half requires the other and both are necessary for the meaning of the whole sentence. The mighty deeds and prophetic words by which God made Himself known to Israel, and which have been recorded for our learning in the Old Testament, were the earlier stages in a series of deeds and words which were destined to be summed up in the deeds and words of Christ. And as the Old Testament is the record of the preparatory revelation, the New Testament is the record of the fulfilment in Christ. The mighty deeds of God wrought through Christ are His supreme revelation to men: in them His salvation, concerning which the

[1]R.S.V.—American Revised Standard Version, 1946.

prophets inquired and searched diligently, has been brought near. And in the words of Christ we have the message of 'a prophet mighty in deed and word' (Luke 24. 19), who was more than simply the last of the series of Israel's prophets, being Himself the One of whom the prophets spoke and the One whose Spirit spoke through them. They *uttered* the word of God; He *is* the Word of God. They said, 'Thus saith *the Lord*'; but He said, '*I* say unto you.' He is the One to whom law and prophecy bear witness; at His advent they recede, for in Him their witness is completed. Moses and Elijah conversed with Him on the holy mount touching His coming decease at Jerusalem—that greater Exodus of which the Exodus of Moses' day was a foreshadowing, just as the redemption associated with the blood of the paschal lamb pointed forward to the cosmic redemption achieved when Christ our Passover was sacrificed for us. Then, having conversed with Him thus and crowned their witness to His glory, Moses and Elijah disappeared into the cloud, which passed to reveal to the disciples no man save Jesus only. For He is the sum and substance of Old Testament revelation (Luke 9. 28-36. The Gk. word translated 'decease' in verse 31 is *exodos*. The subject discussed on the holy mount was the subject which had formed the burden of O.T. Scripture).

The story of 'all that Jesus began both to do and to teach' (Acts 1. 1) was the burden of the apostolic testimony after His ascension. The apostolic preaching (*kērygma*) was the good news of God's saving activity in the passion and triumph of His Son; the apostolic teaching (*didachē*) which was imparted to those who had believed the good news was based on the teaching of Jesus Himself.

But He told His disciples plainly that while He was with them on earth He could not teach them all that they needed to know. The great saving events themselves had to take place before they would be able to receive all that He desired to teach them. And for this purpose, among others, He sent them His Spirit. On the eve of His betrayal He promised His disciples that after His departure from them He would send His *alter ego*, the Holy Spirit, to bring to their remembrance all that He Himself had told them; to guide them into all the truth, and to show them things to come (John 14. 26; 16. 12-14). While these promises are not restricted to any one generation of His followers, they found a special fulfilment in the first generation, and as a result of this special fulfilment we have the Books of the New Covenant. Our New Testament is the written deposit of the apostles' witness to Christ—their narration both of the events which accompanied and followed His coming into the world, and of all that He taught, including not only what He began to teach them in the days of His flesh, but also what He continued to teach them later from heaven by His Spirit. 'The testimony of Jesus is the spirit of prophecy' in Old Testament and New Testament alike (Rev. 19. 10: 'The Spirit of prophecy is the Spirit of Jesus, Who must needs testify of Jesus.'—H. B. Swete, *in loco*). The prophets of Old Testament times testified to Him in advance; the apostles in New Testament times testified to Him as the One whom they had seen and heard and touched—the incarnate Word of life. The prophets knew but dimly the circumstances under which their words would be fulfilled (1 Peter 1. 10-12); the apostles, who lived at the time of their fulfilment, spoke unhesitatingly as those upon whom the end of the ages had come: 'This is that which was spoken by the prophet' (Acts 2. 16).

If we ask how the Holy Spirit so controlled those prophets and apostles as to give their words the unique quality of inspiration which they possess, we must answer in the opening words of the Epistle to the Hebrews, 'in many and various ways' (Heb. 1. 1, R.S.V. The words so translated, Gk. *polymerōs kai polytropōs*, are the first words of the Epistle). And in all the variety of these ways their individuality of thought and diction remained unimpaired. The paradox of Biblical inspiration has been well expressed in these words of Bishop Handley Moule:

> 'He who chose the writers of the Holy Scriptures, many men scattered over many ages, used them each in his surroundings and in his character, yet so as to harmonize them all in the Book which, while many, is one. He used them with the sovereign skill of Deity. And that skilful use meant that He used their whole being, which He had made, and their whole circumstances, which He had ordered. . . . He can take a human personality, made in His own image, pregnant, formative, causative, in all its living thought, sensibility and will, and can throw it freely upon its task of thinking and expression—and

behold, the product will be His; His matter, His thought, His exposition, His Word, living and abiding for ever' (*The Epistle of St. Paul to the Romans*, Expositor's Bible, 1893, pp. 7 f.).

The Biblical writers were not mere penmen or secretaries; they were authors in the full sense of the word, yet authors under the overruling influence of God the Holy Spirit, the Primary Author. Divine control does not suppress a man's faculties and talents, but raises them to their highest capacity.

The Holy Spirit, who spoke through the prophets and who indwelt Jesus in permanent fulness, is the same Spirit whom Jesus, after His ascension, bestowed upon His disciples to reveal to them more fully the things concerning Himself. And these things He also reveals to us as we read the witness of those men of old who spoke from God as they were borne along by the Holy Spirit. For the Holy Spirit is not only the Primary Author of Scripture, but also, in Abraham Kuyper's phrase, the Perpetual Author, continually speaking through the Word to the believing reader and unfolding fresh meaning from it. This abiding vitality is one of the outstanding evidences of the Bible's divine character. No one generation can exhaust its significance. It is as true in our day as in John Robinson's that 'the Lord has more truth yet to break forth out of His holy Word.'[1] Every Scripture, says the apostle (2 Tim. 3. 16), is 'God-breathed' (Gk. *theopneustos*), and just as Adam became a living soul when God breathed into his nostrils the breath of life (Gen. 2. 7), so the 'God-breathed' writings are also living, and life-giving as well. The Spirit who spoke in ancient days to and through the prophets and apostles still speaks to us through the written record of that revelation, saying, 'Hear, and your soul shall live.' In the Bible, therefore, we find not only what the Spirit said to the Churches of the first century, but what He is still saying to those of the twentieth. But what He says to us is in perfect harmony with what He said to them. 'The Holy Ghost,' as John Knox said to Queen Mary, 'is never contrarious to Himself' (*History of the Reformation in Scotland, ed.* C. J. Guthrie, 1898, p. 280).

[1] From the address to the Pilgrim Fathers on the eve of their departure from Leyden in 1620, reported in D. Neal, *History of the Puritans*, ii (1732), p. 129, on the basis of Edward Winslow's 1646 account, and frequently quoted since; see article 'John Robinson' in *Dictionary of National Biography*.

The Scriptures, then, inspired and interpreted by the Holy Spirit, are the rule of faith, by which everything that is commended to our belief with regard to ultimate realities is to be tested. And as they are the rule of faith, so they are also the rule of practice, being 'profitable for teaching, for reproof, for correction, and for training in righteousness, that the man of God may be complete, equipped for every good work' (2 Tim. 3. 16 f., R.S.V.). But when we call the Bible the rule of faith and practice, we do not mean that any part of it can be taken and applied in this way, without regard to its context. The inspiration of the Bible does not imply that all the actions recorded in it, even those of good men, have the divine approval, or that all the words reported, even those of wise men, have the divine authority. Abraham's equivocation about his relationship to Sarah, for example, is not a model for us to imitate, nor is every argument of Job's friends an utterance of the Most High. There are many such deeds and words preserved in the Biblical narrative which are not part of God's revelation of Himself; they are, however, part of the context in which that revelation was given, and they were written down for our instruction.

Much harm has been caused by isolating parts of the Bible from the whole. *All Scripture* is the context in the light of which *any Scripture* is to be understood and applied; the earlier stages in the revelation appear in their true perspective when viewed in the context of the completed revelation in Christ. The Scriptures, in fact, cannot be properly interpreted or used apart from Christ and the testimony which they bear to Him. 'It is they,' He said Himself, 'that bear witness to Me' (John 5. 39, R.S.V.); and only by remembering that shall we be able to handle the Word of truth aright.

Holy Scripture, we believe, is sufficient for the purpose for which it was given—to teach us the way of salvation through faith in Christ and to show us how we ought to live as those who have received this salvation. Is it then immaterial whether it is accurate or not in other matters, which it touches incidentally? This question has been raised, for instance, with regard to questions of physical science and general history. In the former case, the relation of the creation narratives of Genesis to the ascertained conclusions of scientific research is still debated from time to time. It is obvious, at any rate, that the Biblical account of the origin of the world is notably free from the grotesque and polytheistic features which mark most ancient cosmogonies. That the *language* in which it records the beginning of things should differ from the language of modern science goes without saying. When the Biblical language on these matters is criticised as 'pre-Copernican,' one can only ask in wonder what else could be expected. Again, to imagine that we should expect (say) complete conformity between the creative days of the first chapter of Genesis and the geological order as commonly reconstructed nowadays would be to attribute to twentieth-century science a finality which no reputable scientist would wish to claim for it. The Genesis cosmogony has a dignity all its own; and if we could go back through time to the birth of the world we should find ourselves passing in reverse through stages not dissimilar to those successively described in the first chapter of the Bible. It is noteworthy, too, that the origins of matter, life and mind, for which no satisfactory explanation has yet been given by scientific investigation, are all three ascribed in the Genesis narrative to the creative act of God. (This is not to say that God's creative power must be sought only in the gaps unbridged as yet by scientific discovery—gaps which may be closed in our faces to-morrow. 'His tender mercies are over all His works,' and His activity extends continuously throughout all space and time.) Above all, these opening verses of the Bible have their chief value for us in that they emphasize that the God of the Bible, who in the fulness of time sent forth His Son, is the Maker of heaven and earth, and that the race of men, in which the Son of God in due course became incarnate, was in the beginning created in God's image and after His likeness.

As for the historical element which bulks so largely in the Bible, it is particularly important to know how far we can regard it as a trustworthy account of events that really happened, for the simple reason that the Bible represents God as a God who has revealed Himself in history. Our faith is an historical faith; it is based on something which God is said to have done at a particular point in time, when 'Jesus Christ, His only Son, our Lord . . . suffered under Pontius Pilate.' People who say that the Christian religion would not be greatly affected even if it could be proved that Jesus Christ never lived are not talking about a religion of which the Bible knows anything.

There is one event above all others where the supernatural claims of Christianity are so interwoven with the historical process that, if once the historicity of that event is established, the whole of Christianity is logically established at the same time; whereas, if that event could be proved unhistorical, the whole fabric of the Gospel would collapse. That event is the resurrection of Christ. Some theologians regard this as a purely 'theological' event which cannot be proved by historical evidence but must be received by faith alone; others characterize it as a 'myth' (in the proper and not the popular sense of the word) which embodies certain eternal values. But these conceptions of the nature of Christ's resurrection are quite inadequate to convey the true significance of that event, and fall far short of the way in which it is presented in the earliest apostolic preaching. The apostles, who claimed to be eye-witnesses of their Lord's resurrection, described it as something that really happened, and they appealed to the recognized laws of evidence in support of their claim. The circumstances of the event were so public in character that the resurrection narratives of the New Testament lend themselves particularly well to examination of this kind; and we should welcome the closest scrutiny of the record, as the apostles themselves did, by the severest canons of literary and historical criticism. The apostles staked everything on the reality of this event—not only the truth of the message they preached but life itself. And indeed, the more the whole matter is sifted, the more convincingly does it appear that the only account which satisfies all the evidence is the account which the Bible gives—that Jesus of Nazareth, who died on the cross, returned to life the third day thereafter.

But if this is so, the other supernatural features in the Bible story present no great problem. The resurrection is presented as the crowning instance of God's mighty self-revealing works; no reader need be stumbled by the presence of the miraculous in the record of those works once he has accepted the truth of this supreme miracle.

The whole Biblical record, in fact, responds astonishingly well to historical research. We grant that the presentation and proportion of Biblical history differ from those of ordinary history, in view of the distinctive purpose for which Biblical history was written. But Biblical history has had an ever-increasing flood of new light thrown upon it in recent years, mainly from archæological and similar research, and while such research is in the nature of things incapable of confirming the details of the narrative, it does confirm the general picture which the Bible gives us of Near Eastern history, from the first century A.D. back to the fourth millennium B.C., to the picture of antediluvian civilization which we find at the end of the fourth chapter of Genesis.[1]

We welcome all the help which can be given in these ways to the understanding of the Scriptures. We shall appreciate the Biblical record all the more for being able to read it against its contemporary background. While it has a message for every age, we shall be all the better able to learn its message for our own age by seeing the various parts in the light of the age in which each appeared. We wish to be as sure as possible, too, of the faithful transmission and translation of the original text, and we highly value the selfless labours that so many have expended on these important matters. We acknowledge that historical, philological and textual studies have a necessary and honourable place by way of introduction to the exegesis of the Scriptures. It is all to the good that studies like these should throw light on the sacred narrative and help to dispel difficulties which for some readers appear to stand in the way of their accepting the Biblical testimony. But it is not by these means that the real authority of the Bible is established.

God is His own interpreter; He also can best vindicate Himself. If God speaks, His word must be self-evidencing; we cannot suppose that He is dependent on anything other than His own authority to establish His word as being indeed His word. When the prophets spoke for God, the divine origin of their message

[1] *Cf.* such a statement as this by W. F. Albright: 'There can be no doubt that archæology has confirmed the substantial historicity of the Old Testament tradition' (*Archæology and the Religion of Israel* [1941], p. 176). This confirmation goes back through patriarchal times, upon which a flood of light has been thrown in the last 25 years, to the Deluge and even earlier; for archæological evidence bearing on Gen. 4. 16-22 *cf.* J. G. Duncan, *New Light on Hebrew Origins* (1936), pp. 15 ff. As regards the N.T. period I may be permitted to refer to my little book, *Are the New Testament Documents Reliable?* (3rd ed., 1950).

was discerned by those who had the requisite spiritual capacity; when the apostles wrote, they challenged similar recognition in words such as these: 'If any one thinks that he is a prophet, or spiritual, he should acknowledge that what I am writing to you is a command of the Lord' (1 Cor. 14. 37, R.S.V.). The Spirit of God, under whose inspiration the words were first spoken or written, is the One who imparts the power to recognize in these words His word. The things of the Spirit of God are spiritually discerned (cf. 1 Cor. 2. 14), and one of the gifts of the Spirit is 'the ability to distinguish between spirits' (1 Cor. 12. 10, R.S.V.). The Reformers thus rightly maintained that the final and convincing proof of the divine authority and truth of Scripture is provided by the inward witness of the Holy Spirit. (Cf. Calvin's *Institutes*, I, vii. 4, 5.) The Spirit of God, that is to say, bears witness within the believing heart, with an assurance that no counter-argument can shake, that this is indeed His own word. This He does both in the individual believer (which is the justification of the Protestant insistence on the right and duty of private judgment) and in the believing community. It is plain that, in according unique recognition to the books of the New Testament canon, the early Christians were guided by a wisdom higher than their own. The test of canonicity is this testimony which the Spirit bears, within the Church, to the Scriptures as being His own word. This is as true in principle of the Old Testament canon as of the New Testament canon, but in the case of the Old Testament canon there is the further consideration that it is confirmed by the direct testimony, in word and practice, of our Lord and His apostles.

How right and appropriate, then, are the words which, in the British coronation ceremony, the Primate of All England uses when he gives the sovereign a copy of the Bible: 'Our gracious King; we present you with this Book, the most valuable thing that this world affords. Here is wisdom; this is the royal law; these are the lively oracles of God.'

We began with a quotation from the Westminster Divines. When these men drew up the *Westminster Confession of Faith* in 1647, they devoted their first chapter to the theme 'Of the Holy Scripture'; and that chapter is so admirable an embodiment of 'what oft was thought, but ne'er so well expressed' that we cannot conclude our own discussion of this subject in any better way than by reproducing its ten theses:

'1. Although the light of nature, and the works of creation and providence, do so far manifest the goodness, wisdom, and power of God, as to leave men inexcusable; yet they are not sufficient to give that knowledge of God, and of His will, which is necessary unto salvation: therefore it pleased the Lord, at sundry times, and in divers manners, to reveal Himself, and to declare His will unto His Church; and afterwards, for the better preserving and propagating of the truth, and for the more sure establishment and comfort of the Church against the corruption of the flesh, and the malice of Satan and of the world, to commit the same wholly unto writing; which maketh the holy scripture to be most necessary; those former ways of God's revealing His will unto His people being now ceased.

'2. Under the name of Holy Scripture, or the Word of God written, are now contained all the books of the Old and New Testaments, which are these [here follows a list of the 39 books of the Old Testament and the 27 books of the New Testament]. All which are given by inspiration of God, to be the rule of faith and life.

'3. The Books commonly called Apocrypha, not being of divine inspiration, are no part of the canon of the scripture; and therefore are of no authority in the Church of God, nor to be any otherwise approved, or made use of, than other human writings.[1]

'4. The authority of the holy scripture, for which it ought to be believed and obeyed, dependeth not upon the testimony of any man or church, but wholly upon God (who is truth itself), the author thereof; and therefore it is to be received, because it is the Word of God.

'5. We may be moved and induced by the testimony of the Church to an high and reverend esteem of the holy scripture; and the heavenliness of the matter, the efficacy of the doctrine, the

[1] The 'apocryphal' books never formed part of the Hebrew Bible, and were not treated as authoritative by our Lord and His apostles, as the books of the Hebrew Bible were; they were not regarded as canonical by the Palestinian Jews, nor yet (contrary to what is generally believed) by the Alexandrian Jews. The first people to accord them canonical status were Greek-speaking Christians, who probably did so because they found them in close association with the O.T. books in the Septuagint version.

majesty of the style, the consent of all the parts, the scope of the whole (which is to give all glory to God), the full discovery it makes of the only way of man's salvation, the many other incomparable excellencies, and the entire perfection thereof, are arguments whereby it doth abundantly evidence itself to be the word of God; yet notwithstanding, our full persuasion and assurance of the infallible truth, and divine authority thereof, is from the inward work of the Holy Spirit, bearing witness by and with the word in our hearts.

'6. The whole counsel of God, concerning all things necessary for His own glory, man's salvation, faith, and life, is either expressly set down in scripture, or by good and necessary consequence may be deduced from scripture: unto which nothing at any time is to be added, whether by new revelations of the Spirit, or traditions of men. Nevertheless, we acknowledge the inward illumination of the Spirit of God to be necessary for the saving understanding of such things as are revealed in the word; and that there are some circumstances concerning the worship of God, and government of the Church, common to human actions and societies, which are to be ordered by the light of nature and Christian prudence, according to the general rules of the word, which are always to be observed.[1]

'7. All things in scripture are not alike plain in themselves, nor alike clear unto all; yet those things which are necessary to be known, believed, and observed, for salvation, are so clearly propounded and opened in some place of scripture or other, that not only the learned, but the unlearned, in a due use of the ordinary means, may attain unto a sufficient understanding of them.

'8. The Old Testament in Hebrew (which was the native language of the people of God of old), and the New Testament in Greek (which at the time of the writing of it was most generally known to the nations), being immediately inspired by God, and by His singular care and providence kept pure in all ages, are therefore authentical; so as in all controversies of religion, the Church is finally to appeal unto them. But because these

[1] This does not mean that the light of nature and Christian prudence can serve as substitutes for the directions of Scripture in these matters, but that they serve as guides in our application of these directions to varying times and circumstances, that the details of church government and divine service may be carried out decently and in order.

original tongues are not known to all the people of God, who have right unto and interest in the scriptures, and are commanded, in the fear of God, to read and search them, therefore they are to be translated into the vulgar language of every nation unto which they come, that the Word of God dwelling plentifully in all, they may worship Him in an acceptable manner, and, through patience and comfort of the scriptures, may have hope.

'9. The infallible rule of interpretation of scripture is the scripture itself; and therefore, when there is a question about the true and full sense of any scripture (which is not manifold, but one), it must be searched and known by other places that speak more clearly.

'10. The supreme Judge, by which all controversies of religion are to be determined, and all decrees of councils, opinions of ancient writers, doctrines of men, and private spirits, are to be examined, and in whose sentence we are to rest, can be no other but the Holy Spirit speaking in the scripture.'

CHAPTER III

The Holy Trinity

W. E. VINE

THE word Trinity is not found in Scripture, but was used as early as the second century to express conveniently the Scriptural doctrine that, in the undivided unity of the divine nature of the Godhead, there are the personal distinctions of Father, Son and Holy Spirit, each possessed of complete and perfect personality. They are spoken of by some as 'Persons,' and objection has been raised to the use of this word as being non-Scriptural and as suggesting the existence of three Gods; and the objection holds good if the term is used in its customary modern sense. But since the distinctions are not those of essence, but are personal, and are distinctions of unity, and if the word 'person' is understood as simply signifying an intelligent being or agent possessed of reasoning faculty, it may be regarded as not so exceptionable, although its use is not really necessary.

It has sometimes been suggested that there are faint glimmerings of the truth in the religions of the East, but we must emphasise that the doctrine of the Trinity is peculiar to the Scriptures. As Hodge points out, 'The Triad of the ancient world is only a philosophical statement of the pantheistic theory which underlies all the religions of antiquity. With the Hindus, simple, undeveloped, primal being, without consciousness or attributes, is called Brahm. This being, as unfolding itself in the actual world, is Vishnu; as returning into the abyss of unconscious being, it is Shiva. In Buddhism, we find essentially the same ideas, in a more dualistic form. Buddhism makes more of a distinction between God, or the spiritual principle of all things, and nature. The soul of man is a part, or an existence-form, of this essential essence, whose destiny is that it may be freed from nature and lost in the infinite unknown.' The mythological imaginations of false religions are no reflection of the truth and we agree with Hodge's conclusion that 'these trinitarian formulas have no analogy with the Scriptural doctrine of the Trinity, and serve neither to explain nor to confirm it.' The full revelation of God is given in the Bible alone.

Any setting forth of the truth relating to the Trinity must be based upon the fundamental doctrine that there is only one God. It is well to remind ourselves in the first place of the testimony of Scripture in this respect. Moses instructed Israel that God's dealings with them in bringing them out of Egypt had this design, that they might know that 'Jehovah, He is God; there is none else beside Him.' 'Hear, O Israel,' he says, 'Jehovah our God is one Jehovah' (Deut. 4. 35; 6. 4). God Himself declares, 'I am Jehovah; that is My Name: and My glory will I not give to another.' 'Before Me there was no God formed, neither shall there be after Me.' 'I am the first, and I am the last, and besides Me there is no God' (Isa. 42. 8; 43. 10; 44. 6; cf. Zech. 14. 9). For any created being to lay claim to possession of the attributes and powers of Godhood is attempted and presumptuous usurpation. Since all other than God Himself, the Creator, are creatures, He is righteous in requiring their recognition of their relation to Him as such.

The Scriptures teach, however, that, while there is not a plurality of Gods, there is a certain plurality in the Godhead. There is one God, but that God subsists in Three Persons, Father, Son and Holy Spirit, and the Scriptures testify to the essential Deity not only of the Father but also of the Son and of the Holy Spirit.

The plurality is not easy to define, and the Bible does not define it, a fact which is but consistent with the supernatural character of its teachings. It is perfectly clear that the Three, the Father, the Son, the Holy Spirit, are distinguished from One Another as Personal Agents, each at the same time being possessed of the essential attributes of Deity. The Father is not the Son, and neither the Father nor the Son is the Holy Spirit, yet they are the same in substance and are equal in power, honour and glory. Since the divine essence is common to all Three Persons, it necessarily follows that all the divine attributes belong equally to each. Omnipotence, omniscience and omnipresence can be predicated of all Three. Holiness, equity, justice, truth, grace, immutability, and eternity characterize all Three.

No one of the Three is simply an attribute, or a mode of action, or an operation, or an influence. There are distinctions in the Three. Each has a divine personality. They hear, speak, will, act, love, etc., but all have an uncreated divine nature eternally antecedent to all created beings. Each is possessed of infinite knowledge, will, love and power, and all Three are in perfect and inseparable unity. They have one mind and will and purpose and are ever in full harmony. Any distinction lies within this essential unity, neither modifying it nor usurping its place. While there are differences in personality and relation, there are not degrees of Deity. The same honour and worship are paid to each; all are described as responsible for the work of creation; all are supreme in the realms of heaven and earth.

In regard to the question of relation, the Father is the One who 'sent' the Son, the One who 'gave' Him. The Son is the One who came from the Father, became incarnate, fulfilled the Father's will, gave up His life in propitiatory sacrifice, was raised from the dead, and ascended to the right hand of the Father, becoming the Mediator and Intercessor; He is coming again to receive His saints to Himself, and coming in glory to establish His millennial kingdom (1 Thess. 4. 14-17; 2 Thess. 1. 10; Rev. 19. 20). The Holy Spirit is He who was sent by the Father and the Son on the day of Pentecost, who dwells in the bodies of believers, acts for their welfare and convicts the world of sin, righteousness and judgment (Acts 2; John 16. 8-11).

There is quite clearly a subordination of the Persons of the Trinity in regard to the mode of subsistence and operation, but a subordination which does not imply inferiority. The Scriptures teach that the Son is of the Father and that the Spirit is of the Father and the Son. They also indicate that the Father operates through the Son, and the Father and the Son through the Spirit. Certain acts appropriate to one Person are never predicated of the Others. It has been said, for example, that generation belongs exclusively to the Father, filiation to the Son, and procession to the Spirit. Again, the 'Father preserves all things, the Son upholds all things, and the Spirit is the source of all life. The Father creates, elects and calls, the Son redeems, and the Spirit sanctifies.'

It is a significant fact that, while One God and only One is the object of worship and adoration, the Son of God is addressed or spoken of in similar terms of worship and adoration as God (John 20. 28). Further, while there are attributes, prerogatives and functions which are revealed as belonging to Deity, these attributes, prerogatives and functions are ascribed not only to God the Father and to the Son, but likewise to the Holy Spirit, and all this is maintained in the Scriptures consistently with the fact that there is only one God.

The Scriptures, while ascribing to each of the Three the attributes and functions which belong exclusively to Deity, yet do so always in a way which forbids anything like polytheism or tritheism, or any such idea as that divine functions are merely delegated by the Father to the Son or to the Holy Spirit. The Biblical teaching that there are Personal and Divine distinctions in the Trinity of the Godhead is a testimony against the error of Sabellianism, which denies any such distinction, and teaches that the terms Father, Son and Holy Spirit simply represent God under different aspects. That error was taught by Sabellius in the third century.

Again, the teaching of Scripture concerning the Trinity is likewise a testimony against the error of Arianism, which maintains that the Godhead consists of one eternal Person, and that the Son and the Holy Spirit were created by Him, an error promulgated by Arius in the fourth century. It is, of course, equally a witness against heresies of the present day, such as the teachings of Unitarianism, Christadelphianism, Swedenborgianism, Russellism, etc.

There are several indications in the Old Testament of the fact of the Trinity. The names of God are frequently used in the plural forms—and with a singular verb on occasions. Plural pronouns are used by God in speaking of Himself. 'And God said, Let Us make man in Our image, after Our likeness.' 'And Jehovah God said, The man is become as one of Us.' 'Let Us go down, and there confound their language' (Gen. 1. 26; 3. 22; 11. 7). 'And I heard the voice of the Lord saying, Whom shall I send, and who will go for Us?' This use is not simply the plural of majesty. The passage in Isaiah 6, describing the prophet's vision of the glory of the Lord, speaks of Him as 'the King, Jehovah of hosts' (Isa. 6. 8). The Apostle John declares that the glory seen by Isaiah was that of Christ (John 12. 41). Paul states that the message given to the prophet was that of the Holy Spirit (Acts 28. 25). Twice in Isaiah the Son associates the Spirit with Himself and the Father: 'The Lord God hath sent Me (the Messiah) and His Spirit' (the correct order as in the R.V.). Again, 'the Spirit of the Lord God is upon Me, because Jehovah has anointed Me' (Isa. 48. 16; 61. 1).

In the New Testament the intimations are even clearer. At our Lord's baptism, for instance, as the Son stood in the River Jordan to be baptised of John, the Father's voice was heard, declaring His complete approbation of the Son, whilst, at the same time, the Holy Spirit descended from heaven in the form of a dove to abide upon the Lord.

In that marvellous discourse in John 14-16, the Lord referred to both the Father and the Spirit in terms which indicated quite plainly their personality and divinity.

The Lord's commission concerning baptism was, 'Go ye therefore and make disciples of all nations, baptising them into the name of the Father and of the Son and of the Holy Spirit' (Matt. 28. 19) —not the *names*, but the 'name', a plain intimation of the unity of the Three in the Godhead. The Triune benediction with which the Apostle Paul closes the Second Epistle to the Corinthians provides another striking instance, and here there is a change in the order: 'The grace of the Lord Jesus Christ, and the love of God, and the communion of the Holy Spirit be with you all' (2 Cor. 13. 14). 'God sent forth the Spirit of His Son into our hearts' (Gal. 4. 6). This phrase, 'the Spirit of His Son,' does not mean the character, purpose, or general sentiment of sonship; it is to be understood in the sense demanded by the parallel passage in Rom. 8. 16, where the Spirit is said to bear witness with our Spirit; that is the function of a person, an intelligent and active agent.

In the Epistle to the Ephesians the Three are associated in a varied order: 'Through Him (Christ) we both have our access in one Spirit unto the Father' (Eph. 2. 18). 'In whom (Christ) ye also are builded together for a habitation of God in the Spirit' (Eph. 2. 22). The apostle prays 'That He (the Father) would grant you . . . that ye may be strengthened with power through His Spirit . . . that Christ may dwell in your hearts by faith' (Eph.

3. 16, 17). 'There is one body and one Spirit . . . one Lord . . . one God and Father' (Eph. 4. 4-6). 'Be filled with the Spirit . . . making melody with your heart to the Lord; giving thanks always for all things in the name of our Lord Jesus Christ to God even the Father' (Eph. 5. 18-20). In Rev. 1. 4, 5, the Seven Spirits can only mean the Holy Spirit in His sevenfold plenitude of power. In the order of mention there He comes between the Father and Jesus Christ.

The relation of the Spirit of God to Christ the Son of God, so constantly operating in and through Him in the days of His flesh, has an important bearing upon the relation between the Spirit and the believer. He who wrought in the conception of 'that Holy Thing' in the womb of Mary is the One through whose instrumentality a person becomes regenerate. The life which the Spirit thus imparts is the life of the risen Christ; 'he that hath the Son hath the life' (John 5. 12). Christ is his life. A person is thus united to Christ, and is to 'grow up in all things into Him, who is the head' (Eph. 4. 16). Joined to the Lord he is one spirit (1 Cor. 6. 17), and this oneness is imparted and maintained by the indwelling Spirit. In all this 'there is one God and Father of all, who is over all, and through all and in all' (Eph. 4. 6).

Thus, in inseparable operation, the Trinity of Divine Personalities in the one Godhead act for, and in, and through true believers. The Father and the Son receive their worship and their love, their trust, their willing and devoted obedience and service, and the Holy Spirit effects all this through His gracious work within (Phil. 3. 3, R.V.). Without His power and ministry nothing can be done, and all self-efforts on their part are futile and vain. The supreme validity of the claims and operations of the Triune God is manifested in the happiness and true prosperity of those who recognize them. All who bow to these claims, acknowledging with gratitude what has been, and is being, wrought for them by the Father, the Son and the Holy Spirit, and own the divine will as the law of their lives, find therein their utmost satisfaction and joy, and their highest possible welfare. This, after all, is the great compelling evidence of the truth of the doctrine of the Holy Trinity.

CHAPTER IV

The Fatherhood of God

A. RENDLE SHORT

MANY years ago, I heard the preacher at a chapel in a Cornish seaside resort declare that the universal Fatherhood of God and the universal brotherhood of man is the outstanding theme of the New Testament. Dr. Torrey, in his very valuable book, *What the Bible Teaches*, says (p. 299), 'The doctrine of the universal Fatherhood of God is utterly unscriptural and untrue.' Obviously these opinions cannot both be true. They both over-simplify a real problem.

Neither in Scripture nor in common parlance does the term 'father' necessarily imply paternity in the physical sense. Paul, for example, refers to Timothy as his 'own son in the faith' (1 Tim. 1. 2). In the Old Testament, the students of the prophetical schools were termed 'sons of the prophets' (1 Kings 20. 35; 2 Kings 2. 3; 4. 1). Indeed, it was the custom for any teacher to be called 'father' by his scholars and also a master to be so described by his servants (2 Kings 2. 12; 5. 13; 6. 21). Those who followed a certain leader were called his sons and he in turn was called their father, e.g. Jabal was called 'the father of such as dwell in tents and of such as have cattle,' and his brother Jubal was referred to as 'the father of all such as handle the harp and organ' (Gen. 4. 20, 21), whilst our Lord told the Jews who boasted that Abraham was their father that, since they practised the works of the devil, he was their father (John 8. 39, 44). Again, objects of worship were termed 'father' (Jer. 2. 27), and persons who were respected, particularly those who were older in years, received the same designation, e.g., Stephen addressed the council before whom he stood as 'Men, brethren and fathers' (Acts 7. 2) and Paul addressed the tumultuous crowd at Jerusalem in the same terms (Acts 22. 1). Parental authority and supremacy were normally unquestioned and the expression 'father' became generally used as indicative of respect and reverence. It was significantly used of benefactors: Job declared that he 'was a father to the poor' (Job 29. 16) and the Psalmist describes God as 'a Father of the fatherless' (Psa. 68. 5). It was even employed of a creator or originator (e.g. Job 38. 28).

As Creator and Sovereign Ruler, God could be said with some measure of justification to be the Father of all mankind and, at Athens, the Apostle Paul virtually confirmed the propriety of this description when he quoted with apparent approval the words of a heathen poet to the effect that men are the offspring of God (Acts 17. 28, 29).

In the Old Testament, God is several times spoken of as Father of the nation of Israel, and the people are referred to as His sons. When Moses was sent to Pharaoh, God declared, 'Israel is My son, My firstborn' (Exod. 4. 22). Again Moses said, 'Ye are the children of the Lord your God' (Deut. 14. 1) and later he asked, 'Is not He thy Father?' (Deut. 32. 6). 'Doubtless Thou art our Father though Abraham be ignorant of us,' cried the prophet (Isa. 63. 16), and again, 'O Lord, Thou art our Father' (Isa. 64. 8). 'I called My son out of Egypt,' said God to a later prophet (Hos. 11. 1). It will be observed that the passages referring to God's paternal relationship to Israel are not numerous. But the Pharisees in Christ's time were proud of the divine Fatherhood. 'We have one Father, even God,' they indignantly told our Lord (John 8. 41).

If the Biblical references to the Father of the nation are limited, the idea that God might be the Father of an individual is even less often met with. But there is such a reference to Solomon in Nathan's revelation of the divine purpose for David's house. 'I will be his Father, and he shall be My son' (2 Sam. 7. 14) was the promise of God regarding David's seed.

In the New Testament, by contrast, references to the Fatherhood of God simply abound. In the fourth Gospel, God is spoken of as Father ninety times, and in the majority of these cases, it is as the Father of the Lord Jesus. In the other three Gospels, the term 'Father' is used of God sixty-seven times. It is made very plain, however, that a distinction is drawn between the sense in which our Lord is Son of God, and that in which there is a sonship of human beings. Our Lord is unique in that He was the Only

Begotten of the Father. In the parable of the Wicked Husbandmen (Matt. 22. 33-41), the proprietor of the vineyard first sent his servants to receive the fruit and then finally his one son, the well-beloved. The Jews quite recognized that Christ interpreted the title 'Son of God' in a sense which they regarded as blasphemous, because it was a claim to be a Divine Person. It is noteworthy that He never used the term 'Our Father' as though it meant the same thing as applied to Himself and to the disciples. When, for instance, He gave the pattern prayer to them, He said, 'When *ye* pray, say, Our Father' (John 20. 17), as though there were a distinction. He was from the beginning with God.

The Lord Jesus Christ was the Son of God from eternity, and there has never been a time when God was not His Father. In the Johannine Gospel particularly, 'Father' and 'Son' are correlative terms and each implies the other. Lofthouse pertinently remarks, 'The father could not be a father if he had not a son, nor the son a son if he had not a father. To our modern thought, this relation may be fulfilled in the mere begetting of a child; to the Hebrew mind, with its comparative neglect of the physical side of paternity, the relation implies a double or mutual functioning, continued as long as the two individuals exist side by side. The father must not only have a son; he must have a son who knows that he is a son, and who acts and gives and obeys as a son should do.' The Son of God came into this world at His Father's behest (John 5. 37; 10. 36, etc.). His purpose was primarily to reveal the Father and to do His will. Christ was the full and final revelation of God to man and, through Him, God is made known to man.

Selbie writes: 'In that much-discussed saying, "Neither knoweth any man the Father, save the Son, and he to whomsoever the Son will reveal Him" (Matt. 11. 27), we have the clear assurance of a knowledge of God's Fatherhood possessed by Jesus Christ and communicable to others.'

In the Sermon on the Mount there are seventeen references to God as Father, but the sermon was definitely addressed to the disciples (Matt. 5. 1, 2). Christ would not say to a careless multitude, 'Ye are the salt of the earth; ye are the light of the world.' Failure to observe this has led to much erroneous teaching. In the introduction to his epistle to the Romans, and again in that to the second epistle to the Thessalonians, the Apostle Paul speaks of 'God our Father'. Again, John says, 'Behold, what manner of love the Father hath bestowed upon us, that we should be called the children of God, and such we are' (1 John 3. 1, R.V.). In many places where 'the Father' is spoken of, the natural sense is that He is the Father of believers, even when this cannot always be regarded as proven.

It is not taught in Scripture that we are the children of God by natural birth. We need to be born again, in John's phraseology; to receive the adoption, in Paul's. When a convicted sinner exercises faith in the atoning work of Christ, he is born of the Spirit into the family of God. He becomes a child of God, and the Eternal God becomes his Father.

So far, there is no great room for difference of opinion, but when we come to consider whether there is a wider sense in which God is Father, the ground becomes more controversial.

Certain passages may be quoted which appear to support the idea of the universal Fatherhood. The origin of the human race is traced by Luke in his genealogical table back to 'son of Adam, which was the son of God' (Luke 3. 38). Again, the parable of the Prodigal Son is normally used in preaching to the unsaved, not to backsliders. In the discourse, preserved for us in Matthew 23, which was addressed to the multitude and the disciples, and not merely to the latter, Christ said, 'One is your Father, which is in heaven'. He spoke to the unregenerate woman of Samaria of worshipping the Father (John 4. 21). Paul, in his address at Athens, said to idolatrous Athenians, 'Forasmuch as we are the offspring of God' (Acts 17. 29). He wrote to the Ephesians of 'the Father ... from whom every family in heaven and earth is named' (Eph. 3. 14, 15). And again of 'one God and Father of all' (Eph. 4. 6).

It may be that none of these passages, taken by itself, can be regarded as conclusive. And there is much to be set out on the other side. Admission to the privilege of sonship is by the new birth, or by adoption. We are all dead in trespasses and sins. It is to as many as receive Him, that it is given to become the sons of God; they are born, not of the flesh, but of God (John 1. 12, 13). The children of the flesh are not the children of God (Rom. 9. 8). 'Ye are all the children of God by faith in Christ Jesus,' said Paul (Gal. 3. 26). It is those who are redeemed who receive the adoption of sons; such are no longer servants but sons (Gal. 4. 5-7). The first epistle of John marks the signs of those who are born of God (1 John 3. 10). The inspired writer also refers in the same verse, however, to some who are even the children of the devil. The Pharisees who told Jesus that they had one Father, even God, moreoever, were told that they were of their father the devil (John 8. 39-44).

If we are to base our doctrine on all these Scriptures and not on an arbitrary selection of them, it would appear that we must recognise that, whilst the Bible teaches the Fatherhood of God, it is not always with exactly the same meaning. In the Old Testament, God is the Father of the chosen people; individuals, with the exception of Solomon, do not emerge in this connection. Personal sonship of God does not seem to be envisaged under the old covenant. In the New Testament, the Lord Jesus Christ is seen as the Son of God. No human being can be son of God in the exclusive sense in which the Lord Jesus was and is. In Him, Sonship connotes eternal being; all the fulness of the Godhead bodily. But through His work, others become children of God. The believer enters by faith (which is the human approach) and by the new birth or adoption (which is the divine approach) into a sonship that belongs to him, but not to the unconverted; only he can say, 'Abba, Father'. Even this is not all. There is a Scriptural sense in which God is described as the Father of the human race; they are His offspring and their first ancestor was His son. But, on the other hand, all men are not His sons in the more personal sense.

If this seems to be a contradiction in terms, let us consider further. What does it mean when it says that God is our Father? Obviously, the description does not coincide exactly with the earthly relationship between parents and family. It surely means that—quite apart from the question of the new birth—God is Father in the sense that He is the Author of our being, and that He has the feelings of a father for us, however unworthily we treat Him. He loves us, gives us good gifts, instructs us in the right way, disciplines us, protects us, and earnestly desires our love and obedience. In that sense, a relationship exists between Him and every member of the human race, but it is not identical with the relationship enjoyed by the true believer with Him.

The preaching of the Gospel suffers if the doctrine of the Fatherhood of God is not rightly understood. If all men without distinction are thought of as being personally sons of God, the necessity for the new birth disappears, and a kind of universalism takes its place. But if the prodigal son can no longer be sure that God has the feelings of a father for him, the Gospel we preach will seem very hard and legal. Let us take care, therefore, to recognise the perfect balance of Scripture in this matter.

CHAPTER V

The Deity of Christ

J. B. WATSON

THE keystone truth of the Christian faith is the Deity of Christ. That faith differs from all other religions because its central claim is that God has become incarnate and has invaded our world for the ends of redemption. Christianity *has* a philosophy of life, but is itself more than a philosophy: it *has* a code of ethics but is itself more than such a code. It is a salvation; a salvation whose source and stream is God Himself. It is more than a revelation of the eternal nature of God; it is a faith founded on the history of the working of God on the stage of human affairs and on behalf of mankind. It is a coming of God to man on a redeeming mission: a descent of God into this sorrowful planet because to stoop into manhood was essential to the out-working of His plan for man's salvation.

The New Testament is the divine literature of this redemption. God has not only wrought, but has included in His redeeming activities a record of that working, both authoritative and abiding. His work in giving this record has been followed by another work for the preservation of the record given, so that it abides available for men, in whose interest the redemption has been both conceived and accomplished. Of themselves these writings give this account: 'Men spake from God as they were moved by the Holy Spirit' (2 Peter 1. 21). And it is this Word of God written that announces the Word of God Incarnate. All the dependable information we have of the Person of Christ is gathered together and presented here. And therefore it is to these Oracles that we turn for guidance and enlightenment.

Christianity, as the name implies, depends upon Christ. It is the direct result of His work, the product of His impact upon His day and generation. In contrast with other world-religions the faith which He initiated depends not only on His moral and religious teaching but on His character and yet more on certain events which make up His story—His death and its unparalleled sequel, resurrection. But for all we know of Him and the events that befell Him we are dependent on four short pamphlets written by followers of His. These, written within a few years of the happenings they narrate, for the information of the growing number of those who had become His disciples, constitute a fourfold testimony whose veracity and integrity have been established by detailed and long-sustained criticism to which they have been subjected by truth-seeking scholars. From them and a group of contemporary letters by other followers of His we must gather our knowledge both of the nature of the work He did and of His personal claims. It is on the substantiation of these personal claims that the spiritual values of His work depend.

What were the nature and scope of these claims? They were of the most astonishing height and reach. The fact that they were entertained and accepted by multitudes in the generation which followed Him is a fact almost as significant as the claims themselves. Let us see what these were:

He claimed powers which reside in God alone. The power to forgive sins, for instance. On one occasion when His hearers demurred to a pronouncement of forgiveness, made by Him in their presence to a man brought to Him for physical healing, He demonstrated that His words were no mere pious wish but an effectual conferment of pardon by coupling them with words which conveyed instant physical cure to the man, a paralytic. Was the cure effectual? So, it may be concluded, was the pardon. Was the cure instant? So was the forgiveness. Both were displays of divine power. His word must be regarded as equally valid in both the physical and spiritual realms. 'That ye may know that the Son of Man hath power on earth to forgive sins (He saith to the sick of the palsy), "Arise, take up thy bed and go unto thine house".'

'Who *can* forgive sins but God alone?' His critics had justly asked. His word brought peace of conscience to those sinners to whom He pronounced pardon as truly as it brought the awareness of physical cure to those to whom He spoke healing.

He claims a unique relationship to God (Matt. 26. 63, 64). Here He explicitly claims to be the Son of God. Many have discounted this as not being a claim to Deity because the name 'Son' is applied to others as well as to Him, e.g., to angels, Adam, the Hebrew nation and Christians (Job 1. 6; Luke 3. 38; Hosea 11. 1; Rom. 8. 14). But Christ's Sonship differs from and is loftier than any or all these. This is shown by the expression 'His only begotten Son' (John 3. 16; 1 John 4. 9): the mode of the use of the names 'Son' and 'Son of God' in the Gospels and the Epistles as applied to Christ, also clearly implies a unique relationship. Matt. 11. 27 and Luke 10. 22 set forth this relationship in language reminiscent of the fourth Gospel, 'All things have been delivered unto Me of My Father: and no one knoweth the Son, save the Father; neither doth any know the Father, save the Son, and he to whomsoever the Son willeth to reveal Him.'

Dr. James Stalker has drawn attention to the fact that the statement is often made that Christ's Sonship is ethical, not metaphysical. 'No doubt it is ethical,' he says, 'that is to say He is like the Father in feeling, mind and will—but it does not follow that it is not at the same time metaphysical, for the perfection of ethical unity depends upon that which is metaphysical. The Sonship is official, it is part of the qualifications of Messiahship, but a mere official sonship is not adequate: the relation must be ethical and metaphysical as well. To a perfect Sonship all three elements are essential.' Which means to say that Messiah must wear and possess the official standing expressed by the name 'Son of God' and also share the Father's mind and will and be identical in nature with Him. And what is this if it be not Deity? The closing verse of the prologue to John's Gospel (1. 18) speaks thus of Christ: 'The only-begotten Son which is in the bosom of the Father.' This is a strong affirmation of the uniqueness of the Sonship. The words do not refer to Christ's present state of exaltation or to any act of ascension to that place, but to the permanent habitat, the native sphere of the Son, to the indestructible relation of imminence between the Persons of the Godhead. Thus Westcott says of the clause, *ho ōn eis ton kolpon tou patros,* 'It is natural to take the phrase as an absolute description of the nature of the Son, so that the participle (*ōn*) will be timeless.'

The verdict of the Jewish Sanhedrin was given against Jesus because He made Himself the Son of God (Matt. 26. 63-66). This claim, made in the presence of the tribunal, so that its chief member, the High Priest, considered other witnesses unnecessary, was one He had made on previous occasions and was understood by those who heard it as a claim to be equal with God (John 5. 18; 10. 33); an impression He did nothing to correct, which He would have been bound to do had it been a misapprehension. The verdict of the Sanhedrin was right (Lev. 24. 16) if His claim was baseless: it was wrong if the claim was true.

He claims Universal Judgeship, a task which demands omniscience. Using His favourite name, Son of Man, He speaks of the day when, attended by all the holy angels, He will sit on the throne of His glory and before Him all the nations shall stand. Unerringly He will separate them, as a shepherd divides sheep from goats, to right and left, for eternal life, or eternal punishment (Matt. 25. 31-46). Who but God is sufficient for this? God is the Judge of all, but has committed all judgment to the Son because He is a son of man (John 5. 27). No man who shall be judged will be in a position to complain that his Judge was one who had no experience of human conditions and infirmities or that his judgment was lacking in the understanding that only such experience can give. Yet that is only one side of the truth; the other is that absolutely nothing is hidden from the Divine omniscience of the Judge; and omniscience is with God alone.

He Claims an Eternal Pre-existence when speaking to the Father of a glory He possessed alongside Him prior to the present creation. 'And now, O Father, glorify Thou Me with Thine own self with the glory which I had with Thee before the world was' (John 17. 5). These words need no explanation, their import is clear—they claim that the Speaker shared glory alongside (*para*) the Father, not merely before the Incarnation but before the present creation was called into being, and asks that it now be resumed.

'Before Abraham was I am' (John 8. 58) were words He used in answering a question whether He had seen Abraham. The form of the answer is significant. Note the words 'I am'; not 'I was', as might at most have been expected, but the timeless name, the name of Him who spoke out of the bush to Moses, 'I AM THAT I AM.' It is a claim to eternal pre-existence, and the quality of eternity of being is God's attribute and His only.

He Claims to be the Answerer of Prayer. This is a prerogative of God. 'O Thou that hearest prayer, to Thee shall all flesh come' (Psalm 66. 2). An inherent impulse is found in the heart of man, as man, to cry to God when in extreme need—need beyond hope of relief by any human power. 'We all pray sometimes' was the admission of a professed atheist who had been overheard to cry to God for deliverance on the beaches of Dunkirk. Christ calmly puts Himself in the place of God in this matter of answering the heart-cries that arise from His disciples, 'If ye shall ask anything in My Name I will do it' (John 14. 14). This is an assumption of limitless power—the power that belongs alone to God (Psa. 62. 11).

He Accepts Worship. When Cornelius fell down to do homage to Peter, the apostle raised him up saying, 'Stand up: I myself also am a man' (Acts 10. 26). When John of Patmos fell down to worship before the feet of the angel who showed him the vision of the New Jerusalem, the angel rebuked him saying, 'See thou do it not: I am a fellow-servant with thee, and with thy brethren the prophets, and with them that keep the words of this Book; worship God' (Rev. 19. 10).

When the man who had been born blind, but now saw because Christ had healed him, was asked by Jesus whether he knew the Son of God, he answered: 'Who is He, Lord, that I may believe on Him?' Jesus said unto him, 'Thou hast both seen Him and He it is that speaketh with thee.' And he said, 'Lord, I believe,' and he worshipped Him (John 9. 35-38). Nor is there any record of rebuke or refusal of the worship so offered. Christ thus accepted the worship which is due to God alone; an open claim to Deity.

There was no rebuke, correction or remonstrance to Thomas by the Christ when that disciple uttered his adoration in the words, 'My Lord and my God' (John 20. 28). The acceptance of worship expressed in such terms is an emphatic assumption of Deity. 'I am the Lord, that is My name and My glory will I not give to another' (Isa. 42. 8).

★ ★ ★ ★ ★ ★

These are some of the claims of Christ: they are only some out of many but they must suffice for our present purpose. Let us pursue for a little another line of witness to this great truth.

The principal authors of the writings in which the doctrines of Christianity are authoritatively set forth are: Paul, John, Peter, James, and the writer of the Epistle to the Hebrews. Let us ask each of these in turn for a brief answer to the question: Was Jesus Christ God manifest in Manhood?

PAUL. Paul the Apostle was the greatest depositary of Christian doctrine. He spoke of the truth of the faith committed to him as 'the good deposit', which implies that he received it from God. Among the truths he taught, none was more emphatic than that we are considering. In all his epistles it is present and in some of them is stated in the most explicit language. Of these none is more clearly worded than Col. 2. 9; 'In Him dwelleth all the fulness of the Godhead bodily.' 'Fulness', *plērōma*, was a term much in use in the speech and writings of the gnostics. The nature of the fulness is to be gathered from the context. Here the word *theotētos* defines the *plērōma* as the fulness of Deity. The word is to be distinguished from *theiotēs*, divinity. Deity is the being God, divinity is the being godlike.[1] The passage thus asserts the real Deity of Christ. Gnostic teachers represented the *plērōma* as distributed among the ascending ranks of angelic orders (with Christ as the highest of these) but Paul thunders No! ALL the *plērōma* of Deity is permanently housed (*katoikei*) in Him. And he adds the word 'bodily', *sōmatikōs*, in order to indicate that what he says is true not only of the incarnate Christ but of the glorified Man now in the midst of the throne in heaven.

Another very strong passage is Phil. 2. 6: 'Who, being in the form of God.' Here the word 'being', *huparchōn*, conveys the thought of 'subsisting originally' and the word 'form', *morphē*, is important, for the possession of the *morphē* involves participation in the essence also.[2] He who is in the 'form of God' possesses the

[1] *Theotēs*, Deity, differs from *Theiotēs*, divinity, as essence differs from quality or attribute —(*Grimm*).

[2] *Morphē* always signifies a form which truly and fully expresses the being which underlies it.—(*Kennedy*).

Plainly form, *morphē*, has reference to nature; equality with God, *to einai isa Theō*, to a relation.—(*Kennedy*).

Morphē is properly the nature or essence, not in the abstract, but as actually subsisting in the individual, and retained as long as the individual itself exists. . . . Thus in the passage Phil. 2. 6-7 *morphē theou* is the divine nature actually and inseparably subsisting in the Person of Christ. . . . For the interpretation of 'the form of God' it is sufficient to say that (*a*) it

essential divine attributes. Only God can be in the form of God. Light is thrown on the phrase by its antithesis with the succeeding expression in verse 7, 'the form of a bond-servant'. In His humiliation, His assumption of the conditions, obligations and relationships of a bondman were actual, veritable, real. His servitude was no semblance but was of the central essence of bondservice. Similarly the form of God indicates the essence of Godhood. Maclaren says 'there is no room for candid doubt that "being originally in the form of God" is a deliberately asserted claim of the divinity (Deity) of Christ in His pre-existent state.'

JOHN. The impressive opening of the Gospel of John is a carefully constructed statement which sets forth the peerless dignity of the Person of whom John is about to write. His aim in writing is to convince his readers that 'Jesus is the Messiah the Son of God' (Chapter 20. 31) and he introduces Him in these words, 'In the beginning was the Word, and the Word was with God, and the Word was God. The same was in the beginning with God.'

Here is a most exact choice of terms. Not a letter can be moved without loss: no change made but for the worse. 'The Word' is John's name for Christ. Now a word is a vehicle of thought, a means of expression; mind can disclose itself to mind by the medium of words. So Christ is the expression of God. Through Him God utters that which tells His heart to man. He speaks to men through Man; the Word is human, comprehensible. Yet that is not all, 'The Word', he continues, 'was with God.' Far back in the beginning there was fellowship in the Godhead. The life of God has not been one eternal solitude. Fulness of life demands that love shall have a place. And there is room here for this. 'The Word was with God'; the preposition, *pros*, gives the thought of movement toward. So God and the Word dwelt together in the eternal past in an ineffable fellowship of love.

includes the whole nature and essence of Deity and is inseparable from them since they could have no actual existence without it, and (*b*) that it does not include in itself anything 'accidental' or separable, such as particular modes of manifestation, or conditions of glory and majesty, which may at one time be attached to the 'form,' at another separated from it.—(*Gifford*)

The true meaning of *morphē* in the expression 'form of God' is confirmed by its recurrence in the corresponding phrase 'form of a servant.' It is universally admitted that the two phrases are directly antithetical and that 'form' must therefore have the same sense in both. —(*Vine*).

'And the Word was God.' In the former phrases the writer has spoken of the eternity of the Word and the distinction of Persons in the Godhead. Now he adds an expression which states clearly the Deity of the Word. The absence of the article before *theos* is important. Were it present the phrase would imply that the Word comprised the whole of the Godhead; the two nouns would be identical so that the statement would be capable of being turned about to read, 'God was the Word'. But as it stands the expression means that the Word has the characterising attributes of God.[1] And then he adds in verse 2 a sentence which is far from being a mere repetition, 'the same was in the beginning with God': that is, there was no point in time at which the Word was raised to this exalted status. It has been forever His.

In this profound statement then, we have expressed the eternity, the distinction of Person, the divine nature and the unchangeableness of the One of whom John will presently say, 'and the Word became flesh and dwelt among us', thus indicating that the historic Person, Jesus Christ, is the One of whom he speaks under the abstraction 'the Word'.

PETER.—Peter is heard in the Gospels as the confessor, expressing for himself and his fellow-apostles the conviction at which they had arrived about the Person of their Master, 'Thou art the Christ, the Son of the Living God' (Matt. 16. 16). Does he, in his maturer years, stand by that memorable declaration of faith? We will take a point in each of the epistles that bear his name.

In the first epistle he writes: 'But and if ye should suffer for righteousness' sake, blessed are ye: and fear not their fear neither be troubled; but sanctify in your hearts Christ as Lord: being ready always to give answer to every man that asketh you a reason concerning the hope that is in you, yet with meekness and fear' (Chp. 3. 14, 15, R.V.). There is an undoubted allusion here to a passage in the book of Isaiah which reads: 'Neither fear ye their fear, nor be in dread thereof. The Lord of Hosts, Him shall ye sanctify, and let Him be your fear, and let Him be your dread' (Isa. 8. 12, 13).

[1] John 1. 1. 'The Word was God,'—*theos:* not simply *theios* as if He were a sort of second God: nor *ho theos* as though in Him were embraced the entire Godhead, but *theos* to indicate His equality with the supreme Deity.—(*Whitelaw*).

Note the significant exchange of names. Instead of the name of the Lord of Hosts in the Isaiah passage is found the name Christ in the New Testament Scripture. Instead of the Lord of Hosts being sanctified, Christ is to be sanctified in our hearts as Lord. He is to be set apart in the throne-room of the soul as our supreme Lord. He is to be given the place claimed for God in the Old Testament passage—the place which to give to any save to God were rank idolatry. The Lord of Hosts and Christ are alike God. It is right to sanctify Christ in our hearts as Lord, because Christ is God.

In his second epistle too, Peter accords to Christ full equality with God as is shown by the remarkable way in which he addresses Him in the opening verse of the letter, where he speaks of 'the righteousness of our God and Saviour Jesus Christ' (2 Peter 1. 1. R.V.). A Peter to whom Christ had been lower than God could never have so spoken. In the following verse also the close association of the name of God with that of Christ carries the same significance, 'the knowledge of God and of Jesus our Lord'. The very use of the names in this manner is a louder-speaking indication of Peter's conviction of the Deity of Christ than any formal argument could be. Incidental and oblique allusions are often more telling than deliberately chosen and elaborately presented proofs.

JAMES.—The writer of the epistle of James, it is generally agreed, was that James who is called 'the Lord's brother' (Gal. 1. 19). He was not a believer during the ministry of our Lord (Jno. 7. 3) but in resurrection the Lord appeared to him, with the result, it would appear, that he became a follower of Christ and was among the disciples who waited in the Upper Room for the coming of the Spirit (Acts 1. 14). He became an acknowledged leader in the church at Jerusalem, as is evident from the weighty way he summed up at the Council recorded in Acts 15 and from the reference to him in Gal. 2. 9. In his Epistle, he refers to himself as the servant of the Lord Jesus Christ (1. 1.) and the only other reference to Christ by name is that in chapter 2, in which he employs most strikingly the title *tou kuriou hēmōn Iēsou Christou tēs doxēs* (literally, 'Our Lord Jesus Christ the Glory'). There is a note on this passage in Mayor's exposition of the Epistle of James in which after discussing interpretations by many expositors including Erasmus, Calvin,

Laurentius, Lange, Ewald, de Wette, Kern, Alford, Erdmann and others he comes to this decision: 'There is a perfectly natural and easy construction suggested by Bengel which has been set aside by other commentators on what seemed to me very inadequate grounds. The objection made to it is that the abstract term *doxa* by itself is too indefinite to bear this weight of meaning. But other abstractions are used of Christ. He calls Himself the Truth, the Life: He is called the Word: why not the Glory? Why should we object to the translation "Our Lord Jesus Christ who is the Glory"?'

What a claim to Deity is here if the verse be taken so. In Israel's inmost shrine dwelt 'the Glory', it shimmered above the Mercy Seat in the holiest of all. It was the Presence, it was God Himself manifested in His holiness and ineffable purity. It was God as He was pleased to dwell among men. All that (says James) was Jesus of Nazareth, the Christ of God, the Lord of us all; He was 'the Glory'; more indeed, He *is* the Glory!

This is a statement of Deity made all the more striking because of the human relationship borne by the writer to the One of whom he writes and in view of his former blindness to the glory that dwelt in Him.

THE WRITER OF THE EPISTLE TO THE HEBREWS.—The words of this anonymous author bear also the same imprint. For him Jesus Christ in His incomparable greatness carries the full values of God. In his introductory statement (ch. I. 1-3) he speaks of Him as God's Son and describes Him as being 'the brightness, *apaugasma*, of His glory', that is, the shining forth of God's own eternally glorious and unchangeable nature for the purposes of self-manifestation. Moreover, the Son is said to be 'the express image of His substance', *charaktēr tēs hupostaseōs autou*. As the impress is to the die, as the stamp is to the seal, so is His correspondence with God full and complete. Can words more definitely claim full Godhead for the Son than these?

Again, in verse 8 of the same chapter we hear God address Messiah the King in these words: 'Thy throne, O God, is for ever and ever'—God addresses Christ as God.

Since God so witnesses to the Godhead of Christ, let every man bow in adoration and own Him 'God over all, blessed for ever'.

We have followed with the barest brevity two lines of witness: first, the claims which Christ Himself makes to Deity in the words and actions recorded of Him in the Gospels and, second, the doctrine taught by the principal writers of the New Testament concerning His Person. We have selected a few strong points only, adducing proofs from peaks of revelation. It needs to be added that the doctrine of the Deity of Christ is affirmed throughout the whole of the New Testament. For instance, we have mentioned two passages only in Paul's epistles. Dr. Gresham Machen has written, 'The Deity of Christ is all-pervasive in the Epistles of Paul. It is by no means an isolated thing. You do not have to search for it to find it. On the contrary, you cannot get away from it. Open the Epistles where you will and you will find the Deity of Christ.' To these true words we may add that not only in the epistles of Paul but in the whole of the New Testament is this cardinal truth written large. It is implied in a thousand places, and is the key to a multitude of passages. It is the underlying assumption in a great variety of situations and oblique references to it are on most of the pages of the Book. Without it, the bottom falls out of the apostolic Gospel and coherence departs from the divine writings. If it be denied, perverted, minimised or reduced the principal significance of the Scriptures is likewise lost. It is the rock on which the fabric of Christianity rests, indeed it is the Rock on which Christ Himself builds His church and against which the gates of hell shall not prevail, the rock of the great confession, 'Thou art the Christ, the Son of the Living God.'

CHAPTER VI

The Son of Man

JOHN R. ROLLO

THE fundamental axiom of all Christian thinking is the existence of God—a God who is infinite, eternal, transcendent in glory, wisdom and power, dwelling in light ineffable, light so bright as to be 'thick darkness.' 'Canst thou by searching find out God? Canst thou find out the Almighty unto perfection? It is as high as heaven: what canst thou do? Deeper than Sheol; what canst thou know? The measure thereof is longer than the earth and broader than the sea' (Job 11. 7-9).

The poet echoes these words of Job when he exclaims:

Thou art a sea without a shore,
A sun without a sphere,
Thy time is now and evermore,
Thy place is everywhere.

The mysterious infinitudes of the personality of God are inaccessible to the self-efforts of men, and had God chosen to remain unrevealed, we had remained of all men most miserable. There is penetrating wisdom in the statement of Paul the Apostle when writing to the Ephesians, 'having no hope, and without God in the world' (2. 12).

But God has chosen to reveal Himself. The work of His hands in nature, the panorama of variegated beauty throughout the changing year tells of an architect whose wisdom and power are alike without parallel. The writer to the Hebrews speaks of creation as a garment to be folded up, but in which God shows His power to men (Heb. 1. 11, 12). He is might, say the mountains sure and true and dependable. He is unfathomable, saith the ocean. His ways are past finding out: tireless energy and infinite patience is He. Stillness and silence, say the stars. He is glorious, radiant and life-giving, says the sun. The wonder of sunrise and sunset reveal Him, the intimate excellence of spring's carpeted beauty, the exquisite perfection of every flower that grows—all these unite in testimony to the reality of their Creator.

Moreover, to those who have eyes to see, history discloses Him. No one is so bigoted as to think that history is a mere accumulation of events. For at any one moment of time, millions of events are taking place in the universe, whose sole significance in history is the part they play in unrolling the canvas of God's purposes for men. In the truest sense history is His story, and far from causing dismay to the hearts of Christian men, the tumultuous happenings of our times are evidence of the superintendence and sovereignty of God. The fact that much is clothed in mystery is a challenge to faith.

The Scripture further teaches that God has been pleased to reveal His mind and purpose through chosen human vessels. The Old Testament introduces us to men whose importance is that for the time being they were the media of Divine Truth. God spake in time past by the prophets, so that we hear Him as the God of Abraham, of Isaac and of Jacob, while in the New Testament He is seen in Christ as the God of love, of grace and of peace.

All this is preparatory to the main theme. The only complete revelation of God is in His Son. There is the final answer to man's quest. The stoop of Deity into humanity's garb. Matchless wonder!

> That glorious form, that light unsufferable,
> And that far-beaming blaze of majesty
> Wherewith He wont at heaven's high council table
> To sit the midst of Trinal Unity,
> He laid aside; and here with us to be
> Forsook the courts of everlasting day
> And chose with us a darksome house of mortal clay.

At the outset we are confronted with a miracle. Our Lord Jesus Christ was born of a virgin mother, but there is more than that. He was conceived by the Holy Spirit. What happened was a divine creative act. Every other birth is the creation of a new personality. It was not so with Jesus. There was a Divine Person already existing but now entering upon a new mode of existence. The great Christogical passage in Philippians 2 bears this out in clear language. The words 'was made' are the translation of a verb meaning 'to become.' 'The tense of this verb is ingressive aorist which signifies entrance into a new state. Our Lord entered into a new state of being when He became man. But His becoming Man did not exclude His possession of Deity' (Wuest). A miracle alone could effect such a wonder. Great is the mystery of Godliness. God was manifest in flesh. The fact of the virgin birth is vital to a correct conception of the Person of Christ. To deny it makes necessary a miracle of some other sort to explain the deeper meaning of His Person and the efficacy of His work. 'His absolute pre-existence, His relation to the cosmos, His eternal power and Godhead do not seem to be congruent with the manner of birth that is common to men. He bears a name that no one knows but Himself' (McIntyre).

Two facts are crystal clear to the devout reader of the New Testament. First, the humanity of Jesus was real, genuine and true, naturally or physically *like* that of all men; and second, His humanity was perfect morally, possessing the quality of sinlessness, *unlike* that of any other man.

To go back through successive stages of man, boy, child and babe, and question the essential reality of His manhood is impossible. No one who knew Him doubted this. He was known as the carpenter's son. We may picture Him in the workshop, on the desert road and by the lakeside, or on the cobbled streets of the towns and villages of the ancient land. He calls Himself man—'a man that hath told you the truth, which I have heard of God' (John 8. 40). He experiences the effects of purely human emotions. He was 'an hungered' (Matt. 4. 2). He was sometimes grieved and angry (Mark 3. 5). Weary and thirsty He sat thus on the well (John 4. 6). After a day of unremitting toil, they took Him even as He was in the ship (Mark 4. 36). And anon He slept, pillowed on the helmsman's cushion, the sleep of unutterable weariness. The tempestuous billows might bring alarm to the disciples, but they could not disturb the slumber of this blessed Man, tired to the point of exhaustion. One day He stood beside the grave of Lazarus and down His human cheeks there coursed human tears, mute but eloquent symbol of His identification with human sorrow (John 11. 35). Moreover, He suffered and died. He Himself spoke thus: 'My soul is exceeding sorrowful' (Matt. 26. 38). 'Into Thy hands I commend My Spirit' (Luke 23. 46). Then after the resurrection He showed to His disciples the reality of His risen body (Luke 24. 39).

The apostles argue He was true man. Peter in his address at Pentecost calls Jesus of Nazareth a Man approved of God (Acts 2. 22). In Athens, Paul declares, 'God hath appointed a day in which He will judge the world in righteousness by that Man whom He hath ordained' (Acts 17. 31). In 1 Tim. 2. 5 (R.V.) the same apostle bases the rightness of Christ's mediational office on the reality of His manhood. 'For there is one God, one mediator also between God and men, Himself Man, Christ Jesus who gave Himself a ransom for all'. When we come to the Epistle to the Hebrews, the whole intricate argument for His perfect priesthood, built with logical precision, pivots round the certainty of His true manhood (2. 14, 17; 5. 8, 9). In addition to these witnesses the Apostle John writes at a later date ere the first Christian century closes, and asserts that to deny 'that Jesus Christ is come in the flesh' is the mark of a deceiver and an antichrist (1 Jno. 4. 2; 2 John 7). It is clear he was combating a heresy of those days that Jesus was a superhuman being, but was not really man at all. His answer is categorical, and the Incarnation has brought eternity into the confines of human life.

Furthermore, our Lord called Himself Son of Man. This was the designation He constantly employed of Himself, and His choice of this title in preference to more current ones, such as Son of David, King of Israel, is full of deep meaning. Let it be remembered that the Messianic ideal fully accepted among the people was that of a king whose power would deliver and whose setting up of a kingdom on earth would radically change their lot. In identifying Himself with the title, Son of Man, our Lord is impressing upon them the need for a revolution in their expectations. He is directing them away from the Son of David of the Psalms to the Son of Man of Daniel's visions. His life on earth will be a lowly one. 'For even the Son of Man came not to be ministered unto, but to minister, and to give His life a ransom for many' (Mark 10. 45). Suffering belongs to the very essence of His mission, but this suffering will be vicarious, a sufficing ransom. It is no extravagant exegesis to see the development of this truth in the Gospel prophecy of Isaiah 53. It is one thing to regard the suffering servant of that chapter as smitten of God and afflicted, and quite another thing to become aware that such suffering was not penal, but vicarious and expiatory. He was wounded for our transgressions. His soul was made an offering for sin. Since this is so, the Son of Man will rise again the third day (Mark 9. 31; 10. 34) and will come again in clouds with great glory and power to establish the kingdom.

Everywhere our Lord uses this title. He is man after the divine pattern, embracing humanity in His own person. It is enough to say with Canon Liddon: 'Nothing local, transient, individualizing, national, sectarian, dwarfs the proportions of this world-embracing character; He rises above the parentage, the blood, the narrow horizon which founded, as it seemed, His human life. He is the archetypal Man, in whose presence distinctions of race, intervals of ages, types of civilization, degrees of mental culture, are as nothing.'

He adequately demonstrated the marks of perfect humanity which can be summed in two words—obedience and dependence. What unbroken trust marked Him in all His ways. He could say prophetically, 'Thou didst make Me hope when I was upon My mother's breasts' (Psa. 22. 9). The whole tenor of that devoted life was in conscious dependence upon the Father. What else is meant by these wonderful words, 'I live by the Father' (John 6. 57), and again, 'I am not alone but I and the Father that sent Me' (John 8. 16)? When He came to die, His last word was not for the sorrow-laden mother who stood by the cross, but for His Father in heaven, 'Into Thy hands I commend My Spirit' (Luke 23. 46). This is in close consistence with an early incident. As a boy of twelve He spoke of His Father; supremely conscious of whence He came, He listened to the remark of Mary, 'Son, why hast Thou thus dealt with us? behold, Thy father and I have sought Thee sorrowing' (Luke 2. 48), and with tender and courteous rebuke responded, 'Wist ye not that I must be about My Father's business?' (Luke 2. 49). A gentle but necessary correction. And from the grave the Saviour spoke, 'My flesh also shall dwell confidently in hope. For Thou wilt not leave my soul in Hades: neither wilt Thou suffer Thine Holy One to see corruption' (Psa. 16. 9, 10); (cp. Acts 2. 27).

Thus the whole horizon of His human life was marked by trust in God, such as has never been evidenced in the life of any other human being. If the first Adam was seduced into sin by distrust of

God's Word, God's love and God's provision, this blessed One will restore that which He took not away, pillowing His whole life upon the will of God, for the complementary truth to this unalloyed dependence is resolute and unswerving obedience to the will of Him whom He so trusted. That obedience brought Him into incarnation with its humiliation and compass of infirmities, led Him along the path of man's rejection through the temptations of the wilderness, past the short-lived acclamation of the crowd, the great renunciation of the Transfiguration Mount, from the upper room over the brook Kedron to the crisis of the garden glade of Gethsemane, where He sweat those great drops in the acutest throes of anguish, when He was sore amazed in face of the staggering implications of His approaching sacrifice as sin-bearer. Holy ground indeed! Yet from the faith-lit confines of His spirit, there come those words, mysterious in their import, yet majestic in their triumph, 'Nevertheless not what I will, but what Thou wilt' (Mark 14. 36). From Gethsemane He goes to Golgotha where the perfect servant became obedient unto death, *even* the death of the cross. And when once we have begun to plumb the awful depths of this word 'even,' then and only then, are we beginning to comprehend the mystery and significance of that infinite sacrifice, accomplished by Jehovah's obedient Servant. 'There went up from the depths of Christ's sinless humanity a perfect Amen to the righteous judgment against sin.'

Yes, once Immanuel's orphan cry
  His universe hath shaken,
It came up single, echoless,
  My God, I am forsaken.
It came up from the holy lips
  Amidst the lost creation
That of the lost no soul might use
  That cry of desolation.

One of the outstanding proofs of the true humanity of the Son of God is His unwearying resort to prayer, and it is no mere coincidence that the Gospel of Luke which portrays Him as Son of Man is the record which best unveils His prayer life. This is a study in itself—*when* He prayed; *how* He prayed; *where* He prayed. Aside, apart, alone, when night had spread her dark wings over the earth, when others had sought their homes, the Blessed Man knelt in prayer. We praise service. Work kept Him from food. Exhausted He slept on a pillow: at eventide they brought their sick: the speeding hours were occupied with service and ministry, yet the place of prayer was pre-eminent.

No man ever spake like Christ because no man ever listened as He did. For Him to pray was to delight in God. It was bound to be so, for no one had ever a greater comprehension or appreciation of God. He did not seek for gifts but for the Giver, and His hours of prayer were hours of direct strengthening. The reasons which drive us to prayer were never present with Him. Under the consciousness of failure and defeat we seek for forgiveness: Christ never had sin to confess. In moments of high resolve, we re-dedicate ourselves to God. In that life of unbroken devotion to God's sovereign will, there never was any need for consecration anew, sanctified as He was to His Father.

He never joined His disciples in prayer. His asking was of a completely different kind from theirs, and the taking was on a far higher plane, and was concerned with the inward needs of His soul. As we trace those stainless steps and watch with ever increasing wonder that ladder of prayer to heaven's inmost shrine, there breaks upon the spirit an overwhelming sense of adoration of this blessed peerless Man, God's most Holy Son, and with deep humility, we re-echo the request of those others, 'Lord, teach us to pray.'

The second fundamental aspect of our Lord's real humanity is His moral perfection, or what is commonly called the sinlessness of Jesus. The New Testament indicates certain elements in this perfection. First, He was of stainless nature. This point has been noted earlier in emphasizing the virgin birth. 'That holy thing which shall be born of thee' (Luke I. 35). This gives the lie to teaching which asserts that Christ was possessed of a nature, sinful as other men, but that He overcame the sinfulness of it and lived a perfectly holy life. Nowhere in the New Testament is there supporting evidence for such teaching, and it is essential that we hold with tenacity to the sinless nature of the incarnate Son. It is integral to His fitness as Redeemer: if it is not true, how could He offer Himself *without spot* to God?

Second, He was of sinless life. It is not only comparatively He sets Himself above us. The rest of mankind stand in sharpest contrast. Jesus of Nazareth stands alone in His own order. Like everything divine in its origin, His life becomes more splendid the more closely we investigate it. The most searching scrutiny merely confirms the wonder of it. He did not live and work in obscurity, but in the full blaze of public attention. Those who were in closest intimacy are most insistent in their praise. They had the best opportunities of closely observing His life in its every varying phase, yet they unite in testimony.

'He did no sin,' said Peter (1 Peter 2. 22); 'He knew no sin' (2 Cor. 5. 21), was the witness of Paul, and 'In Him is no sin,' was the verdict of the beloved disciple (1 John 3. 5). He never repented or confessed, nor felt unfitted for the great task to which He was called. He it was who first established the fact that sin does not lie merely in the outward act, but in the *motive* behind the act. With piercing and unerring discernment he probed deep into the secret recesses, where character is born and cradled. He went behind the impure act to the look and lust, and beyond the blow to the hate which gave it birth. On nothing was our Lord more scathing in judgment than hypocrisy, for in His eyes the worst fault of all was to conceal sin. Yet He challenged His enemies, whose hearts were bitter towards Him, to bring home by proof to His conscience one word or act which had in it the taint of wrong: 'which of you convinceth Me of sin?' (John 8. 46).

There is a great gulf between external blamelessness and His sinless perfection. Herod (Luke 23. 15), Pilate (John 19. 4), Pilate's wife (Matt. 27. 19), the dying robber (Luke 23. 41), the centurion (Luke 23. 47) and Judas (Matt. 27. 4) bear individual yet concerted testimony to His blameless character. But in the light of His own teaching the only two valid witnesses to His sinlessness are God and Himself. We are told that we know so little of His early days, and we speak of the 'hidden' years at Nazareth. And yet we know all there needs to be known, for at Jordan as He emerges from obscurity, the heavenly voice declares, 'This is My beloved Son in whom I am well pleased' (Matt. 3. 17), and thus the seal of divine approval is placed upon the years of childhood, of youth, and of opening manhood. On the Mount of Transfiguration the teachings, testings and toils were searched in the light of God and approved: 'This is My Beloved Son, in whom I am well pleased: hear ye Him' (Matt. 17. 5). At the close of His public ministry there was another heavenly testimony in answer to His prayer, 'Father, glorify Thy Name.' There came therefore a voice out of heaven, saying, 'I have both glorified it and will glorify it again' (John 12. 28).

So much for the testimony of God the Father. The most saintly believer cannot sit down at the end of one day and look into the face of God with the plea, 'I have glorified Thy name.' But this perfect Man, whose standard of holiness far exceeded any human values, can confidently look into the face of God, after thirty-three years, twelve thousand days, conscious that between His soul and the stainless Throne there had not come one shadow or cloud to dim their communion. And so He is conscious of perfect rectitude. This is the highest and strongest kind of evidence, for with such a knowledge of man and sin as He had, it is impossible either that He could be self-deceived, or that He could say what was not true. He fulfilled all righteousness (Matt. 3. 15). 'He went about doing good' (Acts 10. 38). He lived for the righteousness He loved, and died for the lawlessness He hated.

A final witness to the spotless perfection of Christ is Christianity and the Christian Church. 'How was such a life recorded if it was not lived? Where did such a conception of a perfect Christ come from? Who could imagine or invent it? Whence came the ideas of certain virtues and of such a character as our religion demands? They were unknown till Jesus brought them. The world before Christ did not know such virtues as humility, forgiveness and chastity. It considered them not virtues at all, only weaknesses. Who set up this standard? Jesus did. He is the source of Christian morality. Will the source shame the stream? Never. The stream may be less pure than the fountain but never the reverse' (Prof. Laidlaw).

Here it seems opportune to examine the purposes of His incarnation. Probably there are four main lines of purpose. The words of such a man are clothed with supreme authority. His message as the prophet of God is worthy of all acceptation. He is unfaltering in His teaching about God, about sin, about immortality, about human sorrow and suffering, and the imprimatur of heaven is upon His every statement. These are realms of human speculation where man's philosophy and erudition come to a full stop, summarizing their conclusions in supposition or nebulous theory. Not so with God's last Word to man, whose teaching is stamped with inward certainty. It is impossible to make too much of this central fact in the Gospel story. The searchlight of His radiant life, everywhere consistent with His own doctrine, shines into the sin-conscious soul of man, and His words carry conviction to heart and mind, bringing him, if he be obedient, into the surging joy of Christian belief. He is the Emperor of men's souls. He has come to reveal the Father. 'If I say the truth, why do ye not believe Me?' (John 8. 47). Why, indeed! 'He that rejecteth Me and receiveth not My sayings hath One that judgeth him: the word that I spake, the same shall judge him at the last day' (John 12. 48). A messenger from the court of heaven has come bringing to us, not in word only but in the perfection of His holy character, the final and complete revelation of the Father. We do well to join voice with Peter. 'Lord, to whom shall we go? Thou hast the words of eternal life. And we have believed and know that Thou art the Holy One of God' (John 6. 68, 69, R.V.).

Further, He is the great Mediator, Himself man, Christ Jesus. He came to bring God and man together. The barrier between was sin, and the Daysman must Himself be without sin. Few statements are more awe-inspiring than the words of 2 Cor. 5. 21, 'Him who knew no sin He made to be sin on our behalf, that we might become the righteousness of God in Him.' There are mysterious depths of meaning here. It is not so much the bare fact of Christ's sinlessness that is emphasized as God's knowledge of this fact, which rendered Christ a mediator. Some attempt has been made to whittle down this statement by translating 'made sin' as 'made sin-offering.' Is it likely the same word can have two different meanings in the same clause? Is it not contrasted with 'righteousness' in the following clause? Surely although we cannot comprehend the dread statement, that in itself is no reason for doubting it. Whichever rendering we accept, there is here postulated a reason for the coming of the Son of God into human form. He came that He might die. In flesh He could suffer. Being God He could satisfy. God did not die, but He who died was God,

A corollary of this wondrous truth is stated in 1 John 3. 5, 'And ye know that He was manifested to take away sins: and in Him is no sin.' This is an echo of the words of the Baptist. The stupendous task is committed to the Lamb of God's providing. No other in all the universe of God could undertake this gigantic achievement.

Not all the blood of beasts on Jewish altars slain
 Could give the guilty conscience peace or take away one stain.
But Christ the Heavenly Lamb takes all our sins away,
 A sacrifice of nobler name and richer blood than they.

—*I. Watts.*

The fourth great truth resting upon His perfect manhood is the character and efficacy of His priesthood. 'Wherefore it behoved Him in all things to be made like unto His brethren, that He might be a merciful and faithful high priest in things pertaining to God' (Heb. 2. 17). 'For we have not an high priest which cannot be touched with the feeling of our infirmities; but one that hath been in all points tempted like as we are, yet without sin' (Heb. 4. 15). The writer wishes to preclude the common fancy that there was some peculiarity in Christ which made the temptation wholly different from ours, that He was a 'mailed champion, exposed to toy arrows.' On the contrary, He has felt in His own consciousness the suffering which comes from resisting. Christ *suffered*, being tempted. It is said that before a railway wheel is passed for service, it has to pass the most searching tests. A weight of some ten thousand pounds is brought down upon it. The design of such a test is not to break the wheel, but to prove it cannot be broken. The glorious truth is that the victory of Christ in His conflict with sin and Satan attests His fitness not only to be a priest in offering both gifts and sacrifices for sins, but His competence to supply mercy and the grace to help in time of need (Heb. 4. 16).

Touched with a sympathy within, He knows our feeble frame;
 He knows what sore temptations mean, for He endured the same.
He in the days of feeble flesh, poured out His cries and tears
 And though exalted feels afresh what every member bears.

We have hastened to Bethlehem to see a babe wrapped in swaddling clothes. We have trod the highways of Galilee in the company of the Incarnate God. We have climbed the *Via*

Dolorosa to Golgotha's sacred height where divine love was telescoped into time, and Jesus died. But if it be true that no living Christ ever issued from the tomb of Joseph, then that tomb became the grave not of a man, but of Christianity. If Christ did not rise, His death is no longer a sacrifice but the saddest of earth's tragedies, the very midnight gloom of failure, and hope is a word to mock us. But the flashing wonder is—He rose again the third day according to the Scriptures and our Lord is alive in the perfection of His manhood. 'It was not possible that He should be holden of' death (Acts 2. 24). In this connection it is interesting to note that the designation 'Son of Man' occurs only once in the Book of the Acts, when the dying Stephen declared he saw the heavens opened and the Son of Man standing at the right hand of God (7. 56). This is the only instance in the whole New Testament where the designation is employed by any one except our Lord Himself. This is at once Stephen's testimony to the greatness of His Lord in His divine majesty, and a witness to the genuineness of the whole series of declarations attributed to our Lord in which He saw Himself in the Danielic vision, and declared on that basis His Messiahship in its earthly humiliation, and subsequent elevation to participation in divine glory.

The full implications of this series of declarations would require a full chapter to themselves. Suffice to mention the categorical statement of John 5. 27, 'The Father hath given Him authority to execute judgment also, because He is (the) Son of Man.' The prerogative of judgment is associated with the humanity of Christ. Matt. 25. 31-46 limns for us the impressive picture of the great assize, the general judgment of the nations. The Son of Man shall sit on the Throne of His glory. Those arraigned before Him are acutely aware that He knows by experience the force of the temptations by which they have been beset. Nevertheless He is perfectly consistent with His character in so acting. H. B. Swete points out that our English term and its cognates are forensic; they speak of law, with its rigid formalism, its externality, its occasional travesties of justice. But the series of Greek words which we translate by 'judge' and 'judgment' strikes another note: it tells of the spiritual distinctions which exist between man and man and which must ultimately be brought to light. Whatever else happened to men in the presence of Jesus Christ, they were judged. They knew they were. The living Word of God was active and sharper than any two-edged sword. 'Come see a man that told me all things that ever I did,' says a woman (John 4. 29). 'Depart from me,' says Peter, 'I am a sinful man, O Lord' (Luke 5. 8). None who encountered the Light of the world could remain neutral. 'The Person of Christ divides men now, and will divide them in the end: here and hereafter He is the Judge. But when the Son of Man is revealed on the Throne of His glory, complete manifestation will take place. Still is there a dividing line, echoed in the polar words—"Come"—"Depart."' This tremendous passage in Matt. 25. 34 is the only time that the Lord Jesus calls Himself the King. His every act and word had proclaimed it, but not till now does He use the title. But if He speaks in regal glory, the test of discipleship is the attitude of men to those linked with Him for ever in His humanity, embracing every people and tribe and nation—'Inasmuch as ye have done it unto one of the least of these My brethren, ye have done it unto Me' (Matt. 25. 40).

After the Resurrection our Lord was changed, yet the same. He was no longer subject to the material order. He appears; He vanishes: closed doors are no effective obstruction to His movement. Yet He eats of broiled fish. He reveals the marks of His passion to Thomas in such a way as to humble him to adoring worship. To Mary the cadences of the well-loved voice echo in one word, and recognition is immediate. He is the same, yet changed. 'In Him soul and body in the indissoluble union of a perfect manhood, are seen triumphant over the last penalty of sin' (Westcott). It is a glorious, thrilling fact. The Saviour lives in ascended power, still in His perfection as Son of Man.

In the Ephesian letter, Paul tells us more. In a passage which echoes the grandeur of Psalm 24, he depicts for us the hierarchy of power, dignities and principalities in the vast angelic realm. Like some guard of honour they await the coming of the King of Glory. The challenge reverberates across the vaults of heaven, 'Who is the King of glory?' The answer is immediate, 'The Lord strong and mighty, the Lord mighty in battle, the Lord of Hosts, He is the King of glory.' And the serried hosts are hushed into awed silence for a brief space ere their pæan of praise again bursts forth, for fresh from the conflict of the cross comes the man Christ Jesus, still with the print of the nails. And now He passes the exultant throng until He is 'far above all principality, and power, and might, and dominion, and every name that is named, not only in this world, but also in that which is to come' (Eph. 1 21). These three glowing words, 'far above all,' picture unlimited sway and a name unequalled, in which every knee shall bow, proclaiming the Man of Calvary, Sovereign and undisputed Lord, to the glory of God the Father.

CHAPTER VII

The Saviour

ANDREW BORLAND

THE death of Christ is a subject of fundamental importance and of profound significance. Large portions of the Gospel narratives are devoted to the record of the actual historical event. 'Taking an ordinary Bible it is surprising to observe the space devoted to the last week of the life and ministry of Christ, those days which were spent in full expectation of and preparation for His imminent death. For example, out of thirty pages devoted to the first Gospel, no less than ten are given to the record of the last week. In the second Gospel, out of nineteen pages seven are occupied with the story from Palm Sunday to Easter Day. In St. Luke's Gospel no less than one-fourth is taken up with the story of these days, and out of twenty-four pages in the fourth Gospel ten are actually concerned with the same period. This prominence given to the events of the last few days demands attention and calls for explanation. In view of the crowded three years of Christ's ministry, is it not striking that there should be such fragmentariness in the story of those years until we come to the last few days? Surely the conspicuous place given to the death in the Gospels must mean that the writers regarded it as of supreme significance' (Griffith Thomas: *Christianity is Christ*).

Further indication of its importance is the fact that it occupied a leading place in the thought and teaching of the Lord Himself. The variety of the language He used, the increasing frequency of reference to His approaching end, and the startling minuteness of detail in the closing allusions thereto are evidence of the importance He attached to His appointed exodus. From the moment at the commencement of His public ministry when He hinted at the violence of His death in comparing Himself to a bridegroom rudely snatched from his bride (Mark 2. 20) up to the time when He instituted the Supper by which His death was to be commemorated (Matt. 26. 26-28) He was ever and anon preparing the minds of His disciples for that eventuality. That they were slow of heart to believe (Luke 24. 25) and dull of understanding is witness to the fact that the divine intention in the Incarnation was well beyond their mental grasp until, after His death and resurrection, the former of these events was shot through with eternal light.

So closely related are His death and the truth about His person, that the climax of His ministry was reached when, at Cæsarea Philippi, Peter unequivocally announced the mind of the apostolic band by asserting, 'Thou art the Christ the Son of the living God' (Matt. 16. 16). Thereupon came a startling departure in the ministry of our Lord. '*From that time forth* began Jesus to shew unto His disciples, how that He must go unto Jerusalem, and suffer many things of the elders and chief priests and scribes, and be killed and be raised again the third day' (Matt. 16. 21). That the fact was difficult of comprehension and contrary to Messianic expectation is shown in the intervention by Peter, 'Be it far from Thee, Lord; this shall not be unto Thee' (Matt. 16. 22).

It is considered scholarly and modern, in certain schools of thought, to eliminate from an investigation of this theme such references as throw the mind back to the Old Testament sacrificial ritual, and to justify that procedure by maintaining that the apostolic writers simply interpreted the meaning of the Cross in terms of current Jewish thought. The mental content of those first century Christians was circumscribed, the modernist says, by their religious upbringing, and, consequently, their language, being a reflection of the age in which they lived, must give place now to terms consistent with present-day trends of thought. We are not of that disposition and are content to take the New Testament interpretation as it stands and to accept it as a divine revelation of the meaning of the death of Christ.

The acceptance of the New Testament emphasis upon that death as viewed in the light of Old Testament prophetic announcement leads inevitably to the admission that the exodus of our Lord from this world is in a category all by itself. *It was a planned death*, planned in the sense of Isaiah's strange statement, that it was the good pleasure of Jehovah to bruise Him (Isa. 53. 10). Perhaps it was consciousness of that significance that led John to make such frequent reference to our Lord's use of the expression, 'the hour,' and to record with most touching intimacy the opening words of His prayer, 'Father, the hour is come, glorify Thy Son, that Thy Son also may glorify Thee' (John 17. 1).

Apart from the fact that many Old Testament prophecies had an unexpected and, to the disciples, an unanticipated fulfilment in the circumstances leading to and surrounding our Lord's death (Psa. 22; Isa. 53), numerous statements in the New Testament corroborate our assertion that the death was in accordance with a divine plan, conceived before time and executed in the days of His flesh. It was 'when the fulness of the time was come (that) God sent forth His Son . . . to redeem' (Gal. 4. 4, 5), or, as another passage has it, 'in due time Christ died for the ungodly' (Rom. 5. 6). Such statements lend special meaning to our Lord's own words preserved by John, 'No man taketh it (My life) from Me; but I lay it down of Myself. I have power (i.e. authority, commission) to lay it down, and I have power to take it again. This *commandment* have I received of My Father' (John 10. 18). Consideration of these pronouncements gives additional significance to the statement that His exodus should be *accomplished* at Jerusalem (Luke 9. 31), and His own declarations at the end that He had finished His work (John 19. 30). The witness of many Scriptures to the fact that His death was divinely planned can scarcely be denied without doing violence to the text, so that the conclusion must be reached that a death of such a character must be unique, and must have significances that no other death has.

The constant and unstrained use of the language of the sacrificial ritual of the earlier religious economy points in the same direction. So closely interwoven are the two Testaments that it is impossible not to observe how persistently the writers in the New Testament wittingly related the Lord's death to the types in the Old Testament, and concurred in asserting that the shadows had to disappear when the substance had arrived. The appropriating to our Lord by New Testament writers of the title 'Lamb' reveals how they interpreted the central feature of the older dispensation, and surely it is not without some point that, before the canon of Scripture is closed, there should be repeated mention of the triumphs of 'the Lamb.'

Thus, as another has written, 'The Cross pervades all Scripture: the historical books prove its necessity; the Levitical foreshadow its meaning; the Psalms portray its experiences; the prophets foretell its sufferings; the Gospels describe its fulfilment; the Acts proclaim its blessings; the Epistles explain its doctrines, and the Revelation exhibits its fruits' (W. Hoste, *Bible Doctrines*, p. 93).

The theme of the Bible is the story of the redemptive purpose of God. It narrates the Fall and discloses the enslavement of man to an inveterate foe. Sin is a stark reality. It displays itself in universal and wilful disobedience to the God who is Creator and Moral Governor. Lawlessness is an evidence that man's loyalty has been alienated, and another has become his unlawful master. Moreover, the Bible shows what observation and experience confirm, the impotence of man to encompass his own spiritual emancipation. Slave he is and slave he remains, despite his boasted advancement in planes other than spiritual, so that he is shut up to divine intervention to accomplish what he longs for but cannot enjoy. The Bible reveals the God-devised method by which forgiveness can be realized, the power of the enemy broken and a new life of victory experienced. Moreover, it announces that all the pre-Christian illustrations, given in a variety of ways to the nation chosen as the vehicle for the communication and presentation of divine truth, reach their reality and final objective in the death of Christ, for

> In Him the shadows of the law
> Are all fulfilled and now withdraw.

The fact that the man in the street does not understand such language is no reflection on the theologians who interpret the death of the Cross in the terms of Biblical usage, but on the plain man who is not sufficiently interested to inquire what such references mean. (See L. Weatherhead's *A Plain Man Looks at the Cross*).

The endeavour to relate the facts of that death to the circumstances of each generation is admirable enough, so long as loyalty to the Scriptural revelation is maintained. Otherwise it becomes a display of human wisdom seeking to philosophize on a subject that has already received divine interpretation at the hands of writers chosen of God for that purpose. But why should a distaste for the apostolic witness exist? 'Some who have the distaste explain their attitude on the ground that this is a *theory* of the Atonement—the Substitutionary Theory they call it—and that the Gospel should be detached from any theory. . . . It is not uncharitable to hold that the objection to "theory" is here only a specious reason for the rejection of the apostolic witness. The real cause of the distaste for the idea that Christ died as our Substitute is to be found in the influence of the rationalism of recent generations upon theological thought. Rationalism poured scorn upon the idea of anyone—as if Christ was just 'anyone'—dying in place of others, and the majority of theologians, especially in Germany, felt that they ought to come to terms with the spirit of the age by minimising the apostolic testimony' (Prof. Daniel Lamont in *God's Word and Man's Response*).

The contents of the New Testament are meaningless if the death of Jesus is regarded as an ordinary death. If He was 'God manifest in flesh,' 'pleased as Man with man to dwell,' then, being sinless, death to Him was both unnatural and unnecessary. His being in Manhood had a specific objectivity, and that, in Biblical language, was 'to put away sin by the sacrifice of Himself' (Heb. 9. 26). Statements are so consciously guarded, and words so consistently chosen, as to suggest that no other death is comparable with it. *It is unique, unparalleled.* Human analogies, sincerely used as attempts to explain the inexplicable, all fall short. Peter's declaration is that 'the Just One died for the unjust ones, that He might bring us to God' (1 Peter 3. 18). The Baptist's assertion is that He is 'The Lamb of God that beareth away the sin of the world' (John 1. 29). There is nothing to be ashamed of, either morally or intellectually, to be willing to say,

> Bearing shame and scoffing rude,
> In my place condemned He stood,
> Sealed my pardon with His blood
> Hallelujah, what a Saviour!

The late Professor Denney whose book, *The Death of Christ*, is one of the best on the Atonement, was wont to say that the second line of that stanza contained a statement of the greatest truth in the universe. Many will concur.

All Apostolic writers did regard that death as having a specific objectivity about it. It was *telic* in nature. Nothing spectacular attached to it. In it they saw design for a definite purpose. Beyond its relation to man's need, they saw that its ultimate end was that God might be glorified. John's Gospel records our Lord's momentous words immediately prior to His Crucifixion, 'I have glorified Thee on the earth: I have finished the work which Thou gavest Me to do' (John 17. 4). Such intention carries the death on Calvary into a plane solitary and dignified, and announces the fact that the exodus was not by the accident of a brutal human murder but in consonance with a deliberate purpose. In short, the death of Christ was an incident in a plan—a plan which did not end at Golgotha.

It is, therefore, not difficult to conceive that other important subjects in the New Testament are inseparably related to that death. The whole movement of the divine purpose is seen in that light. The Incarnation points to the Crucifixion—for says Paul, 'Christ Jesus came into the world to save sinners' (1 Tim. 1. 15). Further, the Resurrection takes colour from the nature of the death of Christ, for is it not declared that 'He was delivered for our offences (i.e. because we had offended), and was raised again for our justification' (i.e. because we had been justified) (Rom. 4. 25)? Besides, the continued ministry of our Lord in heaven is dependent upon the nature and triumph of that death. As Mediator between God and man He exercises His office because He 'gave Himself a ransom for all' (1 Tim. 2. 6). His High-Priestly ministry is based upon the fact that 'after He had offered one sacrifice for sins for ever, (He) sat down on the right hand of God' (Heb. 10. 12), while His Advocacy for His sinning people is efficacious because 'He is the propitiation for our sins' (1 John 2. 1, 2).

It may be profitable now to approach the Scriptures to discover what is actually said about the various aspects of our Lord's death.

I. *Consider its relation to Time.* What is time? We can imagine neither a beginning nor an end of it. It disappears into eternity at both ends. Time extends backwards beyond the limits of human history. The foundation of the world is the ultimate backward limit of history as far as this planet is concerned. The dissolution of the world is the extreme limit at the other end. In between these two events is what we call time. Now the death of Christ is stated to have a definite relation to all three. As to the foundation of the world, Peter refers to 'the precious blood of Christ, as of a lamb without blemish and without spot who verily was fore-ordained *before the foundation of the world*' (1 Peter 1. 20). As to time it is stated, 'Once in the end of the ages (i.e. the climax towards which previous ages all moved inerrantly) Christ appeared to put away sin by the sacrifice of Himself' (Heb. 9. 26). The death of Christ has affected time ever since. At the other end, beyond time, we read of the Lamb, the symbol of sacrifice, 'And there shall be no more curse: but the throne of God and of the Lamb shall be in it' (Rev. 22. 3). No death is comparable with that!

II. *Think, too, of its relation to space.* The earth is a mere speck in the vastness of the universe. It is the home of man, created in the image of God. Here was the scene of the life of the Son of God. But, most wondrous of all, this planet was the witness of the death of the Lamb of God. The dearest place to God in all the universe must be the hill outside the city wall of Jerusalem

> Where the dear Lord was crucified
> Who died to save us all.

In this respect, too, it should not be forgotten that the death of Christ had cosmic effects. What tremendous significance is contained in these statements, 'And having made peace through the blood of His cross, by Him to reconcile all things unto Himself (i.e. God) . . . whether they be *things in earth*, or *things in heaven*' (Col. 1. 20), or, He 'became obedient unto death (i.e. His obedience to the will of God took Him that far), even the death of the cross! Wherefore God hath highly exalted Him, and given Him the name which is above every name, that in the name of Jesus *every knee should bow*, of things *in heaven*, and things *in earth*, and things *under the earth*, and that *every tongue* should confess that Jesus Christ is Lord' (Phil. 2. 9-11).

III. Numerous passages, too, disclose *the relation of that death to God, the Father.* A mere recital of passages is most impressive. Peter's testimony is: He was 'delivered by the determinate counsel and foreknowledge of God' (Acts 2. 23). He saw that death as part of a divinely conceived plan, although He had been taken and by wicked hands crucified and slain. 'Foreknowledge is that quality of deity which is cognisant of all that is known as history among men. It is a quality not possessed by creatures.' 'The determinate counsel of God' indicates a plan conceived and approved by God Himself, and executed in accordance with His own inscrutable purpose. Consequently we read that it was 'in due time Christ died' (Rom. 5. 6). Calvary was not an afterthought of God, but the expression of an eternal plan, revealing itself in time, and culminating at that sacred spot in one act of unfathomable significance.

To Peter's testimony we can add the corroborative witness of his fellow-apostle, John, in whose epistle are declarations of unequivocal meaning: 'In this was manifested the love of God toward us, because that *God sent His only begotten Son into the world.*' 'God *sent His Son* to be the propitiation for our sins.' 'We have seen and do testify that the *Father sent the Son* to be the Saviour of the world' (1 John 4. 8-14). These quotations are of a piece with the entire teaching of the Johannine writings, and a closer consideration of them will amply repay the effort. Observe, however, these ideas. The words 'Father' and 'Son' are used to distinguish the work attributed to the two divine Persons. The Father is considered as the actuating Person. He loved and He sent. The Son is regarded as the active Person. He came to be the Saviour. Yet there is harmonious co-operation in the work; the Two are as One. How stupendous is that act which displays the love of God the Father in the gift of His 'only begotten Son,' that the Son might become the Saviour of the world living in lawlessness and rebellion against God!

To the witness of these two apostles can be added that of Paul. His is most varied and comprehensive.

Take two passages to illustrate the Pauline teaching in regard to the relation of the Cross to God, the Father.

(*a*) 2 Cor. 5. 19: 'God was, in Christ, reconciling the world unto Himself, not imputing their trespasses unto them.' The whole section should be read and pondered reverently and deeply, for it contains some of the profoundest asseverations in the New Testament. It pays tribute to the deity of Christ, for only One who was God could co-operate in a work of such tremendous moment. It asserts the uniqueness and fitness of His humanity for such a task as was laid on Him, for He 'knew no sin.' The declaration is absolute and admits of no qualification whatsoever;

and in that respect it is at one with similar assertions by other apostles (1 Peter 2. 22; 1 John 3. 5). Moreover, there can be no doubt that Paul intended to convey that the sufferings of Christ were of a vicarious nature, for God, 'made Him to be sin for us.' Here there is an echo of Peter's application of Isaiah's prophetic announcement, 'by whose stripes we are healed' (1 Peter 2. 24). Observe, too, how uncompromising the apostle is about man's need and Christ's work. Man is guilty of trespasses and has offended a holy God. By such offence the world has become estranged from God, and requires reconciliation. That possibility has been secured in the death of Christ, so that the message of the Gospel is, 'Be ye reconciled to God.'

(*b*) Rom. 3. 25: (Christ Jesus) 'Whom God hath set forth a propitiation, through faith, in His blood.' Here again we are thrown back upon the ritual of the Old Testament for an illustration of the death of Christ. Just as the mercy-seat in the economy of animal sacrifices was the meeting-place between God and His people when they approached Him in His appointed way, by the animal blood shed and sprinkled on the Day of Atonement (Lev. 16), so now, in a new economy of grace and a fuller revelation of the mind of God, Christ Jesus (not His Cross but Himself, because His blood was shed) is the appointed meeting-place, where man can enjoy fellowship with a righteous God to whom He has been reconciled through the work of Christ.

How does the death of Christ affect God? First of all, it should be remembered that it does not change His nature. He remains inflexibly righteous. He does not minimize man's sin and guilt, and degenerate into the indulgent Father of many teachers. The death of Christ vindicates God as the Lawgiver. 'The moral wrong committed by the sinner in defiance of the law is a stain on the honour of the Lawgiver. Our Lord's perfect obedience, extending even to voluntary submission to death, vindicated the Lawgiver' (T. C. Hammond, *In Understanding be Men*). By so doing Christ secured for God and for the sinner a basis for the remission of sins satisfactory to both. He fully met all God's claims against the sinner, and at the same time both upheld the righteousness of God and demonstrated His love towards the undeserving and guilty one. Thus the death of Christ changes the relative attitude of God towards the sinner who *believes the Gospel, repents of his attitude towards God,* and accepts the provision made by God for him in the work of the Cross. God forgives such a one, pardons, justifies, accepts him.

IV. We cannot omit to consider Christ's death *as it is related to Himself.* Men have discussed this aspect of the Cross from various points of view. Some look upon our Lord as an adventurer, a selfish seeker after fame who staged His life to fit in with numerous Messianic prophecies with which He and His disciples were familiar. That is a favourite argument of infidels and rationalists, and needs only to be stated to be proved false to the plainest teaching of the Gospel words. It is the refuge of those who perceive in Christ a challenge to which they are not willing to respond.

Others maintain that He was a self-appointed national Hero who espoused the dying cause of the Jews, and running into conflict with the designs of the Roman authorities, paid for His rashness with His own life. Anyone who reads Otto Borchert's *The Original Jesus*, knows how far that is from the truth, for so contrary were His conduct and character to the contemporary conception of the Messiah that it is impossible to read into the New Testament narratives anything in Jesus remotely corresponding to a national Hero. Such a contention does not explain the mystery of His death.

Others again aver that He died as a Martyr because of the strength of His religious convictions. True it is that He encountered His fiercest antagonism from the fanatical religious leaders whose temporizing He unmasked and whose hypocrisy He mercilessly castigated. Their ire He roused to such an extent that they were willing to compound with one of His own disciples in order that they might destroy Him, making pretence that they were jealous for the liberties accorded them by the imperial authority of Rome (Luke 22. 3-6). But an unbiased reading of the history soon disabuses one's mind, for it is quite apparent that our Lord's death was more than that of a victim of Roman or Jewish outrage. None of these suggestions fits the circumstances of the case, or agrees with the doctrines of first century Christians.

New Testament language puts that death in a light entirely different.

(*a*) It was an act of *obedience to a known divine plan.* 'He took upon Himself bondman's form . . . humbled Himself and became obedient (i.e. obedient to the will of God, as far as) unto death, even the death of the Cross' (Phil. 2. 7, 8). Comment is unnecessary. He was always 'about His Father's business.'

(*b*) It was a voluntary *submission to the will of His Father.* In Gethsemane, on the night on which He was betrayed, knowing that He had come from God and went to God, facing the ordeal of the Cross, in an agony of conflict within Himself, He prayed. '*Nevertheless,* not as I will, but as Thou wilt' (Matt. 26. 39). That resignation had been made earlier in the same week when, after the incident of the Greeks in their desire to see Him, He had said, 'Now is My soul troubled, and what shall I say? Father, save Me from this hour? *but* for this cause came I unto this hour. Father, glorify Thy name' (John 12. 27, 28). That *nevertheless* and that *but* are amongst the most revealing words of the Bible and surround with unspeakable dignity the surrender and submission indicated by their use.

(*c*) That obedience and committal had their *origin in a love that recognized no boundaries, and acknowledged no sacrifice too great in its response to the demands made upon it.* 'That the world may know,' He said, 'that I love the Father, even so I do' (John 14. 31). Here was perfect co-operation with the will of the Father; here was an abandonment that makes all the more mysterious the cry of dereliction on the Cross, 'My God, My God, why hast Thou forsaken Me?' (Mark 15. 34). That mystery is insoluble in terms of human reasoning, but is understandable in recollection of the fact that the Sufferer on Calvary was the Antitype of the goat which, on the Day of Atonement in Israel's history, carried the transferred sins of the people into a desert-place to a land not inhabited. His love was stronger than death. The forsaking was real, an experience the intensity of which is without parallel in the history of mankind.

(*d*) The Lord's death was *a voluntary act, consciously and deliberately undertaken, with the knowledge that it was not an end,* but an incident in a plan of which it was only a part. National heroes have offered themselves in sacrifice for the well-being of their compatriots, but their lives were taken from them by the action of others. No man took His life from Him: He laid it down of Himself. And it should be remarked, He laid it down that He might take it up again. As if He embraced the opportunity of displaying His love and hailed the moment of the execution of the plan He exclaimed, 'Father, the hour is come!' (John 17. 1). He knew that the things concerning Him had an end, and sought, after His Resurrection, to assure the disappointed disciples that Christ ought to have suffered and then to enter into His glory (Luke 24. 26). Viewed in that light there is conscious triumph in the loud voice from the Cross, 'It is finished' (John 19. 30). Nor should it be forgotten that not one of the four Evangelists narrates that Jesus *died* on the Cross. Matthew writes, 'He yielded up His spirit' (Matt. 27. 50). Mark and Luke say, 'He expired' (Mark 16. 30; Luke 23. 46), while John declares, 'He dismissed His spirit' (John 19. 30). Add to the significance of these unusual expressions the wonder of the leg-breaking soldiers when they discovered that He was dead. Pilate marvelled that so it was (Mark 15. 44). Something unusual, something unique, had taken place—the sinless life of the Son of God had been 'laid down.'

The conclusion reached from a consideration of these facts is this: the death of Christ was not the result of the miscarriage of justice, nor the exhibition merely of the undisguised hatred of an antagonized priesthood, but the veritable triumph of divine love and the unquestionable disclosure of a plan, from the execution of which no combination of evil forces and circumstances could deter the Son of God. The acknowledgment of the truth of that conclusion cannot but result in the acceptance of the frequently re-iterated doctrine of the New Testament that there was objective reality in that death—to accomplish for mankind a work that only God could do, and to procure in its accomplishment the blessings which the New Testament assures us are the portion of all who by faith associate themselves with Christ, in union with whom they are accepted before God, and forgiven all their trespasses.

V. Furthermore the death of our Lord may be considered in its *relation to the Devil.* The Bible attributes to the Devil, as tempter, the entrance of sin into the world. His activities have always been bent on hindering the fulfilment of the divine promise to send a Redeemer. He was aware that, in the person of Jesus of Nazareth, God was working out a scheme of tremendous importance, and consequently he redoubled his efforts to disorganize and frustrate the plan. By the edict of Herod he sought to destroy the Babe (Matt. 2. 13). At Nazareth he incensed the inhabitants against the new Prophet who had arisen and had spoken against their unbelief (Luke 4. 28, 29). In the wilderness he endeavoured to divert the Lord from His pathway of obedience (Luke 4. 1-12). It was Satan that entered into Judas, through whom he manipulated the betrayal (Luke 22. 3), while the Saviour recognized the forces of opposition when He faced His foes with the words, 'This is your hour and the power of darkness' (Luke 22. 53). The Cross-work of Christ is stated to have special significance for the spirits of evil. On the Cross, says Paul, He 'spoiled principalities and powers, He made a shew of them openly, triumphing over them in it' (Col. 2. 15). John declares that the purpose for which the Son of God was manifested was 'that He might destroy the works of the devil' (John 3. 8), while the writer to the Hebrews maintains that 'He destroyed him that had the power of death, that is, the devil' (Heb. 2. 14).

Probably one of the reasons why men look upon the preaching of 'Christ and Him crucified' as foolishness, and detest the mention of the 'precious blood' is that their minds are blinded by the god of this age who knows that in the death of Christ is the message of victory over sin and his own evil devices. The triumph of Christ on Calvary is the assurance to the whole universe that Satan is a defeated foe, and that God has conquered the enemy in his own domain of death. John, the Seer on Patmos, heard the thrilling words, 'I am the Living One that became dead, and behold I am alive for evermore, and have the keys of hades and of death' (Rev. 1. 18), and these words have come ringing down the centuries ever since with their note of hope and cheer. Satan's power has been broken.

VI. *We may now relate that death to the sinner.* Here again we must abandon human theorizings about that subjective theory 'which makes the atoning value of Christ's death consist in *its effects on us* and not in any 'objective' expiation for sin. According to it there is no problem of forgiveness on God's side. He is eager and ready to forgive as soon as we turn to Him. The one essential is that we should become forgivable—i.e. that we should have a sincere sorrow for sin and a hearty desire to love and serve Him for the future. The place which the death of Christ has in atonement is simply that it is the most powerful means of winning our hearts to Him, because it is the supreme proof of His love for us' (Guillebaud, *Why the Cross?* p. 164). That theory is sentimental rather than Scriptural.

(*a*) The Bible teaches that the death of Christ provides God and man with a common and acceptable meeting-place on the question of sin. Rom. 3. 25 states that 'God hath set (Christ) forth as a propitiation . . . in His blood.' 'It is God who is propitiated by the vindication of His holy and righteous character, whereby, through the provision He has made in the vicarious and expiatory sacrifice of Christ, He has so dealt with sin that He can shew mercy to the believing sinner in the removal of his guilt and the remission of his sins' (W. E. Vine, 'Propitiation,' in *Expository Dictionary*).

(*b*) The Bible teaches that the death of Christ secures the possibility of the sinner's reconciliation to God. Man, we must remind ourselves, is regarded as an enemy, a rebel, one who has been alienated from God by his sins. The propitiation (i.e. the atoning death) makes reconciliation possible, but it is man who must be reconciled, because it is on his side that the estrangement has taken place. The idea in the word 'reconciliation' as used in the New Testament points 'to the winning rather the pardon of an offended King than the consent of a rebel to yield to His kindness' (Moule). Hence it is the heavenly ambassador's duty to approach the rebel race with the message, 'Be ye reconciled to God.' The enjoyment of that pardon and peace is now dependent, not upon what God has done (for there can be no doubt about His attitude since Christ has died) but upon how the sinner responds. If he acknowledges his enmity, his rebellion, God most graciously responds to him, pardons and receives him. The work of reconciliation is not a process by which the sinner becomes acceptable to God, but a completed act when Christ 'was made sin for us'.

(*c*) The death of Christ enables God to be just, and, at the same time, the justifier of the ungodly (Rom. 3. 26). All human analogy fails, for in this case the Lawgiver Himself becomes the Victim and accepts the responsibility. No moral principle is violated. The wrath of the holy God was exhausted in Christ, so that *the believing sinner* is acquitted of his responsibility and is accepted in his Representative. God can justify (i.e. *reckon* righteous, not *make* righteous) the ungodly, not because of what they merit or because of how they feel towards God as they view the sufferings of Christ, but because Christ died for (on behalf of) the ungodly. The debt has been paid by Another, 'blotting out the handwriting of ordinances that was against us, which was contrary to us, and took it out of the way, nailing it to His cross' (Col. 2. 14), where:

> We stand in wonder viewing
> All our sins on Jesus laid.

(*d*) Again, the death of Christ guarantees the believing sinner's redemption and forgiveness. 'In whom we have redemption through His blood, even the forgiveness of sins,' states plainly what the Apostle Paul thought of the Cross-work of Christ. The word 'redemption' is used in four passages in the sense of the removal of the guilt of sin at the cost of the Saviour's blood. (See Rom. 3. 24; Heb. 9. 12-15; Eph. 1. 7; Col. 1. 14). The context in all these passages throws the emphasis on the Saviour's work of putting us right with God; only in the Colossian passage is there any mention of the accompanying deliverance from the power of sin' (*Why the Cross?* p. 142). How succinctly Charles Wesley put the theology of New Testament redemption,

> He breaks *the power of cancelled sin*,
> He sets the prisoner free!

Sinners are delivered from the authority of darkness into the kingdom of the Son of God (Col. 1. 13), where they are taught that they have been purchased by His blood and are consequently not now their own. In this state, too, they enjoy 'newness of life,' communicated in the gift of the Holy Spirit whom they receive on belief of the Gospel message, and in whose power they are enabled to live in holiness unto God.

(*e*) Resting on the death of Christ and His resurrection which proves its value, the sinner can allay every fear of condemnation, for 'there is no condemnation to them who are in Christ Jesus.' So complete is the work that the challenge is issued, 'who shall lay anything to the charge of *God's elect*? Who is he that condemneth?' None answers, for God has justified, and Christ it is who has died. As if to add assurance to confidence the apostle adds, 'Yea, *rather*,

(He) is risen again, who is *even* at the right hand of God, who *also* maketh intercession for us' (Rom. 8. 33, 34). Nor is this all, for we have been 'made nigh unto God by the blood of Christ' and 'accepted in the Beloved One' (Eph. 1. 6).

VII. The study of the death of Christ may be approached, too, in *its relation to the Church.*

(*a*) The Church is built upon the related facts of the Deity and the death of Christ. Immediately upon the acknowledgment of Peter's confession, 'Thou art the Christ, the Son of the living God,' our Lord proceeded to announce that 'He must go unto Jerusalem, . . . and be killed, and be raised again the third day' (Matt. 16. 16-21). The teaching of the Epistles may be summed up in Paul's words 'Christ also loved the Church and gave Himself for it . . . that He might present it to Himself a glorious Church, not having spot or wrinkle' (Eph. 5. 25-27).

(*b*) His death for all is the basic fact governing the recognition of the 'one Body' including believing Jews and believing Gentiles, 'for He is our peace who hath made both (i.e. Jew and Gentile) one . . . having abolished in His flesh the enmity . . . to make in Himself of twain one new man, so making peace' (Eph. 2. 14-18).

VIII. *How does the death of Christ affect the individual believer?*

(*a*) It is the measure of conviction that God has a real concern for the well-being of those who believe. 'He that spared not His own Son, but delivered Him up for us all, how shall He not with Him also freely give us all things?' (Rom. 8. 32).

(*b*) A recognition of its claims acts as a constraint to consecrated service. 'The love of Christ constraineth us because we thus judge that if One died for all, all died, that they which live (i.e. in union with Him in resurrection) should not live unto themselves but unto Him' (2 Cor. 5. 14).

(*c*) The death of Christ sets an example of the limits of self-humiliation in the accomplishment of the will of God. 'Let this mind be in you which was also in Christ who . . . humbled Himself and became obedient unto death, even the death of the Cross' (Phil. 2. 5-8).[1]

[1] Such example is intended for imitation in communal concerns for the out-working of our salvation when difficult problems assail the peace of the company. The observance of the contextual application would save from erroneous ideas about its reference to growth in sanctification.

(*d*) Christ's suffering unto death should act as an inspiration in the day of suffering for righteousness. That is the teaching of Peter's first letter where the death of our Lord is referred to frequently as His sufferings, not so much as the Sacrifice for sin, although that aspect is always in the background of the apostle's argument, but as a Righteous One who bore testimony against men for the truth of God. In such a way He is the Example whom Christians in like circumstances should follow. 'Forasmuch then as Christ hath suffered in the flesh, . . . arm yourselves likewise with the same mind, . . . that ye no longer should live the rest of the time in the flesh to the lusts of men, but to the will of God' (1 Peter 4. 1).

(*e*) The Cross of Christ should be the very heart of Christian glorying. Nothing else can take its place when its truth is apprehended. As we contemplate the marvel and mystery of that Cross with its significance and its insistent claims, can we refrain from saying with Paul, 'God forbid that I should glory save in the cross of our Lord Jesus Christ, by whom the world is crucified unto me, and I unto the world'? (Gal. 6. 14).

We have touched but the fringe of the subject. As the number of Scripture references indicates, it has been our aim to allow the New Testament to speak for itself and to avoid mere theorizing.

Let us draw our study to a close on practical lines.

First let us summarize the doctrine of the Cross in the words of another. It contains four great truths.

(1) The Representation of the sinner before God.
(2) The Substitution of the Saviour for the sinner.
(3) The Identification of the sinner with the Saviour.
(4) The Revelation of God in Christ to the sinner.

(Griffith Thomas).

Second, let us remind ourselves that the provision made for the sinner in the death of Christ is the only ground for confidence in the hour of the sinner's death. We call to witness the words of dying Dr. Samuel Johnson, the great lexicographer: 'For some time before his death,' said the physician who attended him, 'all his fears were calmed and absorbed by the prevalence of his faith, and his trust in the merits and *propitiation* of Jesus Christ. He talked often to me about the necessity of faith in the *sacrifice* of Jesus, as necessary beyond all good works whatever, for the salvation of mankind' (Boswell, *The Life of Samuel Johnson*).

Third, let us take our place before that Cross with all its insoluble mystery, its profound significance, its poignant appeal, its glorious triumph and its challenging application and, as its message reaches us in this far removed century, let us repeat with meaningful sensibility,

When I survey the wondrous cross
  On which the Prince of Glory died,
My richest gain I count but loss
  And pour contempt on all my pride.

Were the whole realm of nature mine,
  That were an offering far too small;
Love so amazing, so divine,
  Demands my heart, my life, my all.

CHAPTER VIII

The Resurrection of Christ

W. WILCOX

THE Apostle Paul in summarizing the Gospel which he preached, declared to the Church in Corinth that 'Christ died for our sins according to the Scriptures, and that He was buried, and that He hath been raised from the dead according to the Scriptures' (1 Cor. 15. 3, 4). The fact of the Resurrection together with that of the Crucifixion thus stands, in the estimate of the apostle, at the very basis of the Christian teaching. He shows that our Lord's Resurrection is:—

(I) Foretold in Scripture.

(II) Historical, i.e. a fact which occurred in time, and the evidence of which is known and has been tested by man.

(III) Doctrinally important, as forming one of the bases of the Gospel message.

We cannot do better than accept this threefold division of the subject and examine each in turn.

I. *Predicted.* Peter, speaking on the day of Pentecost, quotes from Psalm 16. 8-11, to show that the resurrection of our Lord had been clearly foretold. This Psalm was well-known as a Messianic one and Peter so uses it to show the absolute necessity for Christ's rising from the dead.

Further, in speaking of Christ's exaltation as subsequent to the resurrection, he again quotes from the Psalms, showing both these events to have been predicted long beforehand (Psa. 110. 1).

In many passages which are undoubtedly Messianic, while the fact of the resurrection may not be directly referred to yet it is implied, for, otherwise, the events which are predicted as subsequent to His death could not possibly have a fulfilment. We may take as an example the well-known prophecy of Isa. 53, where, after having spoken of His sufferings, death, and grave, the prophet proceeds to predict for Him prolonged days, the seeing of the travail of His soul and satisfaction thereat, a portion with the great, etc. If these latter predictions are to be fulfilled in any real sense, then the resurrection is a necessity.

Further, our Lord Himself frequently foretold His resurrection (Matt. 12. 38-40; 16. 21; 17. 23; 20. 19; 27. 63; Mark 8. 31; 9. 31; 10. 34; 14. 58; Luke 9. 22; 18. 33; John 2. 19-21; 10. 18). But, while His disciples seemed slow to comprehend what these repeated declarations of His should mean, His enemies seemed to understand them and so recommended Pilate to seal the tomb after His burial and to set a watch, lest His disciples should remove His body and declare that He had risen (Matt. 27. 63, 64). They doubted not that such a story would be believed, for 'the resurrection of the dead' was a well-known article of faith among the Pharisees and those whom they influenced, although the Sadducees refused to accept it.

These predictions of our Lord concerning His resurrection form an important part in the testimony as to His rising from the dead, for the disciples afterwards recalled some of them and *then* understood that He had spoken of it beforehand (John 2. 22). That He had done so confirmed them in the faith and in the assurance that all that the Scriptures foretold must surely come to pass.

II. *Historical.* Here we come to the actual records of our Lord's resurrection as given in the Gospels. Happily, these records are fairly numerous and they tell of the goodly number of witnesses and of the variety of circumstances under which the appearances of our Lord were manifested. It is true that it is not always possible to determine with exactness the order of His appearances, to know the full details thereof, or even to be sure of the number of such appearances. Of the last there were probably many more than those of which we have record, for the writer of the Acts speaks of the many infallible proofs by which our Lord showed Himself alive after His resurrection (Acts 1. 3), implying that there were many more appearances than those which had been related.

Those named seem to fall into the following general order:

1. To certain women, the 'other Mary,' Salome, Joanna, and others as they returned from the sepulchre (Matt. 28. 1-10; Mark 16. 1-8; Luke 24. 1-11).

Here we may note that the evangelists regard the resurrection as an incursion of the supernatural into the sphere of the natural. It is accompanied by 'a great earthquake'; an angel of the Lord descends from heaven to roll away the stone; and this angel communicates to the disciples the fact that the Lord is risen.

This is, perhaps, one of the chief causes for the stumbling of the critics who deny the possibility of the supernatural. But, as we read these records, we are surprised that there are so few stories of supernatural events. Had man alone compiled these Gospels, he would have tried to bolster up his story by multiplying such supernatural occurrences and so give to his account a suitable atmosphere of mystery and wonder.

2. To Mary Magdalene at the sepulchre (John 20. 11-18; Mark 16. 9-11). What more delightful story could have been written! There are certain elements in it worthy of note.

Mary was not expecting such an event as the resurrection. When she found the tomb empty, she thought 'the gardener' had taken away the body of her Lord.

His use of the endearing name, Mary, awoke in her the first consciousness that He who spoke was her Lord, and then she responded with, 'Master.'

Did she still fear that He might be but an apparition and so desired to touch Him to make sure that He was really her Lord? 'Touch Me not,' He replies . . . do not let doubt hamper the joy of belief.

Commission ever follows trust. She becomes her Lord's messenger to His other disciples.

Her straightforward testimony, 'I have seen the Lord,' wins their trust and they are led to belief in Him as the risen Lord.

3. To Peter (Luke 24. 34; 1 Cor. 15. 5). Probably Peter would be the last person to desire a meeting with the Lord. With oaths and cursings he had denied all knowledge of Him, yet his Lord makes known His special desire to meet Peter and commissions the women, 'Go tell My disciples and Peter,' and when the two return to Jerusalem from Emmaus they are met with the news that 'the Lord . . . hath appeared to Simon.'

4. To two disciples on their way to Emmaus (Luke 24. 13-35; Mark 16. 12, 13). Apart from considerations which will come up

later, we may here note that our Lord appears in three characteristic ways, as the

(*a*) Upbraider of the folly of the human heart in its unbelief.

(*b*) Unveiler of the true meaning of the prophetic word.

(*c*) Unknown, until revealed in the breaking of the bread.

5. To ten apostles, Thomas being absent (Luke 24. 33; Mark 16. 14-18; John 20. 24-28). Jesus appears in their midst when they are in the upper room with doors barred for fear of the Jews. He comes with a message of peace and brings to them gladness as they see Him, and shows them the way out of frustration and powerlessness as He gives to them assurance and power.

6. To eleven apostles a week later (John 20. 24-28). Thomas had not been with the ten when Jesus appeared to them in the upper room. But now they were gathered again and they bear a united but simple testimony, 'We have seen the Lord.' But Thomas has a sceptical turn of mind and declares that he must see and touch, and handle the Lord ere he will believe. What a large offspring of doubters Thomas has had, all dependent upon physical sight and touch rather than upon spiritual sense and insight! But, in the presence of the Lord, his scepticism vanishes and he rises to the heights of spiritual worship, speaking of the risen Lord, as 'My Lord and my God,' an ascription which, it is worthy of note, Jesus accepts, but fails not to rebuke Thomas for the fact that he had made his faith dependent upon sight.

7. To several disciples at the sea of Galilee (John 21. 1-23). Disheartened by the night's fruitless toil, the disciples, on approaching the land are accosted by the Unknown One. Enquiry elicits the fact that they have caught nothing, and then, at His direction, they cast the net on the right side of the boat, and immediately the net is full. At once memory begins to work and they remember the One who, on a former occasion, had enabled them to obtain a full draught of fishes. At once John says, 'It is the Lord,' and Peter, impulsive as ever, casts himself into the sea to go to his Lord. When the others arrive, all are made to partake of the meal of His providing and then to listen to His words, words which call forth an expression of love and earn a commission to service. Peter is especially addressed but, doubtless, similar words were spoken to all. The risen Lord is to be loved and served.

8. To the apostles and above five hundred brethren at once (Matt. 28. 16-20; 1 Cor. 15. 6). Matthew tells us of the Lord's appearance to the eleven on a mountain in Galilee, while Paul speaks of His appearance to 500 brethren at once. Many count these as one and the same appearance of the risen Lord, but they may well have occurred at different times. In either case the witness is clear, namely, that Jesus appeared to these numbers of disciples, that they were men, and that when they saw Him they worshipped Him.

9. To James (1 Cor. 15. 7). Of this appearance we have no account other than the brief reference made to it by Paul in his letter to Corinth.

10. To apostles at Jerusalem and later at Olivet where they witnessed the Ascension (Mark 16. 19; Luke 24. 50-52; Acts 1. 3-8). Immediately prior to His ascension, while speaking with His disciples, He lifted up His hands and blessed them. He was then parted from them and a cloud received Him out of their sight. Here the statement of the angelic messengers is important. 'This Jesus,' or, as the A.V. has it, 'This same Jesus,' establishes the identity of the risen and ascended Lord with the Jesus whom they had known and who was crucified, and, they declared, this One would come again.

11. To Saul of Tarsus on the Damascus road (Acts 9. 3-9; 1 Cor. 15. 8; 9. 1). Saul sees Him, *hears His voice and submits* to His direction.

In view of the many rationalistic theories put forward to account for the belief in our Lord's resurrection it is of importance to note:

(*A*) The resurrection of our Lord is everywhere declared as a *fact*, formal evidence for it not being deemed necessary. The evidence could easily have been put to the test had it been necessary, both at the time, and at such a period as that when the apostle wrote to the Corinthians about it. There would be many still living who had seen the crucifixion and who had heard both the first reports of His resurrection and the stories spread abroad by His enemies to discredit the veracity of those reports.

(*B*) The disciples themselves were not such as would *invent* the story of the resurrection. Rather, when they first heard the reports of His having risen, they were most incredulous and sought first-hand evidence ere they would believe. For instance:

(*a*) Two of them ran to the tomb to see if what the women had reported was true. They went in; they looked intently upon the linen clothes lying there tenantless; they noted these details, but saw not the Lord.

(*b*) Only when they saw Him break the bread were the two with whom He had walked to Emmaus convinced that He was the Lord risen from the dead. Afterwards they remembered that His words, as He had talked with them by the way, had had a peculiarly convicting power causing their hearts to burn within them.

(*c*) Others to whom He appeared believed Him to be an apparition until He ate a piece of fish and a portion of honeycomb and at the same time pointed to the tangible evidences (flesh and bones) showing that He was a real Person standing among them.

(*d*) Thomas demanded to see the nail-prints and to be able to thrust his hand into the wound in His side ere he would believe; but seeing, not only did he believe, but his heart was captured and he cried, 'My Lord and my God,' as he worshipped the risen Lord.

(*C*) The stories of the resurrection are told with the utmost simplicity and bear the stamp of truth. The variations in the details of the records of the four writers show that there is no agreed story put forward to account for the disappearance of the Lord's body from the tomb, such as would have been necessary had the resurrection been a theory advanced by the disciples for their own ends, or had the story propounded by His enemies been the true account of what had happened.

(*D*) The chief opponents of the resurrection story seek only to suppress it; they do not deny its veracity, although they must have known that such a denial, with due attention to evidence, would have carried far more weight than did the clumsy methods of suppression they adopted.

(*E*) The records of the resurrection are remarkable for the *variety* of circumstances under which Jesus revealed Himself; in a garden, on the road to a village, in an upper room, by the lakeside, on a mountain-top, etc.; given conditions, similar setting and an arranged set of circumstances are nowhere found or considered necessary as they are in the records of the alleged appearances of spirit-beings or of apparitions to men.

The times vary also; in the early morning at the tomb, during the day as He walked, or toward evening, again showing that no particular time conditioned His appearance. He comes in the course of the natural circumstances of those to whom He would appear, just as to-day He meets and talks with His own as they pursue their normal tasks, gilding them with the light of His presence and bringing with Him the joy of unveiled truth.

(*F*) It is noticeable that the evidence grows in cumulative effect. He appears to *one* woman (Mary Magdalene), or to *one* man (Peter, James), to *two* on the road to Emmaus, to *ten* in the upper room, and later to *eleven*, and then to five hundred brethren at once. It could be argued that a lone woman, or a solitary man might have been deceived, or even that two walking together could have imagined that they saw the loved form of Him about whom they were conversing. But it was hardly possible that ten, eleven, five hundred could have been so deceived.

In this connection Edersheim's words are worth repeating: 'The Evangelists, and afterwards St. Paul, are not so much concerned to give the *whole history* of the resurrection as to furnish the evidence for it. And here what is distinctive in each is also characteristic of his special view-point. St. Matthew describes the impression of the full evidence of that Easter morning on friend and foe and then hurries us from the Jerusalem stained with Christ's blood back to the sweet lake and the blessed mount where first He spake. It is as if he longed to realize the risen Christ in the scenes where he had learned to know Him. St. Mark, who is much more brief, gives not only a mere summary, but, if one might use the expression, tells it as from the bosom of the Jerusalem family, from the house of his mother, Mary. St. Luke seems to have made most full enquiry as to all the facts of the resurrection, and his narrative might almost be inscribed 'Easter Day in Jerusalem.' St. John paints such scenes—during the whole forty days, whether in Jerusalem or Galilee—as were most significant and instructive of this threefold lesson of his Gospel; that Jesus was the Christ, that He was the Son of God, and that, believing, we have life in His Name. Lastly, St. Paul—as one born out of due time—produces the testimony of the principal witnesses to the fact in a kind of ascending climax. And this the more effectively, that he is evidently aware of the difficulties and the import of the question and has taken pains to make himself acquainted with all the facts of the case' (*Life and Times of Jesus the Messiah*, II, p. 622).

And again, 'The importance of all this cannot be adequately expressed in words. A dead Christ might have been a Teacher and a Wonder-worker, and remembered and loved as such. But only a Risen and Living Christ could be the Saviour, the Life, and the Life-Giver, and as such preached to all men. And of this most blessed truth we have the fullest and most unquestionable evidence' (*ibid*, p. 629).

And again, 'It was not the belief previously derived from Scripture that the Christ was to rise from the dead which led to the expectancy of it, but the evidence that He had risen which led them to the knowledge of what Scripture taught on the subject' (*ibid*, p. 634).

III. *Doctrinal.* We shall trace the doctrinal importance of the resurrection as found in (i) the Acts, and (ii) in the Epistles.

(i) *In the Acts.* (*a*) Throughout, the resurrection is regarded as the act of God who thus showed His approval of the obedience of our Lord even of that obedience which was unto death (Acts 2. 24, 32; 3. 15; 4. 10; 5. 30; 10. 40; 13. 30; 17. 31; 26. 8). It thus becomes the first step in the exaltation of the Lord.

(*b*) This resurrection was a necessity arising alike from the moral nature of God and of our Lord. Since He was without sin, death had no claim on Him and hence neither death nor the grave could retain Him and His resurrection had to take place (Acts 2. 24). Peter uses this argument very forcibly. Our Lord had set God always before His face, that is, He had lived in that constancy and sincerity of life which neither hid nor desired to hide anything from His holy sight. That searching gaze found nothing of sin in Him and, therefore, life, even the risen life, could not be withheld from Him.

(*c*) The resurrection together with the death on the Cross, formed the central part of the message of the apostles (Acts 4. 33; 10. 36-40; 17. 18).

(*d*) The resurrection was regarded as of vital importance, for,

(1) In the choice of an apostle to fill the place left by Judas, it was insisted that the new apostle should be a witness of the resurrection (Acts 1. 21).

(2) In the apostolic teaching it is that for which the apostles would stand on a charge before the courts rather than abandon it (Acts 24. 21).

(*e*) The risen Lord stands to aid those of His followers who were being persecuted. He is seen by Stephen at the right hand of God (Acts 7. 56), and by Saul of Tarsus, when He claims that, in the persecution of His followers, He, Himself, is being persecuted (Acts 9. 4, 5).

(*f*) In many places where there is no explicit reference to the resurrection of our Lord, that such resurrection took place is assumed, for Jesus is everywhere regarded as being alive (Acts 25. 19); His Name is powerful, when it is invoked upon the sick and infirm; in His Name His disciples are baptized; His voice is heard and His authority to direct the activities of His apostles through His Holy Spirit is recognised.

(ii) *In the Epistles.* (*a*) The resurrection of Christ forms an essential part of the Gospel preached by Paul (1 Cor. 15.4).

(*b*) It is regarded as necessary that men believe in the resurrection of our Lord in order to be saved, it being the necessary accompaniment of their confession of Jesus as Lord (Rom. 4. 24; 10. 9; 1 Thess. 4. 14).

(*c*) The resurrection was because of our justification (Rom. 4. 25), His death having been because of our trespasses. His resurrection shows God's acceptance of His death and carries with it our acceptance also.

(*d*) If the fact of our Lord's resurrection could be proved false, then Paul shows that this would have fatal consequences (1 Cor. 15. 12-19) for:

Faith would be empty (vain). The story of a Christ who had died and was buried might evoke a fond memory, but could not provide for faith an objective reality.

Forgiveness would be a delusion. If Christ had died only, then, it would be arguable, He had died as other men had died, that is, as a part of the great entail of sin. Then He could not have borne the sins of others, however violent the death to which He had been subjected. It would follow that the thought of obtaining forgiveness through Him would be a delusion and it would be idle for them to continue preaching the forgiveness of sins.

Future life would be a false hope, for, if Christ, the Sinless One, were not raised, how could the sinner, though a believer, ever hope for resurrection and the life beyond?

It follows, of course, that the fact of the Lord's resurrection being affirmed, faith is *not* vain, forgiveness is *not* a delusion and the hope of the future life is assured.

(*e*) The resurrection endues the Risen One with power . . . the power of an endless life, a power which is desired by the spiritual aspirant in his own life. It is a life of victorious conquest; the arch-enemy having been defeated, every other foe is a conquerable foe also. By reason of the fact that the believer shares in this risen life, he also shares in this life of victory, every foe with which he is confronted is therefore a conquerable foe and should be met and dealt with in the light of that fact.

(*f*) In the likeness of His resurrection, the believer, emerging from the waters of baptism, has, in symbol, been raised to walk in newness of life (Rom. 6. 5). The believer thus stands upon a new plane; he is ever to conform his life to the fact that he has died and risen with Christ. That risen life of power and beauty, of vitality and victory, of association with the heavenly rather than the earthly scene is to be used and applied to every circumstance of life.

(*g*) In that resurrection the believer sees the hope of his own. 'Christ the firstfruits and afterwards they that are His at His coming' (1 Cor. 15. 23). As the Lord burst the bonds of death, so will the believer rise triumphant over death. He will have part in that *first* resurrection (Rev. 20. 5, 6) wherein Christ was the Firstfruits. Upon such as have their part in that first resurrection, the second death has no power, and they shall be as priests reigning with Him.

The resurrection of our Lord carries with it many important effects in the life of the believer other than those mentioned above.

(*a*) By it he has the hope of being 'perfected' (Heb. 13. 20), for, in the resurrection, Jesus Himself was 'perfected.' He died to seal with His blood 'the eternal covenant.' But many have died in their efforts to secure an object, to achieve a purpose, but in their very death that purpose has been defeated. Not so with our Lord. The eternal covenant could not have been sealed with His blood apart from His death, but His resurrection gives Him the power to make really effective in the life of the believer the purpose His death achieved. 'Peace' has been secured, hence God is spoken of in that character. 'Protection' is assured by the blood of the eternal covenant; and 'Perfection' is accomplished as the believer works out what He has wrought within.

(*b*) By it he has the hope of an inheritance (1 Peter 1. 3, 4). The resurrection opens out to the believer a life of larger vision and of fuller capacity. Even with our Lord we find Him doing certain things in the post-resurrection state while we have no record of anything similar in the pre-resurrection state, e.g. He appeared in the presence of His apostles when they were gathered in an upper room with doors barred (John 20. 19, 26; Luke 24. 36), and, while seated with His disciples in converse and in the act of breaking bread, He suddenly vanishes from their sight (Luke 24. 33).

The records of these acts have sometimes raised in the minds of doubters the important question of the continuity of the resurrection body with that of the pre-resurrection state, that is, is the body that died merely reanimated or is it in some way changed?

In the case of our Lord, it would appear as if both were true. Both grave and grave-clothes were found tenantless. The body in which He had lived was the body which was raised, and yet, in the sense of the Scriptures noted above, it was a changed body. It was the '*same* Jesus' (Acts 2. 36) whom men had crucified, who was now raised and exalted by God. Yet He Himself speaks of that body as 'flesh and bones' (Luke 24. 39) rather than as of 'flesh and blood,' and it is spoken of as 'the body of His glory' (Phil. 3. 21).

How far this is actually to be a pattern of the resurrection of the believer it is difficult to say. Paul says, 'He will fashion anew the body of our humiliation,' and, again, 'we shall be changed, the corruptible having put on incorruption and the mortal having put on immortality' (1 Cor. 15. 52, 53). So, there is change and the body raised is no longer subject to death. But how is continuity secured? Will these actual bodies with which we are now clothed be raised again? Let it be said, in the first place, that these bodies of ours during our lifetime are continually subject to change. Cells live and die and pass out as waste matter and new cells come, yet the form of the man remains. So, argues Paul, the grain of wheat is sown, it brings forth new grains of wheat which are the same, and yet new. God giveth these new grains a body. In the resurrection the risen body will spring from the old with a God-given body, bearing all the characteristics of the old, yet not subject to death and therefore not subject to sin which issues in death. Here both continuity and the necessary change are found. Hence in the resurrection of our Lord the believer has a 'living hope.'

(*c*) He is able to have a good 'conscience toward God' through the resurrection of Jesus Christ (1 Peter 3. 21). Baptized as one confessedly dead, he does not remain as one dead, with no consciousness of God, but, through the resurrection of our Lord, he enters into the risen life with a full consciousness of God, and whatever questionings and testings of the inner life there may be, he will ever remember that, as Christ died and rose, so He has died and risen again as symbolized in his baptism.

(*d*) It assures him of his place at the return of his Lord (1 Thess. 4. 14), for the apostle assures the Thessalonians that 'if we believe that Jesus died and rose again even so them also that are fallen asleep in Jesus will God bring with Him.' Belief in these cardinal truths and in that which they imply, gives assurance regarding the coming of our Lord. Other conditions are not imposed; the believer's place with a crucified and risen Lord being secured solely through His merits.

(*e*) It gives him a constant consolation when beset with difficulties (2 Tim. 2. 8). Paul says to Timothy that, though beset with difficulties which arise from the preaching of the Gospel, he should remember Jesus Christ risen from the dead. In that resurrection there is both comfort and joy, for it ever shows that man's power has limits while the power of God is limitless, and in that resurrection God approved when man disapproved. In the believer's resurrection also, God will approve even when man has disapproved and shown his disapproval by persecuting unto death those who have stood for the truths of the Gospel.

CHAPTER IX

The Ascended Christ

HAROLD P. BARKER

OF the four Evangelists, only Mark and Luke record the ascension of our Lord after His resurrection. Mark states the bare fact in half a dozen words; but Luke, in his Gospel, and still more in the Acts, gives interesting details in connection with that great and extremely significant event.

Some weeks previously, Bethany had been the scene of a marvellous deed, by which Jesus, as Son of God, was greatly glorified (John 11. 4). By the power of His quickening word, He had recalled to life a man who had been dead for four days. Demonstrated thus to be the Victor over death, He went on to Calvary, to win a still greater victory.

Six weeks after that stupendous miracle, risen from the tomb, He led His eleven faithful disciples once more to Bethany. There, after they had been asking questions regarding the restoration of the kingdom, He suddenly raised His hands to bless them. To their astonishment, it proved to be His farewell act, for while He was in the act of blessing them, 'He was parted from them and carried up into heaven' (Luke 24. 51). Their gaze followed Him until He disappeared into a cloud and upon their wondering ears fell the angelic message that the One who had so gone should one day so return.

The disciples, filled with amazement, seem to have gone off immediately to their wonted trysting-place on the Mount of Olives, a mile from Bethany, to speak together of what they had witnessed. From there, with overflowing joy in their hearts, they returned to their lodgings in Jerusalem, filled with praise to God.

It is recorded that the Lord was taken up into heaven, but the word is used in a very general sense, for, as a matter of fact, He 'ascended far above all heavens' (Eph. 4. 10). He 'sat down at the right hand of the Majesty on high,' being thus 'made higher than the heavens' (Heb. 3. 3).

If we speak of certain things, true of our ascended Lord, that could not be predicated of Him while He was on earth, nor before His death, we must not imagine that He has undergone any *personal* change. He is 'Jesus Christ, the same yesterday, and to-day and for ever' (Heb. 13. 8). His ascension was, however, a necessity in order, not only that God might indicate His satisfaction with the work accomplished by His Son, but also that certain things might now come into effect.

One great result followed ten days after the Lord's ascension and as a direct consequence of it. The Holy Spirit was sent down as the Comforter (John 16. 7). He could not be given until Jesus was glorified (John 7. 39), but the Ascension made the way for the gift of the Spirit. With the coming of the Holy Spirit, Christianity began its course. Neither the Church nor Christianity could have had any existence apart from their risen and ascended Head.

As a result of His ascension, our Lord is now the *Head* of the mystic Body—the Church. During His sojourn on earth He had won the love and allegiance of many true-hearted men and women. They were His disciples, and He called them His friends (John 15. 15). Yet, however sincere their friendship for Him, they remained separate individuals with no vital link between them. Members of His body they could not be, for that body was not formed until Pentecost. It was by the gift of the Holy Spirit that all believers, Jews and Gentiles, were 'baptized into one body' (1 Cor. 12. 13) and of that body Christ is the glorious Head. 'He is the Head of the body, the Church,' says the Apostle Paul (Col. 1. 18).

We know Him as our Head, Head indeed over the whole universe, but even that with reference to the Church, His body (Eph. 1. 22, 23). It is in His capacity as the ascended Head that He supplies His Church with gifts, men, in the first instance, who were apostles and prophets (cf. Eph. 2. 20), and subsequently—and continuously to the present day—evangelists, pastors and teachers, all for the edifying of the body of Christ (Eph. 4. 13).

Just as the human body is governed by its head, so Christ, as Head of His body, directs its members, the sharers of His risen life. It is good to realize our membership of that body, in common with all true believers everywhere, and to act towards our fellow-members in accordance with the unity that this membership implies. In order to do this we must hold the Head (Col. 2. 20), acting under His direction, bearing in mind our relationship to Him.

One of the most significant titles of the Ascended Christ is that of '*Lord.*' Peter, in his Pentecostal sermon, contrasted David, who, he declared, 'is not ascended into the heavens,' with the One who *has* ascended and is now exalted there. And he added that God had 'made that same Jesus . . . Lord' (Acts 2. 36). Of course, Jesus was Lord while on earth. At His birth He was proclaimed as such by the angel, and He was saluted as Lord while yet unborn (Luke 1. 43). But the title took on a new meaning when applied to Him as the One ascended and exalted at God's right hand. On earth He was addressed as Lord often merely as a title of courtesy equivalent to 'Sir' (and sometimes so translated). But now it implies Deity, and no one can say that Jesus is the Lord but by the Holy Spirit (1 Cor. 12. 3). The Roman Emperors claimed to be divine and the law made it a crime to refuse to call them Lord. But the Christians claimed that the title belongs to One alone, and many of them suffered martyrdom rather than call Cæsar Lord, for that would have been an admission of his claim to divinity. In calling Jesus Lord we acknowledge His Deity, and it is essential, moreover, to our salvation (Rom. 10. 9).

The Lordship of Christ implies the subjection of His followers to His sovereign will. They gladly submit their will to His and own His sway in every detail of life.

Peter also declared in that first sermon that God has made the ascended one *Christ* (Acts 2. 36). When He was on earth this Greek title was used as the equivalent of the Hebrew Messiah. He was confessed as the Christ, the Son of God, by people like Peter (Matt. 16. 16) and Martha (John 11. 27). He revealed Himself as the Christ to the woman at Sychar (John 4. 26), and the Samaritan believers knew that He was indeed such (John 4. 42). There was a recognition on the part of a limited few, that He was truly the Messiah, but the mass of the people—even His own followers—were ignorant of the fact. But, like the title, 'Lord,' the title 'Christ' is now a *name*. It has no longer merely a Jewish bearing, but is used to denote the position of believers, Jew and Gentile alike, before God. We are 'in Christ.'

'Lord' and 'Christ,' added to His personal name, 'Jesus,' give the Master His full name as known in Christianity. He is the *Lord Jesus Christ;* as such we worship Him.

There is an office which is our Lord's to-day which was not His prior to His ascension. He was not a *priest* on earth, for He was not of the priestly tribe (Heb. 7. 14; 8. 4). But now, seated at the right hand of the Majesty on high, He is our great High Priest (Heb. 4. 14). Chapters 2 to 10 of the Epistle to the Hebrews describe Him as the One who competently and adequately fills this office. All other priests have failed: He will never fail. A whole volume might be written on this subject, but we must be content with emphasizing four features of His priesthood.

First, He is 'a merciful and faithful High Priest' (Heb. 2. 17). He is *faithful* in that not one of God's children, committed to His charge to be brought to glory (Heb. 2. 10), will be permitted to perish by the way. Not one will be missing in the day when those redeemed by His blood are assembled in their eternal home. He is *merciful* in that He will not drive His sheep by harsh treatment, but will lead us tenderly, with patience and forbearance, with consideration for our weakness, and sympathy with us in our trials. Having Himself suffered, He is able to succour those that are in trial of any kind.

Second, having been tried, just as we are, He is not insensitive to our infirmities (Heb. 4. 15). Think of some of the trials which He endured, the remembrance of which remains with Him to-day. One of the most painful is *bereavement.* He has felt the pangs of this great sorrow. At the graveside of His beloved friend, Lazarus, He groaned, not merely outwardly and audibly, but 'in spirit.' He wept, and His tears made even the unbelieving Jews who saw them exclaim, 'How He loved him' (John 11. 36). He knew what poverty meant; He was tired (John 4. 6); He was misunderstood, slandered, falsely accused, ridiculed. His experiences of life's trials and difficulties, its testings and its rigours, fully qualify Him as our great High Priest to sympathize with us in our trials and meet us with mercy and helpful grace.

Third, because He cannot cease to live, His priesthood can never pass to another; it is unchangeable, in contrast to the priests of the Aaronic order, who died one after another, giving no permanence to the office. But Christ, because He ever lives, is able to continue His ministry of saving us through everything to the end of our pilgrim days and to the uttermost of our need (Heb. 7. 25). Although, as the ascended One, He is 'made higher than the heavens,' He makes intercession for us and prevails on our behalf.

Fourth, on four occasions in the Epistle to the Hebrews, the Lord Jesus Christ is said to be a priest *for ever* (Heb. 5. 6; 6. 20, etc.). His priesthood is not, therefore, connected exclusively with our present needs. In the millennial day, He will combine priesthood with kingship on earth (Zech. 6. 13). For all eternity He will be the One to maintain the whole wide realm of creation in harmony with the will and pleasure of God.

If we fail to come constantly to the Throne of Grace to obtain preserving mercy and grace, we shall surely fall into temptation and sin. Then we come under the hand of our ascended Lord in discipline rather than in grace.

'If any man sin we have an *Advocate* with the Father,' wrote the beloved disciple (1 John 2. 1). Our Lord appears for us in heaven on the ground of having shed His blood on our behalf, and on this basis He meets all the accusations of our relentless enemy, 'the accuser of our brethren' (Rev. 12. 10). Satan finds malicious joy in recounting our sins before God. Our Advocate does not meet his charges by 'putting the best construction on our actions,' as has been said, but by presenting the fact of His shed blood as the effectual answer to all. Then He deals with the one who has sinned, leading him to repentance, self-judgment and restoration. Although the erring saint may have lapsed from the running of the race set before him, the Advocate works to put him back in the ranks of the runners, and then to profit again by the succour and support of the Priest.

There is never a moment when we are out of the thoughts of our Lord. He is ever watching our needs and is constantly interceding on our account, while, in His perfect advocacy, He continues to bear up our cases before the Eternal God.

Another character assumed by our Lord as the ascended One is that of *Bishop*. Peter speaks of Him as 'the Shepherd and Bishop of your souls' (1 Peter 2. 25). What is the difference in thought between the conception of Christ as Shepherd and that of Him as

Bishop? There is, of course, a connection between the two titles. But the Lord was a Shepherd when on earth. He entered the fold (Judaism) in order to extricate His sheep from it, and to unite them in one flock with other sheep (Samaritans, Greeks, etc.) who had never belonged to it (John 10. 2, 3, 16, R.V.). Then, as the Shepherd, He proved His goodness by laying down His life for them. Now He lives to guide and feed His sheep, and none can pluck them out of His hand.

As the Bishop, however, He is the Overseer of our souls, ruling and overlooking us in order to keep our feet in the right course. Once we were 'as sheep going astray,' but it is to Christ, in His character of Shepherd and Bishop, that we have returned. It is true that we have been translated into His kingdom (Col. 1. 13). But while the thought connected with kingly rule is that of a political government, the thought of the Bishop, or Overseer, is that of spiritual guidance and government. In all our need of guidance in life's road, we find the full measure of light in Him. We acknowledge His sway and we gladly receive our direction from Him. We may learn a good deal of what Christ as our Bishop does for us by reading what His servants, the bishops, or elders, are to be and do in the churches in which they serve.

'Within the veil . . . the *Forerunner* is for us entered, even Jesus,' says the writer to the Hebrews (Heb. 6. 20). The idea that Scripture usually presents in relation to a forerunner is that of an inferior going before some important personage to prepare the way for his advance. Joseph, for example, was preceded by runners, who cried, 'Bow the knee before him' (Gen. 41. 43). John the Baptist was a forerunner of the Lord Jesus Christ, crying, 'One is coming after me whose shoe's latchet I am not worthy to unloose' (John 1. 27).

In the case of our Lord Jesus Christ, however, the situation is entirely reversed. It is not some subordinate who has gone before to prepare the way for his master, but it is the most glorious One, the ascended Christ, who has gone up to heaven as the Forerunner of a host redeemed from the ways of sin. The function of the forerunner in the east was to prepare the way for those who were coming after, to clear away all obstacles that would impede their progress. Those who saw one at work would at once conclude that some travellers would soon be coming by that road. But when they saw the forerunner sitting down at the end of the journey, they would know that all obstacles had now been removed and that the way was made clear for the coming travellers.

It is thus with the Lord. Having cleared away our sins, and removed the fear of death and the judgment that we so richly deserved, He has entered heaven and now sits there, awaiting the day when a host of after-runners will reach the goal. He said to His disciples, '*I go to prepare* a place for you' (John 14. 2). It was by His going, His entrance into heaven, not in His own personal right, but in virtue of having obtained redemption for us by His blood (Heb. 9. 9), that He has prepared the place for us there. In this way He has acted as our great Forerunner.

In many respects, our Lord's greatest title in the glory is that of *King* and it may be wondered why this title is mentioned last. The Saviour was born a king, acknowledged as such by Gentiles (Matt. 2. 2). By a Gentile ruler He was declared, by the inscription written on the Cross, to be one. But whilst the title is His by right, He has not yet been manifested as King. In a spiritual sense, His kingdom exists to-day, but the manifestation of the King and of His glorious earthly kingdom is still future. At His future advent, with His saints and His angels, He will come as King of kings, and will be owned as 'King over all the earth' (Zech. 14. 9). The ascended Lord, the Sovereign of the skies, will then be acknowledged universally.

Finally, let us remember that those who believe in Him are said again and again to be '*in Christ*.' That is our standing before God. He sees us linked with the risen, ascended One and, viewed in the light of His purpose, it is said that we have been made to sit together in the heavenlies in Him (Eph. 2. 6). It is a wonderful thought that our eternal destiny is linked up with the glorious One at God's right hand, the Man of God's infinite delight. Let our thanksgiving abound to God for this!

CHAPTER X

The Holy Spirit

JOHN RITCHIE

THE age in which we live is pre-eminently the age of the Spirit. Just as there was a day when the Eternal Son of God entered on His distinctive work on earth when born of the virgin mother at Bethlehem, so the Eternal Spirit began His distinctive work at Pentecost (Acts 2. 1), and this work continues throughout the present age of grace. It is true that the Holy Spirit was active in ages past, as the Old Testament scriptures clearly show. It is also true that He was intensely active during the public ministry of the Lord Jesus, as the four Gospels bear witness. He will again be active on earth in 'the age to come' when the prophecy of Joel will have its complete fulfilment, 'I will pour out My Spirit upon all flesh' (Joel 2. 28). But the gift of the Spirit during the present age as an abiding Presence was contingent on the accomplished redemption of Christ, with His subsequent resurrection, ascension and glorification. Hence the revealing words of John 7. 39, 'This spake He of the Spirit which they that believe on Him should receive; for the Holy Spirit was not yet given, because that Jesus was not yet glorified.' It is of vital importance to understand that the advent of the Holy Spirit means that He has come to announce the arrival at 'the right hand of the Majesty on high' of the once crucified but now risen Lord (Acts 2. 33); otherwise He could not have come. When the High Priest of Israel entered into the holy place of the tabernacle on behalf of his people, bearing the names of the tribes in the breastplate upon his heart, he was 'hid from the eyes of men.' But on the fringe of the priestly robe (the ephod) there was a simple but effective arrangement of alternating bells and pomegranates (Exod. 28. 34, 35) which gave forth a tinkling sound as he moved about, thus announcing to the listening people outside that their representative was alive, and busily engaged on their behalf. So, at Pentecost—

fifty days after the Cross—'there came a sound from heaven as of a rushing, mighty wind' (Acts 2. 2) accompanying the advent of the Spirit—the assurance that our Great High Priest had entered on His office—and that all was well for His people.

The Holy Spirit is a Real Person, and not merely an influence or an emanation from the Deity, as so many vaguely imagine. Although not incarnate 'in fashion as a man' as was the Son of God, the Holy Spirit possesses all the attributes of personality, and should always be spoken of as 'He,' not 'it' (John 16. 13; Rom. 8. 16, R.V.).[1] The very name given Him by the Lord—another Comforter—definitely implies personality. It indicates that, what the Lord Himself had been to His disciples during His sojourn with them, the Holy Spirit would be to His people in His absence in even greater degree, since the Holy Spirit would not be restricted by corporeal limitations as 'the man Christ Jesus' voluntarily was. The blessed Lord sensed the need of the men He was about to leave. They were dreadfully afraid that they would be left helpless without such a Leader and Friend; sorrow filled their hearts. His answer to all this was, 'It is expedient (advantageous) for you that I go away; for if I go not away the Comforter will not come unto you; but if I depart I will send Him unto you' (John 16. 7). In simple language He was saying to them, 'Trust Me to do the best for you; you will be far better off; you will have a living, loving Lord in heaven, and you will have the Comforter on earth.' Let us think of some of the things predicated of the Spirit in Scripture which could only be true of a Person. He has knowledge (1 Cor. 2. 11); He has will (1 Cor. 12. 11); He has mind (Rom. 8. 27); He can love (Rom. 15. 30); He can hear (John 16. 13); He can speak (Acts 13. 2; 2 Sam. 23. 2); He can lead (Rom. 8. 14); He can teach (John 14. 26); He can forbid (Acts 16. 6); He can intercede (Rom. 8. 26); He can be grieved (Eph. 4. 30); He can be lied to (Acts 5. 3); He may be resisted (Acts 7. 51); He may be blasphemed (Matt. 12. 31). Other proofs might be adduced, but the above should suffice. Not only is He a real Person, but be it always remembered that

The Holy Spirit is a Divine Person, equal in power and glory

[1] 1 Pet. 1. 11 should read: 'Searching what, or what manner of time the Spirit of Christ which was in them was signifying, testifying beforehand the sufferings of Christ.'

with the Father and the Son. The divine mystery of three Persons in the unity of One Godhead is clearly recognized in Scripture. For example, the Holy Spirit has equality in Name, as in Gen. 1. 26, where the Hebrew word for 'God' (*Elohim*) is in the plural, as well as the pronouns 'us' and 'our,' yet these are followed by a singular verb, suggesting Trinity in Unity. He has also equality in authority (Matt. 28. 19); He has equality in benediction (2 Cor. 13. 14) as also equality in purpose (1 Cor. 12. 4-6). To the Holy Spirit are ascribed attributes which are only true of Deity. He is 'the Eternal Spirit' (Heb. 9. 14). He is omnipresent (Psa. 139. 7-10). He is omniscient (1 Cor. 2. 10-11). He is sovereign (1 Cor. 12. 11). He is 'the Lord—the Spirit' (2 Cor. 3. 18, R.V.). He is superior to angels (1 Peter 1. 11-12). He is recognised as God in Acts 5. 3-4, where Peter charges Ananias with lying to the Holy Spirit, and in the next verse says, 'thou hast lied unto God.' Several times we have messages in the Old Testament from 'the Lord' (Jehovah) attributed in the New Testament to the Holy Spirit; notably Isa. 6. 8-10 compared with Acts 28. 25-27. In passing, it should be noted, that while there are three Persons in one Godhead, each of the Three is distinct the one from the other. This is evident, for instance, in the scene in Matt. 3. 16-17, where Jesus (the Son) is described as coming up 'out of the water' after His baptism; simultaneously the Spirit descends upon the obedient Son 'like a dove,' while 'a Voice from Heaven,' saying, 'This is My Beloved Son,' proclaims the Father's delight.

The Names and Titles of the Holy Spirit should be carefully and reverently pondered since they reveal His Person; His Deity; His character and His work. There are at least thirty such terms in the Scriptures, each with its own significance. Here are a few examples: the Spirit (Isa. 32. 15; Matt. 4. 1) is the basic name and indicates the uniqueness of His Being; there is none other like Him. The Holy Spirit (Psa. 51. 11; Eph. 4. 30) is the name most frequently used. There is an even more emphatic use of this term in John 14. 26, where the literal translation is 'the Spirit—the Holy,' the definite article being used twice—a fact which might well give us pause for reflection. Other suggestive titles are 'the Spirit of grace' (Heb. 10. 29); the Spirit of truth (John 14. 17); the Spirit of holiness (Rom. 1. 4); the Holy Spirit of promise (Eph. 1. 13); the Spirit of wisdom (Eph. 1. 17); the Spirit of adoption (Rom. 8. 15); the Spirit of glory (1 Peter 4. 14); the Spirit of prophecy (Rev. 19. 10). Nor must we overlook the sevenfold description of the Spirit of Jehovah in Isa. 11. 2—clearly a governmental name and probably associated with 'the seven spirits which are before His throne' (Rev. 1. 4). But of all His names, perhaps the most appealing to us, is the name given Him four times by the Lord Jesus (John, chaps. 14-16)—the Comforter. It is a wonderfully expressive and inclusive term and there is really no single word in the English language big enough to do it justice. It is translated 'Advocate' in 1 John 2. 1, where it is used of the risen Lord, but a simple definition of the Greek word *Parakleetos* would be 'one called to the side of another.' An 'Advocate,' as we understand the word, is a legal epithet. If I have the misfortune to be called before a court of law, I might have to call to my side a competent man who not only knows the law, but who knows me and understands my case, but it does not necessarily follow that he would be a comforter. He certainly would not if he failed in his plea. Both words 'Comforter' and 'Advocate' must be taken together if we are to have an adequate conception of what is meant by the Lord's promise to the disciples whom He was about to leave. 'I will not leave you orphans' (unprovided for and unassisted to fight your way through this cruel world) 'I will call to your side the Comforter.' His coming 'would disannul orphanage.' He would be with them and indwell them perpetually; He would be a never-failing source of power, comfort and courage. Why should we ever feel lonely, afraid or despondent with such a powerful, understanding Friend always beside us, and indwelling us? Let us look briefly at some

Activities of the Spirit in Old Testament Times. While we do not get a full revelation of the Person and work of the Spirit in the Old Testament, there are clear evidences of some of His activities.

In the original creation (Gen. 1. 1) of the heavens and the earth, the plural form of the word God (*Elohim*) suggests that the Spirit had a part. 'By His Spirit he hath garnished the heavens' (Job 26. 13). In the six days' work of Gen. 1, we have the first definite record of the Spirit at work. 'The Spirit of God brooded upon the face of the waters' preparing the way for the fiat of God, 'Let light be—and light was' (Gen. 1. 2-3). The Spirit's striving with sinful man is seen in Gen. 6. 3. It is often said, 'leave men to their own consciences, and they will come right.' The answer to this is found in the antediluvian age, when for some 1,656 years, God did just that, and what was the result? There was material progress undoubtedly, but morally the awful condition of things is summed up in Gen. 6. 5, 'God saw that every imagination of the thoughts of his (man's) heart was only evil continually.' Judgment from heaven must inevitably follow, but 'the longsuffering of God waited in the days of Noah' (1 Peter 3. 20) for 120 years, and during this period the Spirit was striving in the consciences of men, no doubt using the warning words of Noah, 'a preacher of righteousness,' as His agent, and generally retarding the gathering tide of lawlessness, until 'it repented the Lord that He had made man ... and it grieved Him at His heart.' In our own times history is in course of repeating itself. The world is drifting on to certain destruction, but again the Spirit of God is acting as the great deterrent to the power of evil. 'There is One who restrains at present until out of the midst He be gone' (2 Thess. 2. 7). Many of us are conscious how real this is, but even so, it cannot alter the truth of the words of Christ, 'As it was in the days of Noah, so shall it be in the days of the Son of Man' (Luke 17. 26).

Then, throughout Old Testament history, the Holy Spirit came *upon* men for a specific purpose and for a limited time. Generally speaking, this word 'upon' is the operative word about the Spirit's work in these earlier days. He came upon Moses, 'the man of God' (Num. 11. 17) but also upon the ungodly Balaam (Num. 24. 2). He 'filled' Bezaleel for the important work of erecting the tabernacle exactly according to the divine 'pattern'; He 'clothed Himself' with Gideon for the deliverance of Israel (Jud. 6. 34, *margin*). He also 'came upon' the wilful King Saul (1 Sam. 10. 10) so that he surprised the people by prophesying. There seems little doubt that He was the same Sovereign Spirit who took control of Caiaphas, the High Priest—that superbly brilliant and damnable politician[1]—to foretell the atoning death of Christ, and to anticipate one consequence of that death, 'the gathering into one body of the children of God' (John 11. 49-52). Always His work and presence in

[1] Dr. Campbell Morgan, in *The Gospel According to John.*

Old Testament times, was transient. There was no abiding presence of the Spirit such as characterizes the present age. So it is, that David in his great penitential Psalm (51) prays, 'Take not Thy Holy Spirit from me.' No true and intelligent believer of this day, however far away from God he may stray, will ever have to include this poignant appeal in his confession. Before leaving a short survey of the Spirit's activities in Old Testament times, we cannot omit to note that He was then the Spirit of revelation and inspiration. The things of God can only be revealed by the Spirit of God. 'The things of God knoweth no man, but the Spirit of God' (1 Cor. 2. 10-12). Of the Old Testament prophets it is recorded, 'No prophecy in Scripture will be found to have come from the prophet's own prompting, for never did any prophecy come by human will, but holy men of God spake as they were borne along by the Holy Spirit' (2 Peter 1. 20-21, *Weymouth*). Not only did the Spirit fill the mouths of the prophets of old with spoken utterances, but in transmitting these utterances into writings, He inspired the writers. He not only gave the thoughts but clothed them with words of His own choice (1 Cor. 2. 13). We freely admit and admire the individuality of each of the sacred writers, and the adaptability of each to the work in hand, but the verbal inspiration of 'all Scripture' is due to the mysterious power which the Spirit of God exerted on the writers in order that His Word might be adequately transmitted through them. It is quite obvious that many of the revelations given to these 'holy men of God' were far beyond their own powers of understanding (Dan. 12. 8) and that they frequently searched diligently their own writings, if perchance they might discover 'what the Spirit of Christ which was in them did signify.' They were the voice of a power superior to themselves, and for the time being, controlling them. How else, for example, could the writer of Psalm 22 have accurately forecast, hundreds of years before the event, the sufferings of Christ on the Cross so accurately that the Saviour could use the very words there given, as His experience in that awful hour? Coming now to the New Testament, let us think of

The Holy Spirit in Relation to the Lord Jesus. The Holy Spirit was the chief agent in the Incarnation. The angel Gabriel disclosed to Mary at the annunciation, 'The Holy Spirit shall come upon thee, and the power of the High shall overshadow thee; wherefore also that which is to be born shall be called holy—the Son of God' (Luke 1. 35, R.V.). To Joseph, the angel of the Lord said, 'Fear not to take unto thee Mary thy wife, for that which is conceived in her is of the Holy Ghost' (Matt. 1. 20). While 'born of a woman' and thus truly Man, the manner of His birth was absolutely unique. It is a miracle, a profound and inscrutable mystery that no human being can fathom.[1]

The Holy Spirit anointed the Lord Jesus at the beginning of His public ministry. John the Baptist—the forerunner of Christ—knew Him not before His baptism, but he did know the signs by which He would be recognized. 'Upon whom thou shalt see the Spirit descending and abiding upon Him, the same is He'; the Baptist convincingly adds, 'I have seen and have borne witness that this is the Son of God' (John 1. 33-34, R.V.). For the first time the heavenly Dove had found an abiding place in a Man (Cp. Gen. 8. 9-12). All through the brief but eventful years of His ministry on earth, the Lord Jesus was 'anointed with the Holy Spirit and with power' (Acts 10. 38).

The Lord Jesus was continually 'led by the Spirit.' In His first public utterance at Nazareth He began by reading the prophetic words of Isa. 61, 'The Spirit of the Lord is upon Me,' and after closing the book, said, 'This day is this Scripture fulfilled in your ears.'

All His mighty works were done in the power of the Spirit (Matt. 12. 28). The mightiest of them all, the surpassing Sacrifice at the Cross, had behind it not only His own immeasurable personal worth but the active co-operation of the Holy Spirit, 'Who through the Eternal Spirit offered Himself without blemish unto God' (Heb. 9. 14, R.V.). There is at least a suggestion that the Spirit had some part in the resurrection, for we read of 'the Spirit of Him that raised up Jesus from the dead' (Rom. 8. 10-11), while there is definite proof that during the forty days of His post-resurrection ministry, the Lord 'through the Holy Spirit gave commandments unto His apostles' (Acts 1. 2). Let us look now at

The Promise and the Mission of the Spirit in John 14-16. It is characteristic of John's Gospel that most of the great distinctive

[1] Dr. Wolston's *Another Comforter*.

truths of Christianity are first mentioned there. In chap. 1 we have the incomparable declaration of the eternal deity of the Son, as also His holy humanity as the 'the Word became flesh,' then in due sequence His sacrificial death as 'the Lamb of God.' In chap. 2. 18-22 the Lord Himself gives the first hint of His resurrection. In chap. 3 we have the fundamental truth of regeneration by the Spirit and the Word, and how to possess eternal life. In chap. 4 there is a clear reference to what was not yet fully unfolded—the gift of the Spirit as a 'fountain of living water' springing up within the believer—and closely allied with this, the worship of the Father 'in spirit and in truth' to supersede the ritualistic worship of the old covenant. In chap. 7, again the Spirit is referred to—this time as 'rivers of living water'—flowing out of the inner being of the believer in ministry and service. Not, however, until the paschal discourses of the Lord to His disciples, given 'when Jesus knew that His hour was come that He should depart out of this world unto the Father,' do we get the first definite announcement of the coming of 'the Comforter.' There are four specific points to notice here about the Spirit's mission towards believers. (1) His abiding presence in and with His people during this age. 'I will make request of the Father and He shall give you another Comforter that He may abide with you for ever' (chap. 14. 16). (2) As 'the Spirit of truth' He would 'teach them all things' and bring all things to their remembrance—a fact which was soon to become evident, as shown in such passages as Acts 1. 16; 2. 16; 11. 16. (3) The Holy Spirit would bear witness of Christ, and His people would be co-witnesses (John 15. 27). (4) The Spirit would announce to believers 'the things which are to come' (John 16. 13), which includes not only prophetic events, but also events which lay much nearer to them, and of which otherwise they could not know. Then, in John 16 we have the Spirit's mission toward the world, 'And He, when He comes, will convict the world in respect of sin, of righteousness, and of judgment' (verses 8-11, *Weymouth*). It is not so much that the Spirit would convince men of sins, although this is true, but that the Spirit's mission in the world is a perpetual interrogation mark. He is asking men in a thousand voices, 'What have you done with the Son of God?' Of all the sins which stain this deluded world, by far the greatest is its rejection of Christ.

The work of the Spirit is to convince men that by this act (for which all men are held responsible), they are going 'full tilt' against the plan and provision of God, to meet their need.

To turn down the claims of Jesus Christ is the damning sin. 'Of sin, because they do not believe in Me' (John 16. 9). There must be 'repentance toward God, and faith toward our Lord Jesus Christ' (Acts 20. 21). Then, the presence of the Spirit in the world is 'to convince men of righteousness.' Men put Christ on the Cross; God has given Him the highest place of honour at His right hand. The only source of righteousness is in heaven, where He now is, and all who, by the urge of the Spirit, desire salvation, will find it by taking sides with God against themselves, and accepting 'the righteousness of God by faith of Jesus Christ' (Rom. 3. 22). The Spirit also convinces men of judgment because the prince of this world (Satan) is under sentence. What was intended to be a crushing blow against God's eternal purpose—engineered by Satan at the Cross—has completely collapsed; the great arch-enemy has been defeated and now awaits his final doom. God wants men to know by His Spirit that the defeat of the adversary at the Cross is a warning to them to get out of the ranks of his followers at once, else they must share his fate (Rev. 20. 10). Coming to the Book of the Acts we find that

The Promise of the Spirit Becomes a Fact. After His resurrection, the Lord had 'presented Himself alive' to His disciples. 'By many infallible proofs' (Acts 1. 3), He had convinced them that He was actually the same Lord, alive from among the dead, walking and talking with them during the forty days between His resurrection and His ascension. No more the querulous, 'We hoped that it was He which should redeem Israel' (Luke 24. 21); doubt had given place to absolute certainty; they confidently recognize 'His Lordship' and supreme authority. Even when He is 'taken up' to heaven, it is evident He is not 'taken away'; with prayer and expectation they 'wait for the promise of the Father,' as He had bid them do, and they were not disappointed. Exactly on the appointed day—the day of Pentecost—the Holy Spirit came, and a completely new epoch in the dealings of God with men, had begun. From this point onwards the Holy Spirit is the dominant actor in the scene; quite clearly He controls the situation. The disciples were 'all filled with the Holy Spirit'; they were transformed by the new Power which, unseen by mortal eye, had taken possession of them. After the Cross, they had been a disheartened, discredited, discomfited little group; now they move forward like an army which has recovered a lost leader, with the confidence and élan of ultimate victory. It is significant that in the Acts alone the Holy Spirit is mentioned some fifty times; it is not, therefore, without good reason that a well-known Bible teacher[1] has suggested that the book should be called 'The Acts of the Holy Spirit' since from first to last it is the record of His advent and activities. Here are a few points, from among many, of outstanding importance, in the Acts.

The Holy Spirit is not only the promise of the Father (chap. 1. 4) but also the gift of the Son to every believer (chap. 2. 33, 38). 'Being by the right hand of God exalted and having received of the Father the promise of the Holy Spirit, He (Jesus) hath shed forth this.' The Spirit came as the communicator and sustainer of divine life. Not only had believers 'passed out of death into life' but with the coming of the Spirit the life of the risen Christ became their life. The Spirit came as the new source of power to believers. 'Ye shall receive the power of the Holy Spirit coming upon you' (1. 8, *margin*) had been the Lord's promise. 'They were all filled with the Holy Spirit' (2. 4) was the fulfilment of that promise. A mighty dynamic force was now at work in and through the disciples and almost immediately signs followed. To these untutored men the Spirit gave utterance, boldness, a new understanding of the Scriptures; ability to preach Christ so convincingly that hostile hearers were 'pierced through to the heart' (2. 37, *Dr. Young's trans.*) and in an agony of conviction cried out, 'What shall we do?' The result was 'that same day there were added about three thousand souls'—added first to the Lord and then to their fellow-believers, in a vital, organic unity, by the Holy Spirit. The supreme control of the Spirit is observable all through this book of Christian activities. Not always using the same means, but making His will perfectly clear, He peremptorily commands (see chap. 8. 29; 10. 19); He makes choice of certain men for certain work (chaps. 13. 2; 20. 28); forbids His servants to take a certain course of action

[1] Dr. Arthur Pierson in *Acts of the Holy Spirit*

(chap. 16. 7); instructs the leaders of the church in the solution of problems on which they had not formerly been agreed (chap. 15. 28).

The control of the Holy Spirit has never been rescinded. Do we, in our day, recognize it and follow it as simply and as wholeheartedly as in those early days? For

The Doctrine of the Spirit we must turn to the epistles and especially to the Pauline epistles. Rom. 8 is one of the greatest chapters in the New Testament. Take special notice of the frequent mention of the Holy Spirit in it. In fact there is more frequent mention of His activities here than in any other single chapter in the Bible. The reason is that the main subject of the chapter is the practical sanctification of the believer in everyday life, and in this, if allowed His way, the Holy Spirit is the great agent. He has come to indwell the child of God; to claim authority over him on behalf of Christ; to dominate and control his life, and that in spite of the fact that the flesh (the old nature) is still there and 'lusteth against the Spirit.' It is possible to say with the writer of the passage, 'The law (the governing power) of the Spirit which is life in Christ Jesus, freed me from the law of sin and death' (v. 2). If this becomes true in actual experience then the believer is said to be 'in the Spirit' —that is, a state marked by the Spirit's conscious control of his life. He is also enjoined to 'walk in the Spirit'; to 'Mind the things of the Spirit' and in all things to be 'led by the Spirit' and so manifest in his life the characteristic traits of a son of God. The believer will come to experience that 'the Spirit beareth witness with our own spirit that we are children of God' (verse 14). When he finds it difficult to pray because 'we know not what we should pray for, as we ought,' he knows that 'the Spirit Himself maketh intercession for us' because He knows the mind of God. All through this most wonderful chapter, there is an absence of hard and fast legal rules, such as obtained under the Mosaic law. 'Ye have not received a spirit of bondage to take you back again to fear, but ye have received the Spirit of sonship, whereby we cry, "Abba," Father' (verse 15). We obey as sons of a father; not as slaves of a despot. In writing to the Galatians, who were in danger of going back to this spirit of bondage, Paul reminds them of two marvellous gifts God has given. First, 'when the fulness of the time was come, God sent forth His Son . . . to redeem' (chap. 4. 4); and second, 'God hath sent forth the Spirit of His Son into your hearts' (chap. 4. 6). As a result the children of God are not only expected to 'walk in the Spirit' and be 'led of the Spirit' but to manifest in their lives 'the fruit of the Spirit' in all its balanced grace and beauty. In the epistle to the Ephesians we have some new facts about the Spirit revealed, and incidentally it is interesting to note that His Name is mentioned in every chapter of this epistle. In chap. 1. 12-13 we read, 'In whom believing, ye were *sealed* with that Holy Spirit of promise, who is also *the earnest* of our inheritance.' The seal of the Spirit marks the believer as Christ's property. 'If any man have not the Spirit of Christ, he is none of His' (Rom. 8. 9). To use a familiar illustration: a farmer goes to buy a flock of sheep at the local auction sale. He may not be able to take possession of them at once, but he puts his mark on them—a mark known to himself and perhaps to others. They have been paid for; they are his property; as quickly as possible he will come and take them to his own pastures. So with believers in Christ. Purchased by His precious blood, sealed by the Spirit, they await the day when their Lord will return to claim them. In the meantime the Spirit as the earnest gives us in actual experience some foretaste of the joys awaiting us. The word 'earnest' used to be applied to the gifts of a bridegroom to his bride-to-be on their betrothal day; it implied that some day all that he had would be hers.

The Spirit's Work in the Church is especially, although not exclusively, to be found in the first letter to the Corinthians. We read of baptism *in* the Holy Spirit (1 Cor. 12. 12-13). 'In one Spirit were we all baptized into one body . . . and were all made to drink of one Spirit' (R.V.). The process began historically with the advent of the Spirit at Pentecost. Remember the Lord's promise before He left; 'Ye shall be baptized in the Holy Spirit not many days hence' (Acts 1. 5). The Risen Lord was the Baptizer; the Spirit was the element in whom they were baptized. All the believers became part of the 'one body' of which the Head was Christ, and as believers in these early days were added in thousands, and as to-day they are added one by one, all become part of the mystical body of Christ, and all have been once for all baptized in the Holy Spirit. The current idea of baptism of the Spirit is quite unknown to Scripture, as also is the thought of a 'fresh baptism of the Spirit.' There may be many 'fillings' but there can only be one baptism. Still more erroneous is the very common thought of belonging to various Christian bodies, presumably all claiming Christ as their Head. There is only One who has the God-given right to be called 'Head of the Church' (Eph. 1. 22; Col. 1. 18). There is only one Body of Christ (Eph. 4. 4). Only God knows where all the members are; they are never found altogether on earth; myriads of them are already in heaven; those who remain on earth are often separated from each other by varying doctrines and known by sectarian names, and yet the Holy Spirit in the individual believer and in the church collectively yearns to lead all true believers into 'the unity of the Spirit' (Eph. 4. 3) by means of 'the unity of the faith' (Eph. 4. 13). Just as the Holy Spirit seeks to control the individual child of God, for his practical sanctification to God, so the same Spirit is at work in the Church to establish the Lordship of Christ, to distribute and co-ordinate the gifts in the Church for the building up of all saints. We have no space to trace the work of the Spirit in the Pastoral epistles, or in the earnest warnings of John's first epistle against spirits of a very different kind at work in the world now, whose specious appeals may 'deceive the very elect.' We cannot close however, without a glance at

The Message of the Spirit in the Apocalypse. The Apocalypse is a book of supernal glories for those who love the Lord. In chapters 2 and 3 are seven letters to the churches, to those who make at least a profession of Christianity, and each of these closes with the same words—'He that hath an ear to hear, let him hear what the Spirit saith unto the churches.' It is a call from One who knows what lies ahead, to the individual believer, surrounded by failure and declension to stand firm, and to return to God, His Word, His Spirit. These calls from the Spirit show how closely He watches for any sign of response to the Lord's invitation to His people to open the door and let Him come in (chap. 3. 20). Then we come to the last mention of the Spirit in the Bible. 'The Spirit and the Bride say, "Come"' (chap. 22. 17). As the work of Eliezer was not finished until he had safely handed over Rebekah to Isaac, so the faithful Guide and Guardian of the Church having seen her safely through the desert way, senses that His task is almost over. 'The Bright and Morning Star' is about to break through the murkiest stormcloud of the night, and so the Spirit in the Church, and the Church in the Spirit, join in a welcoming shout of 'Come!' May we 'abound in that hope, through the power of the Holy Spirit' (Rom. 15. 13).

CHAPTER XI

Creation

F. A. FILBY

THE supreme purpose of the Bible is to reveal to man His Creator. Man is surrounded by a universe that is mysterious and wonderful. Within the deepest recesses of his soul man knows that this mysterious universe had a Creator, yet that inner voice can tell but little about Him. Indeed, in the past, the inner consciousness has been so often suppressed or distorted that men have worshipped their Creator under the symbol of a serpent, a tree, or a pillar of stone, or they have even denied that there is a Creator at all. (Rom. 1. 22-23; but compare also vv. 19-21 which show that man was responsible for the ignorance).

Man has used many aids to probe into his wonderful environment. Giant telescopes have carried his gaze deep into the recesses of space revealing such marvels that all but the most hardened are hushed in the contemplation of such immensities. Microscopes and balances of wonderful design have enabled man to reveal the mysteries of the ultra-small, until the mass of the tiniest of all nature's particles, the electron, has been determined, and its pathway photographed. But man has still not seen God. He has discovered a universe, full of marvels, and packed with evidences of design, but he has not found the Designer.

So the Creator has revealed Himself. In words that are very simple He has told us who it was that designed the universe. The God whose perfect law was given to Moses on Sinai, and whose perfect Son was given to the world on Calvary, the God who was revealed in part through the prophets of bygone days, and fully in Jesus Christ—He, and He alone, is the Creator of the universe. The synthesis is complete. The Unknown has become known in the person of Christ, and in the pages of the Bible.

All that is really needful for us to know of the Creation God has revealed in the comparatively short space of the first chapters of Genesis and the closing chapters of Job, together with some very beautiful poetical passages in the Psalms and in the prophets.

The story begins with a bygone age, briefly designated as 'the beginning,' in which God created the heaven and the earth. It may satisfy a feeling of natural curiosity within us to seek to determine how many of our years ago this creation was. If we could rely upon certain estimates as to the rate at which the oceans are becoming salt, and compare this with their total saltness at present we might conclude that our earth's surface took shape less than 80 million years ago. If we could rely upon the values for the rate at which uranium and thorium break up into simpler elements, and if we knew that these rates had never been changed throughout the ages by any other 'cosmic' influences, and that our analyses of certain ores really represented the beginning and ending of such a process—some, but not all of these links are fairly well established—we might conclude that the earth was already formed 2,000 million years ago. It really makes little difference. If we were telling this to some children we should say, 'A very long time ago. . . .' God, speaking to His human children says, 'In the beginning.'

God 'created.' What do the words mean? We live in a universe which in some ways resembles a watch running down, or a fire burning slowly out. No one seems quite to have solved the riddle of the universe. Sometimes it seems to astronomers that the vast stellar system is ever expanding. All the distant nebulæ and star clusters are running away from us, and if so, there must have been a time when they were all much closer together—a beginning. Others doubt if this apparent running away is real, but still agree that some vast running down is taking place, and in picturesque language they speak of stars which are growing old. The learned speak of a mysterious quantity called the entropy of the universe—a measure of its progress from order to disorder—which process seems to have had a start, and which will have an end. In other words all scientists are agreed that the present scheme of things had a beginning and that it will have an end. This much God has already revealed in His Word. The 'winding up' process is the creative work of God. He alone produces order out of disorder, a universe out of chaos. The universe as He has made it at present will have an end. 'Thou, Lord, in the beginning hast laid the foundation of the earth; and the heavens are the works of Thine hands: they shall perish; but Thou remainest: and they all shall wax old as doth a garment: and as a vesture shalt Thou fold them up, and they shall be changed: but Thou art the same and Thy years shall not fail' (Heb. 1. 10-12). Our age is but one of many: ages will run their course. He who is the Alpha and the Omega, the Beginning and the Ending is alone unchanged throughout them all. In the magnificent words of Jude (v. 25, R.V.), 'To the only God our Saviour, through Jesus Christ our Lord, be glory, and majesty, dominion and power, before all time, and now, and throughout all ages.'

So, if we may speak reverently, yet simply, God, in the beginning, 'wound up' His great universe. He lit its great atomic fires and set them radiating their energy throughout the realms of space. No possible clue as to how it happened can be given us. We do not yet know enough science to understand, so that certainly no generation before us could possibly have understood. It is not God's purpose in Genesis to tell us 'how.' Instead, He tells us in delightfully simple words that even a child can understand, 'He made the stars also.'

But this little globe, which Job (26. 7) knew to be hanging in space, was yet steeped in darkness. Like its neighbour, the planet Venus, it was wrapped in clouds and vapours. In process of cooling it seems to have lost its original atmosphere and then, as the rocks became solid, they yielded up vast quantities of imprisoned water vapour and gases. Yet throughout all this apparent chaos, the Divine Hand was working out His purposes—for when at last the whole work was finished, and He pronounced it good—then there was left on this earth just *exactly* the right amounts of water, oxygen, nitrogen, and carbon dioxide for the types of creatures which He had designed to live here. We do well to ponder this lesson, that chaos is not beyond the control of the Creator. In the darkest and most chaotic conditions He is doubtless working out some mighty plan.

The idea that the oceans were once imprisoned in the rocks of the still cooling earth was also revealed in the Bible, for what other meaning can we give to the words of God in Job 38. 8, 'Or who shut up the sea with doors, when it brake forth as if it had issued out of the womb? When I made the cloud the garment thereof, and thick darkness a swaddling band for it'—a passage which is followed by an equally beautiful poetical description of the rise of the land masses confining the ocean to its decreed place and saying, 'Hitherto shalt thou come but no further, and here shall thy proud waves be stayed.'

But ere these great continents had risen the Creator had brought light into the scene. So, early in the Book we have the great antithesis—light and darkness. In Genesis, physical light breaks in upon physical darkness. In John's Gospel the True Light shines into a world of moral darkness. In the Epistle to the Colossians the Christians are translated out of the tyranny of darkness into the Kingdom of Light. In the Revelation, the darkness is past; 'they need no candle nor light of the sun—for the Lord God giveth them light . . . and there is no night there.' Light is ever the symbol of God or of some aspect of His activity. His Son is the True Light, His Word is a light to our pathway, His servants are the light of the world. Light is so simple that a child revels in the glories of a sunlit garden, but no scientist really knows what light is. We can measure its wavelengths, we can track its path, and determine its speed; we know that it is essential for our welfare: yet it is best to leave its origin in the words of Gen. 1, 'God said let there be light, and there was light.'

God 'said.' The simple words are but picture language. Throughout the chapter we must always remember that, since God cannot tell us 'how' He created the universe, He can only tell us in simple human words the facts that He did do it all. It is not wise to refer to Gen. 1 as mythology, for the word conveys to our minds an idea of garbled legends of human origin containing indeed some truth though in small proportion. The reverse is true of Gen. 1. The actual truths are much greater than the surface meaning of the words. The style is anthropomorphic—God speaks of Himself as acting like a man, yet always with a dignity which raises the account far above the level of the crude mythologies of the East. God speaks of Himself as a workman performing a task—but He is infinitely greater than a man. His words are not human words made with lips and tongue; they represent His control over the forces of the universe which 'hasten to do His bidding.' His 'seeing' is not with limited human vision depending upon eyes and light, but is His immediate knowledge of the very ends of His universe. Later on in the Bible He explains all this to man. His thoughts are not our thoughts, His ways are not our ways, and His days are not our days; to Him thousands of years are but a day, and our brief lives are but as a tale that is told. It is true that the picture of evenings and mornings refers to our earthly days, just as God's 'speaking' pictures Him as a man with a human voice, but Gen. 1 implies far more than is conveyed by the surface meaning of the words and we must transfer the picture words to their truer, vaster meaning, and what to the Creator was but as a single day's work, measured by our little time scale was a geological age.[1]

So the first day's work was ended: the first great act of the creation story was finished. God said, Let there be light, and there was light, and God saw the light that it was good.

The creative work now enters upon a second phase. The gases which had escaped from the molten rocks had now formed an atmosphere, or open expanse, above the surface of the oceans, and the clouds began to form. God divided the waters which were under the firmament from the waters which were above the firmament. Strictly the expanse is unlimited. The air continues, getting thinner and thinner, for many miles and there are strange layers of particles hundreds of miles up. But the word firmament (expanse, heaven) can also be used for ever-widening spheres—for the air (e.g. the birds of heaven), for the interstellar space (the stars of heaven) or in a spiritual sense (the heaven of heavens). So Gen. 1 speaks of the waters above the firmament (lower atmosphere) and also of the sun and moon as being in the firmament of heaven (i.e. space).

We can only comment in passing on the wonders of this atmosphere in which God has wrapped His world. It contains enough carbon dioxide to feed all the plants in the world and yet not injure man, enough nitrogen to provide all the fertilizers man will ever need, enough oxygen for all living things, all arranged at the

[1] For an alternative view that the days are merely the days on which God revealed the story of creation see P. J. Wiseman, *Creation Revealed in Six Days*.

correct pressures for life as we know it. The atmosphere provides, with the help of the clouds, the blanket to keep us warm. It bends the sun's rays to give us twilight. It gives us winds to modify the extremes of heat and cold, to carry the moisture of the oceans far inland, to provide us with rain, and to carry seeds. It is truly part of a marvellous plan!

A third great creative act of God now comes into view. This is no less than the rise of the land masses—great masses of granite, thousands of miles across—from beneath the oceans. It is an amazing fact: nothing but a divine revelation could have made it known to the writers of Gen. 1 and Psa. 104. The highest mountain ranges were once under the sea. No scientist doubts it. The evidence is conclusive: the Rocky Mountains, the Alps, even the mighty Himalayas—all were formed beneath the sea! These great land masses rest upon layers of basaltic rocks, one might almost say they float on it, for they rose as it solidified. The continents of to-day rest with the bulk of their mass embedded in the layers below, and where the mountains are highest, the foundations are deepest. But this principle, which is now known as isotasy, was revealed in the Bible for, in Job 38. 4-6, God speaks of the 'foundations of the earth being fastened,' and the Revised Version margin correctly translates this as 'sockets made to sink.' The same Hebrew word is used here as is used for the tabernacle boards being set into sockets of silver. So the foundations of the earth are made to sink into the underlying layers. The enormous mountain masses are balanced by deeper foundations, or in the beautiful words of Isaiah (40. 6), 'He weighed the mountains in scales, and the hills in a balance.' The great land masses slowly rose above the primeval oceans: the dry land appeared and the waters drained off into their decreed ocean bed. Dr. Maclaren dramatically translates Psa. 104. 8, ' . . . up rose the mountains, down sank the valleys, to the place which Thou hadst founded for them. A bound Thou hast set that they should not pass over, nor return to cover the earth.'

The dry land was not, however, to be left as a vast desert such as we perceive upon the surface of the moon. The day's work was not complete until the earth was carpeted with grass and herbs and trees. No one to-day has any real idea how these marvellous structures developed upon the earth, nor even how they work to-day. We know that they existed in a bygone geological age known as the Primary, that they became tremendously prolific in an age called the Carboniferous whose remains we are using as coal to-day: we know that they grew where all to-day is snow and ice, for coal exists in Greenland, Spitzbergen, and within 800 miles of the South Pole. But no one knows how they came. God has not so far revealed to any scientist, however painstaking and humble, just how He produced living things from inorganic matter. The theory of evolution of course does not pretend to explain this. And when it comes to the question of how they work to-day, a moment's consideration of God's masterpiece, the seed, will soon humble us. For this tiny seed in a year's time will produce a stalk of wheat, this second seed in a hundred years will be a great elm tree, and yet a third will still be living a thousand years hence as a mighty sequoia—the Californian redwood tree, towering 300 feet into the sky.

On the fourth day the account takes up again the question of light. There seems no reason to doubt that sun, moon and stars had existed from the 'beginning' in verse 1. The task of the fourth day is their appointment as light bearers and time controllers. Some have suggested that with the removal of much carbon dioxide from the air in the carboniferous period the light of these heavenly bodies became clearly visible, or that they had previously been obscured by mists and vapours. Others see here some adjustment of the orbits, for the exact regulation of days and months and years, and of summers and winters. Yet others regard the writer as merely returning to his first theme—light—to develop it more fully, just as he next returns to the oceans and tells what happened in them. Thus Day 4 follows Day 1 chronologically, while Day 5 develops Day 2 and Day 6 completes Day 3, the whole structure being based on the Hebrew form of poetical parallelism. We probably do not yet know enough to decide between these views, each of which has certain facts to commend it. The present writer feels that the passage probably refers to some scientific fact which we have not yet discovered but which will one day be hailed as the very latest discovery of science. The words imply more than we have yet grasped.

'The greater and the lesser lights.' Do the words imply that the original account was written in some language so ancient as to have no other names for the sun and moon? It may be so. But how true they are. The greater light! Greater indeed; over 300,000 times the mass of our earth, with a surface temperature of over 6,000 degrees Centigrade, radiating energy at the rate of 65,000 horse power for every square yard of its surface, transforming the atomic energy of probably 250 million tons of matter into radiation every minute—yet not growing appreciably cooler or fainter during the lifetime of the human race! Truly this bush that burns but is not consumed is a marvel of the Creator's design.

'The lesser light!' Lesser it is indeed, for the sun's light is estimated to be 465,000 times as bright as moonlight. Yet the moon shines brightest, and climbs higher in the sky, and stays up longest when the nights are longest and darkest. What a parable for the Christian Church called upon to reflect that glory of God which shines as the sun in our Lord Jesus Christ, but as the moon in His followers during the long winter of His absence.

The heavenly bodies are also for signs and for seasons. This involves not only months and years but the various periods of vegetable and animal life whose cycles are mysteriously linked with the radiations that come to our earth. On a small number of occasions the Creator has also allowed the heavenly bodies to act as signs to mankind. The chief of these are connected with the Person of Christ, at whose first coming a new star appeared, and at whose death the earth was wrapped in a darkness which cannot be satisfactorily explained as an eclipse. The Bible also insists that before Christ's ultimate triumph considerable astronomical upheavals will take place, and there is more than a hint of some great flare-up of our sun which will literally 'burn up' the present surface of the earth, and all 'the works that are therein' leaving a new earth, devoid of sea, for the next stage of the Creator's activity.

The account now returns to the study of the oceans and the atmosphere. The waters were to bring forth abundantly; literally 'swarm with swarms' of living things. Here again the Creator has produced a marvellous range of types and sizes from creatures smaller than the stickleback to the great 'whales' of verse 21, which may well include the monsters of geological times, the great amphibians whose skeletons adorn our museums, as well as the huge sharks, walruses, whales and crocodiles of our present times. The 30 foot shark and the 90 foot whale are indeed marvels of the ocean, but so, too, is the humble minnow into whose body are packed more wonders than can be found in a modern submarine.

These creatures were commanded to swarm with swarms. A female turbot can produce 8 million eggs in a single season; a cod, 4 million. The numbers of herrings landed at fishing ports is of the order of hundreds of millions per year at each large port. An airman is reported recently to have seen in the gulf of Aden a shoal of fish 18 miles long.

The sky, too, must be peopled. To maintain the wonderful balance of nature, winged fowl must fly in the open firmament of heaven. The words it is true are once used of insects, but almost invariably they refer to birds. These, too, are prolific. Flights many miles long have been seen at migration times; sometimes acres of land have been seen covered with birds. The number of house sparrows in the United States east of the Mississippi was estimated some years ago as 165 million. Even in the frozen wastes of the Antarctic far beyond the homes of men, dwell countless thousands of those strangest of all birds, the penguins.

The story is now obviously moving to its climax. With a delightfully neat and simple style it has handled the vast problems of astronomy and geology leaving only the population of the land masses to be dealt with. With the same simplicity of style it tells that the same Creative Power operated upon the continents to produce cattle, creeping things, and beasts of the earth, each after his kind. The classification is simple: the biologist might term it scientifically crude, but the theologian would well retort that it is a much more convenient classification from the point of view of the majority of Bible readers than would be a list of the zoological orders and species.

No clue again is given as to how the Creator built these marvels of design and plan. Men have from time to time put forward theories, some of which were very simple and pretty, but all of which were most unlikely. Some have held that all of these just evolved without any Creator to start or to guide them. It is just useless to argue with such folk. Others have held that there was an original Creator, but that He left the various creatures to evolve one from the other. But careful thought shows this to be unsound. If there was a Creator at all, He must be Creator of all. It was formerly held by many that all the various forms of life now existing on the earth evolved from a few, probably one, original form. No satisfactory evidence has ever been produced for this and scientists are returning to the more reasonable view that life has 'come' to this earth in many—perhaps very many—forms. The idea that geology would produce endless series of fossils showing almost imperceptible grades of creatures, has completely collapsed. A few series have certainly been worked out showing that some types of creatures can vary quite a long way from their earlier ancestors, but even these series are very few, and considerably overrated, and by no means capable of supporting the hypothesis of complete gradual evolution of all creatures from a single ancestor. In several regions immense numbers of fossils have been unearthed, systematically examined and classified, and they do not show gradual changes—but sudden ones.

It was also thought at the end of the last century that a study of the embryos of various creatures, including man, would reveal the various stages of evolutionary ascent. A few curiosities of embryonic development were hailed by some as proving man's descent from a fish-like ancestor, but most scientists are abandoning this recapitulation theory as not really leading anywhere. That the various stages of the development of an embryo reflect its needs during development is a much more reasonable line of approach.

Some, like Lamarck, had felt that an organism 'tried' in some way to adapt itself to its environment and having achieved a measure of success, handed on its improvement to the next generation, which in turn continued the good work. Others held with Darwin that the offspring always differed in a number of small ways from the parents, and that, in the struggle for existence those with more helpful variations survived in greater numbers, and, handing on the improvement to their offspring, produced a slightly different race. By continuing these small changes over a very long time new species and new orders of creatures were evolved. So we were seriously asked to believe that by a process of natural selection operating on chance variations whales and sparrows and oak trees and men and chickens were all evolved from a single jelly-like ancestor!

A few hours' quiet consideration of the amazing pattern of life —the wonderful powers of the eye, or lungs, or the blood system: the intricacies of the tiniest spider, or its web, the highly organized life of bees or ants, the fascinating stories of nest building among birds—and a host of other studies—will soon convince the unbiased scientist that the theories of evolution so far advanced are far too simple to represent reality. Reality—even a single carbon atom is very, very complicated. The pattern of the organic world is still too complex for our solution. To quote the words of two Cambridge scientists, 'To-day we are only just beginning, not so much to solve the problems of nature, but to learn of what the problems consist.' (Saunders and Clark, *Order and Chaos in the World of Atoms*, p. 249).

So far, then, all theories of evolution have fallen lamentably short of being even likely.[1] While many scientists have doubtless held to their own theories with great sincerity, yet it must be admitted that others had an ulterior motive in supporting such views, namely a desire to do away with any ideas about a Creator, or of a purpose in the universe.

What forces the Creator employed in the formation of the various forms of life, and how many forms were thus developed we do not know. We know of the existence of various forces, electro-magnetic, inter-atomic, gravitational and cosmic. These were doubtless some of His tools. Others may yet be discovered. On the other hand we know that members of a given species, to relieve the world of monotony, do vary quite widely from the mean. Yet it is now established beyond any doubt after experiments on many generations of small creatures such as *drosophila* that the most outstanding factor in even such tiny things is their resistance to change and their ability to breed true to type. The forces compelling the creature to breed true, 'after its kind,' are thousands of times stronger than the forces which produce minor variations either side of the mean.

[1] More recent theories that evolutionary development occurred in definite leaps or mutations caused by factors now unknown, bring us nearly back to the theologians' ideas of special creation.

But we must return from this digression on evolution, to consider the last, and so far as the human race is concerned, the most important stage, of the story—the advent of man, admitted by all scientists to be the last of the living things to appear on this earth. Here this chapter begins to merge into the subject matter of the next; yet we must pause for a few considerations before closing. Questions come crowding into our minds. How far is man related to the animals? Did God make man of the dust? Did He make only two people? Did man appear only 6,000 years ago? What is a soul? Some of these questions I must leave to others to expand in their chapters. I have but space to record my own opinions formed from some years of careful study. Man's body does show a general pattern resembling that of creatures known as the primates. The resemblances are no closer than would have been expected, and the differences are quite sufficient to distinguish him absolutely from any other species. The search among fossil remains for the so-called missing links to bridge the gulf between the higher apes or any other alleged ancestors, and man, has been amazingly fruitless when we consider the time and money and patience expended in the effort. The results regarded scientifically are negligible; regarded from the standpoint of art, in the drawings of ape-men, crude and amusing. Biology can never expect to make the progress that has been made by physics and chemistry if it relies on methods such as these. More sober biologists are coming to the conclusion that life has not evolved by very gradual steps but by leaps, and that the coming of man was one of those great leaps. There were no long generations of intermediate creatures.

I see no reason to doubt that the human race sprang from two parents. Blood tests show that the whole human race has blood of four general types, O, A, B and AB and these can all be derived from two parents. I see no valid reason for making Neanderthal man earlier than, or separate from, the Adamic race—in fact the early chapters of Genesis indicate two main streams, the Cainite and Sethite races. All the excavations on sites continuously occupied by man seem to show that he has not been here for more than the six or seven thousand years indicated by the Bible. The flood level at Ur is just over 40 feet from the surface and this represents very approximately 5,000 years. The remains below the clay, containing evidences of earlier man are less than 10 feet thick. With all allowances for slower rate in earlier times this cannot represent many thousands of years. Nowhere is there any evidence from accumulated remains that the Old Stone Age was many times the length of the New Stone Age. Analyses and estimates of the date of the stages of the Ice Age also lead to the view that the coming of man must be put in the last 9,000 years. The stories repeated in book after book about mankind developing slowly for the first 200,000 years are sheer nonsense. While there have always been backward tribes and peoples, these have been contemporary with very advanced civilizations. Our island was relatively backward while the civilizations of Crete, Egypt and Assyria were at their height. Our civilization is now regarded as very advanced, while those of Crete, Egypt and Assyria have fallen far into arrears. Man, as all the rest of the Bible shows, is capable of great heights—and of great depths. Mud huts can often be found within a stone's throw of the ruins of some magnificent temple or pyramid.

Man's body is made from the dust. Dust he is and to dust he will return. It is true. His body is composed only of elements common to this globe. No strange or unusual element was used in his creation. And of his non-material part, with which he in turn creates, and chooses, and worships, I leave my successor to speak in the next chapter. My task is done. The Creator's work was finished as He blessed our first parents and gave them their home. So God finished His work, and behold it was very good. 'Thus the heavens and the earth were finished and all the host of them,' and on the seventh day God rested from all His work which He had made. Thus far creation. God finished it: it was very good: God rested—the great sabbath rest of creation. The remainder of the Bible has another story to tell—that of redemption. And at Calvary Christ finished that also, and it was very good: and He rested in the tomb on the Sabbath day, for that Sabbath day was a high day.

Creation and redemption meet in the person of Christ, for He who redeemed creation was, together with the Father, its Creator. He was in the world, and the world was made by Him, and the world knew Him not. All things were made by Him, and without Him was not anything made that was made. For by Him were all things created that are in the heavens and that are on earth, whether they be thrones, or dominions, or principalities or powers, all things were created by Him and for Him, and He is before all things, and by Him all things consist.

Creation and redemption merge yet again in the close of the Bible record. In the last great vision granted to mankind the apostle sees the redeemed worshipping Him that liveth for ever and ever, and saying, 'Thou art worthy, O Lord, to receive glory and honour and power; for Thou hast created all things and for Thy pleasure they are and were created' (Rev. 4. 11). In the following chapter Creator and Redeemer together receive the adoration of all creation in the greatest of all doxologies . . . 'and every creature which is in heaven, and on earth, and under the earth, and such as are in the sea, and all that are in them, heard I saying, Blessing, and honour, and glory, and power, be unto Him that sitteth upon the throne, and unto the Lamb for ever and ever' (Rev. 5. 14).

It remains for us all to join in the great AMEN!

CHAPTER XII

Man

J. H. LARGE

THE question is asked four times in Scripture, 'What is man?' (Job 7. 17-20; Psa. 8. 4; 144. 3; Heb. 2. 6). Every thoughtful person has surely asked the question many times. When David asked the question it was not man's insignificance but his mysterious significance which aroused his wonder. He could see that, judged by merely physical standards, man was unspeakably small but against this fact was the extraordinary interest God took in man—He was mindful of man, He visited him. Man was made only a little lower than the angels, he was crowned with glory and honour and had been set over the works of God's hands (Psa. 8. 6-8).

There is evidently some mystery here, of which we have all been conscious at some time or another. Consideration of what Scripture reveals as to man's creation will serve only to increase this sense of wonder. The dignity of man is seen in the deliberate counsel within the Triune Godhead—'Let Us make man' (Gen. 1. 26). God's personal intervention in the creation of man contrasts strongly with the impersonal edicts which called creation into being and afterwards fashioned and furnished it. 'Let light be,' 'Let there be a firmament'—thus were the heavens and the earth finished but we do not read, 'Let man *be*'—no, it is, 'Let Us *make* man.' So God created man—and created him in the image of God. Let us notice God's special pleasure in creation when man crowned the whole—day by day we hear God pronouncing His work (with the exception of the second day) as 'good,' but after man appeared God pronounced the whole as '*very* good' (Gen. 1. 31). Surely, too, man's value to God is seen in the fact that as soon as he had sinned God sought him, and has been seeking him ever since. The amazing lengths to which God went to redeem him, the Saviour's pronouncement as to each individual soul being worth more than the world, and His awful warnings as to the nature of man's doom if unrepentant, as well as the unimaginable heights of glory to which the ransomed will be raised, all testify to the fact that there is some mystery about man (Gen. 3. 9; Luke 19. 10; Matt. 16. 26; Matt. 10. 28; Rom. 8. 29, 30).

In the book of Genesis we are given two accounts of man's creation—the first in 1. 26-28 and the other in 2. 7. Some who have felt obliged to establish harmony between the statements of Scripture and the suppositions of science, have regarded these two accounts as referring to distinct and separate creations. It is questionable whether such an idea would have occurred to anybody had there not been first of all some desire to find a distinction. In the first account we are given in broad outline man's racial relationship to God on the one hand, and to creation on the other —as being in God's image, and given dominion. In the second account we get the details as to how the first man and the first woman were brought into being. Seeing that the first account has to do with the creation as a whole and man's place in it, the consistent employment in Gen. 1 of the divine title *Elohim* is just as understandable as the employment of the title *Jehovah* in Gen. 2, where God is seen in his personal relationship to man as an *individual*. The intermediate title, *Jehovah Elohim*, serves to establish beyond doubt the identification between *Elohim* of chap. 1 and *Jehovah* of chap. 2, instead of pointing, as higher critics assert, to the fact that the early chapters of Genesis were the work of an editor who co-ordinated the separate accounts of different writers, one of these writers having used the title *Elohim*, another *Jehovah Elohim* and yet another simply *Jehovah*. It is a sufficient answer to those who would say that the first account refers to the creation of an inferior type of man, and the second to a man of a higher type, to mention that in point of fact the first account gives the more elevated conception of man's nature as created in the image and after the likeness of God, whereas the second record gives the more distinctly physical side of man's creation. Further discussion of the point is unnecessary since Christ in a short statement on marriage, quoted, remarkably enough, a passage from each record in such a way as to make it clear that He regarded them as referring to the same creation.

It will be simpler for our present purpose to study the second account before the first because it can be taken as it stands, whereas the creation of man in God's image involves questions which can be appreciated only in the light of further investigation.

Man's body was formed out of the dust of the ground, the verb 'formed' suggesting the action of a potter moulding clay—in fact the substantive 'potter' is from the same root. Some have felt that the narrative requires them to believe that the Lord God, in human form, actually operated on a piece of clay and moulded it with His hands into the shape of a man's body; in that case simple consistency will require them to believe the same with regard to the brute creation, for we are likewise told that out of the ground the Lord God formed every beast of the field and every fowl of the air. Elihu spoke of himself as being formed out of the clay, and used a similar, though not the identical, word, whilst Job, speaking of his formation in the womb, said, 'Thine hands have made me and fashioned me together round about . . . Thou hast made me as the clay' (Gen. 2. 17, 19; Job 33, 6; 10. 9).

Much harm has been done by well-meaning people who think they are loyally contending for the teaching of Scripture, when they are but contending for what they think the Scripture means. If we are content with the statements that man's body was formed of the dust of the ground, and that the Lord God did the forming we are on unassailable ground, because scientists have to admit the one and cannot disprove, though some may dislike, the other.

In the Genesis account, God is spoken of as 'creating' (as distinct from forming what has been created) at three special points—at the beginning when the material universe was first brought into existence out of nothing (v. 1), again when the processes of formation were ready for the introduction of sentient, as distinct from non-sentient life (v. 20), and lastly, when the animal creation being completed, God introduced man. It is remarkable that, in relation to man, it is thrice stated in one verse that God created —what could be more emphatic? (Gen. 1. 27).

God now breathed into man's nostrils the breath of lives (plural) and man became a living soul. We are not, therefore, to conclude that man is *only* a living soul—that he is, but he need not, therefore, be only that. It is not as a living soul that man is distinguished from the brute creation, for the same expression is applied to the creatures in vv. 20 and 24, where 'creature that hath life' and 'the living creature' are equivalent to 'living soul.' So far what has been said of man's body, and the life which animates it, has been said of the animal creation. What does distinguish man from the brute in this particular account is that in his case he became endowed with life by the special act of God breathing into his nostrils the breath of lives. Clearly we are to understand that man's life is of a higher order than the brute's. It is difficult to assert that the plural form (breath of lives) teaches that man was endowed, not only with natural (soul) life, but also with a higher (spirit) life, because the plural form often occurs elsewhere, and is regarded by some merely as the plural of excellence—even so, the very idea of excellence may rest upon the fact that man's super-sensuous life is twofold. A hint it may be—but we must look elsewhere for developed teaching as to man's inner nature, and this will come later.

This much is clear from our present passage—man is not merely body—he has life. The question we have now to decide is whether the immaterial side of man's nature is merely the life principle (soul) which animates his body (as in the case of the beast) or whether he has a higher spiritual nature distinct from the single natural (soul) life of the beast.

Scripture seems sometimes content to distinguish broadly between man's physical constitution (his body) and his super-sensuous nature, by simply contrasting body and soul, flesh and spirit, body and spirit (Matt. 10. 28; 26. 41; 1 Cor. 6. 20; Jas. 2. 26). Some have concluded, therefore, that man's nature is dual, his super-sensuous life consisting of one element, sometimes spoken of as spirit and sometimes as soul, the two words being regarded as synonymous, or at the most expressing only different aspects of a single super-sensuous life in man. Adherents of the dual-nature theory favour the idea because it relieves them from some embarrassments involved in the doctrine of the tripartite nature of man. Appeal is sometimes made to our own consciousness. Consciousness is a legitimate but not conclusive argument—in any case it is not difficult to discern within ourselves conflicts which arise between aspirations after higher things and desires after lower things, which are at least consistent with, if not proof of, two elements in the inner life of man.

Scripture, however, makes it plain that spirit is not identical with soul. Paul's exhortation to the Thessalonians clearly indicates a dual element apart from the body—'your whole spirit, *and* soul *and* body' (1 Thess. 5. 23). No doubt the distinction between spirit and soul is very fine, as indeed is suggested by the author of the Hebrews Epistle when he regards it as one of the glories of the Word of God that it can divide between the spirit and the soul (Heb. 4. 12). Mary was clear enough as to the distinction because she could speak of her spirit having rejoiced in God prior to her soul magnifying the Lord (Luke 1. 46, 47). The words Isaiah puts into the mouth of Judah express the same distinction although, curiously enough, in the opposite direction—the soul had desired God and the result was that the spirit would seek after Him (Isa. 26. 9), different tenses being employed in both cases, because spirit and soul are sufficiently distinct to allow of a movement in one subsequently affecting the other.

Some who recognize the force of this line of argument hold that it is true only of the regenerate and that in their case this higher life is but an effect of the indwelling Spirit of God, rather than the existence of an individual spirit in the man. This is sufficiently disproved by the fact that the Spirit of God is spoken of as witnessing with our spirit—they must, therefore, be distinct (Rom. 8. 16). Others recognize a distinct spirit in believers, but not in the unregenerate. Certainly the higher life of the spirit is more generally spoken of in relation to believers and it is only to be expected that the indwelling of the Spirit of God would bring the life of the spirit into greater prominence, but for all that, several Scriptures attribute spirit to man as man, irrespective of the new birth. The unregenerate are dead in sins in the sense that they are separated from God, but their spirits are not dead in the sense of being inert and incapable of performing any function whatsoever (Eph. 2. 1). James says that the body without the spirit is dead—if spirit is possessed only by the regenerate then this Scripture declares that all the unregenerate are physically dead (Jas. 2. 26). Then, again, we are told that only the spirit of man can make him acquainted with the things of a man—if the unregenerate have not spirit they manage surprisingly well under the severe handicap of not being able to understand the things of a man (1 Cor. 2. 11). Zechariah speaks of Jehovah stretching forth the heavens and laying the foundation of the earth, and forming the spirit of man within him. This clearly testifies to spirit being a distinct element in man as man, and incidentally to man's importance seeing that the formation of the spirit within him makes him worthy to be mentioned in the same breath as the creation of heaven and earth (Zech. 12. 1). Others who believe that spirit is possessed by the believer only, explain it as being a synonym for the new nature, but this is disproved by the fact that there can be filthiness of spirit even in the case of a believer, and by Paul's prayer for the Thessalonians' preservation of their spirits from blame (2 Cor. 7. 1; 1 Thess. 5. 23).

We conclude then that man as man possesses not only body and soul, but spirit also—hence we speak of the tripartite nature of man. The passage already quoted from the Hebrews Epistle, whilst distinguishing these three elements, suggests that it is a matter of some difficulty, but the attempt will be profitable.

The Hebrew word for spirit (*ruach*) is translated 'spirit' 232 times, 'breath' 28, 'anger' 1, 'courage' 1, 'mind' 5 times, and by a few other words which need not concern us now. The Greek equivalent (*pneuma*) is consistently translated 'spirit', apart from one instance where it is translated 'wind', and in one instance 'life.' The Hebrew word for soul (*nephesh*) is so translated 428 times, 'appetite' 2, 'desire' 5, 'heart' 15, 'life' 119, 'lust' 2, 'mind' 15, 'person' 30, 'self' 19, and by various other words; the Greek equivalent (*psuche*) by 'soul' 58, 'life' 40, 'mind' 3, 'heart' 1.[1] A comparison of the Scriptures where these words occur will show that while certain functions, experiences and sensations are in different places attributed to both spirit and soul, there are features which are distinctive of one or the other. Sensations of anguish, grief, joy, bitterness, and the enjoyment of knowledge are the frequent experience of both, although it will be noticed that the experiences of the soul usually arise from natural and even bodily conditions, i.e. the man in relation to his circumstances, whereas the spirit is influenced by spiritual conditions, e.g. the man's

[1] In view of the fact that soul, in the sense given to it above, lies at the back of all phenomenal life, it is easy to understand how the word came to be used for the life of which it is the foundation, and even for the person himself. Instances of these two secondary meanings are plentiful in Scripture, but are easily discernible and will present no difficulty to the discriminating student.

relationship to God, and men. (Cp. Gen. 42. 21 with Exod. 6. 9, and Job 3. 20 with Ezek. 3. 14). There is also a certain amount of territory which is common to both—an extent to which they interpenetrate and perhaps permeate each other. Thus some things which are strictly distinctive of spirit can be communicated to soul and *vice versâ*. Thus it is the spirit's function to acquire knowledge but it can be communicated to the soul. We have already noticed how, in the case of Mary, her spirit rejoiced in God and prompted the soul to magnify the Lord. The truth probably is that, whilst spirit and soul are distinguishable, so that we can contemplate them separately, they are not to be regarded as existing independently of each other—they are distinguishable but not separable.

The spirit is evidently that element in man's super-sensuous nature which especially distinguishes him from the brute. No doubt man's soul life, as being imparted by the special inbreathing of the breath of life on the part of God is of a superior order to the brute's but it has much in common—the spirit, however, lifts man immeasurably higher in the scale of creation. It is here, especially, that there is a great gulf between the most highly developed animal, and the most degraded man. It is the region of God-consciousness and the higher region of self-consciousness (Rom. 8. 16; 1 Cor. 2. 11). As in the case of animals the soul gives awareness of sensations, but the spirit enables a man to be conscious of his inner self and to reflect upon his own mental processes. The spirit gives the man intuitive perceptions, is the seat of the intellect, with its powers of reasoning, and capacities for spiritual and moral discernment and judgment. In his spirit man forms convictions, decides on purposes and resolves on action, as distinct from those impulses and emotions which arise from the natural instincts of the soul, and sometimes sway the will (Psa. 77. 6; Job 23. 2; 32. 8; Mark 2. 8; Acts 19. 21). The spirit is the higher region of the will, whereby a man may resolutely pursue a course directly contrary to his instincts—this an animal can never do. An animal's intelligence is subordinate to the rule of instinct—a man's intelligence should control his instincts. In the same way a man's spirit will sustain an infirmity under which the soul, of itself, would languish (Prov. 18. 14). The soul belongs more distinctly to the lower plane of man's life and has much in common with the brute. It is mysteriously but most closely associated with the body. To it are attributed feelings of desire and loathing, loving (naturally) and hating, of pleasure and sorrow arising from material or bodily conditions. The soul loves ease and comfort and tends to repine at pain or sorrow. So close are its associations with the body that even bodily appetites are attributed to it (1 Kings 11. 37; Num. 21. 5; 1 Sam. 18. 1; 2 Sam. 5. 8; Psa. 25. 13; Psa. 107. 26; Prov. 6. 30; Isa. 29. 8).

The divine order is given in the well-known Thessalonian passage—spirit and soul and body. In the ideal state the spirit perceives and decides, communicates its knowledge and resolve to the soul, awakes its powers and through it controls the body. This helps to explain the interaction of the two, and the territory common to both. In the present disordered state of man we cannot expect to find this perfect co-ordination. In the temptation Adam was not deceived—his spirit acquainted him with the true situation. His soul (expressed in his natural affection for his wife) swayed the will instead of the spirit. It is probable that, through the Fall, the spirit has been deposed from its rightful throne and the soul has gained the ascendancy. So now the unregenerate man is a natural (soulish or 'soulual'—*psuchikos*) man. The spiritual man is a man whose spirit, energised and guided by the indwelling Holy Spirit, controls his soul and body. The unregenerate man is a soulish man, his soul overrides his spirit and controls his body. The word translated 'natural' in 1 Cor. 2. 14, 'sensual' in Jas. 3. 15 and Jude 19, is *psuchikos*, and could be rendered soulish (or soulual) being the adjective formed from *psuche*. Thus in the great resurrection chapter, Paul speaks of the body in its present condition as being a natural (soulish) body, that is, conditioned by soul, whereas the believer's resurrection body will be a spiritual body, that is, controlled by the spirit (1 Cor. 15. 44).

It would seem, nevertheless, that God is able so to stir the emotions of the soul as to awaken a movement of the spirit, as in the case already noticed in Isaiah. The soul becoming conscious of its discomforts arising from its distance from God, and desiring God so that its comforts may be restored, influences the spirit to seek God. This, no doubt, often happens when the Gospel produces an emotional effect upon a man's soul. If the movement penetrates to the spirit, a work of conviction is wrought—if the movement terminates in the stirring of the soul's emotions, nothing of abiding value is accomplished. In the disordered state of fallen man's constitution various complications can arise, as seen in the case of Peter. Here the Father communicated to Peter's spirit a revelation as to Christ's Sonship and his resultant confession drew the pronouncement of his blessedness from the lips of Christ. A few minutes later Peter's natural (soulish) emotions were aroused by Christ's announcement of His coming sufferings and (prompted by Satan acting on his soul) he expressed himself in a way which earned the Lord's severe disapproval (Matt. 16. 17, 23).

The other member of man's tripartite constitution is the body —consideration of which is often neglected as though the body were merely a temporary expedient to make life possible in a material world. On the contrary, the body is proper to humanity, whether in the unfallen or fallen state, or whether in eternal glory or eternal ruin. The body is not the man, the man indwells the body, as a traveller dwells in a tent.

But the body is so closely associated with the man that Scripture speaks, for example, of devout men carrying Stephen to his burial, when, of course, it was only the dead body they buried (Acts 8. 2). Popular language reflects this close connection when we feel we can say, without inaccuracy, that we have injured ourselves, when in fact it is only one limb which has suffered. Indeed the body is so much an integral part of our nature that believers cannot regard the disembodied state, though it be in the presence of the Lord, as really satisfactory—they desire to be clothed upon. The believer's condition in the spiritual body is so superior to life in the soulish body that the one is referred to under the figure of a tent and the other a heavenly house (2 Cor. 5. 1). Instead of being a clog and a hindrance as some mystics have felt it to be, the body should be the vehicle through which the will of God is done. In itself it is neutral—the sins of the flesh do not rise in the body but in the fleshly mind—in the desires of a sinful soul (Matt. 15. 19; Eph. 2. 3; Rom. 1. 28). The dispositions of the soul determine the use made of the body, unless in the case of a believer the indwelling Spirit of God enables the man's spirit to exercise dominion. The translation 'our vile body' is unfortunate (although it originally meant merely 'low') since it favours the idea that the body is evil in itself

—an idea which in the early church led to the opposite extremes of self-indulgence and ill-treatment of the body (Phil. 3. 21; Jude 4; Col. 2. 23, R.V.). The meaning of the passage is that this body has been humiliated by reason of the fact that instead of being an instrument for the carrying out of God's purposes by the direction of the spirit, it has been enslaved by the sinful desires of the soul. The same body which once we yielded as servants to unrighteousness is the body which we are now to yield unto righteousness. It is to be presented to God as a living sacrifice. The believer's body is the temple of the Holy Spirit and its members are even spoken of as the members of Christ. This is more than sufficient to prove that the body in itself is not evil (Rom. 8. 12, 19; 12. 1; 1 Cor. 6. 15-20).

Although the body is a part of the man, yet conscious existence is possible to man apart from his body. (In his disembodied state man is usually identified with his spirit rather than his soul). Thus the redeemed enjoy the Lord's presence in the interval between death and the resurrection of their bodies at the coming of Christ to the air. Otherwise we may be sure that Paul would not be willing to be absent from the body, and he would not describe the state as being very far better than happy service for the Lord and for the saints here below. The unbelieving endure conscious punishment in the interval between death and the Great White Throne as is proved from Christ's description of the condition of the rich man in hell, whilst his brethren were still alive on earth. It is obvious that Paul regarded consciousness apart from the body as possible—otherwise he could not have been in doubt as to whether he was in or out of the body when entrusted with those revelations in the third heaven (2 Cor. 5. 8; Phil. 1. 23; Luke 16. 28; 2 Cor. 12. 2).

We do not know what changes the fall of man brought about in the body. It would not seem that Adam's body even in the unfallen state was of itself immune from death. If it was, what was the purpose of directing him to eat of the tree of life? It is evident that this tree had the mysterious property of keeping the body free from death, because after his fall God deprived him of access to the tree lest man should prolong his life indefinitely in his fallen state (Gen. 3. 22). It has been stated that there is even now no satisfactory reason known to science why the repairing process which normally keeps the body in health should cease to operate in advanced age, as, of course, we all know it does. We know that death came by sin (Rom. 5. 12). God warned Adam that the day he ate of the tree of knowledge of good and evil he would surely die—'dying thou shalt die.' Apart from the dire immediate spiritual consequences, his disobedience involved physical penalties. He was denied access to the tree of life and that day he began to die—the process of dying had begun. Owing to his wonderful constitution the body held the inroads of decay at bay for many years, but death won in the end. His descendants seem to have inherited a wonderful constitution from him as their amazing longevity proves, but death claimed them all, save Enoch. This subtle change in the human body no doubt involved other disabilities of which Adam at once became conscious—for example, he was previously unconscious of nakedness and it has been suggested that previous to his sin he had been clothed in a covering of light. It is possible, too, that, prior to the fall, the body was capable of transcending the ordinary laws of nature. Christ had a real human body, but even before His resurrection He walked on the sea. To say that this was a miracle makes no difference to the fact that His body was at any rate capable of transcending the laws of gravitation. In the presence of Christ and acting by faith on His invitation, sinful Peter was able to walk on the water. The believer's resurrection body will certainly be liberated from the bondage of natural laws. The resurrection of the body presents the thoughtful believer with very formidable problems, when he considers the origin and the destination of the flesh and bones, 'dust thou art and unto dust shalt thou return.' Nevertheless it seems clear from 1 Cor. 15 that there is some mysterious identity between the body which is laid in the earth and the body which is raised incorruptible. The contrast between the natural body and the spiritual body points to different conditions rather than to two bodies having no relation to each other.

Having studied the tripartite nature of man we are now perhaps better prepared for the consideration of the difficult question as to what is implied by man being created '*in* the image and *after* the likeness' of God.

We can dismiss the crude idea that man resembles God in bodily shape—God is spirit and although Scripture makes concessions to our feebleness of apprehension by speaking of the eyes, the ears and the arms of the Lord, it nevertheless forbids us to think of God in some material form. Nor does the image consist in any resemblance between man's tripartite nature and the Holy Trinity. The relationship between man's spirit and soul and body bears no analogy to the relationship between the Three Persons of the Trinity.

From the fact that after the proposal to create man in the image and after the likeness of God, we get the word image alone in 1. 27 and the word likeness alone in 5. 1, it has been concluded that these two words mean the same thing, but this is not sufficient ground for the conclusion. Scripture does not indulge in mere tautology—if two words are used it is because there are two ideas to be conveyed. Not only are the two words used in the first mention of the proposal to create man but different prepositions are employed. Possibly 'in' our image suggests what is essential, 'after' our likeness, that which is potential; or, to put it another way, 'image' may refer to man's capacities, whereas 'likeness' may refer to his tendencies. In God's 'image' man somehow represents God—being in His 'likeness' he resembled God. As a result of being created in God's image, man was endowed with those capacities which fitted Him for the accomplishment of God's purposes, e.g. the endowment of will and understanding necessary to exercise rule as God's representative. As being after God's likeness he was blessed with a tendency Godward which made co-operation with God's will a delight, the maintenance of which was necessary if he was to develop along God-ordained lines.

Some have explained 'image' as simply referring to man's God-given dominion over creation but this is inadequate. Dominion is spoken of by God as something additional to, and arising out of, man's creation in His image and after His likeness—'*and* let them have dominion.' Moreover, if this explanation were true, we should be faced with the curious situation that the man with the most power would be most in the image of God. Nebuchadnezzar, for example, was given dominion in almost the same terms as the unfallen Adam, yet his autocratic power was never more forcibly displayed than when he sentenced God's faithful servants to death for refusing to worship the image he had set up (Dan. 2. 37, 38; 3. 6).

The explanation which receives, and probably deserves, the greatest support is that the image of God in man consists pre-eminently in the fact that God is spirit and man possesses an individual spirit formed in him by God—not a spirit in the sense of a general principle of life but a separate distinct spirit in every individual. Thus we read of the spirit of a man, but the spirits of men (Rom. 1. 9; 1 Cor. 2. 11; Heb. 12. 23).

This endowment with a free, self-determining spirit which marks man off so clearly from the rest of the lower creation invests him with the capacity for appreciating and reflecting God, makes communion with God possible, and, within proper limits enables him to represent God in his powers of intellect, free-will, creative initiative and capacity for rule. This intelligence and will in man is a reflection of intelligence and will in God, although we must remember that there is an infinite difference not only in degree but in kind.

We suggest that the first man was not inferior, in moral and intellectual faculties to modern man. Man's intellectual powers have, of course, found their sphere of operations widening with every generation as they have inherited the accumulated knowledge of bygone generations. It is not contended that Adam *knew* what modern man knows, but that his mental powers were not inferior. His ability to discern the natures of the animals brought before his notice and to express the difference in them by names of such appropriateness that God was content to let his choices stand, is full of significance. The command of language required for this and further exemplified in his naming of Eve by employing the feminine form of the word for man suggests a high degree of intelligence. It is interesting to observe, by the way, that it has often been found that the languages of savage tribes bear evidence of a complex grammatical construction with a highly developed system of inflexion, which, while it is not appreciated by the savage who still adheres to the construction without knowing why, furnishes proof that developed language belongs to the primeval state of man.

Another element in man being in the image of God would appear to be the possession of free-will. Men who are slaves to scientific conceptions of the universal prevalence of law will not concede that man's will can be free in the sense that within him is a self-determining cause. To their way of thinking, man's thoughts and intentions are simply the inevitable outcome of certain conditions to which he is subjected. But the so-called laws of nature are not self-existing forces—they simply attempt to define the principles in accordance with which God normally sees fit to regulate the universe. If in ordinary life certain effects could not be relied upon to follow certain causes everything would be uncertain—nothing would be predictable and life, as we know it, would be impossible. Consequently God sees fit to act according to certain fixed principles, but He is sovereign and we must not think of God as being the victim of His own principles. So, man, being a morally free agent, has a mind and will of his own and, within certain limits, God allows him to exercise and even carry out his will. God is able to, and often does, curb man when his waywardness reaches certain limits but this does not do away with the fact that man is a morally responsible agent. God does not coerce, much less compel, man to bend his will to God's. God may bring influences to bear, calculated to turn man's mind and will in a certain direction but never to the extent of over-riding man's power and right of choice. On the other hand, when man has deliberately set himself in opposition to God's will, He may quite righteously fulfil His purposes by hardening the heart or darkening the mind which refused to respond to God's overtures. But this we must maintain, that man has a will and God allows its exercise. Man's decisions are not the inevitable outcome of a combination of circumstances—they depend finally upon the man's free-will. Men can act contrary to God's purpose as did Ahab and many others in the Scriptures. Christ's complaint was not that men *could* not come to Him, but that they *would* not. Thus, alas, those very capacities which constitute man in the image of God are used in ways contrary to God's purposes so that men are very far now from being after the likeness of God—they are very unlike God, ungodly. Likeness suggests that disposition which would gladly embrace God's will and so incline the man to develop along the lines of God's appointing to God's glory and man's blessedness, the man loving what God loved (Psa. 76. 10; Isa. 1. 5; Exod. 9. 12; 2 Thess. 2. 11, 12; 1 Kings 20. 42; John 5. 40).

This man has lost. The image of God he retains, though no doubt greatly defaced, for after the flood, God prohibited violence against man on the ground that he was in the image of God. Similarly Paul speaks of man as being the image of God. That is to say, man's capacities and prerogatives have not been withdrawn —intellect, understanding, self-determination and power of rule are inherent in man. Man retains his intellect even though now it be clouded, darkened, blinded. In view of the amazing intellectual powers of which fallen man gives unmistakable evidence, what must have been the mind of unfallen man? Man retains his power of will even though it be degraded. The determination with which men can pursue their goal, the powers of endurance they can display show the impress of God's image, but alas these powers are misdirected. Man's mind is at enmity with God (Gen. 6. 9; 1 Cor. 11. 7; 2 Cor. 4. 4; Col. 1. 21)—the likeness has gone.

He has powers to be wondered at—but they are encompassing his own destruction. What would have been the result if man had not fallen—if his powers had been used progressively through the generations to appreciate and do the will of God, instead of pursuing his self-willed and godless course?

Perfect manhood was seen in Christ. Much that is usually attributed to His Deity is probably proper to His perfect humanity. This is the glory which is to be the portion of His people, as conformed to the image of God's Son, created in holiness of truth. Since the redemptive purposes of God in Christ undoubtedly go beyond what man lost in the fall, we can only re-echo John's words, 'It doth not yet appear what we shall be.' Who can remotely imagine what is implied in 'we shall be like Him? Conformed to His image and in His likeness. What hath grace wrought!' (John 17. 22; Rom. 8. 29; Eph. 4. 24, R.V.).

We have spoken of man's spirit, his soul and his body, his intellect and his will—yet there remains the mystery of personality. Language by a sure instinct, no doubt implanted by God, recognizes an inner 'me'—the ego. Thus we speak of 'my' spirit, 'my' soul, 'my' will, and so on. We are capable of reflection upon our own thoughts and reasonings, we can analyse our feelings, search our hearts and rebuke ourselves for allowing certain moods to influence us unduly (Psa. 103. 1; 42. 5). What is this inner self? No one has ever succeeded in giving a satisfactory answer. Some philosophers have endeavoured to show that the ego is simply the sum of consciousness, but their theory falls to pieces in their own hands. 'Of all psychological problems "self" remains the most difficult for discussion and definition. Man can do little more than accept what is a matter of common experience—viz. that he is capable of reflecting upon the nature of his own actions' (T. C. Hammond, *Perfect Freedom*, p. 48). Indeed this inner self seems capable of experiences and exercises which are not communicable to the understanding; hence the necessity of Paul's exhortations to the Corinthians to confine their public worship to what they and others can understand (1 Cor. 14. 14).

Perhaps here is the mystery. The difficulty of expressing the truth with regard to the real self, whose identity abides through all the changes of life, even through conversion and on into eternity, seems to come out in Paul's 'I am crucified with Christ, yet I live, yet not I' (Gal. 2. 20). We cannot solve it. Suffice it to know that man was created with a view to bringing God glory and pleasure, and what we know of God's wisdom, love and power is sufficient guarantee that He would constitute man capable (though not in himself) of reaching his glorious destiny with immeasurable blessing to himself (Isa. 43. 7; Col. 1. 16; Rev. 4. 11). To believe otherwise would be to charge God with folly, incompetence and cruelty.

CHAPTER XIII

Sin

MONTAGUE GOODMAN

NO thoughtful student of Scripture can fail to be arrested by the dominant place accorded in its pages to 'sin.' Its existence may indeed be considered the very *raison d'être* of the revelation of God to man as we have it in Holy Scripture. The word and its cognates occur upward of 2,000 times or twice on every page of the Bible. It is impossible to open the Book and not encounter it. The characters depicted (with one notable exception) are all of them sinners and every degree of wickedness is described and recorded with relentless faithfulness throughout the Book. Indeed there is no book in the world that deals so comprehensively with the subject in all its dark ugliness as does the Bible and nowhere is its condemnation so faithfully proclaimed nor the doom of sinners so plainly stated. It is this fact that gives the Book its unique character and its pre-eminently human appeal. Men recognize its truth to life more in its insistence on sin than in anything else. For quite apart from its divine authority it speaks to the heart and reflects the experience of every man. It declares that all have sinned and come short of the glory of God and men everywhere recognize this and know it to be true. By whatever standard man judges himself he is perfectly aware he has come short of it and he has a sense of guilt in consequence. He knows he is not what he ought to be and that somehow he is to blame on account of that fact. The last thing of which a man needs convincing is that he is a sinner. He cannot argue himself out of the fact though he would fain do so if he could. But why this is so he is at a loss to explain. Here all philosophy breaks down completely. Why men should recognize and admire right, should set up standards, rules and laws for themselves and their fellow-men, and yet do wrong, is a problem insoluble outside the pages of Scripture. Why do men will right and commit wrong? Why is it that when I would do good, evil is present with me and the good that I would, I do not and the evil that I hate, that I do? And why is this universal and without exception since the earliest history of man until to-day? That man is a sinner is clear and undeniable but why he is so is beyond natural explanation.

It is to solve this problem and to point a remedy that is the main purpose of Scripture. All else, whether biography, history, prophecy or doctrinal teaching, is subordinate to this one great design of revelation: to make plain the nature, origin and extent of sin and the one and only remedy therefor in the kindness and love of God to sinners.

The subject comprehends the whole content of Scripture, and the most that can be attempted here is to indicate some of the salient features and facts as recorded if only by way of introduction to a closer and more comprehensive study.

(I) *The Fact of Sin.* The Bible presents sin as a fact beyond argument or dispute. Much as it assumes the existence of God as a fact not requiring the support of argument or proof, so it treats sin as an undeniable fact of experience beyond all debate. It addresses men as sinners without apology and without exception. It declares them to be such universally and without distinction. 'There is no difference: for all have sinned. There is none righteous, no, not so much as one' (Rom. 3. 22, 23). Nor is this intended to indicate mere imperfection of otherwise unblameworthy creatures. It is not that all have failed in some measure either great or small to attain the highest. It leaves all men without merit or excuse whatever 'that every mouth may be stopped and all the world may become guilty before God' (Rom. 3. 19). Nor is it limited to men's outward conduct for 'every imagination of the thoughts of his heart is only evil continually' (Gen. 6. 5).

The trouble is radical. It is a case of heart disease. 'The heart is deceitful above all things and desperately wicked (lit.: incurably sick); who can know it?' (Jer. 17. 9). The Bible goes further in declaring the case of man to be irremedial. 'Can the Ethiopian change his skin or the leopard his spots? Then may ye also do good that are accustomed to do evil' (Jer. 13. 23). All this is amply justified in the experience of men everywhere. And never more so than in the fateful days in which we are called to live.

In face of much progress in knowledge, learning, science and culture, man has demonstrated himself in all essential respects the same sinful creature as his ancestors from remotest times, only with vastly accumulated powers to work his wicked designs. In spite of great enlightenment and despite nearly 2,000 years of Christian teaching, the fact of sin remains the dominant problem of human history.

(II) *The Origin and Course of Sin.* The Bible does not only state the fact of human sinfulness and demonstrate it by a wealth of illustration throughout its pages; it enlightens men as to how it came to pass, a mystery that all the philosophies of men have failed to penetrate. Man has freely acknowledged his desperate condition but has sought in vain for an answer to the question, 'Why am I thus?' He knows he ought not to be so, that something has gone amiss with him, that sin is a thing that has entered into his life rather than being an outcome of it, but how and where and why it so entered he is totally at a loss to discover. This mystery the Bible sets out to solve and does so in its opening pages in the story of the Fall whereby we are told, 'by one man sin entered into the world and death by sin' (Rom. 5. 12).

That this story should be so generally discredited by men is a matter of some surprise when one takes into consideration certain points not generally borne in mind in relation to the record.

The first is that, strange as the story undoubtedly is, there is nothing either fantastic or impossible about it. It should not be rejected on the score of improbability. Moreover, it explains as nothing else does the universal recognition of the alien character of evil as being something other than the Creator purposed for His creature man. Again, there is no real alternative to offer in place of the story of the Fall. If man is not a fallen creature, why does he deplore his condition and not acquiesce in it as his natural and proper state without regret or demur? If, on the other hand, some such calamity has occurred to him, it must have been at his earliest beginning since there is no branch of the human family immune. And there is a further consideration. The record of the Fall is not confined to Scripture. 'Every nation and people under heaven have retained its memory. Scattered as far as this wide earth permits and separated from each other by vast stretches of land and sea for thousands of years all alike have clung to these recollections . . . go where we will we find the same story. What does it mean? Have all the nations dreamed the same dream and have they all alike been deluded with the conviction that the dream was a reality? . . . Further reflection will lead to the conviction that the 3rd chapter of Genesis is not merely one of the national myths but that it is on the contrary the history which explains the myth. For here and here alone, all is sober, rational, coherent, and worthy of God and man' (*The New Biblical Guide*, Vol. 1, p. 235).

Such, then, was the manner of the entry of sin into the world. It was occasioned by a conflict of wills between God and man resulting in a break of harmony between the Creator and the creature He had formed for Himself. For God made man in His own image and likeness for the express purpose of fellowship with Himself in a way that He could have fellowship with no other of His creatures. He was to be 'the man that is My fellow.' But fellowship depends always on like-mindedness apart from which each party must go his own way. So sin became a parting of the ways between man and God and this divergence has persisted ever since. 'All we like sheep have gone astray, we have turned every one to his own way' (Isa. 53. 6). What a bitter way this has been, history has demonstrated only too plainly. Thus 'sin entered into the world and death by sin.' For 'this is life eternal that they might know Thee the only true God' and men 'did not like to retain God in their knowledge;' so death, the wages of sin, was all that remained for man, and he died (Rom. 5. 12; John 17. 3; Rom. 1. 28; 6. 23). Occurring in the infancy of the human race, it was a catastrophe of the greatest magnitude which has persisted throughout its course. For fallen man begat progeny 'in his own likeness after his image.' He who had forfeited the likeness of God could do no other. As the mighty Amazon takes its rise as a tiny stream, to pursue its inevitable way throughout a continent in ever-increasing volume, until as an irresistible swelling flood it pours its waters into the ocean, so sin in the history of man from the smallest of beginnings—the single breach of a negative command—has taken its disastrous course throughout the long ages of time, carrying death and untold misery and destruction wherever man is found. This course the Bible traces. It is the link connecting individual narrative with national history. It is the story of sin manifesting itself in every variation of human experience and in defiance of every restraining influence. It is as though God would exhibit to man a dreadful picture of the utter depravity of his fallen nature, that sin might be displayed to him in all its exceeding sinfulness. There is no conceivable form of vice and passion, greed, hatred, deceit and lust that does not find itself portrayed with relentless faithfulness in the pages of Holy Scripture, but all is summed up at length with the terrible words, 'Their throat is an open sepulchre; with their tongues they have used deceit; the poison of asps is under their lips; whose mouth is full of cursing and bitterness; their feet are swift to shed blood; destruction and misery are in their ways; and the way of peace have they not known: there is no fear of God before their eyes' (Rom. 3. 13-18).

Thus sin is exhibited as an incurable disease for which there is no human remedy, however hopefully applied, though man in his pride and vain-glory will not have it so. He is ever boastful of his ability to improve, of the upward trend of humanity, of racial progress, of the advance of civilization. He points proudly to social amenities and improved conditions of life, to provision for the sick and aged, to slave emancipation and other undoubted developments, oblivious of the fact that such things are symptoms not of the abatement of the disease but of the preventive effect of the remedy—the presence among men of the salt of the earth without which it would have no doubt perished in its corruption long ere this. Let but his passions be aroused and the beast in man emerges, as rampant and rapaciously cruel and wicked as he ever was, and with infinitely increased ability to achieve his evil imaginings.

The history of sin, as traced in Scripture, is a history of its persistence and growth in spite of every form of deterrent. It is as though God would convince the world by demonstration of the incurable nature of the loathsome disease under which it labours by the application of a series of restraining influences each of which one would have thought sufficient to effect the needed change, but each of which failed in turn. First He applied *punishment*. The fierce judgment of the Flood proved without avail, the new race which followed it being no whit better than that which had perished. Then He turned to *precept* and gave man the perfect standard of the Ten Commandments to guide his conduct aright. Yet they were broken almost as soon as they had been pronounced and have been ever since. Again God tested men under *privilege*. He chose a race of men to whom He gave special honour, separating them from the rest of fallen man and promising them untold blessing if they would obey Him. He even dwelt in their midst and bestowed miraculous blessing upon them. Yet all to none effect. They proved a stiffnecked and rebellious people in no respect better than the heathen around them. After that came the *prophets*, witnessing and warning and pleading for God. It was the same under every condition. Man continued unchanged and unchangeable, the implacable enemy of God, a sinner in spite of punishment, precept, privilege and the pleading of the prophets. He cannot cease from sin. Go where he will, do what he can, he finds himself still a sinner.

I once heard the late Dr. W. Y. Fullerton tell of a visit he paid to a Trappist Monastery in Italy when he asked an inmate, 'Why did you come here?' He replied, 'I came to escape from the world.' 'And do you find you succeed,' asked Dr. Fullerton; to which the monk gave answer with infinite sadness, 'Well, you see, *we bring ourselves in.*'

(III). *The Nature and Character of Sin.* This may, perhaps, be best indicated by the words employed in Scripture to express it and by certain direct statements which may be said to define it. There are three principal words scattered freely throughout Scripture, whereby we may learn, with some accuracy, those qualities that mark out sin and manifest themselves in every sinner. We find them used in conjunction in certain passages and in particular in the account of the great revelation of God's glory to Moses on the mount, when he hears Jehovah proclaim His name in the majestic words, 'The Lord God merciful and gracious, longsuffering and abundant in goodness and truth, keeping mercy for thousands, forgiving *iniquity* and *transgression* and *sin* and that will in no wise clear the guilty' (Exod. 34. 6, 7). From these words we may perceive that that which constitutes man guilty before God is firstly his iniquity, secondly his transgression and thirdly his sin.

(i) *Sin is Iniquity.* That is anything that is morally wrong or contrary to the eternal, immutable standard of equity or righteousness, and that independently of the existence of any revealed laws or express commandments of God. Thus men who have never heard of God or His laws are yet found to be sinners for 'these, having not the law, are a law unto themselves: their conscience also bearing witness, and their thoughts . . . accusing or else excusing' them (Rom. 2. 15).

(ii) *Sin is Transgression,* i.e. it is the breach of the direct command of God. 'Sin is the transgression of the law' (1 John 3. 4) and, as in nature law knows no mercy for those who transgress it, so with God's injunctions imposed on His creatures, to transgress them is to perish, for 'the soul that sinneth it shall die' (Ezek. 18. 4). And this is justly so for it is the prerogative of God to command and it is the province of man to obey.

(iii) *Sin is to Miss the Mark.* For that is the root meaning of the word sin. This indicates that the essential evil in man is not in positive action and conduct but that he has wholly failed in the purpose for which God formed him: he has come short of the glory of God and is in consequence a fallen creature. The standard of that glory from which he has fallen is the Man Christ Jesus, who alone could say with truth, 'I have glorified Thee on the earth.' God assures us that He will apply this standard on that day when He will judge the world in righteousness *by that Man whom He hath ordained.*

These great basic facts concerning sin are further borne out by certain direct definitions of sin contained in Scripture as follows:

(*a*) '*Sin is the transgression of the law*' (1 John 3. 4), that is, sin is direct disobedience by the creature to the known commands of the Creator.

(*b*) '*Sin is lawlessness,*' which is the Revised rendering of the above. It indicates that sin is more than an act, it is an attitude of heart toward God's law by the natural man who is not subject to the law of God, neither indeed can be (Rom. 8. 7).

(*c*) '*To him that knoweth to do good and doeth it not to him it is sin*' (Jas. 4. 17). It is an arresting fact that almost all the individual instances of judgment in Scripture are on sins of omission. No overt act of sin is alleged against Belshazzar, yet he was weighed in the balances and found wanting in that 'the God in whose hand thy breath is, and whose are all thy ways, hast thou not glorified' (Dan. 5. 23). And our Lord pronounced judgment in His parable on the same basis, 'In as much as ye did it not . . .' (Matt. 25. 45).

(*d*) '*Whatsoever is not of faith is sin*' (Rom. 14. 23). That is to say that the greatest sin from Adam's transgression onward was and is the sin of unbelief. For 'he that believeth not God has made Him a liar' (1 John 5. 10).

So in the most comprehensive manner possible God in His Word searches and exposes to mankind 'the plague of his own heart,' sin. He likens it variously to a *despotic* slave-owner, to whom the sinner is compelled to render service; a dread *disease*, the incurable plague of leprosy, which renders him unclean, unfit for association with God or man; to *dirt* that makes him impure and defiled and unfit for heaven where 'there shall in no wise enter in anything that defileth'; to *darkness*, the antithesis of God who 'is Light and in whom is no darkness at all'; and to *death*, that condition in which a creature ceases entirely to correspond to his environment and man made for God finds himself without God and without hope in the world.

It only remains to add that the supreme revelation and demonstration of sin in the human race was their reaction to the appearing in their midst of God incarnate in the person of Jesus Christ. It was the supreme and final test which God applied to men. 'Last of all He sent unto them His Son, saying, They will reverence My Son' (Matt. 21. 37). And it was the climax and culmination of man's sin that they crucified the Lord of glory.

Finally, the province of the Holy Spirit in His coming among men was to convict them of their utter sinfulness on this very ground, 'When He is come He shall reprove the world of sin because they believe not on Me' (John 16. 8), was the word of Christ concerning the Comforter who was to follow Him. Thus man is shown to be a sinner chiefly and essentially because he is an unbeliever, for sin is unbelief and the only remedy for sin is faith in Him who is called Jesus, 'for He shall save His people from their sins' (Matt. 1. 21).

CHAPTER XIV

The New Life

J. REGINALD HILL

'I AM come that they may have life, and may have it abundantly' (John 10. 10). In view of such an explanation of His purpose by the Lord Himself it would not be out of place to regard the whole of the New Testament as a treatise on the subject of the New Life—its origin, its mode of communication to the natural man, the effects of its infusion into his complex nature, the detailed results of its manifestation in his daily life. But the New Testament cannot be compassed in a single chapter, and we shall therefore attempt to summarize the teaching of some key passages on these topics.

The Origin of the New Life. It might seem a mere platitude to say that the new life begins with the new birth. But it is worse than a platitude: it is a poor half truth, for the first chapter of John's Gospel shows that the new life which comes to the one who is born again is nothing less than the life of God Himself. The children of God, we read, are born (R.V. margin, 'begotten') of God (John 1. 12, 13).[1] And the three contrasts in verse 13 emphasize that this phrase 'the children of God' is to be understood quite literally, and not as a figurative expression, as we might take such phrases as 'children of wrath' or 'sons of disobedience' (Eph. 2. 2). Just as an earthly parent passes on to his child his own type of life, so at the second birth God begets His eternal life within His child, and the child becomes, *ipso facto*, a partaker of the divine nature (2 Peter 1. 4). 'As the seed of physical generation stamps upon the offspring an ineffaceable character . . . so does the germ of spiritual life from the spiritual Father set the impression of a permanent organic character upon the God-begotten' (Law, *The Tests of Life*).

Thus it is not merely that the newly-born one begins to live in a new way, or that a hitherto dead part of him becomes alive, but

[1] All quotations in this chapter are from the Revised Version, unless otherwise stated.

that he now begins to share in the very life of the One in whom all life originates. The essence of the matter is not only that one is born anew, and not even only from above (John 3. 3), but that one is born of God. This is the peculiar quality of this new life, and its quantity stems from its quality. It is because it is the life of God that it is eternal, and its eternity stretches backwards into the past as much as forwards into the future. A radio set stands silent and dead with waves of sound pulsating all round it, but at the touch of a controlling hand it awakes, becoming responsive to, and sharing in, the life which has long been surging past. So a man begins to share in this new life at a certain date; but the life itself is the life of the ages.

As is to be expected, nothing less than this life is necessary to fit one for the kingdom of God: 'except a man be born anew, he cannot see the kingdom of God' (John 3. 3). Only God's children are the natives of God's kingdom; only they have the capacity to fulfil its exacting requirements, and to enjoy its unique blessings. All others are not merely aliens, as though they lived in a different but near-by country; they entirely lack the life that belongs to this other sphere of existence; they are 'dead through their trespasses and sins' (Eph. 2. 1).

It is the realization of this tremendous gulf that calls forth the apostle's glowing words: 'but God, being rich in mercy, for His great love wherewith He loved us, even when we were dead through our trespasses, quickened us together with Christ . . . and raised us up with Him, and made us sit with Him in the heavenly places. . . . For we are His workmanship, created in Christ Jesus for good works, which God afore prepared that we should walk in them' (Eph. 2. 4-10; cf. 2 Cor. 5. 17).

We are so conscious of our own mortality that we tend to emphasize the quantitative aspect of the life, with its guarantee of victory over the dread enemy—death. But the qualitative aspect, while it includes this factor, is immensely significant for life in this world. It is not merely that one is in touch with God, the Creator and Governor of the Universe; not merely that one can confide in the infinite love and tender care of such a God; but that one is lifted from the level of being an insignificant unit in the incessant life and death cycle of this earth, and now knows oneself to be 'bound in the bundle of life' with God (1 Sam. 25. 29). No longer a cog in a mighty and apparently meaningless machine, but God's child, able to cry exultingly, 'Christ liveth in me' (Gal. 2. 20).

Clearly the origin and cause of such a type and quality of life is in God alone. No one can be born into it of his own volition, nor by the will or agency of any other human being; it is of God—'of His own will He brought us forth' (Jas. 1. 18). Such a birth is not to be engineered by the persuasive eloquence that produces a mere mental assent or is adept in 'getting decisions.' It is the sole and mysterious prerogative of God the Holy Spirit, and it is on Him and His work alone that the most powerful preacher must rely for any sure results, and true conversions.

Its Mode of Communication. How, then, does a man believe? Not with his head, say the Scriptures unequivocally, but with his heart (Rom. 10. 9). This marks the difference between crediting a fact and committing oneself, body and soul, for life and death, to another. It is the difference between the reader in the armchair, who does not withhold his assent from what he reads in his newspaper, and the soldier, whose life is altogether governed by the plans and commands of his superior officer. It is the difference between an Agrippa and a Paul, between a human persuasion and a divine conviction.

The preacher who overlooks such a difference will do so at great risk to those whom he may encourage to feel that it is enough to give a mental assent to the reasonableness of the facts and claims he has presented. Such an assent may be a necessary preliminary, but it does not in itself differ from the assent which the persuasive politician might obtain for his ideas. The engendering of life can only take place in the heart, in the depths of a man's being, and this is a region accessible only to the Holy Spirit Himself.

Among the various figures used to illuminate the mystery of this life is the startlingly bold one of the 'eating of the flesh,' and 'the drinking of the blood of the Son of Man' (John 6. 54). How much more than mere belief, more even than complete committal, is involved in the new relationship! Made a partaker of the divine nature at the new birth, he must nevertheless draw from His Saviour daily supplies of grace: constant union and complete identification of the believer with the Saviour is indispensable. He must actively turn to his Saviour and consciously receive and appropriate all the benefits of his sacrifice, and all the virtue of the life of which He is the origin and of which He was the exponent here on earth. 'He that eateth My flesh and drinketh My blood abideth in Me, and I in him. As the living Father hath sent Me, and I live because of the Father; so he that eateth Me, he also shall live because of Me' (John 6. 56, 57).

'How can these things be?' (John 3. 9) we exclaim with Nicodemus of old. The operation itself remains a secret in God's hands, the mysterious passage into a bright new experience. But though the passage is mysterious, the door is clearly marked. Nicodemus' question is at first answered by the Lord only with statements that seem to make the explanation yet more difficult. But suddenly, an unexpected light flashes from the seemingly inaccessible heaven: 'as Moses lifted up the serpent in the wilderness, even so must the Son of Man be lifted up, that whosoever believeth may in Him have eternal life' (John 3. 14, 15). 'Whosoever believeth'; 'as many as received Him'; they 'that believe on His name' (John 1. 12): the simple and familiar phrases describe the bridge across an unfathomable mystery.

The Moral Effects of the New Life. For further enlightenment as to the true nature of this new life, and its infusion into man's being we turn to John's first Epistle. It has been well said that 'in the Gospel he sets forth the divine life as it is exhibited in the person of Christ. In his Epistle he sets forth that life as it is exhibited in the individual Christian. . . . In the one we have the perfect life in God as it was realized in an historical Person. In the other we have the directions for reproducing that life as it might be realized by an earnest but necessarily imperfect Christian' (Dr. Plummer, *Cambridge Bible for Schools and Colleges*, p. 37).

On its opening paragraph Canon Liddon's concise comment may be quoted: 'St. John's position in this Epistle is, that the eternal immaterial Word of Life resident in God had become historically manifest, and that the apostles had consciously seen, and heard, and handled Him, and were now publishing their experience to the world. The practical bearing of this announcement lay in the truth that 'he that hath the Son hath the Life, and he that hath not the Son hath not the Life' (1 John 5. 12). For 'God hath given to us the Eternal Life, and this, the Life, is in His Son' (1 John 5. 11, A.V.). If then the soul is to hold communion with God in the life of light and righteousness and love, it must be through communion with His Divine Son' (*The Divinity of our Lord*, p. 240).

It is in the third chapter of this Epistle that the apostle returns to the thought of God's begetting of His children. Moffatt, taking the closing words of chapter 2, makes the chapter open thus: 'Born of Him! think what a love the Father has for us in letting us be called "children of God"!' Paul had often been led to the idea of the 'sons' of God, with its emphasis on the status of the believer. But John loves to use the word 'children,' with its implication of the kinship between the Divine Father and His human children. And so he is not content simply to write of our being 'called children of God,' but adds delightedly, 'and such we are'! More even than kinship is involved in the term, for it suggests the possibility of a fuller development. 'Beloved,' he continues, as an entrancing additional thought, 'now are we the children of God, and it is not yet made manifest what we shall be. We know that, if He shall be manifested, we shall be like Him' (1 John 3. 2).

What, then, will be the attitude of the child of God to sin? How will it differ from that of others? Will anyone claim 'that he can sin without prejudice to his high standing as a spiritual and enlightened man'! This was the very position assumed by the gnostics of John's time, and this epistle is the complete answer to their pernicious doctrines. They claimed that they were above the moral law, and that the soul remained incapable of pollution whatever the sins of the body. 'My little children,' pleads the apostle, 'let no man lead you astray . . . he that doeth sin is of the devil . . . whosoever sinneth hath not seen Him, neither knoweth Him. Whosoever is begotten of God doeth no sin, because His seed abideth in him: and he cannot sin because he is begotten of God. In this the children of God are manifest, and the children of the devil: whosoever doeth not righteousness is not of God' (1 John 3. 6-10).

It is in language so absolute and uncompromising that the apostle denounces this gross perversion of true Christian morality. The only test of being, he declares, is doing. And this is a principle of which Christians of every age need to be reminded. 'We are too often content with the consciousness that we stand in some special relation to the Lord, and come to regard sin as an unavoidable evil which is not so very harmful as might be thought.' (Haupt: quoted by Law, *The Tests of Life*).

If the immediate cause of the apostle's uncompromising affirmations be borne in mind, much of the difficulty suggested by a first reading of the paragraph will disappear. The true child of God will never claim that he is without sin, for 'if we say that we have no sin, we deceive ourselves, and the truth is not in us' (1 John 1. 8). Yet, says the apostle, he cannot sin. In what sense, then, is this true? We may find an illuminating parallel in the poet's question: 'Can a woman's tender care cease toward the child she bare?' It must be admitted that there are such monstrosities as mothers who can thus forget their children. But if it be *claimed* that a mother can be cruel and neglectful, and that without losing her character as a mother, the right answer, the morally true answer, is an indignant denial. In the same sense it is true that the Christian, because he is "begotten of God," *cannot* sin; and to assert the contrary is to assert a blasphemy, a calumny upon God' (Law, *op. cit.* p. 228).

What, then, is the secret of the maintenance of such an attitude? The one who is 'born of Him' must 'abide in Him' (1 John 2. 27). This exhortation links together and explains the apparent contrast between the two statements already noticed: 'If we say that we have no sin, we deceive ourselves' (1 John 1. 8), and, 'whosoever is begotten of God doeth no sin' (1 John 3. 9). Thus we also read: 'Whosoever abideth in him, sinneth not' (1 John 3. 6). The measure of our abiding will be the measure of our avoidance of sin.

As we have seen, the apostle's argument has rested on the analogy of the communication of physical life by a parent to his child. But the child's life is capable of maintaining and developing itself as a separate existence from that of its parent. With the idea of 'abiding,' however, we are referred to the analogy of vegetable life, as in the familiar conception of the vine and its branches. Each branch, twig, and leaf, may be regarded as a child of the tree itself, but each can exist only as it remains, or abides, in living contact with the parent stem, receiving the constant flow of sap. 'So does the Life of God vitalize him in whom He abides, sustaining and fostering in him those energies—righteousness, love, truth—which are the divine nature itself' (Law, *op. cit.*, p. 199).

Now, while there can be no variation in the abiding of God in His children, the abiding of the individual child in Him is by no means automatic. He may keep himself 'in the love of God' (Jude 21), or he may on occasion fail to do so. He may keep his Lord's commandments and so abide in His love (John 15. 10), or he may be disobedient and so obstruct the channels between himself and the source of his true life. Hence the repeated exhortations in both Gospel and Epistle. 'As the abiding of God in us is the persistent and purposeful action by which the divine nature influences ours, so our abiding in God is the persistent and purposeful submission of ourselves to that action' (Law, *op. cit.*, p. 200).

The Practical Effects of the New Life. The infusion of such a surge of powerful new life into the human being and personality must clearly produce a fundamental change, not only of attitude but of conduct; a change which Scripture describes in dramatic terms. 'It is no longer I that live,' exclaims the Apostle Paul, 'but Christ liveth in me: and that life which I now live in the flesh I live in faith, the faith which is in the Son of God, who loved me and gave Himself up for me' (Gal. 2. 20). 'They who live,' he declares again, 'should no longer live unto themselves, but unto Him who for their sakes died and rose again' (2 Cor. 5. 15).

In thinking of life as lived on this earth it is necessary to distinguish between the existence and activities of the physical frame, and the existence of the personality which directs those activities, and expresses itself through the body.

In the unregenerate man, there are thus two lives in one, an inner and an outer life existing together in a relationship somewhat similar to that of a captain and ship. The captain steers at first with his eyes fixed on earthly landmarks and horizons. But at the new birth wide new horizons are opened up, and he becomes aware of heavenly guiding stars; and the new life demands that these shall be the dominant factors in determining the new course. 'Old things are passed away; behold, they are become new. But all things are of God, who reconciled us to Himself through

Christ' (2 Cor. 5. 17). It is not that the new life demands the death of the captain, but that he himself is called upon to turn his back on the old landmarks, and to refuse any hearing to the pleas of a nature that was at home amongst them—in fact to foil and kill every attempt made by that old nature to turn the ship back again to the old and familiar routes.

This fundamental principle is emphasized in both Gospels and Epistles, from the Lord's 'let him deny himself' (Mark 8. 34), to Paul's astonished exclamation: 'Are ye ignorant that all we who are baptized into Christ Jesus were baptized into His death . . . that like as Christ was raised from the dead through the glory of the Father, so we also might walk in newness of life?' (Rom. 6. 3, 4). 'Into His death,' 'buried with Him, 'mortify' (Rom. 8. 13), 'crucify' (Gal. 5. 24), 'I buffet my body and bring it into bondage' (1 Cor. 9. 27), 'a living sacrifice' (Rom. 12. 1), 'conformed unto His death' (Phil. 3. 10): such phrases leave no doubt as to the necessary corollary of the new life.

The baptism of the believer is an acted parable and exposition of all such ideas. Christ lives in him: but Christ died, was buried, and was raised from the dead by the glory of the Father. Then the believer, united and identified with Him, must share a similar experience in fact and in picture. 'We were buried therefore with Him through baptism into death: that like as Christ was raised . . . so we also might walk in newness of life.' 'We have become united with Him by the likeness of His death, we shall be also by the likeness of His resurrection' (Rom. 6. 4, 5).

'The death that he died, he died unto sin once: but the life that he liveth, he liveth unto God' (Rom. 6. 10): these are the slogans of the new life. How are they to be translated into actual practice? 'Reckon ye also yourselves to be dead unto sin, but alive unto God in Christ Jesus' (Rom. 6. 11). That is to say that, in all his considerations and decisions, the captain of the ship is to recognize that he is under no obligation to the sinful factors which once determined his course; that though sin may call to him, it cannot any longer command him; that in fact he has effected a righteous mutiny and his former master is in chains; and that he has a new power to match his new-found freedom as he looks out along the new course and sets his hands to the wheel.

But the old nature, though it may no longer command, will not cease to call; and thus the advent of the new life initiates a struggle for power between two rivals. The man himself has constantly to decide which voice he will follow, which suggestions he will obey, as 'the flesh lusteth against the Spirit, and the Spirit against the flesh' (Gal. 5. 17). Which is to gain the victory? Is he doomed to cry continually, 'I see a different law in my members, warring against the law of my mind, and bringing me into captivity under the law of sin which is in my members?' (Rom. 7. 23).

It is true that the man described in the closing verses of Romans 7 would seem to be a helpless captive, his active conscience trapped and enslaved by an enfeebled will. But there is another law and another power. Just as the power of the engines and the principles of another law enable the aeroplane to overcome the law of gravity, so the energy of the new life burst his chains and revivifies his will as the 'Spirit of life in Christ Jesus' makes him 'free from the law of sin and of death' (Rom. 8. 2).

So the apostle puts it again, 'This variance between the flesh and the Spirit tends to hinder you from doing what you wish to do; but if you be led by the Spirit you are not under the law' (Gal. 5. 17, 18, Conybeare and Howson). 'Let your lives be guided by the Spirit, and then you will certainly not indulge the cravings of your lower natures. Live by the Spirit's power, and let your conduct also be governed by the Spirit's power' (Gal. 5. 16, 25, Weymouth).

The Christian is thus called upon to live by faith, faith in the new life—its fact, its powers, its possibilities. It is this faith that enables him to consider himself dead to sin, and alive to God; and this is the faith that enables him to put off the old man with his deeds, and to put on the new man which is renewed in knowledge after the image of Him that created him. This is the life of victory; for victory presupposes an enemy, and a life of victory involves a lifelong enemy.

The new life originates in God (John 1. 13; 2 Tim. 1. 10) and was embodied in the Lord Jesus Christ (John 1. 4, 5. 26). Only through His death has it become possible for men to become partakers of it (John 3. 14, 15), and He it is who now has authority to communicate it to them (John 1. 12). He does this through the agency of the Holy Spirit (John 3. 6). From the human side, the life is received as the individual believes in the Saviour (John 1. 12), and is realized and enjoyed as he abides in Him (John 15. 5). The possession of such life radically alters his attitude to sin and, therefore, his daily conduct. But because its realization depends on his obedience, its complete expression is still in the future (John 5. 29), and Frances Ridley Havergal's lines about the 'peace of God' are equally appropriate to the life of God:

Perfect, yet it floweth
  Fuller every day;
Perfect, yet it groweth
  Deeper all the way.

CHAPTER XV

Eternal Security

ERNEST BARKER

ETERNAL LIFE is the gift of God, which is transmitted to every genuine believer in the Lord Jesus Christ. The doctrine of eternal life is emphasized distinctly in the Old Testament, where we are informed that, in the last day, many that sleep in the dust of the earth shall awake, some to *everlasting life* and some to shame and everlasting contempt. It is also recorded that the wise shall shine as the brightness of the firmament; and they that turn many to righteousness as the stars *for ever* (Dan. 12. 2, 3).

In one of the best-known Psalms of David we have the encouraging assurance that goodness and mercy shall follow us all the days of our earthly life, and that we shall ultimately dwell in the house of the Lord *for ever* (Psa. 23. 6). These and other passages leave us in no doubt as to the teaching of the Old Testament on this vital subject.

But if we desire to understand the teaching regarding eternal life in its varied aspects, we must examine the pages of the New Testament, where this great truth is presented as follows:

(I) *As a Gift.* Everlasting life is God's gift to all believers, and truly of all God's great gifts this is the greatest (Rom. 6. 23). It cannot be obtained by human merit. To earn or purchase eternal life are impossible achievements. This gift comes through Jesus Christ our Lord, apart from whom we can receive nothing worth possessing.

The witness of God must ever be greater and more reliable than the witness of men, and the complete witness of God is in relation to His Son. Therefore he who refuses to accept the divine record constitutes God a liar. The question automatically arises: What is God's record? In a very few words it is this: That God has given to us eternal life, and that this life is in His Son. The inescapable conclusion is that the possession of Christ implies the possession of eternal life, and *vice versa* (1 John 5. 9-12).

Eternal life is also presented as a gift in John 3. 16; God loved and God gave. Greater love there could not be. A greater gift could not have been given. God's love embraced the world. His gift was His own Son. Man has simply to accept the gift and therewith he becomes the recipient also of the greatest blessing he can possibly enjoy—'a life that shall endless be.'

One of the titles claimed by the Lord Jesus Christ was that of the Good Shepherd and, in that capacity, He voluntarily laid down His life for His sheep in order that thereby they might receive everlasting life as His free gift (John 10. 11, 27).

When speaking to the Samaritan woman, our Lord reminded her that natural water could never permanently assuage physical thirst. At the same time He declared that He was willing to *give* living water to whoever would accept it and that that gift would constitute an internal, ever-flowing fountain, springing up into everlasting life—satisfying not merely the natural thirst but the deeper desires of the spiritual being (John 4. 13, 14).

(II) *As a Present Possession.* Some of Christ's greatest utterances were couched in the simplest language possible. It was in a sentence of eight words that He announced that all who believe in Him *have* everlasting life (John 6. 47). The will of God is that all who see the Son of God by faith and exercise confidence in Him should have everlasting life, and the Lord Jesus Christ has promised that such shall be raised up at the last day (John 6. 40).

A somewhat difficult phase of this subject is our Lord's statement that, only by eating His flesh and drinking His blood, is eternal life possible (John 6. 53, 54). He had just previously stated that the soul that comes to Him shall never hunger and the soul that believes on Him shall never thirst. All who thus come to Him *have* eternal life. This is, in fact, the equivalent of eating His flesh and drinking His blood (John 6. 35). At the close of this discourse on the Bread of Life, many who had been following Him, went back and walked no longer with Him. The Master then turned to His twelve disciples with the pertinent question, 'Will ye also go away?' Peter, answering for them all, said, 'Lord, to whom shall we go? Thou hast the words of eternal life.' The very utterances of Christ breathed the atmosphere of eternal life. One of the vital objects He had in view when He visited this world was that we might have this life, and that we might have it more abundantly (John 10. 10).

(III) *As a Promise.* The people of God have within them the *hope* of eternal life, which God who cannot lie, *promised* before the world began (Tit. 1. 2). We naturally wonder why eternal life is referred to as a promise when, as we have seen, it is a present possession. The answer is that we shall never realize its full significance until we arrive home. Our present experience is extremely limited and there cannot be the full appreciation of all that is meant by spiritual values in this world. We await the full revelation 'in the last time.' John confirms the statement that God has *promised* us eternal life (1 John 2. 25).

Eternal life is the knowledge of God and of His Son, Jesus Christ (John 17. 2). There is no life apart from this. It is true that God is knowable, but He can only be fully known through Christ, who has revealed Him. One purpose of the Incarnation was that He might give us a divine understanding, that we might know God as the only true God, and be eternally united to His Son, Jesus Christ. This, as the apostle informs us, is the true God and eternal life (1 John 5. 20). Thus the attitude of mankind towards God is indicated by its attitude towards the Lord Jesus Christ. No man can honour God the Father without first honouring Christ the Son (John 5. 23).

Eternal life includes the possession of joy, rest, peace, satisfaction and every other abiding blessing. The Lord Jesus Christ now lives in heaven in the power of an endless life. Because He lives, all His believing people shall live also: and their life will continue as long as His—for evermore (John 14. 19).

The assurance of salvation is enjoyed by believing implicitly what God has said in His Word (Acts 27. 25). Faith is not satisfied by thinking only: it must have a sure foundation upon which to rest. In other words, faith must *know*. When the Apostle Paul was incarcerated in a Roman prison, his soul was filled with a joy which was quite independent of outward circumstances. He was assured of his eternal salvation. He had suffered innumerable hardships, but he was not ashamed because he *knew* whom he had believed (2 Tim. 1. 12). He not only knew that he believed in Christ, but he knew the Christ in whom he had believed. He revelled in the knowledge that he belonged to Christ and that Christ belonged to him; and this certain knowledge is within the possibility of every believer in the Lord Jesus Christ.

We know that Christ died for our sins. We know that He rose again the third day. We know that, after forty days, He returned to heaven. We know that God has highly exalted Him, and has crowned Him with glory and honour. We know that He is now interceding for His people as their Great High Priest, praying for them unceasingly. We know that all authority is His in heaven and earth. We know that He must reign until He has put all His enemies under His feet. We know that He is coming again to receive us unto Himself, that where He is, we shall be also. We know that when He shall appear we shall be like Him. We know that we shall behold His glory and share with Him a wonderful eternity. These things are recorded for us in the Scriptures that we might have assurance (Isa. 32. 17), much assurance (1 Thess. 1. 5), and full assurance (Heb. 6. 11).

The Gospel of John was written that we might believe that Jesus is the Christ, the Son of God, and that believing we might have life through His Name (John 20. 31) The Epistle of John was written that we might have the assurance which results from that belief: that we who believe in the Name of the Son of God might know that we have eternal life (1 John 5. 13). There is no room here for uncertainty. Child-like confidence in the Scriptures is the essential condition for divine revelation and personal persuasion (Matt. 11. 25).

There are other ways by which the Christian may have assurance. The new birth produces new relationships. The believer becomes a member of God's family, and is thereby related to his fellow-believers world-wide. It is therefore incumbent upon him to love his brethren in Christ. Love begets love (1 John 5. 1). Herein we see the divine principle: God has loved us: because of this we love Him. The greater our love is towards Him, the greater it will be towards those who are begotten of Him. By this we *know* that we have passed from death unto life (1 John 3. 14).

The witness of the Holy Spirit also contributes towards the believer's assurance, because He witnesses with our spirits that we *are* children of God (Rom. 8. 16). A new outlook, new desires, new aspirations, new expectations are created within the new-born soul. He is a new creation in Christ Jesus—old things having passed away and all things having become new (2 Cor. 5. 17).

This subject of assurance is vitally connected with the departure from this earthly life. The believer's body is described as the 'earthly house of this tabernacle.' If this tabernacle, which is the soul's temporary abode, be dissolved, we *know* that we have a far superior building awaiting us—a building of God, not made with hands, eternal in the heavens (2 Cor. 5. 1). This is one of the most beautiful pictures of death in the realms of literature. To *know* what will transpire should we approach the parting of the ways brings a calm restfulness which can be appreciated only by those who are willing to accept unhesitatingly the teaching of the Scriptures. Should, however, Christ come in our lifetime, we shall be caught away without the dissolution of the earthly tabernacle becoming necessary (1 Cor. 15. 51).

Eternal Security. When a person embraces Christ as Saviour, he is born of God (John 1. 12, 13), and that divine relationship cannot be dissolved. The same principle is true in the natural world. Absalom was David's son, but, unfortunately, he rebelled and fought against his own father. But, however unfilial Absalom's behaviour was, he continued to be David's son, and when David heard of his tragic end, he mourned for him as only a father could (2 Sam. 18. 33). The analogy is complete so far as it affects personal relationship.

The Bible tells us that the believer is eternally secure because of the greatness of God's love. John twice records that 'the Father loveth the Son' (John 3. 35; 5. 20), and no sooner does the believer endeavour to grasp the true meaning of these five words than he finds himself out of his depth. It is impossible for the finite mind to understand fully that love which is so perfectly reciprocal between the Father and the Son. But, however deep is that love, we are loved in the same measure by the Father and the Son (John 15. 9; 17. 23).

The Lord Jesus Christ loved His disciples 'unto the end,' notwithstanding their failures, their inconsistencies, and even, at times, their self-assertiveness. But all their weaknesses failed to detach them from the love of their Lord. He loved them to the Cross—

and beyond it (John 13. 1). Christ's love towards us is not one whit less than it was towards His disciples. His love is stronger than death, and having loved His own in the world, He will love them to the end.

The epistles frequently refer to the love of God and also to the love of Christ. It is the same love, though mentioned in different ways. 'Who can separate us from the love of Christ?' asked the Apostle Paul. He suggested seven items, all or any of which might appear at first glance as likely to detach us from Christ's love but he dismissed the very thought of separation by affirming that in all those things we are more than conquerors (Rom. 8. 35-37). The apostle then turned his thoughts to the love of God, and having examined every possibility, he finally dismisses them and all other potential means of separation, in the words, 'nor any other created thing' (Rom. 8. 38, 39).

The Bible teaches that the believer is eternally secure because of the greatness of God's power. The Apostle Peter tells us that we are *kept* by the power of God through faith unto salvation which will be revealed in its fulness in a coming day (1 Peter 1. 5). Jude again refers to believers as being sanctified in God the Father and *preserved* in Jesus Christ (Jude 1).

The work of grace which God has begun in His people He will complete in the day of Jesus Christ. This implies that our eternal future lies in His hands. The task of completion is His. He began the good work—He will bring it to fruition (Phil. 1. 6).

One of the most assuring statements ever made relative to eternal security was that of the Lord Jesus Christ, when, referring to His sheep, He said, 'I give unto them eternal life and they shall never perish,' or, in the full force of the original Greek, 'They shall in no wise perish for ever' (John 10. 27, 28). None but the Lord Jesus could have uttered such words. To make assurance doubly sure, He affirmed that no man was able to snatch them (His sheep) out of His hand and, referring to His Father, who is greater than all, He said that no man was able to snatch them out of His Father's hand. Thus the Christian is in the safe keeping of the Saviour's hands. He is in the equally safe keeping of the Father's hand—and they are one. It has been well said that omnipotent love must fail if one of Christ's sheep is lost eternally.

When Christ died, He dealt with all our sins. By that one offering all believers are perfected for ever. By that same sacrifice our sins and iniquities are eternally obliterated from God's memory. Christ's work on the Cross was perfect, and every believer is, in the sight of God, as perfect as was that work (Heb. 10. 14-17). The terrible gulf which once separated us from God, has been bridged so completely that we can never again be shut out from His presence (Eph. 2. 13). The life which the Christian has through the death of Christ is so precious in the eyes of God that He has hidden it with Christ in Himself (Col. 3. 3). Christ is the believer's life, which clearly means that every believer is inseparably linked with Him and forms part of Him (Col. 3. 4). Every believer is the Father's love-gift to the Son, whose sovereign will is that all who have been given to Him shall be eventually where He is (John 17. 24). Every Christian is indwelt by the Holy Spirit and sealed unto the day of redemption (Eph. 4. 30).

God has given unto us eternal life and the continuity of that life can never be broken.

Adoption (sonship) conveys the idea of the Christian's position in God's family, whereas the term 'children' conveys the idea of relationship. When a person embraces Christ as Saviour, he is not only constituted a child of God, but is also adopted into the divine family as a full-grown son, both acts taking place simultaneously.

There are three passages which relate to the truth of adoption. The first is connected with the subject of liberty (Rom. 8. 15). We have not received the spirit of bondage, but the privilege of divine sonship, whereby we are able to call God our Father.

The children of Israel were treated as human chattels in the land of Egypt. At that time they were in the 'house of bondage,' the 'furnace of affliction.' The extent of their miseries was known only to themselves and to their God. The Bible says that their lives were made bitter with hard bondage (Exod. 1. 14). They sighed by reason of their bondage and their cry reached the throne of God (Exod. 2. 23). But God in His mercy delivered His people from their oppression with a mighty hand and with an outstretched arm, that they might know the joys of emancipation, and that they might serve Him all their days. Similarly Christians were at one time in spiritual bondage, slaves to unrighteousness, and servants of sin, walking according to the course of this world. But they have been delivered even more wonderfully (Col. 1. 13). Among the many objects God had in view in delivering His blood-purchased children from the powers of darkness was that the fear of death might be removed. The Lord Jesus Christ died that He might deliver them who, through fear of death, were all their lifetime subject to bondage (Heb. 2. 14, 15). The fear of death having been removed, the spirit of love has been substituted. The spirit of sonship enables each believer to cry, 'Abba, Father,' the same title used by our Lord Himself in the Garden of Gethsemane (Mark 14. 36). The term 'Father' reveals a mine of spiritual wealth. It speaks of One who loves His children dearly, who understands them thoroughly, who ever has their interest in view, who is willing to assist them in every emergency, who is only too delighted to answer their supplications.

The second passage refers particularly to the material creation, which is now awaiting the complete manifestation of the children of God. When sin entered the world, God's fair creation was spoilt, and it is now enduring what the Bible calls 'the bondage of corruption.' In a way, in which, perhaps, it is difficult for the finite mind to grasp, the physical creation is groaning and travailing in pain, and it will continue to do so until the time arrives for its ultimate deliverance. Moreover, the new creation also is awaiting this change—from the natural to the spiritual, from bondage to liberty. This change will take place at the return of our Lord, when the bodies of all believers will be redeemed (their spirits having already been redeemed); when this corruption shall put on incorruption, and when mortality shall be swallowed up of life. This is what the Bible refers to as 'waiting for the adoption' (Rom. 8. 19-23).

The third passage on this theme relates to the privilege of heirship (Gal. 4. 1-7). When the apostle says that the heir, as long as he is a child, differs nothing from a servant, even though he be lord of all, he is alluding to the law with all its exacting obligations. The law was our tutor to bring us to Christ by showing us our desperate need of Him. When all else had failed to meet human need, in the fulness of time God sent forth His Son to redeem us from the curse of the law, that we might occupy the position of sons. What the law could not do with all its ceremonies and sacrifices, Christ accomplished once for all on the Cross. The Son of God became the Son of Man, that the sons of men might become the sons of God. Believers in Christ are therefore no longer under servitude, but are in the privileged position of sons; and if they are sons, they are heirs of God through Christ—heirs of God and therefore joint-heirs with Christ (Rom. 8. 17).

The Father loves the Son and has given all things into His hand (John 3. 35). God has appointed Christ to be heir of all things, having transferred everything to Him; and every believer is now a joint-heir with the Son of God. This means that whatever the Lord Jesus shall enjoy throughout eternity, His believing people will enjoy with Him.

It is impossible for the human intellect to conceive even faintly what God has prepared for those who love Him (1 Cor. 2. 9). The Apostle John has placed the fact on record that it does not yet appear what we shall be (1 John 3. 2). Each believer is destined to be conformed to God's beloved Son (Rom. 8. 29). Compared with this every other prospect fades into insignificance. The fulfilment of these words, 'We shall be like Him,' will be the consummation of all God's eternal purposes for His redeemed people. To see the face of the Lord Jesus will be heaven indeed: but to be like Him and to enjoy as co-heirs all that He will enjoy is beyond human ability to understand. As surely as God's children now bear the earthly image, so surely will they ultimately bear the heavenly image. Every Christian will find himself with a glorified body in the presence of a glorified Saviour. All this and more is to be true of those who have received 'the adoption of sons.' All this and more is included in the phrase, 'If a son, then an heir of God through Christ.'

CHAPTER XVI

Divine Sovereignty and Human Responsibility

E. W. ROGERS

IT should not be a matter for surprise that there are, in Scripture, apparent contradictions and incongruities. That which has its source in the Infinite Mind, must of necessity surpass the apprehension of the finite. God has said, 'My thoughts are not your thoughts, neither are My ways your ways' (Isa. 55. 8). That is to say, His way of reasoning is different from ours. Consequently, apart from the instruction given by the Spirit of God, the harmony of the various doctrines of Holy Scripture with each other is not discernible. The revelation of God is such that He has thereby brought to nought the wisdom of the natural man (1 Cor. 1. 26-29).

The sovereignty of God and the responsibility of man is one of a number of such Bible antinomies concerning which Hammond has written: 'This term (antinomy) is applied (in theology) to what are, in effect, conflicting doctrines concerning the same subject. The limitations of the human mind sometimes render it impossible for us to approach nearer to truth than the statement of the two, apparently, opposing sets of ideas, the truth of both of which is capable of equal demonstration.'

Some of these antinomies are: the human and the divine in both the Living and the Written Word; the employment of fallible men in writing an infallible book; the regular functioning of natural laws and the occasional occurrence in nature's ordered system of miraculous events; the inflexible divine purpose and the human free will; temporal sin resulting in eternal punishment; election and universal grace; predestination and individual faith.

This should place the student of Scripture on his guard against being disturbed by any inability to reconcile with one another all the doctrines of Scripture. There are many human ideas which are not the product of human reasoning, but operate in modification of it. We do not, for example, subscribe to the possibility of nothingness or conceive of a beginning from nothingness. Similarly, we can neither comprehend eternity nor understand that 'time should cease to flow.' We may speak of 'infinite space' but strictly the two words express contradictory ideas, though we may understand what is meant. In certain realms it is apparent, therefore, that reason is not adequate; help must be sought elsewhere. For example, in creation two apparently opposing forces are constantly in operation; namely, the centrifugal and centripetal forces, by means of which the heavenly bodies are kept in their courses. These forces are complementary and contribute to the harmonious operation of the universe. Though our reason may fail to comprehend the co-existence of two opposite forces working harmoniously together, yet the undeniable blending of the two opposing forces just mentioned provides evidence that the Creator is not Himself restricted by those limitations which He has imposed on His creatures. It is not surprising, then, that in other spheres, we discover the contemporaneous existence of other apparently contrary principles which work together in perfect unison.

Butler in his *Analogy*, says: 'I look into nature and Providence and I find certain things hard to be understood which can be explained on the assumption that there are in the entire scheme of God's universe vast issues and circumstances that are beyond my knowledge altogether and I have to accept things as they stand and wait for their solution. Now, supposing for a moment that the Author of the constitution of nature has become the Author of a written revelation, shall I not expect to find that in written revelation are some difficulties analogous to those which I find in the constitution of nature itself?'

As another has written: 'In the revelation of His ways we must be prepared for the phenomena which, at least at present, are to us absolute mysteries, for instance, for actions of His will as He is sovereign and as He is His own eternal end, and as He is infinite, which we cannot formally harmonize with His explicit assurances and proofs of power and universal Love.'

The believer can afford to wait for further light on the matter. And yet another has said: 'Ultimately our human reason cannot resolve the antinomy of the certainty which goes with divine sovereignty and the natural ability with which God has endowed man . . . the Christian faith can relieve the antinomy.' And again: 'Each principle must be faced by the issues involved and all the related principles, so that what we do not understand may not be allowed to shake what we do.'

Recognizing such limitations, we approach the subject of this paper which 'is an outstanding case of the need for adhering to what Scripture actually states and for avoiding the temptation to construct a complete philosophic scheme.'

In order to facilitate the consideration of the subject we will deal with it under the following headings:

(i) The Plan of the Ages.
(ii) Prophecy.
(iii) Old Testament History.
(iv) The Introduction of Sin.
(v) Election and Predestination.
(vi) Man's Free Will.
(vii) Prayer.

The Plan of the Ages

There is one goal towards which God is causing all things to move, and He so controls the actions of men that those which subserve His purpose become details of a system which is the outworking of that Sovereign divine plan. God's purpose is that in the consummation of the ages all things shall be headed up in Christ (Eph. 1. 10) who is the Son of His love (Col. 1. 13). The two particular principles under consideration (*inter alia*) co-exist and work together for the accomplishment of that divine purpose. With that end in view, adversity and prosperity, though the one is contrary to the other, often exist side by side (Eccl. 7. 14). Man's wrongdoing is not allowed to frustrate the accomplishment of God's purpose (Rom. 8. 35). Although God will never change His ultimate purpose, yet as Hammond says: 'Whilst it is true that Scripture teaches that it would be just and lawful for God to do what He wished with His own, the whole Scripture is against the notion of any rigid arbitrariness in God.' Accordingly, at times His intermediate and temporary purposes are altered (Jonah 4. 3), and His promised blessing is withheld (Amos 4. 7) or conversely imminent threatened judgment is postponed suitably to the attitude of those with whom He is dealing (Jonah 3. 10). Nineveh's threatened judgment, for example, was long deferred because of its repentance, and Abraham's intercession for Sodom proceeded from his understanding of God's ways in this respect (Gen. 18. 16 ff.).

'Is it not lawful,' asked the householder, 'for me to do what I will with mine own?' (Matt. 20. 15). 'Whiles it remained was it not thine own, and after it was sold was it not in thine own power?' enquired Peter (Acts 5. 4). It is an elemenatary principle in human affairs that the owner has unfettered rights of disposition over his own property, although such rights have, from time to time, been invaded and limited by man-made laws and regulations. None, however, can deprive the Supreme Lord over all of absolutely unfettered rights concerning His own handiwork. 'The earth is the Lord's and the fulness thereof' (Psa. 24. 1). If, therefore, He is pleased to make the blessing of His creatures conditional He does so in exercise of His own essential rights.

He alone has the right to determine individual and national destinies (Acts 17. 26). He it is who decides what shall be the temporal and territorial delimitations of empires (Deut. 32. 8). The details of His actions are as 'wheels within wheels' (Ezek. 1. 16) and one whole 'cycle' of events may be a complete microcosm of God's vast eternal plan which throughout time is being wrought out. In such small 'cycle' there may be temporal divine purposes and displays of His superintending and irresistible control, which are anticipatory examples of His ultimate triumph. Yet there is no caprice in God's sovereign purposings, but rather a perfect goodness and justice are hidden therein. *How* this is so reason cannot determine: that it *is* so is faith's assurance.

The blending of these two principles in God's government of man and in the history of man is illustrated in every earthly kingdom. The fact that the ruler makes laws in his realm serves to remind his subjects that he is sovereign, whereas the holding of courts of law where offenders are punished indicates that his subjects are accountable to him for their conduct. The one is complementary to the other. God's right to impose law arises out of His sovereignty (Exod. 20. 2); man's duty to observe it flows from his responsibility as a created being.

Prophecy

In the prophetic Scriptures God discloses to man what is His purpose. In them He very often speaks of future things in the past tense, forasmuch as He knows that He will ultimately prevail. When God says, 'I will,' the recipients of His promises may be fully assured, for He is faithful that promised (Heb. 11. 11). His enemies, however, should fear and tremble at His word for His threatenings are no idle words. His 'I will' is always followed by appropriate timely action. 'He goes straight forward' (Ezek. 1. 12), and all that is in His path becomes as nothing. He doeth what He will in the army of heaven and amongst the inhabitants of the earth (Dan. 4. 35).

Moreover, although men are sometimes His instruments in the accomplishment of His word, they are not thereby relieved of their responsibility. Assyria was His rod (Isa. 10. 5) although in doing what he did the Assyrian king was unaware that God was thus using him. Rationalistic arguments on this subject must not be allowed to cause us to have any misgivings as to the justice of God.

'Those things which God *before* had showed by the mouth of all His prophets . . . He hath *so* fulfilled' (Acts 3. 18). Observe carefully the word 'so.' The wicked deeds of man fulfilled the prophecies of God. It is not that God decreed man's deed: He rather decreed the plan which involved the over-ruling and utilization of such wicked deed.

Orr has rightly written: 'Man's free actions are not regarded as being excluded from God's fore-ordination (Acts 2. 23), nor is the latter to be conceived of as in any way over-riding or doing violence to human freedom. Man acts freely, as nature acts necessarily, but it is God who appoints the time, place and circumstances of the free act, permits its happening and over-rules it and its issues for the furthering of His own wise and holy ends.'

Why, for instance, was it upon a tree that men hanged the Son of God? (Acts 5. 30). The answer is because it is written, 'Cursed is every one that hangeth upon a tree' (Deut. 21. 23), so that by the crucifixion of the Lord Jesus 'He became a curse' (Gal. 3. 13), though in a substitutionary manner for those who were irrefutably eligible for it. But this did not absolve man from guilt. 'Ye took

Him and ye slew Him, hanging Him on a tree,' is Peter's charge to the guilty rulers (Acts 10. 39; 5. 30). In fact, Christ died pursuant to God's purpose and plan: He also died at the hand of guilty men, and for our sins.

Or, consider Ezekiel's prophecy: 'I will overturn, overturn, overturn, until He comes whose right it is' (Ezek. 21. 27). This refers to divine sovereignty in human affairs. The Scriptures record some of these overturnings: secular history records others: further overturnings are within the knowledge of the present generation. God thus overrules history with a view to the advent of the true Heir of the Kingdom.

What right, it may be asked, has God to interfere in human affairs if He is not sovereign? Where His claims are despised His hand of judgment rightly falls. Foreseeing this, the Lord Jesus wept over Jerusalem as He foreshadowed the invasion of the armies of Titus and the inevitable horrors of vengeance that were to overtake Jerusalem (Luke 19. 41). Yet the destruction of that city and the scattering of the Jewish people were pursuant to the wider plan that, not in that city nor yet in any other city will men worship the Father (John 4. 21). A period was about to be inaugurated when true worship would not be limited to time or place.

The fact of prophecy pre-supposes God's sovereignty, that the prophetic word is directed to man is because of his responsibility. Hence in those writings are to be found interwoven foreshadowings, promises, warnings, pleadings, exhortations and the like. All the Scriptures, and particularly the writings of the prophets are written on the basis that God has rights over man and that man has duties toward God.

Old Testament History

It is apparent that, if prophecy demonstrates the sovereignty of God and the responsibility of man, fulfilled prophecy which becomes history, demonstrates the same.

The history of the Pharaoh of the Exodus is a case in point, though one of a greater number of instances (Exod. 11. 10). God hardened his heart after he had hardened it himself. But God designed to redeem His promise to Abraham which had been given several centuries earlier (Gen. 15. 14) and to release His seed from Egyptian bondage and to bring them into the promised land. Israel was God's firstborn (Exod. 4. 22) in regard to whom He had a righteous claim: Pharaoh's detention of them made him guilty before God.

Bible history contains many similar illustrations of the interaction of the two principles. The 'Lord of the whole earth' brought Israel, under the leadership of Joshua, into the land of Canaan (Josh. 5. 14). Its inhabitants were destroyed by Israel at God's command because of the prolonged failure of the Canaanites in their responsibility to Him: by that time 'the iniquity of the Amorites' had become 'full' (Gen. 15. 16).

Israel's recurring troubles in the days of the Judges were the result of their delinquencies (Jud. 3. 7; 4. 1, etc.). The raising up by God of deliverers, from time to time, were acts of sovereign compassion.

It is not possible at present to trace these two principles throughout the entirety of sacred history or ancient and modern history. In general, however, it is true to say that history makes evident that God ruleth in the kingdom of men and giveth the thrones of earth to whomsoever He will (Dan. 4. 32). He created all things because of His own will (Rev. 4. 11). He is unlimited by anything outside of Himself. 'He doeth according to His own will in the army of heaven and among the inhabitants of the earth and none can stay His hand, or say unto Him, "what doest Thou?"' (Dan. 4. 35).

In all human history the Providence of God exercises an overruling control: it is operative through animate and inanimate things: through things voluntary and things involuntary: through good and evil. It causes all things so to interact one upon another that they issue ultimately for the accomplishment of the divine purpose and for the good of the creature. 'Every day of our lives we act upon a principle which appears to be absolutely incompatible with sovereignty and yet we recognize this truth of sovereignty in reviewing our actions and their consequences.' They have been over-ruled by God's providential control.

It is not only man who is involved: even such an insignificant event as the fall of a sparrow is within the compass of God's sovereignty (Matt. 10. 29). Seed-time and harvest, summer and winter and all the multitudinous details of the organic disposition by God of His universe give proof of it. Nations and governments are 'distressed' (Luke 21. 25) because of their inability to carry into effect unhinderedly their avowed policies by reason of superior forces which direct them into a channel already prepared beforehand by God.

Moreover, both sovereignty and responsibility are found operative in single episodes or in one series of events. 'God sent me before you to preserve life' (Gen. 45. 7), said Joseph to his brethren although they were verily guilty in having sent him down into Egypt.

The operation of the world-wide registration by Cæsar Augustus was delayed in order that it might occur when the Lord Jesus was born at Bethlehem whither his parents had gone in connection with such registration, thus fulfilling the long-standing prophecy (Luke 2. 1; Matt. 2. 6). The birth, training and position of Saul of Tarsus made him the most suitable vessel (Gal. 1. 13, 14) to carry the Gospel of God to the Gentiles. God pre-arranged His servant's earthly circumstances in order to effect His eternal purposes. Paul, however, acknowledges himself to be the 'chief of sinners' (1 Tim. 1. 15). In responsibility as man he had failed: in sovereignty he was chosen.

The Introduction of Sin

Why God permitted sin to enter into the world is not disclosed in Scripture. The manner of its entry is clearly recorded (Gen. 3). That the event did not take God by surprise is evident in that He had, before time began, determined how to overcome it. 'Sin,' says Moule, 'is both an insoluble riddle, and a terrible fact in the freely created universe of the Holy God. It is impossible to reason *a priori* on the effects of an unknown cause.' God in His sovereignty permitted it, and by its presence took occasion to emphasize the responsibility of man to Himself.

The Scriptural record of the fall of man makes it plain that he was a responsible, willing agent in the matter. God had entrusted him with free-will: that fact in itself incurred the liability of its abuse. That liability, however, did not relieve man of his guilt, nor did man's sin defeat God in accomplishing His purpose. Adam, we are informed, was not deceived (1 Tim. 2. 14): what he did in Eden he did with open eyes, wittingly. Nor did the deception of the woman relieve her of responsibility. The imposition of the respective penalties shows that God recognized individual accountability.

In the sin of Adam was the sin of the race, 'for that all sinned' (Rom. 5. 12) when he sinned. Just as Levi, who was not then born but was in the loins of Abraham, is reckoned to have done what Abraham did (Heb. 7. 5 ff.) so the race is reckoned by God to have sinned when Adam sinned, though none was yet born: all, however, were 'in the loins' of Adam.

In consequence of Adam's sin his will became enslaved to sin, under whose dominion he had willingly put himself. This was true of him and of all his posterity: it is true of the race. Man's free-will is now an enslaved will, in bondage to sin. He, therefore, that sinneth is a slave of sin (John 8. 34).

Further, by the fall man acquired the knowledge of good through evil (Gen. 3. 22). Thereafter for man both right and wrong were open and he was under an obligation to 'discern the things that differ' (Phil. 1. 10). Paul's letter to the Romans deals with this: he there states that, even apart from the written word of God, there is the voice of conscience within (Rom. 2. 15). Moreover, in the physical world without there are evidences of God's eternal power and Godhead (Rom. 1. 20) so that man is declared to be 'without excuse.' Additional privileges increase responsibility, but basically all men are sinners although there are different degrees of guilt.

Lamont has written: 'God who is the Creator and Ground of all has an immediate relation to everything in the Universe. He is related in one way to what is good and in another way to what is evil but both relations are distinct and positive. It is impossible to imagine sin as out of all relation to God. He keeps His hand upon it, deals with it in infinite wisdom, and patience, does not allow it to pass beyond the limit which He Himself has fixed. . . .'

Election and Predestination

That God has chosen some out of the world and destined them to eternal glory the Scriptures plainly teach (1 Thess. 1. 4). It is equally plain from the Scriptures that such as are chosen are personally responsible to receive the message of God's grace and, of their own volition, to believe on the Saviour whom He has sent. As Sir Robert Anderson has said: 'The distinctive truth of election must not be lost in the kindred truth of the sovereignty of God.' Or, to quote Guillebaud: 'Here the will of the infinite is impinging upon the will of the creature and must, in some measure, pass our apprehension. We may, however, reflect that even a human father may afford his child a free choice and yet influence that choice more than the child is aware.' And again, 'If God be infinite there may be many reasons for His choice other than those which we can see or apprehend.' These reasons can only be good, well-founded and altogether just; in fact it may be assumed they are in full consonance with all His other attributes.

To the sinner is proclaimed the message, 'Whosoever will may come' (Rev. 21. 17). Having come and believed in the Saviour the saint learns that he was 'elect before the foundation of the world' (Eph. 1. 4).

To quote Sir Robert Anderson again: 'Though to our finite minds election and grace may seem as far as the poles asunder and as antagonistic as the magnetic currents which set towards them, to the Infinite they may appear but inseparable parts of one great whole.' We may look at a mountain from two vantage-points and view two distinct shapes apparently vastly different from each other, though it be the same mountain. So do the doctrines of election and grace appear.

In an orchestra, for example, there are many diverse musical instruments: and some of them, of themselves, are incapable of producing any pleasant sound; indeed, the particular part of any tune which they play may, of itself, be unpleasant to the ear; but when the whole orchestra is playing, that particular part makes an essential contribution to the harmony produced by the several instruments. 'Doubtless, election and grace may appear incompatible but to maintain that, therefore, they are so in fact is to put reason above revelation: in other words, to place man above God.'

Man has learned those laws which operate in the sphere which he is able to investigate: who can tell whether or not directly contrary laws operate in the sphere which he cannot examine?

Election and predestination on the one hand, and the free-will of the person on the other hand, are not the only factors involved in such a great work, but they are essential and integral parts of it: if regarded as unrelated to all the other factors they seem to be inconsistent and illogical, but when the whole plan is revealed their harmony will also become plain. 'The good pleasure of God is the ground of election.'

Problems connected with this subject have for many generations engaged the thoughts of many, but it still remains an unexplained mystery so far as human philosophy is concerned. In handling it, reason must give place to faith. There must be unreserved acceptance of God's Word pending the revelation which will be given in the perfect day.

The two principles are not, as some have affirmed, mutually exclusive: and they are not contradictory. Each is an essential feature of a moral universe in which God has inscribed His rights on the conscience of man, and in which He is working out the counsels of His will.

The late Dr. Moule when discussing this matter said: 'It must be owned a mystery whose explanation and harmony lie within the secret things of God.' Man's destiny is not altogether in his own hands. The elect are prepared before unto eternal glory (Rom. 9. 23). The unsaved are fitted by their own disobedience for judgment (Rom. 9. 22). Moule again says: 'The sovereignty of God viewed abstractly as one attribute amongst many must, of course, be conceived of as qualified by all the rest. It cannot be otherwise than an infinitely wise, righteous and merciful sovereignty.'

God's sovereign election is not confined to those who comprise the Church. The nation of Israel was chosen by God (Deut. 7. 7), as also was Abraham (Acts 7. 2—one out of the three sons of Terah). Isaac was chosen and not Ishmael (Rom. 9. 7). Jacob was preferred to Esau (Rom. 9. 12). Those not so elected had no grounds for complaint, no more than the clay is entitled to say to the potter: 'What doest thou?' (Rom. 9. 20). God's sovereign rights are unchallengeable. Christ was ever before the mind of God: and in His choice of Abraham, Isaac and Jacob He had the people of Israel and their Messiah in view all the time.

Lamont has wisely written: 'The Christian confesses with his whole heart that the initiative in his salvation was not with himself but with God, but he is not permitted to say in the case of a man who may have finally rejected Christ that God took the initiative in that rejection. Many steps have preceded the fatal rejection. Every step in the fatal descent has meant a man's expenditure of the providential freedom which is his birthright. It has, however, meant increasing bondage. This is the inevitable corollary to the rejection of the overtures of the divine Spirit who has kept knocking at the door.' And again he says: 'We must repudiate a statement of this doctrine in terms of a severe logic which makes it equivalent to a scientific theory of determinism.'

Both Peter and Paul, in writing to the saints speak of their 'calling' (1 Peter 1. 2; 1 Thess. 1. 4; Rom. 1. 7), but each of them when announcing the glad tidings to the sinner employs the word 'whosoever' (Acts 10. 43; 13. 39). Neither allows the truth of election to modify the universality of the offer of God's grace. Neither divulges the secret to the unsaved sinner, but each discloses it to the believer.

God is entitled to say, 'I will have mercy on whom I will have mercy'; God, in His providence, acts in this way as is shown by His dealings with Israel under Pharaoh, cited by Paul in Rom. 9. 15-18. Salvation is entirely of grace and no one can either complain if passed over or boast himself if saved.

Man's Free Will

Man, as we have seen, is a moral being who is possessed of a conscience: that is, he possesses the knowledge of moral differences. He is aware of a Supreme Being to whom he must give account (Heb. 4. 13). God has written His claims both in man's conscience (Rom. 2. 15) and in the Scriptures, warning him of punishment for default of duty. The way of life and the way of death are revealed therein (Deut. 30. 19). The way of blessing and of cursing are there explained. Man is responsible to choose one or the other (Josh. 24. 15) and according to that choice, he determines his destiny.

In the words of the late Bishop Moule again: 'Man has free will. He is not the product of circumstances: he is responsible amongst them for moral choice. This is always assumed in Scripture, especially in divine reasonings and appeals. True, Scripture is always jealous for the supremacy and sovereignty of the will of God. This is one of its great and conspicuous characteristics. His will has sovereign relations to all events such that somehow all contribute to the perfect realization of its purpose. But among these "all things" is the reality of the will of the created personality such that man is a true though secondary cause. We fail, by the necessary limits of our viewpoint, to see mentally the harmony of the absolute sovereignty of the will of the Holy Creator, and the true freedom and so true responsibility of the will of the personal creature. But the two facts are equally plain in revelation and equally important in a true theology.'

Parallel lines are said to meet at infinity and it is possible that when the children of God have bodies of glory they may understand the true interaction of these two apparently contradictory principles. 'True human will has been created by the divine Will and is subordinate to it.' One part of a machine may appear to be moving in an entirely different direction from another part; yet without either one or the other the machine could not function. So it is in the realm of morality. Men are free to choose, but in so choosing they are responsible to their Sovereign Creator.

Moreover, man's choice and God's purpose for the believer operate in unison. As another has written: 'When the gift of life was proffered us we were conscious in accepting it that we did so freely, voluntarily. Since then . . . we have come to learn that in a sense deeper and fuller still grace is sovereign.' And yet again: 'God has embedded in the human nature an element of free will (sovereignty) as a feature of His own image, and He will not violate it to coerce the unsaved or saved. The will is the turning-point both in the fall and in salvation. The eternal relationship is established in the reciprocity of God's will and man's.'

Such scriptural terms as guilt (Rom. 3. 19), trespass (Eph. 2. 1), choose (Josh. 24. 15), repent (Acts 2. 38), believe (Acts 16. 31), and indeed all God's specific commands to man, whether given in the Decalogue or other parts of the Holy Writings imply that man is under a duty to obey. A wrong choice involves him in guilt. The inability of man to do the right is but one facet of a many-sided doctrine. God never requires a man to do a thing of which he is morally incapable. If he is required to believe, his unbelief would not be culpable if it could be shown that he was incapable of exercising faith. The Lord's words, 'Ye will not to come to me that ye might have life' (John 5. 40) demonstrate the wilfulness of the Jews although it afforded the occasion for the fulfilment of God's wider purposes of grace. While all that the Father had given to Christ will, surely, come to Him (John 6. 37), it is the responsibility of all such, no matter how deeply into sin they may have fallen, to come, and the promise is certain that all that so come unto Him He 'will not cast out.'

If a man is not responsible for his actions, how (it may be asked) could judgment be 'according to man's works?' (Rev. 20. 12). 'How, then, shall God judge the world?' (Acts 17. 31). How could degrees of guilt be determined? or, how could few or many stripes be awarded (Luke 12. 47, 48). Why, indeed, should God punish man at all?

Man cannot claim exemption from guilt on the ground that God overrules his wickedness in order to carry out His own purposes. God originally endowed men with free-will, and this became evident when Adam chose to disobey in the Garden of Eden. All his posterity, like him, are capable of choosing and all have chosen wrongly. They have turned to their own way (Isa. 53. 6).

Prayer

Events sometimes occur which give rise to the questions, Hath God forgotten? (Psa. 42. 9), and has He 'withdrawn Himself' from the affairs of men? (Isa. 40. 27, ff.). It must have seemed thus to Job. Mordecai, too, probably thought so. But *fronti nulla fides*; it is unsafe to judge from outward appearances. When the whole is viewed, when God has manifested Himself by action, it becomes plain that He has not been a neutral onlooker but has, in fact, been an active participant in each event.

It is when the sovereignty of God is not apparent, that saints pray for help and deliverance. Prayer, however, in itself is an acknowledgment that God is sovereign. Why, indeed, should prayer be made unless God is the Controller and Disposer of all things? It is because the suppliant believes that God has both the right and the power to alter the course of events in his favour, or in the favour of those for whom he prays, that he petitions Him. Prayer offered in a right spirit, moreover, will produce an exercise of conscience through a sense of moral responsibility. 'If I had regarded iniquity in my heart the Lord would not hear' (Psa. 66. 18). God will not satisfy desires of mere self-gratification. Even what are called unanswered prayers, though constituting a perplexing problem, demonstrate the principles we are considering.

Summary

The sovereignty of God and the responsibility of man are thus found to be compatible with and complementary to the working out of God's eternal plan. These concepts are assumed in the prophetic writings of Scripture, and are evident in history. The entry of sin into the world, with all its baneful consequences, has not affected these principles: God has elected poor sinners and destined them to eternal bliss, they meantime exercising their own free will in accepting His gracious offer of salvation. 'From the first day' they believed they have been aware of their indebtedness to God's free grace, ever owning their accountability to Him in all things, and trusting Him in the midst of circumstances which defy rational explanation. Prayer casts them upon God's power and God's love.

'O the depth of the riches, both of the wisdom and the knowledge of God! How unsearchable are His judgments, and His ways past finding out! . . . For of Him, and through Him, and to Him, are all things; to whom be glory for ever. Amen' (Rom. 11. 33-36).

CHAPTER XVII

The Christian Path

GEORGE E. HARPUR

'BUT the path of the just is as the shining light, that shineth more and more unto the perfect day.' The Christian path is entered by the gateway of justification: its course is sanctification and its terminus glorification.

The doctrine of *justification* deals with that act of God by which the sinner's life in the old path is brought to an end, and his feet set in the new one. The doctrine of *sanctification* deals with the method by which God works in the man who has thus been placed in divine favour, leading him on from the starting-point of the Christian Path to its terminus. Logically rooted in justification, it just as logically ends in glorification. The doctrine of *glorification* deals with that act of God by which the justified man completes his journey and enters into the full possession of eternal glory.

These three doctrines are consecutively examined in Romans 1 to 8: Justification, exhaustively, in chapters 1 to 5; Sanctification, in chapters 6 to 8; and Glorification briefly in chapter 8. Bible doctrine, where possible, is best approached through a passage of Scripture where it is set out in a comprehensive way. Other scattered references can then be properly related to the central teaching. The teaching of Romans then, gives us our starting-place.

We are concerned in this chapter only with the two doctrines of justification and sanctification, both of which are of enormous importance in the Christian pathway. The first gives a man that assurance of being right with God, without which all his steps must be uncertain. The second shows him the most expeditious way of growing Christlike and of overcoming the great obstacles to his progress.

These two doctrines are often confused, to the great detriment of the believer's joy and liberty. The distinction between them is clear. To justify is to declare a man to be right; to sanctify is to make holy. The former is to set a man in a clear and correct position before some law; the latter to place within the man all good and Godly graces.

Justification

Justification may be examined in three parts:

(I) What justification is.
(II) How it operates.
(III) What are its effects.

(I) *The sense of the word 'justify.'* The verb 'to justify' occurs in the New Testament about forty times, just (or righteous) about eighty times, and justness (righteousness or rightness) about one hundred times, if we include a few cognate words of infrequent use. The meaning of the word is in precise accordance with its accepted usage, which is 'to pronounce righteous,' 'to declare free from guilt or blame,' 'to show to be just or conformable to law.'

It is, properly, a legal term, and declares that a man, having been brought under critical observation, is judged to be without offence in the eyes of the legal authority before which he has been brought to stand. Justification represents a satisfied law and an acquitted person. The law thus declares itself to have no further interest in the man, for his standing before it is perfect and proper.

The word, therefore, is used about God Himself (Luke 7. 29), where it cannot possibly mean to make righteous. God cannot be made righteous, He *is* righteous: but He can and ought to be declared righteous by man (Rom. 3. 4). Indeed God was anxious to declare Himself righteous and made the declaration in Christ crucified (Rom. 3. 25).

Justification is therefore the opposite of condemnation, and the two words are used closely together to indicate their mutual exclusion (Rom. 8. 33, 34). To condemn a man is not to make the man wrong—his sin made him that—but to *pronounce* him to be wrong. Justification includes acquittal, just as condemnation includes being penalised.

Justification, then, by its definition, usage and its antonym, is seen to refer to a man's standing in law, and declares that so far as the law is concerned he is a righteous man and not a guilty one.

That none of us can take such a place before God is palpable from both conscience and Scripture (Rom. 3. 10; 2. 15). It is, therefore, good news that God can justify the ungodly (Rom. 4. 5), and it is of the utmost importance that we perceive and receive His method of justification.

Justification is an act in which God declares that a believing man is just or righteous, that he is free from condemnation because sin is not imputed unto him (Rom. 4. 8), that justice is satisfied and he is rightly entitled to the blessedness of the status and rewards of perfect righteousness (Rom. 4. 6).

This act of justification is God's answer to the faith of him that believeth in Jesus (Rom. 3. 26). It is gratuitous, springing from the grace of God (Rom. 3. 24). It is provided for those who are ungodly (Rom. 4. 5). It is apart from legal works (Rom. 3. 28). It is given, not to those who seek to establish their own righteousness, but to those who submit to that which God provides in Christ (Rom. 10. 3, 4; 1 Cor. 1. 30).

Justification does not affect a change in the sinner's character (that is done by the new birth and sanctification), but it does affect a change in his status. In himself he is sinful, guilty, condemned, awaiting the second death and, indeed, dead already (Rom. 3. 23; 3. 19; John 3. 18; Rev. 20. 14; Eph. 2. 1, 5). Justified in Christ, he is righteous, conscience-purged, uncondemned, awaiting eternal life, and, indeed, enjoying it already (Rom. 5. 19; Heb. 9. 14; Rom. 8. 1; Jude 21; 1 John 5. 11).

Because man is the kind of sinner that God's Word declares him to be, God's justification of the sinner makes necessary two things, viz.:

(*a*) The non-imputation of all that offends God's holy law.

(*b*) The imputation of a righteousness which satisfies God's holy requirements. For man's law often merely requires the absence of guilt, but God's law requires in addition the doing of His perfect will. His tribunal investigates 'those things which we ought to have done' as well as 'those things which we ought not to have done.'

(*a*) *Non-imputation, Pardon, Forgiveness or Remission.* The first definite statement in Romans about justification occurs immediately upon Paul's having conclusively proved the guiltiness of all men before God. He declares in the same sentence that men are guilty and yet are declared righteous by God (Rom. 3. 22-24). Provided of course, that they are 'believing ones.' Out of this fact spring the strong human objections to 'justification by faith' (as, for example, they are introduced in Rom. 6). This doctrine seems to imply that God is shutting His eyes to facts, and winking at sin. Yet the reverse is the truth. Other supposed schemes of justification must minimize sin and treat guilt as of little account, but the Gospel shows sin in all its awful iniquitousness, and guilt in all its terror. For, since a just God cannot ignore sin, the actual, historic sin of these justified sinners must be imputed to another (qualified and capable of bearing that burden) and not to the sinner himself, and this Paul immediately shows to be the case for Rom. 3. 24-26 plainly attributes justification to our Lord's Cross-work. He was set forth 'a propitiation by His blood,' and that specifically to show forth his righteousness. Peter endorses this, saying, 'Christ suffered for sins once, the righteous for the unrighteous, that He might bring us to God.' Thus the forgiveness of sins is not merely a sovereign act of God, as if He said, 'I will not raise the question of your sins at all.' (It *is* sovereign in the sense that all the plan and work originated in God and not in man). God's action in justifying is in strict accordance with His justice, for the sins have been actually dealt with, and the guilt borne by a substitute acceptable to God, and in a way acceptable to Him.

All that we are in ourselves as sinners is made over to Christ (2 Cor. 5. 21). The sinner who believes is as legally freed from his sin and guilt, condemnation and punishment (penal evil) as the debtor on whose behalf another makes full payment to the creditor, obtaining a receipt of discharge. Moreover, this justification extends to all sins, even to those such as murder and adultery, for which the law prescribed no sacrificial remedy (Acts 13. 38, 39).

(*b*) *The Imputation of a Righteousness which satisfies God's holy requirements.* 2 Cor. 5. 21 mentioned above gives us also the positive side of justification—'that we might become the righteousness of God in Him.' Even so Paul proceeds in Rom. 4 to show that God reckons those whom He saves as not deficient before Him in any particular, but accounts them as possessing righteousness and, therefore, such as on whom He can load His blessings and promises.

It is necessary here that a perfect righteousness be produced which is satisfactory to God. This perfect righteousness is found in Christ (1 Cor. 1. 30). It is perfectly satisfactory to God, for God raised Christ from the dead. 'He was raised for our justification' (Rom. 4. 25). 'When the debtor is proved insolvent, his surety is thrown into prison; but as soon as the latter succeeds in clearing the debt, the debtor is legally set free, and his surety is liberated with him. For he has no debt of his own.' By the resurrection of Jesus Christ we know that God is satisfied, for He died on account of our sins. It is also necessary that this righteousness be available to be made over to the man who needs it. That it is available is stated in Rom. 3. 22; the method whereby it is made over is outlined in Rom. 5. 17-19, R.V. This righteousness, having been provided entirely by God is called a 'righteousness of God' (Rom. 1. 17), or, 'God's righteousness' (Rom. 10. 3). It is without works, because it is provided for those who bring forward no merit of their own. Therefore it is received as a gift (Rom. 5. 17). A gift which is preached (Acts 13. 38, 39), but which may be rejected and spurned (Rom. 10. 3, 4). It is 'of faith' (Rom. 10. 10) because it can be received in no other way than 'by faith of Jesus Christ,' for 'Christ is the end of the law unto righteousness to every one that believeth.' That gratuitous righteousness was testified by the Old Testament (Rom. 3. 21; Jer. 23. 6; 33. 16) is proved in Rom. 4 by the cases of Abram and David. It is not the sinner's own production, it is therefore imputed unto him (Rom. 4. 6-8). It carries the promise of God with it (Rom. 4. 13).

Rom. 10. 5-13 shows clearly the difference between the righteousness of the law which cannot justify and the righteousness of faith which saves. One consists in self-effort and the other in believing.

(II) *How justification operates.* God Himself is the originating cause of justification (Rom. 8. 33). This is an astounding thing, when it is considered that those whom He justifies are 'ungodly,' that they need to be justified from many offences (Rom. 5. 16) and that their sins are lawless acts of rebellion against HIM. That God should condemn and punish sinners is natural and obvious; that He should be able, without contradicting His character, to justify sinners is beyond reason and must be accepted as a matter of revelation. This, Scripture declares it to be (Rom. 1. 17) and further shows that He has not lowered His personal standard of righteousness in bringing this about (Rom. 3. 26). Further this justification is the united work of the Triune God, for 1 Cor. 6. 11 shows how the Lord Jesus Christ and the Spirit of God combine to bring it about. That Paul should express such certainty and assurance about it (Rom. 8. 30-39) is due to the fact that the origin and effectiveness of justification lie in God Himself.

The spring is in HIS grace (Rom. 3. 24), both that of the Father and of the Son (Rom. 5. 15, R.V.; Tit. 3. 7). Hence the word 'gift' and the word 'gratuitously.' It is sometimes said that if the demands of the law have been fully satisfied, as they have, then the acquittal of the sinner is a matter of necessity, not of grace. This is not so, for the matter in question is not merely a debt, where the creditor is satisfied whoever pays. Criminal guilt demands that the person of the offender should answer at the bar of justice and a substitute is rarely possible or accepted. This is where grace steps in, for God, the absolute Judge has power to accept a substitute (the law, with its sacrifices, completely endorses this), so much so that our Lord is called 'the Lamb of God' (cf. Isaiah 53. 4-10). The Saviour also presents his right to lay down his life as a Sin-bearer (John 10. 18). Here is the grace of our God and the Lord Jesus Christ so often referred to at the beginning of Paul's letters (e.g. 1 Cor. 1. 3); God's grace in giving His Son and Jesus' grace in sacrificing Himself. It merely remains now for the third party, the sinner, to accept the provision so graciously made for him.

The effective cause of justification is the blood of Christ. Three Scriptures will establish this without question:

'Being justified through the redemption that is in Christ Jesus: whom God set forth to be a propitiation, through faith, by His blood' (Rom. 3. 24, 25).

'Being now justified by His blood' (Rom. 5. 9).

'So then as through one trespass the judgment came unto all men to condemnation; even so through one act of righteousness the free gift came unto all men to justification of life' (Rom. 5. 18).

No words could more plainly declare that the instrument of our justification is 'His decease which He accomplished' (Luke 9. 31). The heart of redemption's scheme is the propitiatory sacrifice of Christ, and the heart of the propitiation is the blood and these three are set forth in Rom. 3. 24, 25 above. It is an infinitely righteous (or just) Person whose death provides the infinite merit by which God justifies the sinner (1 John 2. 1, 2; Acts 3. 14; 7. 52; 22. 14; 1 Peter 3. 18; Heb. 1. 9; 7. 2).

God's justifying grace comes into operation through faith. This is stated at least thirty times in Rom. 3. 22-5. 2 and Gal. 2. 16-3. 26. Few things are so much insisted on, and few things have encountered such opposition. 'Justification by faith' was not only the war cry of the Reformation; it is the heart of the Gospel message. Article XI of the Church of England states it simply and admirably: 'We are accounted righteous before God, only for the merit of our Lord and Saviour Jesus Christ, by faith, and not for our own works or deservings. Wherefore, that we are justified by faith only is a most wholesome doctrine.'

God does not justify *on account of* faith, but *by* faith; that is, faith has nothing to do with the ground of justification. Neither as an act nor as a state of mind does faith afford any basis for God to justify man. Neither does God accept faith in lieu of righteousness. Faith is the reception of God's offer (John 1. 12). Saving faith comes from the heart (Rom. 10. 9, 10). It is there by reason of 'hearing' and the 'word' (Rom. 10. 17).

When Paul has fully dealt with the doctrine of justification by faith, he raises immediately (Rom. 6. 1) the question that men have ever raised against evangelical teaching about justification, clear proof that this teaching is in line with that of the New Testament. The objection is that, if justification is not on account of personal moral goodness, then all necessity of good works is denied; a man may just as well go on with any sin he likes. If good works are needed for justification (whether after or before), as Romanists and others assert, then this objection cannot be raised. If Paul had only meant that ceremonial works cannot justify, how easily he could have explained it by just saying so. But he answers the objection completely by showing how and why sanctification follows justification, without in any way qualifying his doctrine about justification.

That good works of any kind have no part in our justification is evident from the fact that the ground of justification is always presented as something objective to us, not subjective, something done for us, not in us. Further, good works of any kind have a show of merit, or provide ground for boasting (Rom. 11. 6; 3. 27) and this would exclude grace (Rom. 4. 4). Anything, however good in itself, is expressly rejected in this matter (Phil. 3. 6-9; Tit. 3. 5).

James, in 2. 14-26, is often supposed to be in opposition to Paul's teaching in Romans, but the cases and viewpoints are entirely different. Paul wrote to believers and discusses the 'works' of unbelievers, James wrote to Jews of the Dispersion (Jas. 1. 1, R.V.) about the works or lack of works in professing believers—'if anyone *say* he has faith.' Paul dealt with human merit and legalism, James with intellectual but dead orthodoxy. Paul took Gen 15. to show how Abraham was justified, James took Gen. 22 to manifest the proof of Abraham's justification. Calvin says, 'It is faith alone which justifies and yet the faith which justifies is not alone.' The New Testament speaks a great deal about the works of believers, whether as morally good or attractively good (Tit. 2. 14; 3. 1).

(III). *What the effects of Justification are.* Justification effects three things for those who receive it. These are discussed in Rom. 5.

(*a*) It brings peace with God. The justified man has entered into a new standing with God and all the great question of sin has now been settled. Purged and at peace he can now serve the God against whom he formerly rebelled (Heb. 9. 14). The conscience is satisfied because the justification has been pronounced by God (Rom. 8. 33). If the death of Christ has not only satisfied, but glorified God, then the believer finds absolute peace. First, because his sins are gone, God does not impute his trespasses unto him (Rom. 4. 7, 8). Second, there is no legal charge can be brought against him (Rom. 8. 33), for as our Lord Himself explained, he does not come into judgment (John 5. 24), but third, he has been brought into a position of favour, accepted in One beloved (Eph. 1. 6).

(*b*) Justification not only produces peace because it includes pardon, it also brings about reconciliation (Rom. 5. 10). A pardoned murderer may go free, but he has no reason to believe that his judge, or even his pardoner, will fraternize with him. But our justification produces reconciliation, the transaction is a real one; it is a spiritual fact, not a legal fiction. God remembers our sins no more (Heb. 10. 17); we remember them, but have no more conscience of them (Heb. 10. 2, 22). The death of Christ has effected peace (Eph. 2. 13, 16), as God Himself planned (2 Cor. 5. 18, 19) and now God bids men accept His message of reconciliation (2 Cor. 5. 20). The reconciliation is so complete that our Judge becomes our Father, adopting us into His bosom and family (Gal. 3. 24-26).

(*c*) Justification also gives a title to life (Rom. 5. 17, 18, 21). Since it gives us a title to sonship, sonship gives us a title to the inheritance of God (Rom. 8. 17; Gal. 4. 7). The man whom God counts righteous is thus entitled to eternal life (Rev. 22. 14, R.V.; Rom. 8. 30). This title rests not on anything we are in ourselves, nor on anything that we may possess in the way of righteous acts: our sole title to it is in the justifying blood of Christ. The latest born child of God is as certain of it as the oldest saint. The earliest Gospel explanation of our Lord's ministry makes it crystal clear (John 3. 15, 16): John's own summary of the content of his Gospel reiterates the truth (John 20. 31).

Sanctification

Paul finishes the proof of his doctrine of justification before he embarks on that of sanctification, thus keeping them absolutely distinct. While they are inseparable in experience—every justified man is sanctified too—they are logically distinct. To justify is to count righteous, but to sanctify is to reckon and make holy: the one is something done *for* us, the other is something done *to* us. Justification removes the believer from the custody of God's judgment court, sanctification translates him into God's presence chamber (Heb. 10. 19-22).

The development from justification to sanctification is shadowed in Rom. 5. 12-21. Those from Adam to Moses died, solely because of their relation to Adam and not because they personally had sinned by breaking the law for which he died (Rom. 5. 13, 14). Those in Christ live (justification of life) solely because of their relation to Christ, established by faith, and not because of any righteousness of their own, whether inherent, legal, or imparted. But those from Adam to Moses, and all his descendants, were in fact sinners and unholy and this fact also springs from their relation to Adam; so believers are in fact holy and this springs from their relation to Christ. Thus Rom. 6 plunges into the believer's union, or identification with Christ.

The believer is a holy person. This fact is established from the following considerations:

(*a*) God says so, by express statements in His Word.

'Them that have been sanctified by faith in Me' (Acts 26. 18).

'Them that have been sanctified in Christ Jesus' (1 Cor. 1. 2).

'Ye were sanctified . . . in the name of the Lord Jesus Christ' (1 Cor. 6. 11).

'By the which will we are sanctified' (Heb. 10. 10).

'Them that are sanctified by God the Father' (Jude 1).

Notice the tenses used, and to what the sanctification is attributed.

(*b*) The name which the New Testament adopts for believers is 'saints' (about sixty times from Acts 9. 13 onwards). The name derives from our Lord, 'the Holy One of God' (Luke 4. 34), and our title to it is found in our union with Him (Heb. 2. 11; John 17. 19). It has nothing whatever to do with canonized celebrities, but everything with our divine calling and election (1 Peter 1. 1, 2). We are 'called' saints (Rom. 1. 7; Eph. 1. 4; 1 Thess. 4. 7, R.V.).

(*c*) The experimental access which believers have into the presence of God, the boldness with which they are invited to draw near (Heb. 10. 19), the 'Abba' which springs up in their heart (Rom. 8. 15, 16) proves that they are at ease in His presence, they must be holy. It is in this connection that the Lord says 'Behold I and the children' (Heb. 2. 13, 11).

It was in virtue of the sanctifying blood of the Day of Atonement (Lev. 16) that the Israelite could draw near to God for a whole year. That blood needed annual renewal (Heb. 10. 3, 4), but the blood that sanctifies the believer is perpetually efficacious (Heb. 10. 10, 14). No stronger words could be found—'He has perfected the sanctified ones in perpetuity'—'we have been sanctified once for all.'

Rom. 6 proceeds from this point. Christ died to sin once for all (Rom. 6. 10, R.V., marg. Gk.), even so are we counted dead to sin. He lives to God, and so do we, in Him. As He is, so are we (1 John 4. 17).

We are not yet speaking of the *attribute* of holiness or of cleansing from defilement, but of that position occupied by the believer in virtue of the blood of Christ. It is not to be dismissed as a mere technicality. Practical holiness depends on this. We are not sanctified positionally because we practise holiness (we can never say that we are perfectly holy in our walk or character) (1 John 1. 10), but we can practise holy living because we have been set apart by God Himself in union with our Holy Lord, by the Holy Spirit. 'To set apart,' is, of course, the primary significance of 'to sanctify'; from the usage of the word we can see that one personally and perfectly holy like our Lord can be sanctified (John 17. 19), or even one unsaved and unholy can be set apart (1 Cor. 7. 14). Amoral things can be sanctified, too, like the tabernacle and its furniture (Lev. 8. 10, 11).

Rom. 6 sets out this 'setting apart' as a transfer. Taken from the unholy grasp of sin's tyranny, we are now slaves of God. That which is God's is holy, devoted and sanctified.

Just as a vessel, once devoted to God, was sacred for ever and had to be maintained holy by use and cleansed if defiled, so holiness of life is enjoined on the believer. He must practise holiness (1 Peter 1. 15, 16, R.V.). He must not practise sin (1 John 2. 1). Rom. 6. 12 immediately makes this demand and it is continued and stressed down to the end of the chapter. To practise truth, godliness and holiness is the simple duty of those that are Christ's and it is the evidence that they are His (1 John 3. 7).

In Rom. 7 Paul shows from his own experience, that doing the will of God cannot be achieved by the law, or by self-effort, any more than justification can. In chapter 8 he reveals the secret of the new spiritual law by which the righteous requirement of the law is fulfilled in those who walk after the Spirit (see R.V.). Just as justification sprang from Christ's work *for* us, so sanctification springs from the Spirit's work *in* us. Wedded to law, our members brought forth abortions, death (Rom. 7. 5). What is required of us is that we submit to be led of the Spirit of God (Rom. 8. 14). He will never lead into sin, but into a faith contemplation of Christ (2 Cor. 3. 17, 18) which produces spiritual growth.

So that practical holiness consists of two things:

1. That we are not to let sin reign in us, for we are not bound to obey sin (Rom. 6. 12, 22; 8. 12).

2. That we are to be governed by the Spirit, who will develop in us the image of Christ progressively (Gal. 5. 18, 22).

It is on this ground that consecration is introduced (Rom. 12. 1, 2). Because he is holy and acceptable, the believer can and ought to be consecrated to the performance of God's will for him, whatever that may be (Rom. 12. 3-8). Consecration is not, as commonly supposed, the bringing of an imperfect, stained life to God for deliverance and empowerment, but it is the bringing to Him of a set-apart, Spirit-led person, soul and body to be used of Him as He will.

The Believer's Conflict and the Two Natures. It is abundantly clear that every provision has been made for the believer's deliverance from sin's power and for his being like Christ (Heb. 7. 25; 2 Cor. 7. 1; 2 Peter 1. 3, 4). It is equally clear that no believer is perfectly free from sin in this life (1 John 1. 8, 10). This is due to the fact that in every Christian there is a mixture of good and evil. There is the new nature, created in true holiness (Eph. 4. 24), which is to be worn and there is the old, the flesh, as bad as the other is good (Rom. 7. 18), which is to be discarded. These two are in continuous conflict, being utterly contrary the one to the other (Gal. 5. 17). Paul not only asserts this of the Galatian believers, but gives it as his own personal experience (Rom. 7. 14-25). This conflict is unremitting while in the body, but the way of victory is clear. As we walk by the Spirit the flesh is rendered powerless (Gal. 5. 16, 18, 25; Rom. 8. 2).

The last step of the Christian pathway is final deliverance from 'the law of sin which is in my members,' when the body shall be changed into the image of the Lord Jesus (Phil. 3. 20, 21; 1 John 3. 2).

CHAPTER XVIII

The Church and the Churches

G. C. D. HOWLEY

THE normal Christian life as seen in the New Testament has a double-sided character; it is lived out personally and individually, but it is also lived in conjunction with other Christians. Dr. J. S. Whale puts the matter thus tersely: 'Though an intensely personal matter, faith is never a purely private matter. Man, as God has made him, is an individual ego, but not an isolated ego' (*Christian Doctrine*, p. 126). From the first moments of our Christian experience there rises within us an urge for the company of others like-minded, a desire for their fellowship. And we are being true to this sound spiritual instinct when we find our place in a congregation, or church, of believers. 'I do not think,' says Dr. James Denney, 'the New Testament contemplates the existence of unattached Christians—persons who have accepted the Christian salvation, and embraced the Christian ideal and vocation—but who are not members of a church. The Christian end can never be attained, either for ourselves or for others, except by the mutual action and reaction, the reciprocal giving and receiving, of all who are in fellowship with Christ. What the brethren have is indispensable to us; what we have is indispensable to them' (*Studies in Theology*, p. 188).

But where may we look for this company? The sad divisions of Christendom warn us not to take all that we see as being necessarily right. Indeed, we can find almost every degree of variation in thought among them until the extremes pass far beyond all legitimate Scriptural boundaries. But despite the confusion, we need not be groping in the dark. All life is one, and the New Testament was given to us to provide for Christian life and godliness, in all its aspects. We may find there direction for our private spiritual life, but also—and this must not be overlooked—we are given all necessary guidance for the right observance of our corporate life. It is a curious thing that this fact is not always acknowledged. Many evangelical Christians will readily admit the authority and sufficiency of the Bible for personal life, yet fail to see how illogical it is to dispute its adequacy for matters of church life.

The teachings imparted to the first disciples (Acts 2. 42, R.V.) were derived from Christ Himself; and this is certainly true of the New Testament teaching concerning the Church. Our Lord's use of words was always discriminating and in His references to the Church (*ekklesia*) He was using a term familiar to His disciples. The word is found in the Septuagint as a translation of the Hebrew *qahal*, meaning the congregation or assembly of Jehovah. It was also in common usage in Greek life, denoting the assembly of free citizens of a Greek city. 'In the actual usage of both *qahal* and *ekklesia* the primary idea of summoning is hardly to be felt. They mean simply an assembly of the people' (*The Christian Ecclesia*, p. 6).

Simon Peter's confession of faith at Cæsarea Philippi was the result of a divine revelation, and it is this fact of revelation, the truth of Christ's Person, which is the rock-foundation of the Church. This Peter himself is careful to explain to us, in his illuminating commentary on the words of the Lord: 'To whom coming, a living stone . . . ye also, as living stones, are built up. . . .' (1 Peter 2. 4, 5, R.V.). The thought of the congregation of God (i.e. Israel) would be replaced in the minds of the disciples, by the larger thought of the congregation of the redeemed, the spiritual edifice composed of living stones, that the Lord spoke of building (Matt. 16. 18). The Church as seen here is, then, the Church universal, the whole company of believers of the Christian age, being viewed as one. And this is the conception that dominates Paul's thinking in his Prison Epistles, when he speaks of the exalted Christ as 'Head of the Body, the Church' (Col. 1. 18). 'The Church, which is His Body' (Eph. 1. 22, 23) is Paul's description of what Christ called 'My Church,' the Church viewed in its all-embracing sense, as comprehending *all* the redeemed from Pentecost until the Lord's return. The Church holds a place in relation to the purposes of God that is altogether unique and which will be seen fully when it stands before Christ, presented 'to Himself a glorious Church, not having spot, or wrinkle, or any such thing; but that it should be holy and without blemish' (Eph. 5. 27).

But Christ used the word in another setting, and an examination of the passage (Matt. 18. 15-20) makes evident that here He refers not to the Church universal, but to a congregation of disciples meeting together locally in His name, that is, with His authority and as partaking in some degree, of His character. The perfection and triumph that characterize the Church universal is not fully seen in the church local, for this very passage treats of the imperfection that is seen in some of the members, being manifested in a personal difference. But those two passages are all-important, providing as they do, not only the germ of all later New Testament teaching, but a standard by which we may test all conceptions or interpretations of men as to the Church. It may be said, therefore, that the Church, viewed universally, is invisible, spiritual, a living organism; but viewed locally it is a visible and (to some extent) organized community. Viewed universally we may contemplate its heavenly calling and relationships; but viewed locally we must consider the purpose of its existence against an earthly background. Bishop Hooker has said, in a well-known passage, 'That Church of Christ, which we properly term His body mystical, can be but one; neither can that one be sensibly discerned by any man, inasmuch as the parts thereof are some in heaven already with Christ, and the rest that are on earth (albeit, their natural persons be visible) we do not discern under this property whereby they are truly and infallibly of that body. . . . For the lack of diligent observing the difference, first between the Church of God mystical and visible, . . . the oversights are neither few nor light that have been committed' (*Ecclesiastical Polity*, Book III, 1).

The Acts of the Apostles is Luke's inspired record of the origins of Christianity, and, as we consider it side by side with the Epistles, we may compare the historical account with the theological explanation. Christ's ascension was followed by the descent of the Holy Spirit at Pentecost, and His advent vitally linked the disciples on earth with their risen Lord. They thus became members of His mystical Body, therefore 'members one of another' (Rom. 12. 5). The direct result of the Spirit's coming was the preaching of the Gospel, and as the message of Christ spread abroad, those who believed, spontaneously acknowledged the bond uniting them, by associating together; in this manner local 'societies' or congregations sprang into existence wherever disciples were found. R. W. Dale said, 'Only those who are in Christ have any right to be in the Church' (*Essays and Addresses*, p. 123), with which we may couple the words of Ignatius, 'Wherever Jesus Christ is, there is the Catholic Church' (*Epistle to Smyrna*, c. 8). Men and women were being converted to God and united to Christ, thus His presence was with them, and so the churches developed and multiplied. The Church was in process of construction, according to Christ's words, and its life was finding local expression in the churches of the saints (1 Cor. 14. 33).

These Christian assemblies were marked by fellowship; *koinonia* is one of the great New Testament ideas, that of partnership, a sharing in common. The disciples shared a common life derived from the ascended Lord. The Pentecostal phase of having 'all things common' (Acts 2. 44) might pass, as far as community of goods was concerned, but it has always persisted in its deepest sense, through the long centuries of Christian history. Those who composed the membership of local churches were, at the first, all of them persons with a saving experience of Jesus Christ, and there is no justification for enlarging the scope of membership to-day. A local church, is, properly, an assembly of *Christians*, though ever seeking to embrace others as members by the spread of the Gospel. The bond uniting disciples is, therefore, real, vital, spiritual, and Scripture enjoins us to be 'giving diligence to keep the unity of the Spirit in the bond of peace' (Eph. 4. 3, R.V.); to 'be at peace among yourselves' (1 Thess. 5. 13, R.V.); to 'follow after things which make for peace, and things whereby we may edify one another' (Rom. 14. 19, R.V.). The recognition of our oneness in Christ should create in us a desire to strengthen and help one another, by every means at our disposal, so that there is a common growth evident, a growing up together into Christ. It has been well said, 'Christian character needs the community for development, for it is only possible in fellowship with members of the Christian Church' (W. H. G. Thomas, *Principles of Theology*, pp. 267-8). The inner strengthening and integration of character of the members of a church by their sharing in common both privilege and responsibility produces the finest type of Christian, for it is certain that we cannot attain unto the higher reaches of spiritual experience apart from this nourishment derived through the mutual contribution of our 'fellow-members of the Body.'

The increase in the number of churches in apostolic times reveals the instructive fact that the ordinary practice of the missionaries was to consolidate their work and then leave each church to stand directly responsible to Christ. 'They commended them to the Lord, on whom they had believed' (Acts 14. 23, R.V.). There was no federating into one large group, or even smaller, national or district groups of churches—each church developed and maintained its own administration of affairs, under Christ. An excellent definition of an independent church has been given as follows: 'An "Independent Church" is one which possesses all the ordinances appointed by its Lord for ministering Him to the world and which is therefore able to stand on its own spiritual feet and to act responsibly as the Church of God in the place where it is set' (D. T. Jenkins, *The Nature of Catholicity*, p. 105). And Denney observes: 'Their internal independence is plain from every page of the epistles. . . . But these local churches, reciprocally independent as they were, were nevertheless one. . . . The bond that united them to each other as churches was the same as the bond which united the members in any one of them among themselves; it was their common reception of the love of God in Christ Jesus; their common acceptance of the obligations which receiving that love imposed. They freely recognized each other's Christianity—each other's membership in the Church—in various effective ways. They sent commissioners, duly elected, to each other; they gave letters of commendation to their own members, which found welcome for them in Christian societies elsewhere; they had a lively interest in each other, and in times of distress contributed liberally for the relief of those most hardly pressed. They formed a living and sympathetic unity, a new humanity within the bosom of the old; . . . it was one body, only because there was one Spirit in it' (Dr. Denney, *Studies in Theology*, p. 187-8).

The autonomous character of each local church is a divine principle, but the tendency has ever been for churches to federate, form their unions, make circles from which some believers are almost inevitably excluded. Yet each church derives its life, as a church, from Christ, and must, ultimately, work out for itself the very purpose of its existence. The New Testament never conceives the mystical Body as being made up of the aggregate of the churches, but as composed of all the members of Christ. This may appear self-evident, but history does not lack examples of the readiness of some, often earnest Christians, to 'un-church' others, equally devout, from whom they may happen to differ. The principle of the independence of the local church, once perceived, will deliver men from forming circles of fellowship that would degenerate simply into sects, for sectarianism is essentially a failure to consider and embrace in our affections *all* who belong to Christ. No local assembly on earth is subject to the jurisdiction of any other such church, nor need it submit to the ruling of visiting evangelists or teachers or those other than its own spiritual leaders. Federation may appear to strengthen, as things become controlled from some centre, but it is really a constant source of weakness. Let an enemy strike at the nerve-centre of a movement and it will become paralysed to its remotest bounds; but maintain the purity of New Testament truth—that of independency—and each church will stand, flourish or fall, according to the manner in which it maintains its living relationship to Christ. But will this make for disharmony and indiscipline? Surely not: for the bond linking the churches is the strongest of all bonds, that resulting from the presence of the living Christ in the midst of each one. *He* unites His people, yet deals with each assembly according to its spiritual condition. This is the beautiful conception given us in the vision and messages delivered to the aged John in Patmos—the Lord standing, and walking in the midst of the golden lampstands; each church standing separately, yet all united in Christ. Thus independency never becomes independency of Christ, nor, in the last analysis, anything other than a gracious acknowledgment of and friendly disposition towards the life and activities of other such churches (Col. 4. 16).

But the administrative independence of the local church not only concerns its relations with other Christian congregations, but also its relation to the State. This question of State control has frequently been a matter of controversy in Europe, particularly during and since the Reformation. James I was the hope of the Puritans. He had been 'brought up in Scotland, where episcopacy had been abolished and the State Church had become Calvinistic and Presbyterian. James was destined to disappoint the Puritans. . . . Presbyterianism he rejected because he hated its democratic tendencies. "No Bishop, no king," he remarked; adding, "A Scottish Presbytery as well agreeth with a monarchy as God and the devil. Then Jack and Tom, and Will, and Dick shall meet, and at their pleasure censure me and my Council, and all our proceedings: then Will shall stand up and say, it must be thus; then Dick shall reply and say, nay . . . but we will have it thus"' (A. C. Underwood, *A History of the English Baptists*, pp. 32-3). This gives an amusing sidelight on the outlook of those times. It appears to have been the set purpose of the king to wield an influence in ecclesiastical affairs, and to this end to maintain episcopacy in the Established Church. The unadorned picture of the New Testament is of churches independent of all outside control, whether that of the State or of other churches, but expressing and developing the life that God had implanted.

While these churches were spheres of loving fellowship, we must not fall into the error of viewing them as groups possessing no order. In his remarkable outline of Church history, *Christianity*, (p. 60) Dr. Edwyn Bevan has said: 'Christianity from the very beginning had in it two strains which might seem contradictory, which have in fact often led to conflict in the history of the Church, but which were both necessary to the life of the Body. There was the note of obedience to authority, and there was the note of free individual action and utterance according to the impulse of the Spirit.' From the first, we read of elders in connection with the churches, never merely one presiding elder but a group, referred to collectively as 'the presbytery' or 'elderhood' (Darby) (1 Tim. 4. 14). The brief summary of the manner in which Paul and Barnabas consolidated their missionary work is instructive, for it appears to be recorded as a sample of the normal practice of the apostolic age (Acts 14. 21-28, R.V.). The disciples were confirmed in the faith; 'they appointed for them elders in every church, . . . they commended them to the Lord, on whom they had believed' (Acts 14. 23, R.V.). The churches seem hardly to have been properly constituted until elders had been appointed. And this was a feature of all the New Testament churches—they were not left in disorder or even to develop their own system of order, but guidance was given by those who founded the work, missionaries or evangelists.

Assemblies of Christians need spiritual leadership, and God has indicated plainly His will in this matter. The later letters of Paul reveal the need for maintaining a succession of godly elders, whether in churches recently established (as may have been the case in Crete, where Titus went for a period), or in those that had been in existence for a longer time (as in the case of Ephesus, where Timothy had gone). The language used leaves no doubt that apostolic churches were marked by definite government. The word 'elder' refers to the office, while 'bishop' (Anglo-Saxon *biscop*, from Greek *episkopos*, 'overseer') has reference to the function of the elders, exercising oversight. We read of them that are 'over you in the Lord' (1 Thess. 5. 12), those who stand before, supervise, or take the lead, whose jurisdiction is a spiritual one exercised 'in the Lord.' Diligence is to mark their rule (Rom. 12. 8). The New Testament also describes them as 'them that have the rule over you' (Heb. 13. 17, 24); the verb here (*hegeomai*) means 'to lead' and gives, again, the idea of governing. While these terms lay emphasis upon rule, leadership and guidance, certain pastoral verbs are used also, so that we read of 'feeding' and 'tending' the flock (Acts 20. 28; 1 Peter 5. 2, R.V.), and thus find that the rule of the elders is not dictatorial but that of shepherds. The people of God will always need this element of guidance, and we can discern, even in apostolic times, the need of saints, in such widely separated areas as Macedonia, Rome and Asia Minor.

When we turn to consider the kind of persons who are to hold office as elders in an assembly, the principal stress is laid upon qualities of character. They are to be persons of discretion and sober judgment, blameless in reputation, maintaining all purity in their domestic affairs, revealing in their homes the very qualities of leadership, that will be seen in the larger family circle of the assembly of believers. If the church is described as a house (or household) of God, the elders are God's stewards in His household

(Tit. 1. 7), and must conduct themselves and the affairs of their ministry as those 'that must give account' (Heb. 13. 17). Those who take the oversight of the saints should be veritable princes of the church, princely in spiritual demeanour. Thus the criticism of the world is silenced, and the flock of God will gladly follow such shepherds. Their ministry will involve guidance and direction; they will encourage all true gift where it is evident; they will give counsel in spiritual matters; they will deal firmly with disorderly elements, should these appear; they will lead with the force of moral authority, their labours being their credentials to rulership; in short, all that is involved in the words 'admonish you' (1 Thess. 5. 12) will mark their service. In addition, they are to uphold a standard of sound (i.e. wholesome) doctrine, which will provide a stable background for all the life and service of the church (Tit. 1. 9, R.V.).

The matter of the placing of elders in their office is of considerable importance. There are those who teach that, because there are no apostles to-day, elders cannot be appointed. This is a mistaken judgment. In apostolic times there were not two alternative methods for installing elders in their office; all were elders by appointment. But by no means all the churches had been established by apostles; many were the result of the labours of servants of Christ unknown to us by name, and without apostolic status. It seems clear, therefore, that when Paul and Barnabas appointed elders, they did so, not in their capacity as apostles, but as missionaries and evangelists.

It is significant to observe, in this connection, that in Acts we find two balancing elements in regard to elders: 'They appointed for them elders in every church' (Acts 14. 23, R.V.), yet when Paul addressed the elders of Ephesus (obviously elders by appointment, according to Paul's custom), he speaks of them being made overseers by the Holy Spirit (Acts 20. 28). There was firstly, the evidence of God's call to this work, seen in loving care for the flock; this was followed by the appointment of such persons to office. Passing over some years to the Pastoral Epistles, we can find these same two elements, for, when writing to Timothy, Paul speaks of the inborn desire for the 'good work' of an overseer (i.e. the Spirit-given burden of care for God's people) (1 Tim. 3. 1); but writing to

Titus, he charges him to appoint elders in every city (Tit. 1. 5). It must be carefully noted that the gap of several years saw no alteration in the mode of installation to office and that, throughout that period, men who gave evidence of a divine call and fitness for this ministry, were duly appointed as elders, not by popular election, but by those already exercising spiritual authority. To-day the churches are never to be at the mercy of any persons who may imagine themselves suitable to take oversight, but those who are already elders in a church, as they discern the qualities of an overseer in one and another, will appoint such men as elders, 'without prejudice, doing nothing by partiality' (1 Tim. 5. 21, R.V.). Such elders will command the respect and affection of God's people, who are enjoined so to regard them and, if necessary, to obey them (1 Thess. 5. 12, 13; Heb. 13. 17).

In his book, *The Primitive Church*, the late Canon B. H. Streeter strongly urged that there were considerable divergencies of church order in the different apostolic churches, and he says, 'The history of Catholic Christianity during the first five centuries is the history of a progressive standardization of a diversity which had its origin in the Apostolic Age' (p. 47). Against this theory must be set the frequent statements of the Apostle Paul, when writing to the Corinthians, to the effect that his rulings, for both personal and church life, were not for Corinth alone but for 'all the churches of the saints' (1 Cor. 14. 33; 1. 2; 4. 17; 7. 17; 11. 16; 16. 1). The ordering of the churches was essentially the same throughout the Empire, in the first age of Christianity, and we have no authority for modification, nor is this necessary.

The claims of episcopacy have been reasserted in a large volume edited by the Bishop of Oxford, entitled *The Apostolic Ministry*. In its review of this book *The Times Literary Supplement* said, 'All these contentions will be firmly rejected by non-episcopal communions as well as by some at least within the Church of England. And the hard fact is that nothing approaching proof is possible on the evidence that is available. . . . And, in the last resort, there is only one way in which such claims may be tested: that is by reference to the biblical doctrine of the Church' (May 17th, 1947). Eusebius mentions in his *Ecclesiastical History* that, for some years before his time, pilgrims were shown the episcopal chair actually used by James, the brother of the Lord (Eusebius, H. E., VII. 19. 1). Streeter shrewdly comments, 'What explanation was given of its marvellous survival through two destructions of the city we are not told; possibly no one asked so tactless a question' (*The Primitive Church*, pp. 42-3). We need not press the lesson on our readers, except to quote an admission by Dr. Edwyn Bevan: 'If we read to-day the letters of Ignatius, Bishop of Antioch (martyred in Rome about 115), with their continued insistence on each local church obeying its bishop, they seem to strike a note very unlike that of the first-century documents included in our New Testament' (*Christianity*, p. 70). The simple fact remains that we cannot improve on the Scriptural 'elderhood'—a number of saintly men guiding the Lord's flock heavenward.

The churches were, however, marked also by the provision of other ministries; the reference to the 'overseers and ministers' (Phil. 1. 1, Darby) reveals two distinct groups serving the assembly. The first we have already considered; the second would suggest certain persons engaging in specific ministries in the local congregation. The transliteration of the word 'deacon' is unfortunate, as we always tend to interpret the Bible by current practice, rather than putting everything first to the test of Holy Scripture. The word *diakonos* is used elsewhere but it is always translated 'minister' or 'servant' except in two passages (Phil. 1. 1; 1 Tim. 3. 8-13). Now who were these deacons? They may have engaged in caring for the temporal side of the business of a church, but undoubtedly their ministry ranged wider than that only. We may say that their scope of service would embrace ministries both spiritual and temporal, and that they were, as serving publicly amongst the believers, to be persons of proved fitness for their tasks. The counsel to 'women' (1 Tim. 3. 11, R.V.) in the context dealing with deacons, indicates that there would also be certain Christian women having specific service to render in connection with the church, and their requisite qualities are therefore similarly indicated. Phoebe is the New Testament example of this 'sisterly-service' and is described as 'a servant of the church which is at Cenchrea' (Rom. 16. 1). Her succouring ministry had apparently left its impression on the district of Corinth, and she travelled to Rome with a reputation enhanced by apostolic commendation.

There is a sense in which *all* the members of a local assembly have responsibility, and 'fellowship' implies this very idea. This does not contradict, but supplements, the fact of particular ministries that may be entrusted to a minority. The provision of ministries in a gathering of Christians, through development from within the church of that which lies latent, is explained through the sovereign endowment of God, by the Holy Spirit. Many will be given service of a private nature, while others will express their gift in the church meetings. 'God hath set some in the church' (1 Cor. 12. 28) and His ordering is always perfect. The early churches made provision for the recognition and development of spiritual gifts, and the gatherings were characterized by a freedom for those gifts to be exercised. It is not to be supposed that an assembly meeting is an occasion for any persons to act just as they think fit, without reference to their general capacity and a sense of the fitness of things. Edification and order were to mark the assembly, and Paul laid down valuable ruling principles for the guidance of the churches, both then and for all time (1 Cor. 14). The company of believers coming together in dependence upon God, will find that His mind will be made known in their midst, as He leads them by the Spirit. But let us try to understand what this 'leading of the Spirit' is: it is not necessarily indicated by emotion or impulse. The combination of the two ideas, 'with the spirit' and 'with the understanding also' (1 Cor. 14. 15) shows that the guidance of the Holy Spirit will come to those with subject spirits, and minds quick to judge the suitability of the occasion for any particular contribution they may be exercised to make. In other words, the emphasis is laid by the apostle, upon the use of spiritual judgment on the part of the brethren, and in their discerning participation in the meetings, the mind of God will be revealed. This is no claim to infallibility for any person, but as brethren take part according to the guiding principles laid down for us there will be peace, order and edification marking the gatherings of the church, and men will discern that God walks amongst His people (1 Cor. 14. 25). How different this from what might be supposed to prevail, were we to judge from the unfortunate statement made by the late Dr. Hensley Henson, 'The Dissenters are handicapped by the weakness of their systems, the crudity of their distinctive beliefs and the repulsiveness of their "corybantic" methods' (*The Church of England*, p. 238).

All this leads us on to the question of human ordination, for it is frequently overlooked that there was no suggestion in the early churches of any special person or status being required for the celebration of the Lord's Supper. Similarly, in the assemblies of believers, those who participated publicly were those gifted of God for the purpose. One of the pioneer lay-preachers of the seventeenth century was Captain John Spencer, an officer in the Parliamentary Army. 'In 1641 he published *A Short Treatise concerning the lawfulness of every man's exercising his gift as God shall call him thereunto*. This produced a reply which throws some light on the times. *New Preachers, Greene the Feltmaker, Spencer the Horse-rubber, Quartermine the Brewers Clerke, with some few others, that are mighty sticklers in this new kind of talking trade, which many ignorant Coxcombes call Preaching*' (A. C. Underwood, *A History of the English Baptists*, p. 76). Captain Spencer's tract seems to have stirred some vested interest of the day! History reveals the readiness with which men turn away from the freedom of action so characteristic of the primitive churches and fasten upon believers, man-made regulations, forming minority-groups of special ministers with unique powers, so that, in its extremest expression, 'the Church' is equated with the hierarchy rather than with the whole congregation. There is, however, no finer training-ground for the service of God than a local assembly of believers, where the members develop and fulfil their particular ministry. The Apostle Peter gives us a glimpse of such a church at work: 'According as each hath received a gift, ministering it among yourselves, as good stewards of the manifold grace of God; if any man speaketh, speaking as it were oracles of God; if any man ministereth, ministering as of the strength which God supplieth: that in all things God may be glorified through Jesus Christ' (1 Peter 4. 10, 11, R.V.). Here is an ordered freedom—liberty, but in subjection to Christ as Lord, the diverse spiritual ministries of a church confirming that its members have been 'enriched in Him, in all utterance and all knowledge' (1 Cor. 1. 5, R.V.).

While men are permitted to lead the proceedings in the church gatherings, the apostle lays it down that the women are to be in quietness (1 Cor. 14. 34). Women are not permitted by Scripture to lead publicly in the assembly, though their presence and spiritual influence is of an importance second to none. They have, however, a wide range of service in church life, and their ministries amongst other women-folk, in young people's work and in other spheres, have been abundantly owned and blessed by God, both in the home-land and in missionary service abroad.

We have already seen that the churches appear in the Apocalypse under the symbol of golden lampstands (Rev. 1-3). They stand as witness to Christ and His truth. Their internal life, fellowship and ministries are to the end that they may work out that which God is working in them and that they 'shine as lights in the world, holding forth the word of life' (Phil. 2. 15, 16). The local church is a sphere illuminated by the very light of God, as revealed in Christ, and the light is to be conveyed to men. This must be primarily the work of God, but His people are called to co-operate with Him, that the witness of Christ may be carried to those in darkness. Let the church be in a right attitude and spirit towards God, then the Holy Spirit will operate through the believers, and the work of 'sounding out the word of the Lord' (1 Thess. 1. 8) will readily be done, with spiritual power and signs of blessing.

The ministry of the Gospel is *one* work, wherever it may be done; and while the primary duty of an assembly is to convey the truth of God to those immediately around, it carries a responsibility also to consider the wider field of the world. The earliest missionary impulse was awakened by the scattering of the Jerusalem church through persecution. Later, we find the hand of God laid upon two of His choicest servants, whose divine call to travel with the Gospel was confirmed by the discernment of their brethren at Antioch. So they released them for this fresh ministry, and they went forth, 'being sent forth by the Holy Ghost' (Acts 13. 1-4). They travelled, not as the servants of the church at Antioch, but as God's servants (Acts 16. 17), subject to no central authority but following, as God opened their way, the divine leading. The direct result of their preaching was that those who had believed came together and formed local churches, and thus fresh centres of light and testimony sprang into being over the ground they had covered.

The pattern of apostolic missionary enterprise abides; it has been tried and found still to be entirely adequate for modern requirements. As the Holy Spirit burdens men and women with an urge to carry the Gospel to the regions beyond, their divine call will find confirmation in the hearts of their brethren and they will go forth, commended by the church, but sent forth by the Holy Spirit. Such persons go 'for the sake of the Name . . . taking nothing of the Gentiles'; they are therefore to be set forward on their ministry 'worthily of God' (3 John 6, 7, R.V.). They will travel, labour for Christ and preach His Word, and it is the privilege of the believers to provide them with adequate support and provision for the expenses of their service, because 'the Lord ordained that they which preach the Gospel should live of the Gospel' (1 Cor. 9. 14). Thus, as the Gospel-seed is implanted in men's hearts, it bears fruit in lives saved from sin, in those lives becoming linked in the bonds of fellowship and in their pure and united witness to the One who has loosed them from their sins by His blood (Rev. 1. 5, R.V.).

A Christian assembly is distinguished from all human associations, societies or groups by virtue of the fact that God dwells amongst His people. And in the free exercise of the gifts He has bestowed, and in the overflowing of divine love through Christ's members, in the midst of the sin and darkness of this world, the presence and glory of God are manifested. To this end we should ever be 'with one soul striving for the faith of the Gospel' (Phil. 1. 27, R.V.); and as the believers assemble in the fear of God for their church gatherings, He will manifest Himself amongst them, and it will be known that He is among them indeed. We can crave no higher dignity nor sweeter blessing in the church, than such evidence of the overshadowing glory and presence of God.

It may be objected that the ideal of a church sketched in this paper is impossible of attainment, that this is merely a counsel of perfection; and we may be pointed to gatherings of Christians that seem far from the realization of such spiritual condition. Yet that is no reason to forego apostolic counsels; and it is well to remember that almost every church figuring prominently in the pages of the New Testament had its own peculiar difficulties and troubles. The perfect assembly of Christians has not yet been seen, but it is necessary to keep ever before us the pattern, that we may press forward unto a closer attainment to the revealed will of God.

In the early years of the seventeenth century a young man named John Smyth, who had been a Fellow of Christ's College, Cambridge, and who had developed a strong Puritan turn of mind, separated from the Church of England after much anxious consideration. He found a body of Separatists at Gainsborough and laboured amongst them until they were uprooted and many of them fled to Holland. Their solemn dedication to Christ as a church, marked by a genuine humility, modesty and expectancy, is worth recording and stands as an abiding challenge to us to-day. They had, 'as the Lord's free people joined themselves, by a covenant of the Lord, into a Church Estate in the fellowship of the Gospel to walk in all His ways made known or to be made known unto them, according to their best endeavours, whatsoever it might cost them, the Lord assisting them' (W. T. Whitley, *A History of British Baptists*, p. 20). May we, in all our church relationships, be found marked by a similar spirit.

CHAPTER XIX

Church Practices

WILLIAM HERON

AN examination of Church practices in apostolic times must be based on accurate and trustworthy historical knowledge. For this we need not go beyond the Acts of the Apostles by 'the beloved physician,' of whom Sir William Ramsay has said, 'this author should be placed along with the very greatest historians,' and again, 'Luke's history is unsurpassed in respect of its trustworthiness.' Before writing this treatize he had given in the Third Gospel an ordered account of 'all that Jesus began to do and to teach until the day in which He was taken up after that He, through the Holy Ghost had given commandment unto the Apostles whom He had chosen' (Acts I. I, 2), his aim being the assurance of Gentile believers in the trustworthiness of what they had learned. For historical authorship Luke was uniquely equipped. He had at his command the heritage of Greek historical writing and he had enjoyed the fellowship of some who had been Christians from the first and also the intimate companionship of Paul himself. The latter must have left nothing undone after his conversion to ascertain and communicate all he could about the Lord's commandments to His apostles. Luke knew how to use his material as a trained historian but infinitely better he enjoyed what we call inspiration, the guidance of the Holy Spirit whose acts he so faithfully records in his second writing. We thus have in his two 'books' a continuous history of Christian origins from the birth of John the Baptist to 60 A.D. approximately, an invaluable record for our present study.

When the baptism of His Cross and Passion had been accomplished and He was no longer straitened, our Lord continued through His Spirit and His Church the deeds and doctrine of His public ministry. In the Acts, Luke devotes his attention to the deeds rather than the doctrine, giving us 'the history which is the birthplace of every great doctrine,' and leaving it to the apostolic writings to expound the 'doctrine which controls and models practice.' As Rackham says, 'We can hardly overestimate the importance of the Acts of the Apostles—it is our chief authority, whether within or without the Bible for the history of the founding of the Church and its early growth.' Here we are right back at the beginnings and can examine their underlying principles in the written Word, the only permanent, unfailing standard of truth. This is especially needful to-day when human tradition, which naturally flatters the flesh, has led to the substitution of human rule for subjection to God's Word. With this record before us we dare not assert that the primitive Church was perfect nor can we expect to find perfection now but it is our duty to be zealous for the Lord's honour and to eschew everything in doctrine and Church practice contrary to God's order. 'We must obey God' was the controlling principle of the apostles and it should be ours.

The Church in the Acts is but a communion of believers in an exalted Saviour and can only be recognized as the House of God or Body of Christ with the help of the revelation given to us elsewhere. The nucleus consisted of the small company assembled in the upper room in Jerusalem, awaiting at the Lord's command the promise of the Father. Upon them, 'all together in one place' came the mysterious baptism of the Spirit with the audible 'sound of a rushing mighty wind,' and the visible 'divided tongues as of fire,' and 'they were all filled with the Holy Ghost and began to speak with other tongues as the Spirit gave them utterance.' Henceforth it was the will of God that the newly-formed assembly should be characterized in its walk, witness, worship, and work, by unquestioning submission to the one Spirit who alone could interpret the things of Christ for them and realize these in them. Our Lord had commanded 'that repentance and remission of sins should be preached in His name unto all nations beginning at Jerusalem,' but they were to remain till they were 'clothed with power from on high' (Luke 24. 47, 49). This enduement was now an accomplished fact and repentance and remission of sins were preached in His name by Peter but with an important and significant addition, namely baptism.

Baptism

From the earliest days of the Christian Church the authority for the baptism of believers has been derived from the command of Christ recorded in Matt. 28. 19. In recent years, however, doubt has been cast on the authenticity of this record, formerly accepted as unchallengeable. But the practice of the Church from its inception cannot readily be explained without such a command.

From Pentecost, when Peter called on his audience to 'repent and be baptized every one . . . in the name of Jesus Christ for the remission of sins,' baptism seems to have been commanded rather than commended. Indeed, on a later occasion, when the command was repeated, it is clear that it was given in direct conformity with a definite divine injunction (Acts 10. 33, 48). In practice baptism was consistently regarded as an act of obedience and the immediate and spontaneous accompaniment of true faith. Even when analogies are drawn and ancient types are cited (1 Cor. 10. 1-4; 1 Peter 3. 19-21) the context suggests compliance with a command of God.

Outside Acts there are only nineteen references to baptism and these are confined to seven Epistles, but as Dr. Machen says in another connection, 'Some things are omitted from the Epistles not because they are unimportant but on the contrary just because they are fundamental; instruction about them had to be given at the very beginning and except for special reasons did not need to be repeated.' Such instruction about baptism can be inferred from the fact that 'they that gladly received the Word were baptized,' obviously in compliance with the teaching of the apostles and in acquiescence with the will of God. Baptism was not new to them in its form even if its significance was deepened. John's disciples were baptized on the confession of their sins and in anticipation of a Coming Messiah. It was a baptism unto death, the due reward of their deeds, but not to Christ's death. It was related to repentance as an outward act, in which an inward change found visible expression, but it was quite distinct from Christian baptism.

At Pentecost, Peter, in the power of the Spirit, had made an orderly proclamation of the truth of the Gospel, presenting Jesus of Nazareth in the perfection of His Person, His Passion, His resurrection, His exaltation, His divinely attested Lordship, and His reception and outpouring of the Spirit. The happenings he described had been witnessed not more than two months before, but now in the light of God the Spirit they were revealed as steps in the evolution of the divine plan and purpose. From the place of contempt where the rulers, the religious and the rabble thought they had for ever left Jesus, He is pictured ascending to the throne. Finally Peter delivered the divine shaft which pierced the consciences of men—'This Jesus whom ye crucified,' and to their cry of conviction, he answered, '*Repent and be baptized* every one of you in (in dependence on) the name of Jesus *unto the remission of sins* and ye shall *receive the Holy Ghost*.' Here we have the twofold requirement of God from Israel and the twofold blessing which He promised them. Professor James Orr has well said, 'Repentance . . . means literally change of m*i*nd. . . . The change, however, is one in which not the intellect only but the whole nature (understanding, affections, will) is involved. It is such an altered view of God and sin as carries with it heartfelt sorrow for sin, confession of it and decisive turning from it to God and righteousness. Its reality is tested by its fruits.' Those who heard Peter had with darkened understanding, hatred and self-will condemned and crucified Jesus as a blasphemer. Now He had been revealed as dying not for His own sins, for He had none, but for theirs. Straightway there followed a galling repentance, a glad reception of the Word, and a willing submission to baptism as a public confession of the change and an open identification with the death of Christ. This evidence of true repentance was followed by the divine assurance, the gift of the Spirit. 'Repentance and faith, rightly viewed, are but the positive and negative poles of the same state of mind. There can be no evangelical faith which does not spring from a heart broken and contrite on account of sin; on the other hand there can be no true repentance which has not the germ of faith' (Orr). Their baptism was 'in the name of Jesus Christ' which Grimm translates 'so as to repose their hope and confidence' in Him.

In the case of Saul, the persecutor of Jesus, the divine requirements were similar. 'Arise and be baptized and wash away thy sins, calling on the name of the Lord' (Acts 22. 16). This last expression, so reminiscent of Peter's words, 'Whosoever calleth on the name of the Lord shall be saved' (Acts 2. 21) is significant. 'This calling on the name of Christ, thus closely associated with baptism, *and preceding it*, necessarily involved belief in Him' (Dr. Knowling). Moreover, the use of the causative or permissive middle voice in the Greek for 'Be baptized and wash away thy sins,' or 'Get thyself baptized and thy sins washed away,' as Dr. A. T. Robertson translates it, surely puts the individual responsibility of the believer in the matter of baptism beyond doubt.

The immediate dependence and sequence of baptism on the confession of faith are made more explicit in the case of the Samaritans (Acts 8. 12), of the Ethiopian eunuch (Acts 8. 36, 37), of Cornelius (Acts 10. 47, 48; 11. 17), of Lydia (Acts 16. 14, 15), and of the Philippian jailor (Acts 16. 31-34), but in these instances there is not the same emphasis on the inter-relation of repentance and baptism *unto the remission of sins*. It should be remembered that there was not the same immediate and evident responsibility as with the men of Israel who had crucified the Son of God or with Saul who shared the national sin of Christ's rejection and death and who became the very embodiment of Jewish malignity. But in every case baptism was a public confession of faith in Him and a complete renunciation of the past.

Some received the gift of the Spirit before baptism in water without the laying on of the hands of the apostles; others received the Spirit when their hands were laid on them; on others again the Spirit was bestowed after baptism. 'As the wind bloweth where it listeth,' so the Spirit of God is sovereign. If God was entitled —and who shall dispute it?—to institute the difference between Jew and Gentile, He is no less free to annul it or to vary the order of their obedience and the reception of His blessings.

The deep spiritual significance of baptism is not revealed to us by Luke. For this we must turn to Romans, the epistle which expounds our individual relationship to God. In it we are seen as those brought from the house of bondage and made children of God with the Spirit of sonship. As a result of personal identification by faith with Christ crucified we are brought into vital union with Him, with the Father, and with the Holy Spirit. As these new relationships are apprehended, we are expected to manifest them practically on earth. 'How shall we who are dead to sin live any longer therein?' says the apostle. 'Do you not know that we all when baptized were baptized into His death? We were entombed, therefore, with Him by means of our baptism into His death that just as Christ rose from the dead by means of the glory of the Father, so we should begin to walk in newness of life. For if we became vitally connected by the likeness of His death, we shall be vitally connected with Him also by the likeness of His resurrection. This knowing that our old man was crucified that the body of sin might be cancelled. . . .' (Rom. 6. 3-6, Moule's translation). As Drs. Sanday and Headlam put it, 'Baptism expresses symbolically a series of facts . . . Immersion—Death; Submersion —Burial (the ratification of death); Emergence—Resurrection.' There can surely be no doubt, then, about the mode of baptism. On immersion we must insist for it alone is adequate as a symbol. These same writers add, 'When we descended into the baptismal water that meant that we died with Christ—to sin. When the water closed over our heads, that meant that we lay buried with Him in proof that our death to sin, like His death, was real. But this carries with it a third step in the process. As Christ was raised from among the dead by a majestic exercise of divine power, so we also must from henceforth conduct ourselves as men in whom has been implanted a new principle of life.'

Faith's vision produced in the early Christians the spirit of obedience for 'the new nature lives in obedience in the consciousness of sonship.' The Lord had commanded His servants to baptize believers in the name of the Father and the Son and the Holy Spirit and these early Christians regarded it as a duty and privilege to conform to His will, though few of them could have grasped the significance of the rite with spiritual intelligence. Moreover, the command had been connected with discipleship and how could they be disciples if they remained unbaptized? Their forefathers had been 'baptized unto Moses in the Red Sea,' thus expressing their allegiance to him as leader and now it was for them to follow their example. Baptism by immersion was the Lord's will and way. Is there a true believer who would suggest by his neglect that he is wiser than his Lord?

"The Breaking of Bread and the Prayers"

Christians in apostolic times realized that they not only had individual responsibilities but a corporate testimony to maintain. To the small company of the upper room 'there were added in that day about three thousand souls,' and 'they continued stedfastly in the apostles' teaching and fellowship, in the breaking of bread and the prayers.' 'And the Lord added to them day by day those that were being saved' but 'of the rest durst no man join himself to them' (Acts 2. 41, 42, 47; 5. 13, R.V.). A new association distinct from the old congregation of Israel had been formed with a *fellowship* of divine life established by the Spirit, a fellowship with the Father and the Son which only the Spirit could initiate and maintain. The newly-formed Church was the living expression of that fellowship which was not an abstraction but a relationship of which corporate consciousness sought and found corporate manifestations. As the house of God, the pillar and ground of the truth, they could present in communal practice a living commentary on *the apostles' doctrine* which only the interaction of so many lives could produce. As a spiritual house, a holy priesthood, they could offer up spiritual sacrifices of praise and thanksgiving in the energy of the Spirit. As the household of God, the family of the redeemed with all the privileges of sonship, they could exhibit the full and distinctive character of Christian *worship*, and in that holy institution, *the Lord's Supper*, which forms such an affecting and important centre for the worship of the assembly, they could give that distinct outward expression to the unity which the Holy Spirit had produced. As a holy temple in the Lord they were privileged to show forth that characteristic feature of God's house—holiness and its characteristic activity—*prayer*. The most important of these manifestations of the fellowship of life, love and power was the breaking of the bread.

The Lord's Supper. We stress the corporate nature of the breaking of the bread as an expression of fellowship for in no other gathering of the assembly is the stress so strongly on communion and union the one with the other. 'The cup of blessing which we bless is it not a communion of the blood of Christ? The bread which we break is it not a communion of the body of Christ? seeing that we, who are many, are one loaf, one body: for we are all partakers of the one loaf' (1 Cor. 10. 16, 17, R.V.). As Dr. Plummer says of this passage, 'However we may unravel the construction, we have the parallel between many fragments, yet one bread, and many members, yet one body.'

The record of the institution of the Lord's Supper is found in all three synoptic Gospels. A matter so emphasized in the story of our Lord's life and work on earth should be very near to the heart of every Christian.

The circumstances of the institution were significant. 'The feast of unleavened bread drew nigh, which is called the passover. And the chief priests and scribes sought how they might put Him to death. . . . And Satan entered into Judas who is called Iscariot . . . And he went away and communed with the chief priests and captains how he might deliver Him unto them' (Luke 22. 1-4). The day of unleavened bread came and the Lord sent Peter and John to make ready for the eating of the passover. As He foretold, an unknown guide carrying a pitcher of water, so symbolic of a body indwelt by the Spirit (John 4; 2 Cor. 4. 7), unwittingly led them to a place where the master of the house (evidently a disciple since he at once recognized the title and the prerogative of 'the Teacher') answered the question, 'Where is *the* guest -chamber where I may eat with My disciples?' by showing them a large upper room furnished. How this action of a nameless man stands out against the dark background of hatred, betrayal and Satanic intrigue!

The Character of the Supper is then revealed. 'And when the hour was come, He sat down with His disciples and He said unto them, "With desire I have desired to eat this passover with you before I suffer."' He knew that this passover typified Himself, sacrificed for them but 'the knowledge of the intensity of the suffering did not conceal the intensity of the desire' (Plummer). 'And He took bread and, when He had given thanks He brake it and gave to them saying, This is My body which is given for you: this do in remembrance of Me. And the cup in like manner after supper, saying, This cup is the new covenant in My blood, even that which is poured out for you' (Luke 22. 19, 20, R.V.). To this account of Luke, Matthew adds the Lord's invitation, 'Drink ye *all* of it,' and Mark gives the response, 'And they all drank of it.'

Paul's first Epistle to the Corinthians gives us the only other detailed account of the Supper and it is important because it was written before the Gospel and because it is this epistle which contains the doctrine of the Church as a fellowship of Christians in the world. After dealing in Chapters 1 to 10 with the sufficiency of Christ and His Cross as the wisdom and power of God and as that which brings us into communion with God and with one another, Paul turns to the theme of the assembly, its order, its testimony in gathering, its spiritual manifestations and its spirit of love, the pervading and controlling principle and the perfect uniting bond. But division had unfortunately come into the Church at Corinth and was unfortunately manifest at the Supper. So he says in rebuke, 'When ye come together into one place ye cannot eat the Lord's Supper. For in eating each one takes before the rest *his own* supper' (1 Cor. 11. 20, 21, margin). In other words, 'Each anticipates the partaking in common and thus destroys the whole meaning and beauty of the ordinance' (Plummer).

The Significance of the Supper can be deduced from the above. Like baptism it stands in relation to His death but whereas baptism is a single individual act, the Supper is communal and continuous. Moreover it is *the Lord's* Supper. It was He who on that night 'when He was being delivered up' (not only betrayed by Judas but surrendered by the Father), gave this proof of His faithful love so that His own might in His absence respond to that love in remembrance of Him and in identification with His death till He should return. The symbols used were bread and wine, presented separately for they spake of a *broken* body and of *outpoured* blood. The special aspect of His death seems to be that of the peace offering in which a part ascended to God, a part was eaten by the priests and a part was shared *by the offerers*, for His words were, 'This is My body which is given *for you*,' and 'This is My blood which is shed *for you*' (1 Cor. 11. 24, 25). This interpretation is supported by the parallel which Paul draws between the Lord's Table and Israel's altar and to that offering in which those who eat of the sacrifices were 'partakers with the altar' (1 Cor. 10. 18). But when we remember Him in this way there is no limitation on an appreciation of Him either as the burnt offering or the sin offering.

The Partakers of the Supper are clearly distinguished. The recurring word 'all' in the accounts of Matthew and Mark to which reference has been made, finds its counterpart in the opening words of the Epistle to the Corinthians, 'the Church of God at Corinth—with *all* who in every place call upon the name of Jesus Christ, our Lord, both theirs and ours,' and again in the words, 'We are *all* partakers of that one bread' (1 Cor. 10. 17). It is clearly the prerogative of all believers to enjoy this privilege unless sin has excluded them (1 Cor. 5). But every one who appreciates the true significance of 'the breaking of the bread' will seek to maintain not only the unity but the purity of the assembly, purity in doctrine, practice and association and will obey the injunction, 'Let a man prove himself and so let him eat of the bread and drink of the cup.' It is our duty to 'receive one another as Christ also received us' (Rom. 15. 7), if we are to maintain the unity of the body but it must be 'to the glory of God' if we are to preserve its purity.

The Time of the Supper appears to be made clear for, though it was not instituted on the first day of the week, Acts 20 makes it evident that on that day it was regularly observed. Moreover, there is a fitness in the celebration on the Lord's Day which witnessed the triumph of the resurrection. The truth that Christ was risen indeed had an immediate gathering power. The two disciples of the Emmaus walk 'found the eleven gathered together,' and a week later the experience was renewed. By the time we find Paul at Troas the breaking of the bread had become, as Rackham points out, the distinctive feature of the worship of the first day of the week.

The Prayers. We now come to the last of the four elements which consituted the holy walk of the assembly from the day of Pentecost. The word translated 'prayers' in Acts 2. 42 is used of prayer in general and literally means 'a pouring out.' One of the main forms of prayer must ever be *worship.*

Worship is such a characteristic feature of the assembly at the Lord's Supper that it has become customary for some to speak of this as 'the worship meeting' though no such expression is found in the New Testament. As C. F. Hogg has pointed out there is no suggestion that the Corinthians met explicitly for this purpose 'nor indeed is there any New Testament reference to a worshipping company save in the Revelation, where the scenes are not earthly but heavenly. . . . Worship is not something done on occasion and in association with others; it is the characteristic and normal attitude toward God of the regenerate soul. . . . If we are not worshipping alone we shall not be able to worship when we join a company.'

Worship generally considered is the overflow of the heart, in the consciousness of infinite blessedness, giving its full homage and adoring reverence to the only worthy one—God. Perhaps no better expression of this can be found than in the opening of Psalm 45, 'My heart overfloweth with a goodly matter: I speak the things which I have made touching the King: my tongue is the pen of a ready writer. Thou art fairer than the children of men.' Worship for believers is the free adoration of the soul which, brought nigh to God by sacrifice and having no more conscience of sin, approaches Him in the enjoyment of His love and in the knowledge of Him as Father.

The Character of Worship is determined by the manner in which God is pleased to reveal Himself in any given time and circumstance. To the patriarchs, consciously dependent on His power for the supply of their needs as pilgrims and strangers and for the fulfilment of His promises, He revealed Himself as the Almighty and this determined the character of *their* worship. To Israel, Jehovah was the title which He took as the Deliverer of His people on the ground of His covenant of sovereign grace and to them He revealed Himself as the great self-existing Source of redeeming love. But *their* relationship was not immediate nor intimate and their worship centred around typical rites and ceremonies invested in a priesthood set apart from the rest of the people. In our dispensation with its full revelation of God in Christ worship has passed from the material to the spiritual. The type has gone for the reality has come; the shadow has given place to the substance and we offer the adoration of filial affection, the response begotten of His love. Our Lord revealed this to the woman at the well when He said, 'The hour cometh when ye shall neither in this mountain nor yet at Jerusalem *worship the Father*' (John 4. 21) Worship had assumed a new character based on the personal relationship, not previously known, of which John writes, 'Beloved, now are we the children of God' (1 John 3. 2). As from the heart of the only begotten Son there ever ascended the sweet odour of worship to His Father so this new generation, entirely after His order, whom He is not ashamed to call brethren, offer the adoration of children. In the consciousness of being before God in Christ and with loving appreciation of Him who made the Father known they express to Him the delight of their souls in all that He is. This is worship.

The Place of Worship is no longer a material centre nor are the worshippers merely a people looking up to heaven. In spirit they are in the presence of God. As Westcott says, 'The object of worship determines its conditions.' 'The filial character of the new worship emancipates it from every limit of place and time' (Godet). In the Tabernacle's typical teaching the worshipper could only go as far as the blood of the sin-offering. But the High Priest on the Day of Atonement carried the blood into the very holiest of all and sprinkled it before the mercy seat. It could go no further. Typically this sets forth what Heb. 10 19-22 declares doctrinally—that the believer has boldness of access into the very presence of God as a purged worshipper.

The Theme of Worship is the perfections of Christ, divine and human as revealed by the Spirit and the Word and our appreciation of the Father as revealed by the Son. Sharing God's thoughts concerning the Son and the Son's thoughts concerning the Father, the believer learns the holy exercise of adoration in spirit and in truth. 'By the Incarnation men are enabled to have immediate communion with God and thus worship in spirit has become possible: at the same time the Son is a complete manifestation of God for ever and thus a worship in truth has been placed within our reach' (Westcott).

The Power of Worship is clearly revealed to us in Philippians. 'We are the circumcision who worship God in the Spirit and rejoice in Christ Jesus and have no confidence in the flesh' (Phil. 3. 3). The word for worship here signifies the yielding of the whole being in willing priestly service by the Holy Ghost. No one individual can grasp the blessedness of God and the greatness of Christ: it takes the whole assembly to render to Him worthy homage and adoration and this in its fulness can only be attained when 'His servants shall serve Him and they shall see His face' (Rev. 22. 3). Meanwhile our highest joy in worship is usually experienced when we gather with Christ in the midst and in His Supper recollect the mystery of godliness and ponder the unfathomable love of Calvary.

The 'prayers' of Acts 2 did not only include worship but also the 'systematic, positive praying, not as individuals only but in connection with one another' (Campbell Morgan). Dr. Plummer has drawn attention to the fact that Luke gives remarkable prominence to worship, praise and thanksgiving in his Gospel, which begins and ends with worship in the temple and that more than any other evangelist he brings before his readers the subject of prayer. When we come to Acts we are impressed with the same feature. The company in the upper room 'all continued with one accord in prayer and supplication.'

United Prayer resulted in a wonderful external sign and a remarkable internal experience. It is little wonder that the new converts 'continued stedfastly . . . in the prayers.' The apostles 'gave themselves continually to prayer,' that is, they surrendered themselves to it with urgency, perseverance and unanimity and their prayers were characterized as 'earnest,' literally 'stretched out,' not in length but in intensity. But we have an actual example of such a prayer meeting in Acts 4. 23 ff. where the assembly is seen lifting up their voices to God with one accord. The principles which governed their united prayer are revealed there.

1. *Their Attitude to God* is remarkable. Firstly, they addressed Him as absolute ruler, as 'sovereign master and disposer of all' (Kelly), acknowledging His glory in creation like Hezekiah (2 Kings 19. 15) in the face of his enemies. Evidently, therefore, to them God was more than all. 'This was the subconscious conviction that underlay the prayers of these men. Prayer always begins there' (C. Morgan). Secondly, they revealed their acquaintance with and faith in the Scriptures as the divinely inspired expression of the wisdom and will of God which must be carried out despite the opposition of men and nations. Thirdly, they manifested a quiet confidence, in God's gracious care for His own.

2. *Their Attitude to His Holy Servant, Jesus,* was equally remarkable. They acknowledged Him as the Holy One who, as God's anointed

servant, had accomplished His will by suffering and death, and by whose name signs and wonders could still be done through their testimony.

3. *Their Attitude to Men* was in accordance with these facts. As implacable hostility had been shown to God and His Christ, so they, His followers, were being threatened. Like Hezekiah again they spread the matter before the Lord but unlike him they did not ask for deliverance from the persecution but for boldness to speak His word while He stretched out His hand to heal. The utter selflessness and abandonment to God's interests of these believers, whose very prayer shows how much they had still to learn, contrasts strongly with the self-centred attitude of much of our praying. Their one desire was that God's will should be done in them, that His word should be proclaimed with fearlessness and faithfulness and that His blessing might be experienced by others.

Can we wonder that 'When they prayed, the place was shaken wherein they were gathered together: and they were all filled with the Holy Ghost and they spake the word with boldness' (Acts 4. 31)?

CHAPTER XX

Israel

ROWLAND C. EDWARDS

THE earliest narratives of the Bible survey the whole Adamic race. It is with the introduction of Abram in the later part of the eleventh chapter of Genesis that the attention is focused on the family of God's choice, 'who,' says Paul, 'are Israelites.'

The nation took its name from Israel its ancestor (Jacob, the younger twin-brother of Esau). Israelites they are, not Edomites. The choice of God before their birth was that 'the elder shall serve the younger.' This 'purpose of God according to election' is coupled with a statement from Malachi's prophecy, 'Jacob have I loved, Esau have I hated.' In the New Testament a comma separates them, in history a millennium (Rom. 9. 4; Gen. 25. 23; Rom. 9. 12, 13; Mal. 1. 2, 3).

In the review of the Lord's dealings with His earthly people given in Psalms 105 and 106 it is said, 'Israel also came into Egypt and Jacob sojourned in the land of Ham.' With this sojourn Israelitish history begins. Introductory to it were the call of Abraham, God's choice of Isaac rather than Ishmael, and the personal and official history of Joseph. How long were they in Egypt? This was the subject of prediction.

Gen. 15. 12-16 foretells their entry, and also their exodus in the fourth generation. It speaks of servitude and strangership. It is clear that as four generations were covered by Levi, Kohath, Amram and Moses, the servitude of this passage could have extended over only a part of the four hundred years. Evidently, then, the thirteenth verse should be read as an introversion, thus: 'Know of a surety (*a*) that thy seed shall be a stranger in a land that is not theirs; (*b*) and shall serve them (*c*) and they shall afflict them (*d*) four hundred years.' Read, first (*a*) with (*d*), then (*b*) and (*c*) together.

It was the strangership that was to last four hundred years: the servitude covered the shorter period of four generations.

When did the strangership begin? Gen. 21 connects it with Isaac as the seed of Abraham. As the giving of the law took place 430 years after the Abrahamic covenant of promise, so did the exodus, for both exodus and law-giving happened in the one year. The strangership therefore began 30 years after the call, the covenant, the promise. Abram being then 75 years old at the onset of the strangership, he must have been 105, and Isaac a boy of five years. The latter being of the age of 60 when he became Jacob's father, and Jacob 130 years old when he went into Egypt, the strangership must have begun 185 years before the entry into Egypt (Exod. 6. 16-20; Gen. 15. 12-16; Gal. 3. 17; Gen. 12. 1-3; Exod. 12. 1-6, 41; 19. 1; Gen. 12. 4; 21. 5; 25. 26; 47. 9). The sojourn in Egypt of the children of Israel therefore lasted 215 years (the difference between 400 and 185). During these 185 years Abraham's seed was a stranger in a land not their own, namely, Canaan, and in Egypt, another land not theirs, for 215 years. (The 430 years of Exod. 12. 40 are 30 years longer than the 400 years of Gen. 15. 13, because they include the sojourning of Abraham himself). (Anstey, *Romance of Bible Chronology*, p. 117).

The weaning of Isaac and the feast celebrating this event in acknowledgment of him as Abraham's heir took place therefore when he was five years old (Gen. 21).

In Egypt, in the wilderness, in Canaan, Israel was a theocracy. The journeyings are to be distinguished from the wanderings. With God leading them, they take their journeys. They arrive at Kadesh, eleven days distant from Horeb, but they take a year to reach it. From Kadesh they could have entered the land of Canaan at once, but they were faithless, as Numbers 13, 14 narrate. Divine judgments overthrew the adult generation. The younger became wanderers for about thirty-eight years, which period lies between Num. 13. 26 and 20. 1, and verses 36 and 37 of Num. 33. Of it 'there is no record save the stoning of the Sabbath-breaker and the sin and doom of Korah and his company' (John Ritchie, *From Egypt to Canaan*). Then Num. 33. 41 and later verses, a summary of that part of their history which commences at 20. 1, speak of their journeyings being resumed. After Judges 16 the chronological order is broken for a time. The historian now selects certain topics in the period of the Judges for special mention. Thus the seventeenth and eighteenth chapters constitute an appendix, the next three chapters another, and the book of Ruth another.

The transition from the theocracy to the monarchy is covered by the first seven chapters of the first book of Samuel. They tell of two judges, Eli and Samuel. The latter is the first of the prophets (Acts 3. 24; 13. 20). The next chapter introduces Israel as a monarchy. The rest of this book deals with the first king, Saul, and the next book with David, though the last four chapters are of the nature of appendices. In the first two chapters of the next book David's history is carried on. Solomon's reign is described in 1 Kings 2. 12 to 11. 48.

At his death the kingdom, united as it has been for 120 years, splits into a northern Israel and a southern Judah. The former lasts about a century and a third, the latter about four centuries. (Anstey's figures are 133 and 397). Israel under Hosea is subjugated by Assyria, Judah under Zedekiah by Babylon (2 Kings 17. 1-18; 25. 1-21). The times of the Gentiles now begin, which evoked the Lamentations of Jeremiah and to which the Lord Himself sorrowfully alludes (2 Chron. 36. 17-21; Jer. 1. 3; 39. 1-10; 52. 1-27; Ezek. 24. 1-15; 33. 21; Luke 21. 24).

In the relations between Judah and Babylon there are to be distinguished the Servitude, the Captivity and the Desolations. The last four Kings of Judah were Jehoahaz, Jehoiakim, Jehoiachin, and Zedekiah. The promise, 'after seventy years be accomplished for (R.V.) Babylon, I will visit you and perform My good word toward you in causing you to return unto this place,' that is, Jerusalem, was fulfilled in the first year of Cyrus, King of Persia (Jer. 29. 10; 2 Chron. 36. 22, 23; Ezra 1. 1-4; Dan. 1. 1-4). Reckoning back seventy years reaches the third year of Jehoiakim, when Daniel and his princely companions were taken to Babylon. The supremacy of Nebuchadnezzar is now acknowledged, as in Jeremiah's reference in Jer. 25. 1, the first such acknowledgment, though the prophet has been prophesying for 22 years.

Nebuchadnezzar had intended to imprison Jehoiakim in Babylon but relented and released him in vassalage (2 Chron. 36. 6; 2 Kings 24. 1). He served thus for three years, then rebelled. After disposing of more pressing affairs which detained him some years,

Nebuchadnezzar again marched against Jerusalem. By this time Jehoiakim's young son, Jehoiachin, was on the throne. He submitted with little force or delay. Thousands of captives were taken, including Ezekiel and Mordecai (2 Kings 24. 12-16; Ezek. 33. 21; 40. 1; Ezra 2. 1, 2; Neh. 7. 7; Esth. 2. 5, 6). This is the epoch of the Captivity, eight years subsequent to that of the Servitude.

'Seventy years was the appointed duration of the Servitude to Babylon. But the stubborn refusal of the people to submit to that judgment or to profit by the further chastisement of the Captivity . . . brought on them the terrible scourge of the Desolations. The essential element in the last judgment was not merely ruined cities, but a land laid desolate by a hostile invasion, the effects of which were perpetuated by famine and pestilence' (Sir R. Anderson, *Daniel in the Critics' Den*). The Desolations date from the tenth year of Zedekiah, commemorated ever since by a yearly fast (Ezek. 24. 1, 2; 2 Chron. 36. 8-21; Jer. 25. 1-11. Their *terminus ad quem* is in Hag. 2. 15-17). To Daniel, exercised about them, the further revelation of the seventy weeks or hebdomads was given. Israel is to suffer from desolations other than those of which Jeremiah spoke. The awaited Messiah will certainly come but He will be cut off without taking His kingdom. Thereafter, abominations other than those Ezekiel saw, are to usher in a mighty desolator, whose end, however, is pre-determined and certain (Dan. 9.).

Babylon, the head of gold of Nebuchadnezzar's image, was succeeded by Medo-Persia. This is the dominant world power of the times of Ezra, Nehemiah, Esther, Haggai, Zechariah and Malachi. A remnant returns to Jerusalem, rebuilding the temple and restoring its worship, building the city wall and repairing its gates. Always there are some who fear the Lord and think upon His name, but the sad tale of degeneration of the people in general and the priests in particular has to be told by the prophet whose words close the Old Testament writings.

The bane of the chosen people was idolatry. Abraham himself came of idolatrous stock and from an idolatrous environment, as Scripture shows and archæology illustrates. Rachel took with her the stolen teraphim of her father. Jacob's household had idols in

Canaan, and in Egypt the people served other gods. They are out of Egypt only two months when Aaron makes the golden calf. The nations in and around Canaan were all idolators, with Baal as chief god of the Syrians and Phoenicians, Ashtoreth his consort, Chemosh the national god of Moab, Dagon of the Philistines, Moloch of the Ammonites. Solomon for all his wisdom was a devotee of many idols. After his death, in both Israel and Judah idolatry continued to be rife. The prophets ceaselessly denounced it. Hezekiah cast out Nehushtan and other idols. Even after the fall of Jerusalem under Zedekiah the people obstinately persisted in the worship of the queen of heaven, attributing to her favour their former ease and prosperity. As Psalm 78. 58 says, 'They provoked Him to anger with their high places and moved Him to jealousy with their graven images' (Gen. 31. 19; 35. 2; Exod. 12. 12, 32; Josh. 24. 14; Jud. 2. 1-3; 1 Kings 11. 1-8; Jer. 44. 15-19; Ezek. 20. 7-10).

But those who returned from Babylon brought with them a detestation of idolatry. One people owning one God, they were bent on the practice and preservation of their religion. Though without prophets since Malachi, the prophetic writings they had they studied as never before.

The period between the Testaments saw the rise of the Sanhedrim and the synagogues, the Pharisees and the scribes. The Sanhedrim was the supreme judicial body for the administration of Jewish law. Consisting of 72 members it had its origin as far back at least as about 200 B.C. and met in Jerusalem.

With the destruction of Solomon's temple and the erection, after a long interval, of an inferior building, the importance of the temple was eclipsed by that of the synagogue, instituted during the Exile.

The Pharisees took rise in the Maccabean period (which began *c.* 168 B.C.), being known then as the 'Chasidim' or 'Pious Ones.' They called Israel to a study of the law and a conscientious observance of its precepts, such as tithing. How they degenerated is revealed in the Gospels.

The scribes came to be an important section of the people during this period. At first their business was to copy the Scriptures; then they gradually became recognized as authoritative interpreters, with increasing domination of individual consciences.

The scribes and the Pharisees are often found together in the Gospels, maintaining the tradition of the elders. This traditionalism expressed itself in a mass of Rabbinical additions to the law of Moses, connected with or foisted on the text of Scripture, of the nature of explanation, illustration and decision. Referring to Exod. 24. 12, 'I will give thee tables of stone and a law and commandments which I have written, that thou mayest teach them,' an eminent Rabbi argues, 'The "tables of stone" are the ten commandments; the "law" is the written law (in the Pentateuch); the "commandments" are the Mishnah; "which I have written" refers to the prophets and the Hagiographa, while the words, "that thou mayest teach them" refer to the Gemara. From this we learn, that all this was given to Moses in Sinai.' This is the background of such chapters as Matt. 15 and 23. 'The traditions of the elders' were accorded a place equal to that of the Scriptures, indeed they were often held to be of greater authority, as being explanatory of them. Thus, 'teaching as their doctrines the precepts of men,' did they 'transgress the commandment of God.'

Almost four centuries intervene between the time of Malachi and the advent of the Christ. The events of Daniel 11 occur in that period. Greece displaces Medo-Persia, to be itself displaced by Rome, and the writer of the first synoptic Gospel is a collector of taxes whose business it is to see that God's chosen people Israel pay tribute to their heathen overlords the Romans.

The time being fulfilled, the sixty-two hebdomads of Daniel's great prophecy having expired, the Messiah came. He preached, 'Repent ye; for the kingdom of heaven is at hand.' He was cut off, rejected, without taking His kingdom. On the following Day of Pentecost Peter called upon all the house of Israel to recognize that God had made the crucified Jesus both Lord and Christ. Many individuals, from scattered parts of the Empire, welcomed the news, but official Israel persisted in unbelief. Peter's subsequent appeal for a reversal of this attitude (Acts 3. 19) so that the appointed Christ should come to them again in restoration of the kingdom and with long-promised seasons of refreshment was spurned. Stephen's indictment intensified the wrath of unbelieving Israel and brought martyrdom on the speaker. The perverseness so tenderly mourned by the Lord Himself became even more blatant.

The sacrifice which the bigoted and cruel Caiaphas hoped would propitiate Rome failed to do so. False Messiahs arose, duping many, even to death. The Roman authorities became incensed at the rebellious fanaticism of the nation. Titus, the son of the Emperor Vespasian, marched against Jerusalem at the head of 100,000 trained and seasoned troops. It fell to him in 70 A.D. after a siege of nearly five months. More than 1,100,000 perished, the survivors were sold into slavery, the Temple was demolished and the city devastated (Josephus, *Wars of the Jews*, Book VI, chap. ix).

After this outline of the history of the chosen people, it seems fitting briefly to notice certain salient manifestations of God's favour towards them. The chief of these was their being made stewards of the oracles of God, the sacred Scriptures, for their own observance and the blessing of others (Rom. 3. 2, 9; 4. 5).

Individuals varied in their attitude to these writings, as is shown, for example, in the prophecies of Jeremiah (Jer. 15. 16; 36. 21-32; 44. 16). History shows that this most outstanding of all advantages lost its good effect on them as pride of possession displaced humble realization of God's unmerited favour in their being thus entrusted.

'Whose is the adoption,' says Paul. The word is *huiothesia*. It means the son-placing or sonship. Sonship in Scripture is varied. It is of descent, immediate or remote (Mal. 1. 6; 3. 3, 6, 17). There are references also to sonship of nature or character (Matt. 5. 9, 43-45; Mark 3. 17; Luke 10. 6; 16. 8; 20. 34; John 12. 36; 17. 12; Acts 4. 36; Rom. 8. 14; Gal. 3. 7; Eph. 2. 2; 5. 6). Adoption from without into God's family, with a definite background of Roman custom against which it should be viewed, is another aspect of sonship (Eph. 1. 5; John 1. 12; Rom. 8. 15). (Both Cæsar Augustus and Tiberius Cæsar entered the royal family by adoption). An altogether different Roman custom gives its tone to Gal. 3. 23-4. 7, in which passage, alone in the New Testament, all believers of this present season of grace are viewed as sons, adults in standing, in contradistinction to the minority attaching to saints under the law. In other aspects, too, sonship pertains to the believer.

But Israel's sonship is national, not personal. 'My son, my firstborn' is called out of Egypt, called in love to be 'a people, a name, a praise, and a glory for the Lord' (Exod. 4. 22; Hos. 11. 1-4;

Jer. 13. 11). Rebellion brought chastisement and they became numbered among 'all the nations' for judgment (Jer. 25. 15, 18, Amos 3. 2), though the word of the Lord through Amos was 'you only have I known of all the families of the earth.' Thus Israel was 'the people' in contradistinction to 'the nations' (Num. 23. 9; Deut. 2. 4; 4. 6-8; 7. 6, 7; Luke 2. 32), but the Hebrew word *goyim* thus translated is found applied to Israel in rebellion. To use another's words, 'Israel had become Gentile.' John, later, looking back, speaks of 'that nation,' and the 'Great Commission' of Matthew's Gospel surely includes Israel among 'all the nations.' Nevertheless it is to be realized, despite all the darkness of departure, that 'the gifts and calling of God are without repentance.'

'To whom pertaineth . . . the glory,' says Paul (Rom. 9. 4). After Moses had finished the work of setting up the tabernacle, 'the cloud covered the tent of meeting and the glory of the Lord filled the tabernacle. And Moses was not able to enter into the tent of meeting because the cloud abode thereon, and the glory of the Lord filled the tabernacle.' The cloud covered the tabernacle by day and the appearance of fire by night, for guidance. The glory was within, the Shekinah, visible manifestation of the presence of God. Later, the glory of the Lord filled Solomon's temple, which temple after 400 years was destroyed by Nebuchadnezzar. He 'burnt the house of the Lord and the king's house; and all the houses of Jerusalem, even every great house, burnt he with fire' (Exod. 40. 34, 35; Num. 9. 15-23; 1 Kings 8. 11; 2 Chron. 5. 14).

Ezekiel saw visions of the glory. From the cherub on which it was it departs to the threshold of the temple, standing over it, the court being full of its brightness, and later, removing from temple and city to the Mount of Olives (Ezek. 8. 1-4; 9. 3; 10. 4, 18, 19; 11. 22, 23). Subsequently, Zerubbabel returns with a remnant and builds another temple. The glory is not in it. But, 'I will shake all nations and the desirable things of all nations shall come, and I will fill this house with glory, saith the Lord.' The expression, 'this house' seems to be used in accordance with the principle of identifying each of the temples as 'the house of the Lord.' The Lord Jesus cleansed the temple of His day, erected as it was by an Edomite usurper wholly for personal and political reasons. There is yet another, the millennial temple of which Ezekiel the priest speaks in prophecy, 'and, behold, the glory of the Lord filled the house' (Hag. 2. 7; Ezek. 40. 1-5).

As to 'the covenants' to which Paul alludes in his enumeration of Israel's blessings, Scripture tells of the Edenic, Adamic, Noahic, Abrahamic, Mosaic, Palestinian and Davidic. In relation to Israel the New Covenant is to come.

The 'giving of the law' was through Moses to Israel in a threefold manner. First, the 'ten words' were given orally, accompanied by (*a*) judgments covering relations between Israelite and Israelite; (*b*) directions for keeping three annual feasts, and (*c*) instructions for the conquest of Canaan (Exod. 20. 1-17; 24. 3-8; 21. 1-23; 33. 14-33).

Next time the law was given them on tablets of stone, which Moses was called to the mount to receive. While he is thus engaged, receiving instructions about the tabernacle, priesthood and sacrifice, the people demand of Aaron to 'make us gods.' He makes the golden calf, which they worship, at this early stage thus breaking the first commandment. Moses descends and shatters the first tablets.

For the third time the law is given them, on the second tablets (Exod. 34. 12-31; 32. 1-6; 34. 1, 28, 29).

Certain relevant connections as to time can readily be determined. Two months elapsed from the exodus to the giving of the law on Sinai. Another nine months and a half passed ere Moses set up the tabernacle. The book of Leviticus covers another month. The spies were sent to view the land twenty days after the first census (Exod. 12. 1-6, 41; 19. 1; 40. 17; Lev. 1. 2; Num. 1. 1; 10. 11).

From Num. 10. 11 to the death of Aaron over thirty-eight years go by, and another nine months till, on the eve of the entry into the land, 'on this side Jordan in the land of Moab began Moses to declare this law.' He reviews their past history (three chapters), re-affirms the law (eight chapters) and gives further instructions and warnings (Num. 10. 11; 33. 38; Deut. 1. 5; Josh. 5. 10). The events from Deut. 1. 3 to Joshua 5. 10 required two months and a half.

To keep the law was Israel's very life. Its being observed secured their being preserved from idolatry and associated immoralities, sexual and other. It was a fence, an enclosure, a fold. Holding them in bond, as a warder or gaoler while protecting them, it was a temporary provision against the advent of the Messiah. It came in by the way. Paul taught the Galatians that its transitoriness impressed on the saints under it the characteristic of immaturity. He likened it also to the *paedagogos* of his day, the slave whose duty it was to care for the children on their way to school and to deliver them to the schoolmaster. Christ having come, it has now no standing, having given place to Him in whom is finality, who came to buy out Jewish saints from the law and to give to all believers of this present season of grace the place of sonship, that is, adulthood in the public economy of God, in contradistinction to minority (Deut. 4. 6, 9; 5. 33; 6. 23; John 10. 16; Rom. 5. 20; Gal. 3. 23; 4. 7). The background of this last passage is Roman custom. The Roman boy was taken from school at about seventeen to have legal adulthood conferred on him by his father. Hitherto regarded as a child he is now saluted as a son.

The 'service of God' is thus summarized in the Epistle to the Hebrews, 'The first covenant had ordinances of divine service and its sanctuary of this world.' For there was a tabernacle prepared, having an outer and an inner part, 'the first, wherein were the candlestick, and the table, and the shewbread, which is called the Holy place, and after the second veil, the tabernacle which is called the Holy of holies, having a golden censer and the ark of the covenant overlaid round about with gold, wherein was a golden pot holding the manna and Aaron's rod that budded, and the tables of the covenant and over it the cherubim of glory overshadowing the mercy seat. . . . The priests go in continually into the first tabernacle accomplishing the services,' these 'being only carnal ordinances (with meats, drinks, and divers washings) imposed until a time of reformation.'

Those actions described in the last sixteen chapters of the book of Exodus, in Leviticus and in parts of Deuteronomy in connection with the tabernacle, and those subsequently connected with the temple, comprise 'the service.' (The words, 'of God,' are not in the Greek of Rom. 9. 4; it is at least doubtful whether their insertion is helpful). The word *latreia*, used here for 'service,' occurs five times in the New Testament, and its verbal form twenty-one times. Israelites, as 'worshippers' were 'earnestly serving night and day,' through priests who 'offer the gifts according to the law, who serve' the tabernacle, that 'copy and shadow of the heavenly things,' according to Mosaic ritual. To this only is the term 'divine service' applicable in a Scripture sense, as denoting God-ordered ritual. All other appropriations of the expression 'divine service' have to look beyond Scripture for their warrant.

In conformity with it, an individual Israelite under the law, such as the aged Anna, departing 'not from the temple,' could be described as 'worshipping with fastings and supplications night and day.' But the day of rectification having come, we Christians are 'the circumcision,' who, if true to character 'worship by the Spirit of God' (that is, who subject ourselves to Him in thought and action, belief and testimony), 'and glory in Christ Jesus' (which the Jew clinging to the ancient Mosaic 'service' scorns to do), 'and have no confidence in the flesh' (Heb. 9. 1-10; 10. 2; Acts 26. 7; Heb. 8. 5; 13. 10; Luke 2. 37; Phil. 3. 3).

Paul continues his enumeration, 'and the promises.' A promise may be extracted, as by bargaining, negotiation, or request. Or it may be given voluntarily and spontaneously. The Greek language expresses these shades of meaning by different words. Invariably in the New Testament the word *epangelia* is used, denoting an undertaking made without outside pressure. With the one exception of Acts 23. 21, it is used of the promises of God.

'To Abraham were the promises spoken, and to his seed.' Very definite they were. 'I will make of thee a great nation, and I will bless thee, and make thy name great; and thou shalt be a blessing, and I will bless them that bless thee, and curse him that curseth thee, and in thee shall all the families of the earth be blessed'—a sevenfold unconditional promise of grace. It is repeated to Abraham, confirmed and enlarged, extended to Isaac and to Jacob (Gal. 3. 16, 18; Gen. 12. 2, 3; 13. 14-17; 15. 18; 17. 1-14; 21. 12; 22. 15-18; Heb. 7. 6; 11. 17; Gen. 26. 2-5; 28. 13-15; 35. 9-12).

The promises of God converge in Christ. 'How many soever be the promises of God, in Him is the yea; wherefore also through Him is the Amen, unto the glory of God through us.' In Gal. 3 it is argued that faith is greater than law-keeping, in conformity with the fact that the law coming after the promise to Abraham, is inferior to it, and cannot annul it.

Of Israel it is said, 'whose are the fathers.' The term in itself is indefinite. The context, with other references, seems to identify these 'fathers' as Abraham, Isaac and Jacob (Rom. 9. 4; Deut. 9. 5; 10. 15; Acts 3. 13; 13. 32; Rom. 11. 28). The sons of Israel 'are beloved for the fathers' sake.' Literally the wording is, 'beloved through the fathers,' that is, in conformity with God's promises to Abraham, Isaac, and Jacob, through which blessing came to the people. It is not for their sakes, but for the sake of, on account of, God's revelation to them that Israel is beloved.

Out of Israel came the Christ: she it was who 'brought forth a man child' (Rev. 12. 5; Gen. 3. 15; Matt. 1. 20; Luke 1. 35; Gal. 4. 4). The first prediction concerning the Christ depicts His final triumph. With His bruised heel He crushes the serpent's head. His adversary vanquished, the wounded Christ stands forth from the conflict as Victor. This 'protevangelium' foretells in symbolic terms the gladdening advent of the Man of all men, the Seed of the woman. 'The goal towards which all history is moving is here announced in this graphic, cryptic oracle' (D. L. Cooper). It is graphic, with bold outlines; cryptic through lack of details.

In point of time the next prophecy of the Christ is Enoch's. In this, as in Job's, which is next, a Person is in view, Judge of the ungodly, Vindicator of the godly. Proceeding chronologically, in the next passages the seed is multiple and of a heavenly order as well as of an earthly. But the wording 'in Isaac shall thy seed be called,' demands a Person as Seed, coming through Isaac, as does Jacob's blessing his sons, and as do the visions of Balaam. The Seed of the woman is not only the coming Lord and Redeemer, but the Seed of Abraham and Isaac, of Jacob and Judah, the Salvation of Jehovah, the Shepherd of Israel, the Stone of Israel, the Star out of Jacob, the Prophet-like Moses, and the Seed of David (Jude 14, 15; Job 19. 25-27; Gen. 12. 1-3; 15. 13-16; 17. 7; 21. 12; 26. 2-4; 28. 13, 14; 49. 18, 24; Num. 23 and 24; Deut. 18. 15; 2 Sam. 7. 14-16; 23. 1-5).

As in drawing a figure, an artist first limns a few lines which require many others for final identification, so the first lines of the figure of Israel's Messiah are laid down in the protevangelium and additions made throughout the Old Testament so that when His advent drew nigh He could be recognized by the intelligent eye of faith. Thus Matthew pointed to Jesus of Nazareth and said this and that happened in connection with Him 'that it might be fulfilled which was spoken by the prophet' (Isaiah or Hosea or Zechariah or other) about the Christ (Matt. 1. 22; 2. 15; 4. 15, 16; 8. 17; 12. 18-21; 13. 35; 21. 5; 27. 35).

The Spirit of Christ through the prophets foretold both the sufferings of Christ (the Greek preposition is our 'unto') and the subsequent glories. These worthies found themselves unable to co-ordinate the two themes. They diligently exercised their powers of thought and discernment to discover what period in God's dealings with men or what characteristics of such period might effect the desired adjustment. The clue continued to elude them. It was not God's purpose to reveal it till much later. Had they been acquainted with 'this present season,' this day of salvation, this very season of most favourable acceptance adumbrated in Isaiah 49. 8 (though this looks forward even now to its primary fulfilment) they would have been more successful in their search. But though Isaiah sees nothing between the acceptable year of the Lord and the day of God's vengeance, the Lord Jesus unerringly rolls up the scroll of the prophet to put at least nineteen centuries between the onset of the two. (1 Peter 1. 9-12; 2 Cor. 6. 2; Luke 4. 20).

The full elucidation belongs elsewhere. It is relevant to note here, however, that there is more said in Scripture about the glories than the sufferings, and that the former are connected with the second advent of Messiah, as the latter are with the first.

God's objective by present Christian testimony is to take out of the nations a people for His name. 'And to this agree the words of the prophets' (though what we call Christian testimony was an unknown subject to them) as they foretold the re-gathering of Israel into Palestine, the re-establishment of Davidic rule, and the blessing of the Gentiles through Israel and Israel's Messiah. Now dispersed as never before, scattered and peeled, they are abiding without king, prince, sacrifice, image, ephod or seraphim in subjection to 'parvenu' nations of whose very existence the fathers and the prophets could know nothing (Acts 15. 14; Hos. 3. 4, 5; Jer. 9. 16). Of their impacts on trade and commerce, art and science, politics and war during the last nineteen centuries of their triumphs and trials, this is not the place to treat. It may be noted, however, that the old division into Judah and Israel no longer obtains. Indeed, before the Exile there fell to Judah many Israelites of other tribes. Moreover, since Nebuchadnezzar's 'Babylon' embraced Assyria, to which many among the northern tribes had been deported, his Israelitish subjects were of all the tribes. The edict of Cyrus embraced all Israel. They are called Jews or Israelites alternatively. Returned to the land, they sacrificed 'for all Israel.' And in apostolic days Peter speaks to 'all the house of Israel,' and Paul of 'our twelve tribes' without distinction (2 Chron. 11. 13-16; 15. 9-15; 31. 6; 34. 9; 2 Kings 17. 6; 2 Chron. 36. 23; Ezra 1. 1-4; 6. 17; 8. 35; Acts 2. 36; 26. 7), as does James (1. 1).

Of the seventy hebdomads of Daniel's great prophecy one only remains. For its duration 'the prince that shall come' (not Messiah) will make a pact with Daniel's people, the Jews. This necessitates a return to their own land and it also implies their political unity. How this will take place need not concern us here. It is revealed that the covenanting prince will break his agreement when but half its course has run. Jewish sacrifice and oblation will be prohibited. The implication is that these have been offered, in rejection of the Christian faith. The 'abomination of desolation' (presumably an idol) will be set up in the sanctuary in Jerusalem. 'Jacob's trouble' will set in, 'for then shall be the great tribulation.'

In this time of terror lawlessness will abound among the apostate people, as is to be expected. But others, a remnant, will turn to the Lord, by their faith averting, again, from the whole nation the reproach of being as Sodom and Gomorrah. A remarkable accompaniment will be the proclamation of the truth among the Gentiles over widespread areas, evidently by Jewish believers, leading to many conversions. For, as the Lord said, 'these good tidings of the kingdom shall be preached in the whole inhabited earth for a testimony unto all the nations.' These Gentiles are seen by John to come out of the great tribulation, blessed for earth serving God 'day and night in His temple; and He that sitteth on the throne shall spread His tabernacle over them . . . and God shall wipe away every tear from their eyes.' The Jewish remnant, the elect, will either suffer martyrdom or will be preserved through the dreadful trials for millennial blessing (Dan. 9; 12. 1, 11; Matt. 24. 1-22; Rev. 7. 4, 9, 14-17; Isa. 1. 9, 10).

The Old Testament prophets frequently refer to 'the day of the Lord,' during which, while 'Jacob's trouble' is proceeding, Jehovah's wrath is being visited on Israel's oppressors. Their chief is described in the Revelation as a wild beast. Judgments of mounting intensity fall on him and his supporters, both Jewish and Gentile, those denoted by the seven 'vials' or bowls being the climax of 'the wrath of God.' These are preparatory to the 'wrath of the Lamb,' when the Lord Jesus comes in glory and judgment. He reaps the harvest and treads the winepress, thus ending the present and introducing the coming age, when He will 'at this time restore the kingdom to Israel.'

The exodus under Moses was 'with much substance.' The return from the Exile was on a much smaller scale. Both will be eclipsed by the restoration yet to be, to which the prophets bear enthusiastic witness.

'When the Most High gave to the nations their inheritance . . . He set the bounds of the peoples according to the number of the children of Israel.' But their land, in its entirety, has yet to be possessed. Even David, who in the later years of his reign, called no man lord and who extended the kingdom as never before, did not possess the whole.

Further, 'all Israel shall be saved' (that is, after the purging from apostacy), born of water and Spirit, cleansed from sin's uncleannesses, the new covenant writing God's law in their inward parts, in their heart. 'The earth shall be filled with the knowledge of the glory of the Lord.' The 'fulness' of Israel shall abound to the blessing of the nations, the 'receiving of them,' the clothing of the dry bones with new life, will be like new life also to the Gentiles. The 'King of kings and Lord of lords' will have undisputed sway, reigning in righteousness, for Satan will be bound and cast into the abyss for the kingdom's duration, which Revelation intimates will be a millennium.

In the rebuilt Jerusalem will be a temple, as described by Ezekiel. A prince of the house of David will have his dwelling on Mount Zion, from which shall go forth the law.

The contour of the land will be changed. The Mediterranean will be connected with the Dead Sea by a water-way, passing through the Mount of Olives. The earth will yield prolifically, the desert blossoming like the rose. Nation will not make war on nation and the very beasts of prey will have their ferocity changed into docility (Rev. 13. 1-10; 15. 1-19; 14. 14-20; Isa. 11; 63. 1-6; 66. 8-20; Jer. 16. 14-16; 23. 3-6; 31. 31-40; Ezek. 36 and 37; Deut. 32. 8, 9; Josh. 1. 4; Rom. 11. 12-15, 26).

> And the Lord shall be King over all the Earth,
> In that day shall there be one Lord and His name one.

CHAPTER XXI

Angels

W. R. LEWIS

THE word 'angel' means a 'messenger' and it is applied in various ways in Scripture. It is frequently used, in both the Old and New Testaments, in the ordinary sense of human messengers, for example, of those who came to Job (Job 1. 14) and of those sent from John the Baptist (Luke 7. 24). It is used of prophets, such as Haggai (Haggai 1. 13) and John the Baptist (Mal. 3. 1) and of priests, whose lips should keep knowledge (Mal. 2. 7) and to whom men's vows were declared (Eccl. 5. 6). It is used also of the disciples (Luke 9. 52) and of the representatives of the churches (Rev. 2-3).

The word 'angel' is further used of providential circumstances, for these, too, convey a message. God 'makes winds His messengers; His ministers a flaming fire' (Psa. 104. 4). These restless, untiring agents of God's will constitute His voice to men. The forces of nature are instinct with the powers of the spirit realm. Men see only material results whereas God is fulfilling His Word through these forms of elemental action (Psa. 148. 8). In ignorance and blindness men think of nature as secular only and look upon the ordinary course of events as a series of cold operations governed by law and force, having nothing to do with any divine purpose. But these outward and visible actions are in reality the means whereby men can feel after God and find Him. They bring Him very near (Acts 17. 27) and, throughout the Scriptures there is a readiness to attribute every kind of outward blessing, as well as external calamity, to their divine cause, and to see in them the voice and hand of God. How true it is that in the seen and temporal there is a constant presence of a Power that is Divine (Rom. 1. 20)! At every point, the natural and supernatural are blended, conveying a divine message to the soul that is ready to receive it. Everywhere and always man touches God though he knows Him not. His lovingkindness can be discerned in the earth and stars, the sun and moon (Psa. 136. 7-9), and in His handiwork in ourselves (Psa. 139. 13-18). When the Lord looked upon the lilies of the field He thought at once of the Father (Luke 12. 27), whereas how often men observe His works merely as objects of admiration or curiosity instead of as excitements to wonder and praise, simply, perhaps, as naturalists or scientists, instead of as children of their Creator. The believer can say, they are our Father's handiwork. 'O Lord, how manifold are Thy works! in wisdom hast Thou made them all: the earth is full of Thy riches' (Psa. 104. 24). What messages and lessons they contain for the adoring heart!

We need not be surprised, then, to find that the word angel is even applied to the Living Word Himself, for He is frequently referred to as 'the Angel of Jehovah.' In His incarnation He became God's final Message to men, but even before He became flesh He seems to be clearly indicated by this title (Exod. 3. 2; Acts 7. 30-32). Unlike the created angels, this 'Angel of the Lord' accepts the worship offered to Him, whereas they, as mere creatures, refuse it. He even, at times, appeared in human form before His incarnation but since He became flesh and dwelt among us He is never called 'the angel of the Lord.'

But the word angel is chiefly used of those superhuman creatures whose abode is heaven and who are the unseen agents in executing the purposes of God. To them are assigned functions in the administration of nature and of nations as well as in communications to men. They act as God's messengers and as personal agents in the fulfilment of His Word. They are the hosts of the Lord, innumerable and mighty, and endowed with faculties which fit them for their higher sphere of existence. They excel in strength, and, intently listening to the voice of His word, they are ready instantly to catch the slightest intimation of His will (Psa. 103. 20). They formed the retinue of Jehovah when the Law was given (Deut. 33. 2; Heb. 2. 2; Gal. 3. 19). They are 'holy ones' accomplishing perfectly the will of their Creator (Mk. 8. 38). They are 'elect' for, by means of divine preservation, they refused to be partners with Satan and his angels when they fell (1 Tim. 5. 21). They stood victorious in the test of the fierceness of that terrible defection and hence are fitted to help and sympathize as they behold how we have need to stand in the conflict that is ours (1 Cor. 4. 9).

In their ministry there is a marked economy both of word and of the display of power. Their words are always few and directly to the purpose and, as for the power they exercise, it is always ample but never more than ample. There is nothing superfluous in either case. Like the flame of fire and the winds to which they are likened, when the purpose is effected the flame dies down, the wind drops. They never indulge in the slightest self-display and in their obedience they never over-pass the limits of their commission. They never add to or diminish the message they carry. Again, they have no preferences in their service. No errand is beneath them. Whatever it may be, it is equally an honour to serve their Lord. It is all one to them whether they are sent to control the opposing forces of Persia or of Greece or to maintain the cause of Israel, or, on the other hand, to spread a meal for a weary traveller like Elijah (Dan. 10. 20; 12. 1; 1 Kings 19. 5). They consider not the nature of the command but alone its Author.

How readily they wait upon the heirs of salvation (Heb. 1. 14)! Yet they are never permitted to be the objects of our personal regard or to receive the worship due alone to their Creator (Col. 2. 18; Rev. 22. 9). They never receive the gratitude of the objects of their care for it is not intended that thanks should be rendered to them. With us the lack of thanks for any help we may bestow on fellow-mortals disturbs our spirits, but never theirs. How unselfishly they render service to those who are beneath them in the scale of creation but who are destined to administer the habitable earth to come and to occupy a place nearer to the Throne than theirs throughout eternity (Heb. 2. 5; Rev. 5. 11). They are never envious of our high destiny. How gentle, too, is the manner of their service! If they bear us up in their hands lest we dash our foot against a stone, yet is their care so softly rendered that we are rarely conscious of their protection (Psa. 34. 7; 91. 11, 12). It was an exceptional case to be smitten, like Peter, on the side, but Peter needed to be disturbed for he was fast asleep (Acts 12. 6). It is to the One who sends such messengers to our relief that thanks and praise are due. However lightly and contemptuously the conversion of a soul may be thought of among men, angels behold it with delight, whereas how trifling must human discoveries, exploits and victories appear to them! Nothing so pleases them as the deliverance of a sinner from the power of darkness and his translation into the kingdom of God's dear Son. They do not originate the joy; it is joy in their presence. They share the joy of the Father, Son and Holy Spirit (Luke 15. 10).

In all these perfections they can, indeed, be our example: in their instantaneous obedience for they have never to be told twice to do a thing; in their entire absence of self-display; in their absolute impartiality, for as spectators without fear or favour they observe us, having been themselves upheld as 'elect' in the great apostasy of Satan and his host (1 Tim. 5. 21); in their alacrity to help those who need it, though they never get from us a 'Thank you'; in their unselfishness and contentment, though the object of their care is quite unconscious of their deed; and in their thorough sympathy with the heart of God towards the lost and perishing.

How they must have wondered, to see their Creator upon the Cross of shame and curse and how their loyalty must have again been tested as they heard His unanswered cry of anguish, 'My God, My God, why hast Thou forsaken Me!' (1 Tim. 3. 16). But with what acclamations they would receive Him as He took His seat at God's right hand, the glorious work completed! Yet, though they have a high intelligence and can interpret visions (2 Sam. 14. 17, 20; Dan. 7. 16; 9. 21; Rev. 22. 8), they desire to look into the things which concern the scheme of our salvation (1 Peter 1. 12). It is not theirs, personally, to enjoy its blessedness. Relatively they do, for they sang with joy at the Advent of our Redeemer and rejoice over the repentance of a sinner. They have, indeed, their songs to sing, but the song we sing is

> A song unknown to angels' ears
> A song that tells of banished fears
> Of pardoned sins and dried-up tears.

Nor can they be the direct channel of the communication of life and blessing for in this human, not angelic, instruments are used.

Their ministry may be employed indirectly in furthering the bringing of the good news to men but it is not theirs to impart spiritual instruction; that is the work of the Spirit of God through the Word. Hence since the Scriptures have been completed, how few have been angelic messages! An angel may bid Peter gird himself, put on his sandals and cast his cloak about him, but he conveyed to Peter no spiritual instruction. The angel may open the prison doors, but when that is done he leaves (Acts 12. 7-12). It was an angel that directed the outward circumstances of Philip; but it was the Spirit who gave him directions for his spiritual service (Acts 8. 26, 29, 39). So far as men are concerned, angels deal with material, rather than with spiritual things, though they may avert evils which might hinder the progress of the Gospel and they may be used to bring about results which promote the reception of the message. All that they do appears to be done by means of natural causes and only by intensifying or in some particular way, directing these, do they seem to exercise any decisive influence on events in progress.

If, as we have seen, they can be to us examples of obedience and other graces, they can learn, by means of the church, the much-varied wisdom of God (Eph. 3. 10). They watch the behaviour of assemblies as well as of individuals and notice the slightest tendency to immodesty or irreverence in those they serve (1 Cor. 11. 10). If these holy beings are accustomed to veil their faces and cry, 'Holy, Holy, Holy,' in the presence of the Lord of Hosts, how much more should we, who are sinners by nature and by practice! As those who themselves have never sinned, who can tell how even they are edified by the obedience of mortal men and by their stedfastness in trial (1 Cor. 4. 9)? Before these angels the Lord is going to confess or deny those who have confessed or denied Him before men (Luke 12. 8).

Doubtless He who calls the stars by name, has given names to the angelic host, but of these, apart from Satan, we know but two, Michael and Gabriel. Michael is an archangel and Gabriel seems to be in some nearer relationship to God than others less elevated in power, for he speaks of himself as 'standing in the presence of God' (Luke 1. 19). There are also cherubim and seraphim, an order of heavenly beings not sent to earth at all but who are always in attendance upon God and are the bearers of His throne. There seems to be a variety in angelic ministry, for Gabriel's ministry is on behalf of men, whereas Michael's seems rather to be in opposition to Satan. Gabriel is a messenger of mercy, peace and restoration (Dan. 9. 21-23; Luke 1. 26), whereas

Michael is a warrior prince, apparently in charge of Israel, a messenger of wrath against movements hostile to the Kingdom of God (Dan. 10. 13-21; Jude 9; Rev. 12. 7). There are diversities amongst them of strength, for a 'mighty' angel is spoken of as though all were not precisely such, though all of them excel in power (Rev. 18. 21; Psa. 103. 20). There are gradations of rank amongst them, for we read of 'thrones, dominions, principalities and powers,' all of whom have been created by Christ and for Him (Col. 1. 16). He who once was made a little lower than the angels for the suffering of death is supreme over all the angelic host (Heb. 2. 9; 1 Peter 3. 22).

We read of their 'council' (Psa. 89. 7; 1 Kings 22. 19) as well as of their 'general assembly' (Heb. 12. 23; Psa. 82. 1; 89. 5), but beyond this we know but little of the angelic hierarchy. They spoke usually in human voice, though ordinarily their tongue is distinguished from man's (1 Cor. 13. 1). They are spoken of as 'men' and never 'women' for there are no sex distinctions in their case any more than there are amongst the redeemed in resurrection (Matt. 20. 30). Though created before the foundation of the world, they never grow old; they are always in their prime and appear as 'young' (Mark 16. 5). Their numbers never diminish and never increase and they need no means to perpetuate their race as mortals do.

Angels not only rejoiced at the birth of Jesus but they ministered to Him in the days of His flesh, both after His temptation in the wilderness and in His agony in the Garden. But what form that service took is hidden from us. It would seem to have been in the nature of physical rather than of spiritual assistance (Matt. 4. 11; Luke 22. 43; Matt. 26. 53). They announced His Second Advent (Acts 1. 11) and they will all worship and accompany Him when He comes in the glory of His Father and of the holy angels (Heb. 1. 6, R.V.; Matt. 25. 31). They will then be the instruments in the execution of the judgments that will attend that Coming (Matt. 13. 41-49; 2 Thess. 1. 7).

These myriads, continually ascending and descending on errands of mercy, render instant service to the heirs of salvation during life and cease not their office till they have carried the souls of the righteous to their heavenly abode (2 Kings 2. 11; Luke 16. 22).

How many a deliverance has been ours, did we only know it, whether through their personal agency or through the natural agencies under their control!

Yet though they occupy such an exalted position in creation, neither against Satan (Jude 9) nor against false teachers (2 Peter 2. 11) do they bring railing accusation; they leave the rebuke these merit to the Lord. The final end of Satan is yet future but already he is a defeated foe for at the Cross he met his Conqueror (Col. 2. 15). He will yet be bound and cast into the abyss (Rev. 20. 2). Meanwhile he finds in every triumph of the Gospel a pledge of his defeat, for the same power of God, which in the Gospel is salvation to everyone that believes it, is the death-knell of Satan's power (Luke 10. 18).

The Fallen Angels

Satan did not fall alone; a mighty host followed him in his rebellion. For this leader and for those he leads everlasting fire has been prepared (Matt. 25. 41). Some of these fallen ones appear to be at liberty in the heavenlies, while others, in still further rebellion, keeping 'not their own principality, but leaving their proper habitation, giving themselves over to fornication and going after strange flesh, are set forth as an example, suffering the punishment of eternal fire and are kept in everlasting bonds under darkness unto the judgment of the great day' (2 Peter 2. 4; Jude 6; Gen. 6. 2). As with the elect angels, so also amongst these fallen ones, there appear to be in Satan's kingdom ranks analogous to those occupied by the angels in Christ's Kingdom, and they can be compared, in respect of strength, only with the angels of Christ's power.

These evil angels have been passed by in the scheme of redemption. They fell without being tempted as man has been and their ruin is irretrievable. They fell each one for himself and not like Adam and his posterity as a race. Of this apostacy little has been told us save the fact and the awful future that awaits them. They will, apparently, be judged by the redeemed (1 Cor. 6. 3). There is no hope of salvation for them. 'He layeth not hold of angels, but He layeth hold (that is, to deliver and to help) of the seed of Abraham' (Heb. 2. 16-18), not, it is to be noticed, the seed of Adam, for that would mean the whole human race, as the universalist would teach, nor even the nation of Israel, but He layeth hold of the seed of Abraham, that is, those who, like Abraham, are justified by faith (Rom. 4. 11; Gal. 3. 29).

The Demons

Besides Satan's headship of fallen angels, the partners of his fall, he is also prince of demons (Matt. 9. 34), vassals in his kingdom, and forming part of a vast organized realm of evil governed by the prince of the power of the air (Eph. 2. 2). While angels are 'spirits' (Heb. 1. 14), they are sometimes distinguished from 'spirits' as they are certainly distinguished from 'demons' (Acts 23. 8, 9). They are never said to indwell the bodies of men, whereas the human body seems to be the normal abode of demons when a man lays himself open to their ingress (Matt. 12. 43-48). Some have suggested that demons are the discarnate spirits of beings who were once on earth before man appeared, but Scripture is silent as to this. Certain it is that they seem to favour the bodies of men as their temporal abode. They are spoken of as 'unclean,' as 'lying spirits,' and as manifesting every form and degree of evil (Matt. 12. 45). They can perceive and understand, can hate, and rage, and speak, and act, and tremble. They are 'spirits of error,' 'seducing spirits' (1 Tim. 4. 1), oppressing and tormenting men (Matt. 15. 22), seeking their ruin and hurt (Rev. 16. 13; 18. 2). They attack, especially, the minds and bodies of men, tempting them with unclean thoughts and afflicting them with bodily disease (Mk. 9. 17; Luke 13. 11). They take and seize and use the bodily organs and mental powers, for mind as well as body can be subject to demoniacal tyranny. Mental disease may, at times, betray symptoms of a hostile spiritual power behind it, whilst at other times, demon possession is distinguished from such disease (Matt. 4. 24). They subjugate the reason and imagination in their torment and oppression.

The real workers behind idolatry are demons and as gods they are worshipped (1 Cor. 10. 20; Rev. 9. 20). They are 'knowing ones' for that is the meaning of the word 'demons.' They have supernatural knowledge and could recognize the Lord before Peter had revealed to him the glory of His Person. They have doctrines of their own, emanating from the pit and inciting men to rebellion against God. What are the distinctive doctrines of Rome, that inveterate enemy of the Gospel, but doctrines of demons? (1 Tim. 4. 1). We need to remember that there is a filthiness of the spirit as well as of the flesh (2 Cor. 7. 1). The moral can abominate many of the unclean ways of the flesh and seek to fetter and prevent them, but how few regard with loathing the filthiness of the spirit, that uncleanness, for example, that tampers with the Word of God, which belittles Christ and exalts man, and seeks in various ways to disseminate various heresies (Rev. 16. 14). This unclean spirit deludes the soul, for it is very subtle in its influence and works unsuspectedly with the cultured and refined. The Lord and His apostles never accepted the testimony of demons even when such testimony was true (Mk. 1. 34; Acts 16. 18). On the other hand they can be 'fierce' (Matt. 8. 28) and can make their victims a terror to the neighbourhood. The very consciousness of the man possessed becomes merged in that of the fiend within him. From Mary of Magdala alone seven demons were cast out and a multitude may possess a single victim. Like a Roman legion, containing from 2,000 to 6,000 men, they can act in concert to crush the intellect and moral being of the man (Mk. 5. 9).

These malignant foes are filled with dread of the abyss awaiting them (Mk. 5. 12). Their one wish is not to be sent to hell for they have no doubts concerning everlasting punishment. They would rather have a swine's heart and brain and life for the time being than be there. When they take possession of a man, it is of his whole personality; they become a part of the man's very being, and swine chose death itself rather than to become possessed of these evil beings. What a contrast to those who, in modern spiritism, invite the entrance of such emissaries of Satan![1] Little do men know what it is to be in Satan's power. He hates to see his dupes cured of their spiritual disease; he dreads the display of the Saviour's power; he strives his utmost to hinder the spiritual progress of the soul, and when that soul begins to come to Christ, he sets in motion every kind of opposition. As long as men are regardless of their need of Christ he keeps them in peace, but the

[1] W. E. Vine deals with this subject in a fuller way in *Spiritism Unmasked.*

awakening conscience finds the trial of opposition greatest when a man's foes are those of his own household; when the persecution comes from those he loves and ought even to obey—only in the Lord—and greatest of all when opposition takes the form not of violence and threats, but of kindness, entreaties and tears. Whatever impedes our coming to Christ is of Satan, and must at all costs be resisted, for whatever difficulties we may encounter, come to Him we must if we would be blessed. It is the one thing needful.

'Our wrestling is not against flesh and blood but against the principalities and powers, against the world-rulers of this darkness, against the spiritual hosts of wickedness in the heavenly places' (Eph. 6. 12). The character of the rulers is indicated by the description of the realm they rule. The world-rulers of this darkness have made it a kingdom of darkness like themselves. The scene of this conflict is the 'heavenly places.' This is not heaven, for there is no conflict there, no wrestling, no spiritual wickedness there. 'Heavenly places' describe the spiritual atmosphere in which the heavenly-minded have their being. It is entered here on earth and constitutes our present position in Christ, where alone our spiritual blessings can be enjoyed. The word 'wrestling' means a contest in which one combatant 'shakes' the other in the endeavour to throw him down and in our case, to cast us down from our excellency (Psa. 62. 4), to shake our hold upon our most holy faith (Eph. 4. 14). It is not only a 'wrestling' but an armed 'combat,' a personal engagement for which we must be individually prepared. The stratagems of the enemy demand that fullest preparation for it should be made. Were our foes men like ourselves, human devices might suffice, but with this enemy the preparation must be outside of and above this human sphere. Only in the armour which God supplies can we successfully meet this foe.

We are confronted not by a single foe but by spiritual hosts of wickedness, by bands of evil spirits, all under the control of one like unto themselves. The god and prince of this world has around him hosts, whose nature, like his own, is spiritual and whose aim it is to advance, in his interest, in their several provinces, the progress of his kingdom, and they lend all their powers to their fell design, without intermission and in full accord. These foes have no need to draw their bow at a venture, they know full well the weak spot at which to aim, and what can mere flesh and blood do as opposed to such superhuman might and unseen terrestrial and celestial foes?

Assuredly no demon can enter the body of a child of God where the Holy Spirit has taken up His abode, and as regards our conflict with the angelic hosts full provision has been made for heart and will and understanding. If the divine armour is upon us we can hold our ground, however cunning the enemy's schemes may be, but only with this armour on can we resist the onslaught that may be made against us, and, especially, in a season of abounding wickedness. The enemy seems to know that his day of opportunity is shortening and is summoning to the attack all his forces to overwhelm us. Even when victory has been gained the field must still be kept. The grace of constancy is needed as well as the grace of victory.

The divine panoply of truth, of righteousness, of peace, of faith, of salvation, of the Word of God and prayer, renders the wearer, however timid he may be, invincible. The shield is intended for the defence of the whole man, turning every way, catching every blow or dart. Faith defends the whole being. It is not heroic courage we require; it is trust in God. It is only as we have the assurance of acceptance in the Beloved, peace through the blood of Christ, a conscience void of offence, the heart's affection true to Christ, that we have any strength to war against such foes. Satan aims at faith, and success there ensures his victory.

To the Captain of our salvation all authority has been given in heaven and on earth. He has been set at God's own right hand in the heavenly places, 'far above all principality and power and might and dominion,' far above every title or dignity that has been or can be given as a designation of majesty, good or evil, present or to come, and the same power that wrought in Christ and set Him there, in all its exceeding greatness, is wrought in the redeemed (Eph. 1. 18-22). He is there as Son of Man at God's right hand (Acts 7. 55), angels and authorities and powers being made subject unto Him (1 Peter 3. 22). To know the power of His resurrection is to experience it in ourselves in view of the vital union that subsists between Christ and the believer (Phil. 3. 20).

Let us, then, take courage. They that be with us are more than they that be with those who may oppose us. 'Elisha prayed and said, Lord, I pray Thee, open his eyes that he may see. And the Lord opened the eyes of the young man and he saw, and, behold, the mountain was full of horses and chariots of fire.' These were Elisha's bodyguard (2 Kings 6. 11). While there is no room for carelessness or sloth, there is no room for despair on the part of the one who remembers that his Helper is omnipotent.

CHAPTER XXII

Satan

FREDK. A. TATFORD

THE apparent existence of two conflicting principles in nature early gave rise to what Dr. Réville has termed 'an eminently dualistic conception of the forces or divinities which direct the course of events,' and this really lies at the root of the dualism which is inherent in all forms of nature worship. During the captivity, the Israelites were brought into contact with the teaching of Persian Zoroastrianism—which had the same basic features—and it has been suggested by many that it was in the mythological conflict of the evil Ahriman with the good Ormuzd that the doctrine of a personal devil first found its origin. It is quite plain that neither pagan conceptions nor mythology formed the basis of the Biblical doctrine, however, for the Scriptures had clearly referred to the existence of this mighty being at a much earlier date.

It is sometimes maintained that the devil is merely a personification of the principle of evil and is not an actual being, but this is patently irreconcilable with the teachings of Scripture (Matt. 13. 39; John 13. 2; Acts 5. 3; 1 Peter 5. 8). 'The personal existence of a spirit of evil,' says Barry, 'is revealed again and again in Scripture. Every quality, every action, which can indicate personality, is attributed to him in language which cannot be explained away.' He is capable of movement (Job 1. 7, 12), he enters into men (John 13. 27), he lays snares for them (1 Tim. 3. 7; 2 Tim. 2. 28), he tempted Christ (Matt. 4. 1-9), he is described by our Lord as a liar and murderer, whilst activities and characteristics are credited to him which can only be applicable to a person. If our Lord's testimony is to be accepted, there is no question as to the personality of Satan. Findlay says, 'In the visible forms of sin, Jesus saw the shadow of his great antagonist. From the Evil One He taught His disciples to pray that they might be delivered. The victims of disease and madness whom He healed were so many captives rescued from the malignant power of Satan. And when Jesus went to meet His death, He viewed it as the supreme conflict with the usurper and oppressor who claimed to be "the prince of this world." '

Satan is neither self-existent nor eternal. He is a created being and came into existence by the hand of God. In his first estate, he was one of the cherubim, of the highest angelic order, and standing in closest proximity to God Himself. He was 'the anointed covering (or protecting) cherub' (Ezek. 28. 14). 'Like the golden cherubim, covering the visible mercy-seat in the holy of holies of the earthly tabernacle,' writes Chafer, 'he was created a guard and covering cherub to the heavenly centre of glory.'

Ezekiel's 'lamentation' upon the king of Tyre (Ezek. 28. 12-15), whilst addressed to an earthly potentate, obviously goes beyond the earthly king and applies to one of greater power—even to Satan himself, the real, though unseen, ruler of Tyre. The prophecy reveals that this mighty spirit was created by God for immediate attendance upon Himself and that he was placed in a position of close relationship to His throne, being connected, as one of the cherubim, with the holiness and governmental purposes of the Almighty. From the day of his creation, he received honour and dignity and was in 'Eden, the garden of God'—not the Adamic Eden, but as Torrey suggests, 'an earlier one. The Adamic Eden was remarkable for its vegetable glory. This early Eden for its mineral glory. Compare the New Jerusalem (Rev. 21. 10-21). . . . In the Adamic Eden, Satan was present, not as here, as a minister of God, but as an apostate spirit and a tempter. The glory of the early Eden seems to have been specially prepared for Satan. There was also the pomp of royalty, tabrets and pipes.'

Surpassing all other created beings in his marvellous beauty, it is recorded that he was 'perfect in beauty'; taught by the Almighty, he possessed divinely-given wisdom; cherished and honoured above all created intelligences, he was the anointed covering cherub, dwelling in the mountain of God, walking in the stones of fire, and possessing the mark of God's approval in a covering of gold and precious stones. From the reference to musical instruments and to his anointing, it has sometimes been deduced that he was also connected with the worship of the angelic hosts and that he was possibly the leader in this service.

Set in authority in the midst of the heavens, it is possible that the whole hierarchy of angels was in subjection to him, but little is recorded of the exact extent of the original power of the great Lucifer.

The recipient of such blessing and favour might have been expected to exhibit the utmost loyalty to his benefactor, but an inordinate pride and overweening ambition led to his tragic fall (1 Tim. 3. 6). In amazing arrogance, he sought the supreme place in heaven. Whether he endeavoured to divert the worship of the angelic hosts from the Creator to himself, or whether he put himself at the head of a rebellious army of angels in heaven in a desperate attempt to overthrow God and to establish himself on the throne of the Almighty, is not explicitly revealed. But, with the dejected hosts of his followers, he was expelled from the immediate presence of God and deprived of his glory and dignity. 'Thou wast perfect in thy ways till unrighteousness was found in thee,' declared Ezekiel. 'Thou hast sinned; therefore have I cast thee as profane from the mountain of God, and have destroyed thee, O covering cherub, from the midst of the stones of fire' (Ezek. 28. 15, 16). Isaiah gives a further glimpse of that dark hour when he writes: 'How art thou fallen from heaven, Lucifer, son of the morning! And thou that didst say in thy heart, I will ascend into the heavens, I will exalt my throne above the stars of God, and I will sit upon the mount of assembly, in the recesses of the north; I will ascend above the heights of the clouds, I will be like the Most High: none the less art thou brought down to Sheol, to the recesses of the pit' (Isa. 14. 12-15). The devil was the original sinner (1 John 3. 8) and a bitter price has he already paid for that act of sin.

Deprived of his former estate, Satan became, not only the author of sin, but the great arch-enemy of truth and holiness, and the title he will carry into the lake of fire—'that old deceiver, the devil'—will perpetuate the memory of his iniquity and the origin of sin.

Some of the angels who fell with him were divinely seized and imprisoned in chains, to await the execution of the judgment which will cast them, with their leader, into the lake of fire (2 Peter 2. 4, 5; Jude 6). Satan evidently has a greater liberty than his former satellites, but has been appointed well-defined limits, beyond which he cannot go.

From the moment of his downfall, Satan set himself in opposition to God and sought particularly to frustrate the divine purposes in relation to man. To unfallen man in the garden of Eden, he appeared in the guise of a serpent and enticed to a deliberate transgression of the commandment of God (Gen. 3. 4-7). In the antediluvian period, there seems to have been an unprecedented demonstration of Satanic activity ('the sons of God' in Gen. 6. 2 seem to have been fallen angels who had left their proper estate—although it is suggested by some that they were descendants of Seth). He tempted David to number Israel (1 Chron. 21. 1). He consistently attacks God's people to-day and attempts to seduce them from the path of loyalty to Christ.

His efforts were particularly directed against the Messiah, however. When Adam fell, God revealed that a Redeemer would come: the Seed of the woman should bruise the serpent's head and he should bruise His heel (Gen. 3. 15). From that moment commenced a long-drawn-out struggle on Satan's part to prevent the fulfilment of the promise. The murder of Abel (Gen. 4. 8), the universal corruption and consequent judgment of Noah's day (Gen. 6), the murder of the Hebrew babes (Exod. 1. 16), are all illustrations of his attempts to blot out the line through which the Redeemer should come. In the time of Athaliah, an attempt was made to destroy the whole of the royal house and it was only through the intervention of his aunt, Jehoshabeath, and the fidelity of Jehoiada, the priest, that the sole survivor, Josiah, was preserved (2 Chron. 22. 10-12).

When the forerunner of the Messiah appeared in the person of John the Baptist, as foretold by Isaiah and Malachi, prophecy had prepared the devil for the Coming One Himself. Hence his instigation of Herod to destroy the children of Bethlehem (Matt. 2. 16).

When our Lord was about to enter upon His public ministry, Satan took the step of personally assailing Him, in the severest of temptations, to entice Him to sacrifice the object of His incarnation. Suffering from the pangs of hunger, Christ was tempted to satisfy the appetite by a miracle. From the pinnacle of the temple, the tempter urged Him to show His power and majesty by a miraculous descent. Arraying all the kingdoms of the world before Him,

Satan offered Him all their glory and sovereignty in return for His swerving from the path of allegiance to God (Matt. 4. 1-10). But every temptation was completely unavailing.

In due time, however, the Lamb of God was delivered into the hands of those who sought His life. In order to secure the achievement of his purpose, Satan entered into Judas Iscariot (Luke 22. 3) and inspired the man of Kerioth in his treacherous betrayal. The subsequent agony of Calvary told something of the devil's power, and the Psalmist reveals the depths of Satanic malignity: even in those moments of untold suffering, the forces of evil gathered exultantly around the Cross. 'Great bulls have encompassed Me; Bashan's strong ones have beset Me round. . . . Dogs have encompassed Me; an assembly of evildoers have surrounded Me' (Psa. 22. 12, 16). What transpired during those hours of darkness will never be fully known.

In that hour of Satan's greatest victory, the Christ of God turned defeat into victory. He undid the works of the devil (1 John 3. 8), annulled his power (Heb. 2. 14), and defeated him who had the power of death. From the depths of Hades, Christ released the souls of the blest and wresting from the devil the keys of death and Hades, rose triumphantly on the third day, carrying back with Him a multitude of captives (Eph. 4. 8; Heb. 2. 14, 15). He spoiled the Satanic principalities and authorities and made an open show of His triumph over them (Col. 2. 15). The first great blow towards the complete bruising of the serpent's head had been struck; the bruising of the heel of the woman's Seed had been fulfilled at Calvary, and the final crushing of the Evil One was now ensured (Rom. 16. 20).

Despite his fall, Satan has not yet been deprived of all his dignity. Indeed, so exalted is his position still that even Michael the archangel 'did not dare to bring a railing judgment against him' (Jude 9).

He is still 'the ruler of the authority of the air' (Eph. 2. 2). The Jewish rabbis taught that the terrestrial atmosphere was his abode and that it was peopled with spirit beings. This is supported by the apostle's statement that 'our struggle is not against flesh and blood, but against principalities, against authorities, against the universal lords of this darkness, against spiritual powers of wickedness in the heavenlies' (Eph. 6. 12). It is sometimes maintained that the reference to the air is simply to spirit or breath and that 'Paul refines the Jewish idea of evil spirits dwelling in the surrounding atmosphere into an ethical conception of the atmosphere of the world, as that from which the sons of disobedience draw their breath and receive the spirit that inspires them' (Findlay). Beck, for example, says, 'The power of the air is a fitting designation for the prevailing spirit of the times, whose influence spreads itself like a miasma through the whole atmosphere of the world. It manifests itself as a contagious nature-power.' But it seems quite clear that what the Ephesian letter was intended to convey was that the Evil One was the sovereign of hosts of evil spirits who made their abode in the physical atmosphere. Our Lord specifically uses the title Beelzebub, the chief of the demons, of him (Luke 11. 18, 19).

In addition to the angels of God, the air is apparently populated by apostate angels—still retaining the ranks and titles (principalities, authorities, lords) which were theirs before their fall—and by the demons, or unclean spirits, whom our Lord cast out whenever He found them inhabiting a human body on earth. We know little of the former, but much is said in the New Testament of the latter. Dr. C. I. Scofield says of the demons that 'they are capable of entering into and controlling man and beast (Mk. 5), and earnestly seek embodiment, without which apparently they are powerless for evil (Matt. 12. 43, 44; Mk. 5. 10-12). They are unclean, sullen, violent and malicious, and inflict physical maladies' (Matt. 8. 28; 10. 1; Mark 5. 2-5; 9. 20). These evil spirits recognized Christ and are fully aware of their coming doom (Matt. 8. 29; Jas. 2. 19). They are all subject to the direction of Satan: he is their unseen lord and it is his behests they obey.

The devil is also described as 'the prince of this world,' and our Lord recognized his right to this title (John 12. 31; 14. 30; 16. 11). 'Was this world a department assigned to him of God as separate kingdoms have been assigned to different celestial potentates?' asks Torrey. 'Did he drag down his dominion with him in his own fall?' It has sometimes been suggested that this earth was the scene of his former glory and that it suffered a pre-Adamite judgment as a result of his fall, and some colour is given to this by references in Isaiah and Jeremiah (Isa. 24. 1; Jer. 4. 23; cf. Gen. 1. 2 with Isa. 45. 18).

Whether this be so or not, there are not wanting evidences that spiritual as well as human powers are concerned in the administration of the earth. Isaiah, for example, declares that, in a coming day, God 'will punish the host of the high ones on high, and the kings of the earth upon the earth (Isa. 24. 21), that is, both the spiritual and the human rulers. Again, when the angel of the Lord came forth to speak with Daniel, he was confronted by rebel spirit princes, whose titles indicated their terrestrial authority (Dan. 10. 21). Satan evidently still has authority over the world and, as Pember has said, 'divides the world into different provinces according to its nationalities, appointing a powerful angel, assisted direct by countless subordinates, as viceroy over each kingdom, to its energies and bend them to his will.' He is 'the head of the kingdom of darkness, which embraces all evil beings,' says Hodge.

'The powers that be' are ordained of God, but, within the restrictions set him by the Almighty, Satan is behind the whole system of world government, and powers are but puppets in his hand. He exercises all the rights of sovereignty in a scene which so readily subjects itself to him. The greed and ambition of nations, the diplomacy and deceit of the political world, the bitter hatred and rivalry in the sphere of commerce, the organization of many forms of government itself, proceed from a Satanic source. It was this sovereignty that he offered to Christ (Luke 4. 6), and his right to offer it was not disputed by our Lord. 'Though under the restraining hand of God,' says Chafer, 'Satan is now in authority over the unregenerate world, and the unsaved are unconsciously organized and federated under his leading. . . . This federation includes all of the unsaved and fallen humanity; it has the co-operation of the fallen spirits, and is but the union of all who are living and acting in independence of God.' The Satanic system is utterly evil and at enmity with God (Jas. 4. 4). It is corrupt (2 Peter 1. 4) and polluted (2 Peter 2. 20). 'The whole world lies in the wicked one' (1 John 5. 19). With the exception of the redeemed, the entire mass of men rest supinely in Satan's embrace. The death-knell of that mighty dominion was sounded, however, at Calvary (John 12. 31).

The cause of Satan's original downfall was a desire to be on an equality with God and that deep-seated ambition is still buried in his breast. Not content with the rule of men's ways, he seeks supremacy over their hearts and cleverly directs the religious worship of mankind to himself. 'The god of this age,' wrote Paul, 'has blinded the thoughts of the unbelieving' (2 Cor. 4. 4). In order that the glory of the Gospel might not shine into their hearts, Satan presents himself to their gaze. To some he becomes the great Mammon, the god of money; to others he takes the form of the Muses or Arts; others worship him as fame or fortune, or even as the personification of religion. Through each channel, by every idol he sets up, he gains the worship of a section of the inhabitants of the world, blinding them to the light of the Gospel. Behind every phase and facet of man's objects of worship is the central figure of the 'god of this age.'

The early Christians believed that evil spirits were behind all the deities of the ancient pantheons and that all worship of false gods was therefore directed to Satan himself. This belief was fully confirmed by the Apostle Paul when he wrote, 'What the nations sacrifice, they sacrifice to demons and not to God' (1 Cor. 10. 20). Even to-day, it is impossible, as one writer remarks, 'to explain all occult phenomena and phrenetic moral aberrations by physical causes,' and there is little doubt that behind the idols of the heathen even to-day are the spiritual forces of Satan.

During the present day, the devil has power over the physical bodies of unbelievers (Luke 13. 16; Acts 10. 38) and, where permitted by God, can also inflict malady and physical suffering even upon believers (Job 1. 9-12; 1 Cor. 5. 5; 2 Cor. 12. 7). He had formerly 'the might of death' (Heb. 2. 14), i.e. authority in the realms of death. But the Son of God descended into death, faced and defeated the mighty foe, and rose again triumphantly, having broken the devil's power.

Throughout the present age, Satan is permitted to have a part in the sifting and testing of believers (Luke 22. 31), but the Lord is ever watching and ready to supply all needed help in the hour of temptation. Indeed, the testings are often divinely permitted in order that faith may be proved. Whilst he is thus engaged on earth, the devil also finds an access before God to draw attention to the faults and failings of those who seek to live godly lives (Job 1. 6-12; 2. 1-7), but the day is not far distant when he will be ejected for ever from that heavenly sphere (Rev. 12. 9, 10).

'Satan is the consummate form of depraved and untruthful intellect,' writes Findlay. 'We read of his thoughts, his schemes, his subtlety and deceit and impostures (2 Cor. 2. 11; 11. 3; 2 Thess. 2. 9, 10; 2 Tim. 2. 26); of his slanders against God and man (Rev. 12. 7-10; Gen. 3. 4, 5; Zech. 3. 1), from which, indeed, the name devil (*diabolos*) is given him. Falsehood and hatred are his chief qualities. Hence Jesus called him 'the manslayer' and the 'father of falsehood' (John 8. 44). He was the first sinner, and the fountain of sin (1 John 3. 8). All who do unrighteousness or hate their brethren are, so far, his offspring' (1 John 3. 10). As Barry points out, he does not 'act directly and openly, but needs craft and dissimulation in order to get advantage over man by entangling the will. The wiles, the devices, the snare of the devil are expressions which indicate the indirect and unnatural character of the power of evil (Eph. 6. 11; 2 Cor. 2. 11; 1 Tim. 3. 7; 6. 9; 2 Tim. 2. 26)'.

Although his power is so great, Satan suffers from restrictions placed upon him by God and is, in many respects, virtually only a servant of the Almighty. His power, through his demon and angelic forces, is almost beyond comprehension, but the power of God is greater than all the forces of the evil one and Paul declares emphatically that not even angels, principalities or powers shall separate the Christian from the love of God (Rom. 8. 38, 39). In dependence upon the Holy Spirit, there is victory for the believer over all the powers of evil and James definitely declares: 'Resist the devil and he will flee from you' (Jas. 4. 7). Depicting the devil as a roaring lion, Peter again exhorts both vigilance and resistance (1 Peter 5. 8). The armour of God alone will suffice for this fray (Eph. 6. 11).

Satan's limitations are very clearly indicated in Scripture. Although his evil hosts make his power felt throughout the world, he is not omnipotent since, as in the case of Job, he has to seek permission before he may do certain things. Although his intelligence is as great as can be conceived for a creature, his lack of knowledge is apparent from the many errors of judgment he has made in history, particularly in his dealings with Christ; he is definitely not omniscient. Nor is he omnipresent, as he revealed in his statement in Job's day that he came 'from going to and fro in the earth, and from walking up and down in it' (Job 1. 7; 2. 2).

With the myriads of his demon and angelic hosts, Satan possesses a power which might well cause men to quail in fear were it not for the fact that that power is at present held in check by the restraining influence of the Holy Spirit and the Church of God (2 Thess. 2. 6, 7). At the coming of Christ, however, the Holy Spirit and the Church He indwells will be removed (1 Thess. 4. 15-17; 1 Cor. 15. 51-54, and the devil will be at liberty to produce his masterpiece—a complete travesty of divine things. In place of the church, he will present to the world a great counterfeit, Babylon the harlot (Rev. 17); in the stead of Christ, he will introduce Antichrist (2 Thess. 2); and in lieu of God's king, he will enthrone the Beast (Rev. 13. 1-10).

His access to the heavenlies will be taken from him and after bitter warfare with Michael and his angels, he will be cast down to the earth (Rev. 12. 7-12). His days of liberty numbered, Satan's fury will be unleashed, but when wickedness has reached its culminating point, the Son of Man will appear in glory, with the hosts of His saints, to execute judgment upon all (Jude 14). The armies of Satan's two puppets will be destroyed, the leaders taken and cast alive into the lake of fire (Rev. 19. 11-21), whilst the devil, who inspired them, will be judicially bound and sealed in the abyss, there to remain impotent for a thousand years (Rev. 20. 1-3).

Throughout the millennium, Satan will necessarily be inactive, but at its close, he will again be loosed for 'a little season' (Rev. 20. 7). Unchanged in character, his undeviating purpose will remain the frustration of God's will. With bitter hatred he will use his liberty to organize a last desperate effort to overthrow the Almighty, gathering together all the forces of evil and all the nations of the earth against the beloved city. Inspired by their mighty leader, the tremendous armies will seek to make war on the Lamb and the saints, only to find bitter retribution in consuming fire from heaven (Rev. 20. 9). His plans dissolved and his power for ever broken, Satan will be powerless before God, who will pronounce his eternal, irrevocable doom. Once the anointed cherub and the favoured one of God, he will be cast into the lake of fire, long reserved for him (Matt. 25. 41), to be 'tormented day and night for ever and ever' (Rev. 20. 10).

Well has Chafer written, 'The present time is, for Satan, the struggle for his own existence, as well as the realization of all that has been his ambition in the ages past. The warfare is no mere passing amusement for him, for he, in desperation, is facing a terrible and awful judgment if he cannot succeed in his purpose. The spectacle now presented to all enlightened beings of the universe is that of a mighty celestial being, the god of this earth, who was by creation the full measure of perfection, both in wisdom and beauty, making his last and most desperate warfare, both to realize his own ambition and to thwart every movement of the Most High; knowing that in failure there is no ground for mercy, but only the terrible destruction that has been so long predicted. He knew when he formed this God-dishonouring purpose that it must either wholly succeed or he himself fall into terrible judgment.'

Well might we fear but for the knowledge that greater is He that is for us than he that is against us.

CHAPTER XXIII

Christ's Second Advent

J. M. DAVIES

THE coming of Christ, the Messiah, into the world was the main burden of the promises and the prophecies of the Old Testament. The first of these is given in Gen. 3. 15 and the last in Mal. 3. 1 and 4. 2. These portions, like many others, partake of certain common characteristics. They are couched in enigmatic terms, which could only be fully understood in the light of further revelation and in some cases only in the light of their fulfilment. Then again the time element is not introduced. The fact that 4,000 years would elapse before the seed of the woman would come, or that another long period (already nearly 2,000 years) would intervene between the coming, the bruising of the heel of the Saviour, and the final bruising of the head of the serpent is not hinted at. Similarly in Mal. 3. 1 the reference to John the Baptist has already been fulfilled, whereas the second half of the verse still remains to be fulfilled.

Owing to the absence of the time element in the prophecies of the Old Testament, predictions concerning the first and second advent of our Lord are brought together as in Zech. 9. 9-10; Isa. 61. 1-3 and Dan. 9. 26.

The Old Testament prophecies of the Messiah fall into two groups:

(*a*) Those which speak of Him as suffering,

(*b*) Those which speak of Him as reigning.

While we may with ease harmonize these now, it was difficult for the Jews to do so. Even after the resurrection the Lord had to rebuke the disciples for being slow of heart to believe *all* that the prophets had written. Little wonder that to preach Messiah crucified was a stumbling-block to the nation.

This dual aspect of Old Testament prophecy was manifest in the ministry of our Lord. He spoke of His decease, which He was to accomplish at Jerusalem, and foretold His rejection, crucifixion and resurrection, while the Old Testament prophecies concerning the triumphant character of the coming Messiah were continued in the parables, and applied to Himself as the Son of Man. These parables have in view His relationship to Israel, to Jerusalem, to the Land and to the world.

But 'in the night in which He was betrayed,' during the time in which Judas was consulting with the chief priests and elders, our Lord, for the first time, spoke of His return in a new way. 'If I go away, I come again, that where I am, there ye may be also.' In keeping with the gradual and progressive method of revelation, much was left undisclosed in the discourse in the upper room as to His return for them and their reception to glory. This was revealed later through Paul.

Teaching concerning the Lord's return and its contingent events is scattered with much profusion throughout the whole of the New Testament. All the writers refer to it in one aspect or another. The late Dr. A. T. Pierson computed that in all there are over 350 references to the subject in the New Testament. But while this is so, it is in the Church epistles of Paul that explicit teaching is found regarding the rapture of the Church, and what is vitally connected with it, the redemption of the body, which involves the resurrection of those who 'died in faith, not having received the promises,' and of 'those which have fallen asleep in Christ,' the saints of both Old and New Testament days respectively.

Peter in his epistles says he is a confirmatory witness, bearing corroborative evidence to what Paul had taught. Such is the force of the word 'testifying' in 1 Peter 5. 12 (Bengel).

Dr. McNicol, late Principal of the Toronto Bible College, in an article on the 'Hope of the Church,' in Vol. IV of the *The Fundamentals*, points out that this hope is the personal return of the Lord and shows among other things that redemption is not complete until the coming of the Lord. This is true of the various phases of the work of redemption. The redemption of the body awaits His return. It will only be effected when He comes. In view of this we read that the believer is 'sealed until the day of redemption.' He has been given the Holy Spirit as the 'earnest of his inheritance, until the redemption of the purchased possession.' The gift of the Holy Spirit is the 'first-fruits,' a technical term used with reference to the birth certificate of a free person.

Justification is unto life. Hence the believer's spirit has already been quickened. The spirit, the spiritual element in the believer is life because of righteousness; but the body, the physical element, being the 'body of sin,' with the law of sin engraved upon its members, is a body of humiliation. Having been sold under sin, and not yet redeemed, it is still a 'mortal body' and is referred to as this 'body of death.' The apostle yearned for deliverance from it; he groaned within himself 'waiting for the adoption, to wit, the redemption of the body,' and gave thanks as he contemplated the consummation of redemption in relation thereto. As Bengel suggests, this longing for deliverance is a life-long yearning, and says the body is stated to be 'dead,' instead of 'about to die' with great force. 'The contrast between the spirit and the body leads us rather to apply the former term to the spiritual element in the believer. The spirit is already quickened: the body must be also. The spirit having been quickened because of righteousness must be understood in the sense of justification' (Godet. Rom. 8). The effect of sin upon the body has not yet been removed. It is dead, that is, not yet quickened, and is therefore mortal, subject to death, corruption and disintegration. But as the body is dead *because* of sin, and the spirit is life *because* of righteousness, so the believer's body shall be quickened *because* of the Spirit of God indwelling him.

The apostle then shows that the redemption of the body is an integral part of the purpose of God and involves the resurrection of the dead. It is more especially the resurrection of those who are fallen asleep in Christ that the apostle is referring to in 1 Cor. 15. 'How are the dead raised up? and with what body do they come?' he asks. The body is spoken of as being sown in corruption, in dishonour, in weakness, and a natural body; and as being raised in incorruption, in glory, in power and a spiritual body.

Immediately connected with the resurrection of the dead is the physical change that will be effected in all them that are Christ's at the coming of the Lord. Our bodies as at present constituted cannot inherit the Kingdom of God. They must undergo a change so as to fit us for the conditions of the heavenly sphere. God will impart the life, give the body and grace it with glory (1 Cor. 15. 36, 38, 41). All believers will not die, but all will be changed. This change will be accomplished in a moment, in the twinkling of an eye, at the last trump. This is tantamount to saying that we shall all be changed at the same moment. This precludes the possibility of the change affecting any section of the redeemed only, or that some will have priority over others. It is all based upon our relationship to Christ, and will include all who are labelled by the apostle as 'they that are Christ's.'

The Rapture

The resurrection of the body not only embraces the resurrection of the dead but the rapture of the saints also. In Rom. 8 it is involved in the term 'glorified,' but in 1 Thess. it is spoken of in more detail. 'The rapture is defined as the act of conveying a person from one place to another. It is the translation of a Greek word which is rendered "snatch" in John 10. 12, 28, 29 and "caught away," in Acts 8. 39. Thus the rapture of the saints or of the church is an entirely Scriptural expression, and describes vividly the instantaneous removal of those who are in Christ, whether living or dead at the word of the returning Lord' (*Touching the Coming*, Hogg and Vine, p. 43).

In 1 Thess. 4 the coming of the Lord is introduced as a message of comfort in relation to those who are fallen asleep. In chap. 5 it is introduced as a message of warning to Christians, who, instead of being watchful or sober, as being of the day, had become like those who go down to the pit, those that are of the night or of darkness and were asleep. They were in the grip of spiritual sloth. In chap. 4 the dead in Christ and living believers are the two classes referred to, whereas in chap. 5 it is the slothful and the sober, the two classes of living believers that the apostle has in view. In accordance with this important difference the resurrection of Christ is mentioned in chap. 4 in relation to those who have died. But in chap. 5 it is only the death of Christ that is mentioned. In this, one of the simplest of Paul's epistles, written to a young assembly, not long saved out of idolatry, there are but two references to the death of Christ. This is made to be the one basis of our part in the coming rapture. Irrespective of death on the one hand, or of spiritual sloth on the other, the trumpet sound will usher us all into His presence. Some will be ashamed before Him in His presence or *parousia* (1 John 2. 28). In connection with salvation in its past, present or future aspects (and in the places where the word is used in 1 and 2 Thess, it is the future aspect that is prominent), it is important to keep ever before us that it is obtained through Christ alone, by grace alone, and through faith alone.

As the Cross of our Lord stood between the two thieves and became the meridian which separated them eternally, so in 2 Thess. the Gospel is the great divide between destruction, or the punishment of the wicked, and glory, the portion of the redeemed. Those who obey not the Gospel are punished with everlasting destruction from the presence of the Lord (2 Thess. 1. 9). By the Gospel we are called 'to the obtaining of the glory of our Lord Jesus Christ' (2 Thess. 2. 14).

1 Thess. shows that the dead in Christ rise *first*. Therefore no living saints are to be translated until they are raised. There is no hint that only some who may have attained a special undefined state of holiness are to be raptured.

The Judgment Seat

The rapture of the saints will usher in the 'day of Christ,' otherwise designated as 'the day of Jesus Christ,' 'the day of the Lord Jesus'; 'the day of the Lord Jesus Christ'; 'the day' and 'that day.'

From the context in which these expressions are used, and from the fact that they are used in relation to believers only, it is evident that they refer to the period when our Lord will be present with His people between the rapture and the revelation. This period is covered by the word *parousia*. This word is used some twenty-four times in the New Testament. It is twice rendered as 'presence,' and twenty-two times as 'coming,' fifteen of which are in connection with the return of the Lord. Liddell and Scott in their Lexicon give its meaning as 'a being present, presence.' Dr. Young in his Concordance gives its meaning as 'a being alongside, presence.' This meaning may be verified by the use of the word by the apostle of himself and others, in which connection it is used some six times. Paul's detractors said that his bodily 'presence' was weak. The apostle urged the saints at Philippi to constant and continued obedience, not only in his 'presence' but in his absence. In this verse the words presence and absence, *parousia* and *apousia* are set over against each other antithetically. In speaking of the time spent on the Mount of Transfiguration with the Lord, Peter refers to it as the power and presence, or *parousia* of our Lord. 'In a document of almost the same period as that in which the New Testament was written a person states that attention to her property necessitated her *parousia* in a certain city' (Hogg and Vine, *Touching the Coming*).

Hence, while of necessity the thought of arrival is implied in the use of the word, it by no means satisfactorily exhausts it or adequately defines its true meaning. 'It signifies more or less a prolonged period following the arrival' (C. F. H. and W. E. V., *Touching the Coming*, p. 60).

The R.V. gives in the margin of the references in which it is used in connection with the Lord's return the literal meaning of the word as 'presence.' A comparison of these fifteen references will reveal that the emphasis in them varies, in that some of them have the commencement, others the course, and others the consummation of the *parousia* in view.

The reconciliation in the body of His flesh through death has as its aim the presenting of those thus reconciled holy and unblameable and irreprovable in His sight. The apostle confidently looked forward to this as far as he and his fellow-workers were concerned. 'Knowing that He which raised up the Lord Jesus shall raise up us also by Jesus and shall present us with you.' The Lord would recognize and reward his services then. Thereby he would be vindicated. Along with Jude he was convinced that the Lord was able thus to present all His own. He was assured that 'Christ loved the Church and will eventually present it to Himself a glorious Church, not having spot or wrinkle or any such thing.'

Moreover the apostle anticipated the joy of presenting 'every man perfect in Christ' and the assembly 'as a chaste virgin to Christ.' In view of this he desired that he would have whereof to glory in the day of Christ that he had not run in vain or laboured in vain (Phil. 2. 16). This he speaks of as the 'prize of the high calling of God in Christ Jesus.' The prize is the reward conferred by the Lord at the end of the race, and toward this Paul was pressing on, counting as dross and refuse all that would hinder his progress.

18

Thus connected with the 'day of Christ,' the *parousia* of the Lord with His own is the fact that it will be not only a time of rejoicing, but of review and rewards.

As all believers are to be caught up, so all believers are to be at the 'Judgment Seat of Christ.' As no unbeliever will be caught up to meet the Lord in the air, it logically follows that there will be no unbelievers at the Judgment Seat of Christ. As, moreover, we are assured that there is no condemnation to them that are in Christ Jesus, and that they will not 'come into judgment,' it is evident that the Judgment Seat of Christ is not to be confused with the Great White Throne, before which there will be gathered those whose names are not in the book of life and from whence they will be cast into the lake of fire.

The word 'Judgment Seat' is used in the New Testament of the tribunal before which our Lord was brought, and of a similar one at which the Apostle Paul stood accused. It was the symbol of the imperial authority of Rome as exercised by its delegates. As used in the Epistles, 'judgment seat of God' (Rom. 14, R.V.), 'judgment seat of Christ' (2 Cor. 5), it emphasizes the fact that the Father judgeth no man, but that all judgment has been committed to the Son. 'He that judgeth me is the Lord' are the emphatic words of the apostle. That tribunal will be invested with all authority and power. We may be assured that nothing deserving of praise or commendation will pass unrewarded.

'The Lord is a God of knowledge, and by Him actions are weighed' (1 Sam. 2. 3). 'He weigheth the spirits and pondereth the heart' (Prov. 21. 2; 24. 12). In view of this the apostle says that at the *bema* the counsels of the heart shall be made manifest (1 Cor. 4. 4-5). The motives which have moved us in our service will be brought to light. Hence the need for spiritual integrity, moral honesty and transparency of purpose in connection with all life's activities and our *in*activity.

The word 'manifest' is a key-word in the portions dealing with the *bema*. Not only will our motives be manifest, but what we are will be manifest. Every believer will appear in his true character. There will be no mask, and nothing hidden. Each will receive a reward for the things done in the body, that is for service rendered. The word *receive* is a technical term for receiving wages. 'The words good and bad are singular, and as abstract, may refer to the character of what we will receive. Reward will be good: loss will be bad' (Alford).

The apostle was guided by a wholesome apprehension of the fear of the Lord and endeavoured to live in the light of it, antedating the judgment seat.

'Every man will receive a reward according to his own labour' (1 Cor. 3. 8), and besides, 'every man's work will be made manifest. The day shall declare it, because it shall be revealed by fire; and the fire shall try every man's work of what sort it is. If any man's work abide, he shall receive a reward. If any man's work be burned, he shall suffer loss: but he himself shall be saved; yet so as by fire' (1 Cor. 3. 13-15). The eyes of the Lord will be a flame of fire (Rev. 1) and His word is like a fire (Jer. 23. 29). As in the Grecian games it was necessary to run lawfully if the prize was to be won, so all work will be tested by the revealed will of God in His Word. In this portion in 1 Cor. two types of workmen are contemplated. It is possible to be a good workman that needeth not to be ashamed, building things that will abide into life and character. On the contrary, it is sadly possible to be poor workmen building with material that will produce nothing but a heap of ashes in that day. Later the apostle speaks of a bad workman who defiles, corrupts, or destroys the temple. Him, we are told, God will destroy. This would seem to be a reference to those whom he later described as 'false apostles, ministers of Satan.' The apostle warned the saints against them and against being deceived by them (1 Cor. 6. 7-9).

The importance of the judgment seat is again emphasized in that it is introduced when exhorting the saints to mutual grace, care and love. Happy will be the man, who, in the exercise of his liberty, has not been the cause of stumbling to a fellow-believer.

Those who will be recompensed at the resurrection of the just will enter into the joy of their Lord, and will be rewarded according to their fidelity to Him in looking after His interests, by being given positions of honour and responsibility in the administration of the coming kingdom (Luke 19). Crowns will be awarded. These correspond to the thought of position and honour. They are spoken of as: an incorruptible crown, the crown of life, a crown of glory, a crown of rejoicing, and a crown of righteousness.

To teach, as some do, that believers will be cast from the judgment seat of Christ in their glorified bodies into the outer darkness, to weep and wail for a period of 1,000 years along with the wicked and hypocrites, is devoid of Scriptural foundation, derogatory to the value of the death of Christ and a denial of His own word of assurance that believers will not come into judgment. It savours of the teaching of Rome, borrowed from heathen cults, as to purgatory.

The Great Tribulation

Our Lord forewarned His own of tribulation 'because of the Word,' and that in the world tribulation was to be the portion of the believer, seeing he is the follower of a rejected and crucified Lord. In keeping with the testimony of our Lord, the apostle warned the Thessalonian saints that it is through much tribulation we are to enter the kingdom. Moreover, the Church at Smyrna was told that the tribulation through which it was passing was to last a specified time, and believers were exhorted to endurance and to be prepared for martyrdom.

But these and many other Scriptures of a similar character do not touch upon the subject of the 'Great Tribulation'—'The Tribulation—The Great One.' 'This points to a definite prophetic period, and not simply to tribulation in general, in which all saints share. The insertion of the definite article marks its speciality' (W. Scott on *Revelation*, p. 171). This period of suffering was the subject of prophecy. Isaiah, Jeremiah, Daniel and others refer to it.

In a passage that predicts the disannulling of the covenant with Anti-Christ, and the overflowing scourge that will follow like a flood sweeping away their shelters, Isaiah tells of the consumption determined upon the whole earth—more especially the land of Palestine (Isa. 28. 14-22, R.V.). Foreseeing that day Jeremiah cried: 'Alas for that day is great, so that none is like it: it is even the time of Jacob's trouble, but he shall be saved out of it' (chap. 30. 7). Daniel, who was told to seal up his prophecy as it pertained to the time of the end, says it 'shall be a time of trouble, such as never was since there was a nation, even to that same time, and at that time thy people shall be delivered' (12. 1).

In the Olivet discourse these prophecies were expanded by our Lord. 'Then shall be great tribulation, such as hath not been since the beginning of the world till now, no, nor ever shall be. Immediately after the tribulation of those days, the sun shall be darkened . . . and they shall see the Son of Man coming on the clouds of heaven' (Matt. 24. 21, 29, 31). This discourse was given in response to the questions of the disciples, 'When shall these things be? What shall be the sign of Thy coming? and the end of the age?' '"Thy coming" here means the Lord's presence with them on the earth, the end of the time during which our Lord would be absent from them. They wished to know the sign of His presence. They knew there could be no such desolation if their Messiah was reigning over them' (W. Kelly, *Matthew*).

The terms 'Jacob's trouble' and 'thy people' point clearly to the fact that the Jewish people were the ones to undergo this suffering and eventually to be delivered. In keeping with the general character of prophecy the references to this period in the Old Testament are brief. The details were to be filled in later. These are given to us in Matt. 24 and Rev. 6-19. All these portions have certain features in common:

(*a*) Prominence is given to the land, to Judah and Israel (Jer. 30. 4); to the city, the holy place (Matt. 24. 15); and the temple of God and Jerusalem (Rev. 11. 1-8).

(*b*) Gentile domination. They were to hear 'another tongue' (Isa. 28. 11) and were to bear the yoke of bondage in captivity (Jer. 27. 12).

Daniel's reference to 'the time of the end' follows the prophecy concerning the King that shall exalt himself. In the Olivet discourse the Lord refers to the prophecy of Daniel, and says that Jerusalem is to be trodden down of the Gentiles until the times of Gentiles are fulfilled. Revelation gives us another and fuller picture of the consummation of the 'times of the Gentiles' in its relation to Jerusalem and the Jews.

(*c*) A remnant will be preserved. 'To the residue of the people, the Lord of Hosts shall be for a crown of glory in that day' (Isa.

28. 5). 'I will not make a full end of thee' (Jer. 30. 11). 'Those written in the book will be delivered' (Dan. 12. 1). 'For the elect's sake those days shall be shortened' (Matt. 4. 22). 'The number of them which are sealed of the children of Israel' (Rev. 7. 4).

(*d*) Final and complete deliverance will be brought about suddenly. 'The Lord of hosts shall be . . . for strength to them that turn the battle to the gate' (Isa. 28. 5-6). 'He shall be saved out of it' (Jer. 30. 7). 'The judgment shall sit, and they shall take away his dominion.' In its place the everlasting kingdom shall be inaugurated (Dan. 7. 27). 'They shall see the Son of Man coming in the clouds of heaven . . . ' (Matt. 24. 30). 'Behold He cometh with the clouds and every eye shall see Him.' 'And I saw heaven opened, and behold . . . the King of kings and Lord of lords' (Rev. 1. 7; 19. 11, 16).

(*e*) The overthrow and judgment of the enemies. 'In that day the Lord shall punish . . . the kings of the earth' (Isa. 24. 21). 'I will make a full end of all nations' (Jer. 30. 10). 'He shall come to his end and none shall help him' (Dan. 11. 45). 'As the flood took them all away . . . so shall the coming of the Son of Man be' (Matt. 24. 39). 'The beast and the false prophet . . . were cast alive into the lake of fire' (Rev. 19. 20).

Neither the Church nor the rapture are in view in Matt. 24, but Israel, the elect nation, referred to as 'this generation.' Hence we read of the land, Judæa, the Sabbath, the holy place, etc. As the remnant will be waiting for the coming Messiah, false prophets will seek to deceive by saying 'Here is Messiah.' They will adduce his miracles as his credentials. The remnant is told to flee, and not to delay by returning to the house, and they are encouraged to pray that their flight should not be in the winter for that would mean added suffering. How different this is from the rapture!

To interpret verse 31, 'And He shall send His angels . . .' as prophetic of the coming of the Lord for His Church is false for many reasons.

(*a*) The Church is not referred to in the discourse. The 'elect' spoken of are those referred to in Rom. 11. 28 as 'beloved for the Father's sake.' The elect of Matt. 24 wait for the Messiah according to the prophecies of the Old Testament and not for 'His Son from heaven' in fulfilment of the New Testament revelation. The word 'generation' is elsewhere translated 'nation' (Phil. 2. 15; Isa. 45. 4; 65. 9-22).

(*b*) It confuses the words, 'The Lord shall descend from heaven . . . ' with the 'angels blowing a great trumpet.' The one gathers the redeemed to meet the Lord in the air, and is the subject of a later and special revelation through Paul. The other gathers Israel back to the land and is the subject of Old Testament prophecy (Isa. 27. 13).

(*c*) The chapter contains no reference to the resurrection of the dead either directly or by implication. The terms 'four winds, from one end of heaven to another,' refer to the reclamation of the Jews from the countries whither they had been dispersed. Their dispersion to the utmost part of heaven and to all the winds had been prophesied by Moses and Ezekiel (Deut. 30. 4; Ezek. 5. 10-12), and is illustrated in the judgment pronounced upon Elam by God through Jeremiah (Jer. 49. 36).

(*d*) Moreover, if in v. 31 we have the rapture, then the appearing of the Lord described in v. 30, when all the tribes of the earth shall mourn, will actually precede the rapture. Thereby the portion is made to teach what is contrary to other plain statements of Scripture, that the saints will accompany Him on His return.

(*e*) In keeping with the fact that the Church is not in view in the chapter the Lord says: 'This Gospel of the kingdom shall be preached . . .' The Gospel of the grace of God emphasizes that grace reigns: the Gospel of the kingdom's emphasis is on the imminent approach of the King.

The tribulation will be the closing hours of man's day of opportunity and liberty and will demonstrate his complete and absolute failure to govern. It will also be the closing days of the 'times of the Gentiles.' Its consummation will be marked by the same gross idolatry as characterized its commencement. Moreover, as Israel's national history was marred by its worship of the golden calf in its earliest days, so it will be marked by worse idolatry during the last week of the 'seventy weeks determined upon them' (Dan. 9. 24).

As there was a remnant of Jews that would not bow to Nebuchadnezzar's image and in consequence were thrown into the fiery furnace, so there will be a remnant which will not bow to the final image. For this they will pass through the unprecedented sufferings foretold by our Lord. This period will also be the days of vengeance when the Jews will suffer nationally and collectively for the sin of crucifying the Messiah.

The Revelation gives us the last and fullest description of this terrible period. There are no references to the witness of the churches in the section, prophetic of the 'things which shall be hereafter,' which begins with chap. 4. 1. There are, however, references to saints. They are the object of the enmity of the beast. War is made on them by him. They are overcome. Who are these saints? Do they constitute a part of the redeemed known as the Church?

One essential feature of the Church age is that the middle wall of partition between Jew and Gentile is broken down. As a nation they have no priority now. But in Rev. 6-19 the nation of Israel is again prominent. A remnant is sealed from among the tribes. Therefore it must be concluded that the period of Church testimony will be over before then.

Moreover, Jerusalem was superseded in the Acts by Antioch. Hence it has had no place in the programme of evangelization since. But the testimony of the two witnesses of Rev. 11 is to be borne in Jerusalem. It is there they testify and perform their miracles, which like those of Moses and Elijah are to be miracles of judgment in contrast to those of the apostles. It is in Jerusalem they are slain, and we are told that 'they of the people . . . shall see their dead bodies.' This evidently refers to those Jews who will have been gathered back in unbelief to Palestine. Of this gathering and its purpose Ezekiel had spoken after foretelling of their dispersion. 'I will scatter . . . Behold I will gather . . .' (Ezek. 22. 15-22). While on the one hand they will be gathered from among the peoples and nations to their own land in unbelief and will pass through persecution, yet as prophesied by Joel it will be a day of visitation and of the outpouring of the Spirit in a marked manner (Joel 2. 23). The initial and partial fulfilment of this on the day of Pentecost resulted in thousands of Jews being saved and incorporated into the Church. That was the early rain. The latter rain will come when the prophecy of Joel is completely fulfilled.

Then from amongst the oppressed nation there will be a company which no man can number who, in response to the word of the Lord, will call upon Him and will be delivered. This company will be from among those of the dispersed and regathered peoples. They are viewed as a collective company. Over them the Lord will spread His tabernacle. The deliverance and maintenance of the nation from Egypt and in the wilderness will be repeated on a far greater scale. They will hunger no more, daily manna will be provided. They will thirst no more—their bread and water will be sure. The terms used in Rev. 7 are reminiscent of Israel and describe the experience of a people still on earth, and not in heaven. There is no reference to resurrection in the chapter.

Hence, as the Church is later seen in heaven, and coming out of heaven, it must have been caught up before this period. This harmonizes with the promise to the church at Philadelphia. 'Because thou hast kept the word of My promise I also will keep thee from the hour of temptation which shall come upon all the world. . . .' (3. 10). While the rapture is not directly mentioned in the book it would seem to be symbolized in the translation of John in spirit to heaven. 'After chapter 3 the Church is never again referred to as on earth, and it seems evident that the judgment of a guilty world is suspended until the Church has been removed from the scene' (Tatford, *Prophecy's Last Word*, p. 75).

Furthermore, in the Epistle to the Thessalonians we are told definitely that we are not appointed to wrath, but to obtain salvation through our Lord Jesus Christ (1 Thess. 5. 9). He is our Deliverer from the coming wrath (1 Thess. 1. 10).

During this final phase of man's day, and of the 'times of the Gentiles' there will be distress of nations, perplexity owing to the apprehension concerning what will be happening and what those happenings portend. Political chaos, with wars and rumours of wars; national and international confusion and economic crises will strike fear into the stoutest hearts. The mystery of iniquity is already working, but there is a restraining hand. When that restraining power is removed, out of the midst of this chaos and confusion, heralded as the superman, the final world-ruler will appear. He will be the head of the resuscitated Roman Empire, a confederacy of the western powers. Along with him will appear the False Prophet, who will work miracles with all lying wonders. The counterpart of the image that was erected on the plains of Dura will be made and worship will be ascribed to the beast. Whilst these will be the two main actors they will not be the only ones. We read of the King of the North and of the King of the South and of the final gathering of the armies to the valley of Armageddon.

Manifestation of Christ

Whereas the rapture of the saints to meet the Lord in the air is a truth especially revealed through the Apostle Paul, the appearing of Christ, or His coming in glory, was the subject of Old Testament prophecy, and of much of the teaching of our Lord as recorded in the Synoptic Gospels. It is inextricably interwoven with the visions of the Messianic Kingdom granted to the prophets of Israel.

The earliest of all the prophecies was that of Enoch, the seventh from Adam. 'Behold the Lord cometh with ten thousands of His saints . . .' (Jude 14). To Abraham, God promised, 'Thy seed shall possess the gate of his enemies, and in thy seed shall all nations of the earth be blessed' (Gen. 22. 17, 18). Again, He declared, 'The Lord at thy right hand shall smite through kings in the day of His wrath . . . He shall wound the head over many nations' (Psa. 110. 5).

In accordance with the blessing bestowed upon Judah by Jacob the sceptre and law-giver was to come through his family (Gen. 49. 10). In confirmation of this we read: 'The Lord hath sworn in truth unto David; He will not turn from it; of the fruit of thy body will I set upon thy throne' (Psa. 132. 11). Consequently it was said of the Lord Jesus, 'The Lord God shall give unto Him the throne of His father David; and He shall reign . . . forever; and of His kingdom there shall be no end' (Luke 1. 32, 33).

Daniel lived and prophesied at the commencement of what is spoken of as 'the times of the Gentiles,' a period which began in the second year of Nebuchadnezzar. At that time the nation was taken captive and the land of Palestine came under Gentile dominion, as it has been ever since and will be till the end. 'Jerusalem shall be trodden down of the Gentiles until the times of the Gentiles shall be fulfilled' (Luke 21. 24).

Daniel prophesied that Gentile rule would consistently deteriorate in character and cohesion. This was signified by the metals and materials used in the composition of the image to symbolize the four successive world empires. In the dream the image was seen to be crushed as the dust of the summer threshing-floor by the stone smiting it upon the feet, and ushering in the kingdom set up by the God of heaven. Nebuchadnezzar saw, in his dream, these Gentile kingdoms according to their outward character, but Daniel saw them as devouring beasts of prey, depicting their method of conquest and general attitude to Israel as the people of God. The last beast seen by him was the most ferocious, and diverse from all the others. It was a monstrosity, seemingly a composite beast, combining in itself all the characteristics of the first three. Its final head would speak great words against the Most High and wear out the saints of the Most High.

Corresponding to the vision of the Stone cut out of the mountain without hands, smiting the image, Daniel saw the Son of Man coming in the clouds of heaven, to whom the kingdom and universal dominion were given.

When the Lord began to show unto His disciples how He must suffer, be killed and raised again, He also told them that the Son of Man shall come in the glory of His Father with His angels. This clearly connects it with the prophecy of Daniel and was later confirmed in the Olivet discourse. Moreover, when before Caiaphas, the Lord not only affirmed His Deity, and equality with God, but asserted His title to Messianic and universal dominion. In Him the prophecy of Daniel was to be fufilled. To Caiaphas the Sadducean High Priest, that was blasphemy. Hence they crucified the 'Lord of glory.'

In connection with the rapture of the saints to meet the Lord in the air, we read of the 'day of Christ' and kindred expressions unique to the Church epistles. These refer to the period during which our Lord will be present with His own in the air, before the manifestation of His *parousia*, rendered the 'brightness of His coming' in the A.V. More literally the phrase is: 'The epiphany of His parousia.' It refers to the 'blessed hope, the appearing of our great God and Saviour Jesus Christ,' the sudden apocalypse, or the unveiling of Christ to destroy the wicked one, the man of sin, and deliver His people Israel. His coming will be 'as the lightning which cometh from the east . . .'; 'as a thief in the night'; and 'as travail upon a woman with child sudden destruction will come upon them.' This will inaugurate 'the day of the Lord,' so often spoken of by the Old Testament prophets, and referred to five times in the New (cf. Acts 2. 20). 'It will be a great and notable day: a day of darkness and gloominess,' a day without comparison in human history.

While God was still lingering in longsuffering over Israel, Peter referred to this aspect of the Lord's return shortly after the Day of Pentecost as 'the times of refreshing from the presence of the Lord,' and 'the times of restitution of all things spoken of by the mouth of all His holy prophets' (Acts 3. 19-21).

Before this 'day of the Lord' shall be ushered in by the revelation of Christ coming with clouds, when 'every eye shall see Him,' we are told definitely that certain things are to take place.

(*a*) The apostacy must set in. Truth once acknowledged will be entirely repudiated and denied. This will be the culmination of that which has been insidiously working all along. But as salt hinders putrefaction from setting in, so there is 'that which hinders' or withholdeth the full development of the apostacy (2 Thess. 2. 6). Once the restraining influence is removed, the complete disavowal of all the truth of Christianity will rapidly spread and ripen. The presence and power of true Christian witness is undoubtedly that which is as light arresting the deepening darkness, counteracting the process of corruption. At the rapture this will be removed and Christendom will be spued out. The Gentiles, the wild olive tree, now brought into the special sphere of blessing will be broken off, and the natural branches grafted into their own olive tree (Rom. 11. 24). Christendom will be abandoned to believe 'the lie' (2 Thess. 2. 11). Satan is a liar from the beginning, he is the father of lies, and has been indefatigable in the denial of the truth and the propagating of that which is false. But 'the lie' would seem to be personified in the Antichrist, the man of sin, as 'the truth' is in Christ. That apostacy will not only be departure from certain truths, or even from the truth, but its total, complete and absolute repudiation along with the acceptance of 'the lie.'

(*b*) The man of sin is to be revealed (2 Thess. 2. 8). This, the son of perdition, will be the antichrist and would seem to be the same as the false prophet of Rev. 13. 11-18. He will be energized by the Dragon, and will perform works of power, signs and lying wonders. These three words, 'miracles, signs and wonders,' were used by Peter to describe the ministry of the Lord Jesus. They were the credentials of His Messiahship, as those performed by the apostles were the evidence of their apostleship.

The very fact that he will sit in the temple of God in Jerusalem (2 Thess. 2. 4) and perform these miracles in opposition to the two witnesses shows that by then Palestine will once more be the storm centre and the cockpit of the trouble.

(*c*) The fig tree and all the trees will be showing signs of spring (Luke 21. 29, 30). The spirit of nationalism will again become a virile and potent factor in world affairs. Not only among the Jews and Zionism will this be true, but in other nations also. This has been witnessed to a marked degree of late years, and is on the increase. This is very evident from that which is taking place in the Middle East at the present time. Not only is there movement among the 'dry bones' of Israel, but the other powers contiguous to Palestine are waking out of their long slumber. The Pan-Islamic world will undoubtedly become more and more pronounced in its enmity to the Jew and his rehabilitation in the land.

(*d*) Conditions that characterized the world in the days of Noah and of Lot will prevail before the advent of the Son of Man in glory (Matt. 24. 27). In the pursuit of the material the spiritual was absolutely forgotten. Along with this materialism, and born out of it there was gross immorality. All moral barriers were removed. 'They gave themselves over to fornication, going after strange flesh' (Jude 7). This brought its own harvest of shame and ruin. The flood came and took them all away. Likewise the incendiaries from heaven turned Sodom and Gomorrah into ashes. Only a small remnant was saved in either case. So shall it be when the 'Son of Man is revealed.' As by the sinister force of blast many will be taken away in judgment. Others will be spared, left to enter millennial blessedness. The reference to the carcase and the eagles in this connection (Matt. 24. 28) points to the fact that Palestine will be the scene of this. The Gentile nations, like unclean birds of prey, will be gathered there in their armies to dominate the land and devour its wealth.

(*e*) What has characterized human history in general, 'wars and rumours of wars,' with their associated evils—famines and pestilences—will become more and more accentuated and more universal (Matt. 24. 6, 7). The discord between nations, the distress that will come upon them, with death in its cruellest forms ever on the horizon will be accompanied by seismic disturbances on an unprecedented scale. Stars will fall and the powers of heaven will be shaken (Matt. 24. 29). Because of these things men's hearts will quail for fear of the things which are coming on the earth.

(*f*) According to the Old Testament prophecies regarding the final phase of man's day, and the times of the Gentiles, there is to be a certain alignment of nations in view of the consummation of the long drawn out conflict. The issue is to be decided finally at Armageddon. It will bring about the complete overthrow and destruction of the forces of evil. We have no authority in the New Testament to look for the fulfilment of these alignments during the Church age. Failure to recognize that the Scriptures are silent as to these during the present interim period of grace has led many to precipitate conclusions and vain prophesyings which can only prove false.

(*g*) In Dan. 12. 10-12 a certain time-table is given which seemingly will enable the wise to understand from the course of events the conclusion of the time of the end, even as Daniel had understood from the prophecy of Jeremiah that the time of the nation's captivity was finished. Moreover, the way in which the advent is symbolized clearly indicates a certain moral and spiritual condition which must precede the advent in glory, and will be discernible to the wise. Associated with the lightning is the storm; with the thief's coming the midnight darkness; and with the sudden destruction—the travail—the gradual, consistent and final culmination of evil.

But we read the New Testament with its revelation of the truth relative to the rapture of the saints and the *parousia* of the Lord in vain to find any hint of the possibility of fixing a date. All attempts at doing so have only served to discredit such prophets, and what is more serious, to do untold harm to the cause of truth. His coming is taught as being imminent so that we may be preserved in a state of watchfulness awaiting His return. The night is far advanced, the day is at hand. Our salvation is nearer than when we believed.

The Millennium

The millennium is the Latin word for the expression 'a thousand years,' used six times in Rev. 20. 1-7. From these references we learn certain facts.

(*a*) At its commencement Satan, the arch-enemy of God and man, referred to as the dragon, the old serpent, the devil and Satan, will be bound and banished to the abyss. He will be kept there for the duration! At the close he will be loosed again for a season before he is eventually cast into the lake of fire to be tormented for ever and ever.

(*b*) During the whole period Christ will reign in triumph, and associated with Him will be all those who will share in the first resurrection. These will comprise all who are spoken of as 'they that are Christ's' to be raised at His coming or *parousia*, and those referred to as having been slain for the witness of Jesus during the tribulation period. These all belong to the one 'order.'

(*c*) The rest of the dead will only be raised after the consummation of the thousand years, and then to stand before the great white throne, whence they will be cast into the lake of fire.

On his death-bed Jacob gathered his sons together and told them what should befall them in the last or latter days. In the blessing of Judah, reference is made to Shiloh, the peacemaker or the Prince of peace, who was to come and to whom the peoples will be obedient (Gen. 49. 10), 'Judah should bear the sceptre with lion courage until his rule over the tribes was widened into the peaceful government of the world.' 'Messiah antitypically fulfils the "prophecy."' (*Gesenius, Keil, Fausset's Enc.*). The R.V. gives in the margin an ancient rendering as 'till He come, whose it is.' This seems to be echoed by Ezekiel in the words: 'He will overturn, overturn, overturn until He come whose right it is' (chap. 21. 27).

The Lord made with David an everlasting covenant ordered in all things and sure. His seed was to sit upon his throne, and his kingdom would be established in perpetuity. 'In His days shall the righteous flourish, and abundance of peace as long as the moon endureth. He shall have dominion from sea to sea, and from the river to the ends of the earth. Yea, all kings shall fall down before Him. All nations shall serve Him' (Psa. 72. 7-11). Then it will be said, 'The Lord reigneth.' 'For the kingdom is the Lord's: and He is the governor among the nations' (Psa. 22. 28). Moreover, He is to have dominion over the creation. 'Thou hast put all things under His feet' (Psa. 8. 3-6). Thus the dominion that was lost in Adam is to be restored in Christ, the Messiah, the second man, the last Adam.

Isaiah reverts to the Davidic covenant when announcing that there shall 'come forth a rod out of the stem of Jesse, and a branch shall grow out of His roots' (11. 1). He shall be the Prince of peace. Of the increase of His government and peace there shall be no end' (9. 7).

The later prophets, living in darker days were also borne along by the Holy Ghost and caused to focus attention on the future with its coming glory. Their prophetic utterances were not their own interpretation of the course of history, but the Spirit of Christ which was in the prophets was testifying beforehand concerning the sufferings of Christ and the glories to follow (1 Peter 1. 11).

During the reign of David's Son and David's Lord the abundance of peace will be such that swords shall be made into ploughshares and spears into pruning hooks. Nations will wage war no more, neither will they *learn* war any more (Isa. 2. 4). There will be no expenditure of wealth on armaments as is the case now.

In Babylon, Daniel was given to see that the period of Gentile domination and misrule would be brought to an end catastrophically, and in its place an everlasting dominion would be set up, in which the saints of the Most High would share the glory of the kingdom with the Son of Man (Dan. 2. 44; 7. 13-18). Ezekiel, his contemporary, was also carried forward and given visions of that coming day of glory.

The post-captivity prophets likewise herald the overthrow of the nations (Haggai 3. 22); the establishment of the Messianic kingdom with the one whose name is 'the Branch,' building the temple and ruling as King-Priest—the true Melchizedek.

When we turn over to the New Testament it is to find that the forerunner is proclaiming the kingdom as being at hand, and calling for repentance in view of it. But the leaders were deaf. He was 'a voice crying in the wilderness.' In the ministry of our Lord the teaching regarding the kingdom is given in parables. For the present the kingdom is in abeyance. Some of the parables deal with its mysteries—its present character, others deal with its manifestation in great power and glory.

With these and many similar Scriptures filling their minds, little wonder that the disciples were concerned, even after the resurrection, with the restoration of the kingdom. In His answer, the Lord gave them to understand that it was not for them to know the times and seasons which are in the Father's own power. In the meantime they would be empowered by the Holy Spirit so as to enable them to be witnesses unto Him world-wide, even to the uttermost part of the earth. The coming kingdom and its glories were not abandoned. On the contrary, it formed an integral part of apostolic preaching and teaching. This is evident for many reasons:

(*a*) The messages recorded in the Acts. To the people of Jerusalem Peter spoke of the 'times of refreshing' and the 'times of restitution of all things . . .' to be inaugurated at the return of Christ (Acts 3. 19-21). Paul preached the kingdom of God (Acts 20. 25; 28. 31).

(*b*) The enemies accused Paul, not only of affirming that Jesus was alive, but that He is King (Acts 25. 19; Acts 17. 7).

(*c*) It is the uniform teaching of the Epistles of the New Testament that this period of grace is not going to be brought to a conclusion in a different way from those already ended. Each preceding age has ended in judgment. So will this one. The darkness is going to deepen, wickedness is to increase, and wicked men shall wax worse and worse until at last the 'man of sin' shall be revealed, whom the Lord will consume and destroy with the appearing of His glory, the epiphany of His *parousia*. Under the beast and false prophet the forces of evil will be marshalled for their final attempt at a Satanically controlled world-government. It will be the consummation of evil in a most concentrated form. The preaching of the Gospel will not bring about millennial conditions in the world. The kingdom will be established suddenly and with terrible judgments. The Scriptures of both the Old and New Testaments bear witness to this with one voice. There is no discordant note struck by a single writer. 'He must reign.'

It remains to note briefly some of the main features of the millennium, the mediatorial kingdom of the Son of Man.

(*a*) Christ will not only be accepted as the Messiah and King of Israel, but He will be 'King of kings and Lord of lords' (Rev. 19. 16). His dominion will be universal. 'All the ends of the world shall turn to the Lord, and all kindreds of the nations shall worship before thee' (Psa. 22. 27). His reign will be characterized by righteousness and faithfulness (Isa. 11. 5; Acts 17. 31).

(*b*) The enemies shall be completely overthrown (Rev. 19. 11-19; 2 Thess. 1. 7-10; 2. 8). He will thoroughly purge His threshing-floor. Everything that offends will be removed.

(*c*) Satan will be bound and cast into the abyss (Rev. 20. 2-3). The world will be free from his deceptions. The heavenly places will be purged of all evil spirits. The prince of the power of the air will no longer be at liberty to do his nefarious work. For the first time in man's history he will be free from the evil influences of the powers of darkness.

(*d*) The saints, both those of Old Testament days and the present time will share in the reign with Christ. He will enter into the possession of His inheritance in and with His saints. The apostle prayed that the eyes of the saints might be opened to see, among other things, the glory of this inheritance, and the riches of its glory (Eph. 1. 18). This inheritance is of vast dimensions, and includes more than the millennial reign.

(*e*) Israel will be delivered *and regenerated*. At the commencement of man's history the ominous word 'curse' was used. Ere Moses died he warned the nation of the 'curse' and solemnly enough the last word in the Old Testament is that same word 'curse.' The curse has rested upon the nation (Deut. 27. 26; 28. 8-9); upon the land of Canaan (Jer. 44. 22; Lev. 26. 33; Deut. 29. 27); upon the temple (Matt. 23. 38; Jer. 44. 22; Mic. 3. 12); and on the city (Luke 19. 41-44). These will all be lifted. *The land* will become a 'delightsome land' (Mal. 3. 12); and the nation will possess all of it according to the boundaries mentioned in the Abrahamic covenant, from the river of Egypt to the river Euphrates (Gen. 15. 18). *The city*, now forsaken, and a desolation (Isa. 62. 4; 64. 10; Lam. 2. 15), will no more be termed 'Desolate' but 'Hephzibah' —my delight is in her, and thy land Beulah . . . thy land shall be married' (Jer. 32. 37-41). The city will be called the 'city of the Great King' (Matt. 5. 35; Zech. 14. 16) and 'Jehovah-Shammah —the Lord is there' (Ezek. 48. 35).

From Jerusalem there will flow a river to the west, and to the east to the Persian Gulf (Isa. 33. 21; Ezek. 47; Zech. 14. 8). Jerusalem will thus become an inland port with access both to the east and to the west. This tremendous change will be brought about by the earthquake which will take place at our Lord's return, when He will place His feet upon the Mount of Olives (Zech. 14. 4). On account of this river flowing to the east, that which is now barren and waste will blossom as a rose (Isa. 35. 1-2).

Moreover *peace* shall be extended to Jerusalem like a river and the glory of the Gentiles like a flowing stream (Isa. 66. 12).

The *temple* will be rebuilt and its glory will exceed and eclipse all its previous glories, for He will glorify the house of His glory (Isa. 60. 7).

The *nation* will be restored to favour. 'All Israel shall be saved.' The veil, now upon their hearts will be removed. They shall be a crown of glory in the hand of the Lord, and they shall be called the 'holy people' (Rom. 11. 26; 2 Cor. 3. 17; Isa. 62. 1-12). To-day they are an astonishment, a proverb, a byword among the nations in fulfilment of the word of God by Moses (Deut. 28. 37). Then, instead of being a curse as they are to-day among the nations, they will be a blessing (Zech. 8. 13) and a joy (Isa. 65. 18).

(*f*) Creation will be delivered. Things in heaven and things in earth are to be reconciled (Col. 1. 20). This will be brought about at the appearing of our Lord. It will be the 'times of refreshing from the presence of the Lord,' and 'the times of restitution.'

The curse pronounced upon the animal world (Gen. 3. 14) will be removed, with the exception that the serpent will still go on its belly and dust shall be its meat (Isa. 65. 25; 11. 6-9).

The curse that rests upon the ground will be lifted also. Instead of the thorn shall come up the fir tree, and instead of the brier the myrtle tree (Gen. 3. 14; 4. 12; Isa. 55. 13; 29. 17). Productivity will be such that a handful of corn on the mountain will yield a rich harvest, and the ploughman shall overtake the reaper (Psa. 72. 16; Amos 9. 13).

Creation will be delivered from its bondage to corruption into the liberty of the glory of the children of God (Rom. 8. 21). The prophecy of Psa. 8 envisages the complete dominion of the Son of Man, not only over all nations, but over all creation.

As the dominion lost to man is to be restored to the redeemed we are told that we shall reign in life by one, Jesus Christ (Rom. 5. 17). As the restoration of the principal was an essential part of the trespass offering so the restitution of this dominion is an integral part of the redemptive work of Christ. Moreover, as a fifth part was added to the principal when restitution was made, even so we shall enter into possession of greater glory than Adam ever had. It is important to note that this is vitally related to the value of the death of Christ and is not dependent on any meritorious faithfulness on the part of the believer. But position and responsibility in the kingdom will be based upon faithfulness, as is evident from the teaching of Christ.

With the lifting of the curse and the reconciling of things in heaven and in earth, death and disease will be so rare that for a man to die when he will be a hundred will be considered to die in infancy, and will be a penal act (Isa. 65. 20).

(*g*) With all these wonderful things it must be remembered that the millennium will not be heaven! There will be those who will only yield feigned obedience (Psa. 18. 44; 66. 3; 81. 15). We read of the sinner being accursed when a hundred years old (Isa. 65. 20).

The emissaries of the King will 'declare His righteousness unto a people that shall be born, that He hath done it' or that it is finished (Psa. 22. 31). Yet all will not accept the message, for when Satan will be loosed for a season at the end of the thousand years, he will find people in the four corners of the earth, i.e. the parts most remote from Jerusalem, ready to respond to his deceptions and act in rebellion. Forming an army they will encompass the camp of the saints and the beloved city, when fire will fall from heaven and devour them. That will bring to a close man's rebellion with a final proof of the innate wickedness of the human heart, and demonstrating the truth that the flesh is not subject to the law of God nor can be. The best of governments and of environments will not affect the heart of man. It is incorrigibly evil. A man must be born of God if he is to be subject to the will of God.

In view of the weight of Scripture teaching regarding the millennium, we may with confidence look forward to its accomplishment.

> Jesus shall reign, where'er the sun
> Doth his successive journeys run:
> His kingdom stretch from shore to shore,
> Till moons shall wax and wane no more.

CHAPTER XXIV

The Last Things

HARRY LACEY

AT the beginning of the Apocalypse it is recorded that John prostrated himself in worship. The glory of the Lord left no more spirit in him (Rev. 1. 17). A similar effect resulted from the vision of the last things (Rev. 22. 8, 9). Unless restrained, he had worshipped the angel who showed him the vision. The record is for our learning. The critical faculty should be counter-poised by the exercise of that of wonder lest the vision fail of the moral effect desired. What effect, indeed, should contemplation of the catastrophic dissolution of the heavens and the earth, the last great assize, the judgment and eternal woe of unforgiven human souls have! What effect a view of the new heavens and the new earth, the eternal city of God and the felicity of the redeemed! The record of John's reactions is intended to be salutary.

The vision of the last things is described in three paragraphs with an attendant epilogue at the close of the book of the Revelation. The first paragraph describes the Great White Throne and its judgment (chap. 20. 11-15); the second the New Heavens and the New Earth (21. 1-8); and the third the Holy City (21. 9-22. 15). The epilogue consists of sundry declarations and appeals associated with these subjects and those which have gone before in the book (22. 16-21).

The Great White Throne

'And I saw a great white throne,' wrote John (20. 11). He had seen the emblem of royal power, the seat of a king earlier in the Apocalypse (5. 2-4). Then it was rainbow-encircled to describe the manifold attributes of the One whose crystal Being sheds the lights and colours of flame as He holds court to assert His authority and to invest the Lion-Lamb with universal dominion. The pre-eminent hue of the encircling iris was then emerald—the restful colour, suggestive of mercy—and all that proceeded from the throne passed through the circle of enthroned men. On a later occasion he saw people worshipping and rejoicing before a throne, like Levites in a heavenly sanctuary (7. 9-17). They were sinners from the darkest hour of earth's history who had washed their robes and made them white in the blood of the Lamb. Consequently, their adoration, their anthems and their joy were abiding. No want should be theirs to eternal day.

Now, in the vision of the last things, there is no rainbow, there are no worshippers, there is no distinguishing of the Persons of the Godhead. The emblem of sovereignty is said to be great and white—great above all greatness—the very earth and the heavens flee—white above all whiteness—the white light of divine holiness shines in full glare unrefracted. 'To this nothing is ascribed, but greatness and whiteness, indicative of immeasurable power, and of pure, complete, unmingled and invincible justice' (Seiss, *Apocalypse*, p. 478).

Isaiah records an oath which will take effect in a final way in the day John saw (Isa. 45. 20-23). When asserting His sovereignty and uniqueness, in contrast to the idols of the heathen, and calling upon the ends of the earth to look to Him for salvation, Jehovah declared He had taken oath by Himself that every knee should bow to Him and every tongue make confession. The context suggests that the oath takes effect in God's present moral government. A New Testament passage applies its principle to believers (Rom. 14. 11). At the return of Christ they will give account to God for their works—Their guilt was put away at the Cross. But at the end of man's last probation, when the thousand years have run their course, the widest range of God's creatures will give account to Him.

The day when God shall judge the secrets of men is mentioned in the great treatise on the Gospel (Rom. 2. 16). Therein it is designated, 'the day of wrath and revelation of the righteous judgment of God' (Rom. 2. 5). The knowledge of it which was common to the Jew and the Greek of those days was confirmed in the preaching of the Gospel (Rom. 2. 16).

The judgment of that great day is described as righteous, universal and inescapable (Rom. 2. 5, 9, 3). Moreover, it will be impartial, according to each person's degree of light and therefore proportionate to the measure of responsibility (Rom. 2. 11, 12, 15). Of it, all are clearly and solemnly forewarned, 'It is written, As I live saith the Lord, to Me every knee shall bow, and every tongue shall confess to God' (Isa. 45. 20-23).

The ineffable One who sits on the throne is the Lord Jesus Christ. It is by Him that God will judge the secrets of men (Rom. 2. 16). The irrevocable oath will be implemented in Him. This is clear from the way in which the words are applied to Him in later revelation (Phil. 2. 9-11).

The Lord Himself stated this much. He declared that, 'the Father judgeth no man, but hath committed all judgment unto the Son' (1 John 5. 22). He also stated that the Father 'hath given Him authority to execute judgment also, because He is the Son of man' (John 5. 27). The Lord favoured the designation, 'the Son of man' and most frequently used it of Himself. However, there is a difference in this passage which is noted in the Revisers' margin. They have, 'a son of man' to indicate that the article is omitted in the original. This omission heightens the sense of the humanity of the Person and diminishes the idea of office. Authority to judge is His because He is 'man.' By a man will men be judged.

In the consciousness of this right and the impending exercise of it at the Great White Throne, Jesus stated in the same discourse that some would not come into judgment (John 5. 24). These are they who have already passed from a state of death into that of life. They already possess everlasting life. In no more positive terms could complete exemption from judgment be conveyed.

Evidence that Christ Jesus is Himself the Judge is found in Paul's last-written Epistle (2 Tim. 4. 1). He solemnly charged Timothy before God and Christ Jesus, the Judge, and also by His appearing and kingdom to preach the Word (verse 2). The consciousness of Christ's judgeship thrusts upon preachers the responsibility to do the work of an evangelist, as well as to reprove, rebuke and exhort those who profess salvation (vv. 2-5).

With the passing of heaven and earth the dead, the great and the small, were seen to stand before the Throne (Rev. 20. 12). This involves resurrection. Christ plainly stated that all that are in the tombs shall come forth (John 5. 28, 29). Instances of return to life were known in Old Testament days (2 Kings 13. 21, etc.). Those cited and the others referred to in the Gospels manifest that Christ is the resurrection and the life (John 11. 25, 43). To His apostles He delegated for a short time as a sign of the supernatural origin of their message the power to raise the dead (Acts 9. 40; 20. 10). All of these miracles are powers of the world to come (Heb. 6. 5). What was shown in them in a very limited way will be enacted upon the fullest scale in the future.

Resurrection is divided into a first resurrection and a last resurrection. The former is to be completely fulfilled before the start of the millennium (Rev. 20. 6). Christ is its first-fruits (1 Cor. 15. 20, 23), the 'rapture' its harvest (1 Cor. 15. 23, 51), the resurrection of 'tribulation saints' its gleanings (Rev. 20. 4). What John saw with the passing of heaven and earth fulfils the prediction of Christ that they that have done evil shall come forth unto the resurrection of judgment. Singularly enough, this event which John saw is not termed in his record, a resurrection. This raising of the body, and uniting of the being to enter that eternal experience of separation from God and His blessings is termed, 'the second death.'

The fearfulness of standing before God unforgiven is inferentially indicated by the ejaculatory character of one of the closing beatitudes of Holy Scripture, 'Blessed and holy is he that hath part in the first resurrection: on such the second death hath no power' (Rev. 20. 6).

When the dead appeared before God, John saw books opened (not 'the books' as A.V., but simply 'books'). The fact that records of human conduct exist is thus emphasized (Rev. 20. 12). David realized vividly that God kept records when he spoke of a book in which the details of his physical being were recorded before his birth (Psa. 139. 16). Job's demand that his adversary write a book and record all his sins was needless (Job 31. 35). All is recorded and each unforgiven soul will face its record in that day. Men are not held responsible for inheriting the nature of Adam. They will each receive according to their own works. During life, thoughts might be hidden, words of evil whispered in secret and deeds of wrong done clandestinely. Now, whatsoever was spoken in the darkness shall be heard in the light and whatsoever was spoken in the ear shall be proclaimed (Luke 12. 2, 3).

Angels are reserved unto judgment against that day (Jude 6). The wicked antediluvians, the inhabitants of ancient Sodom and Gomorrah and such as Dives, though now suffering judgment, will appear before that Great White Throne (2 Peter 2. 4-6; Luke 16. 23; Rev. 20. 12). With the exception of the Beast and the False Prophet (Rev. 19. 20), all the unforgiven of the human race will be called to account at that Great Assize. 'The Lord knoweth how to keep the unrighteous under punishment unto the day of judgment' (2 Peter 2. 9). For some that judgment will be more tolerable than for others (Matt. 11. 22-24). Degree of light and measure of privilege will weigh then. It seems that the salvation of those who lived under lesser light will prove the condemnation of the unrepentant who lived under greater (Matt. 12. 41, 42).

Dissolution of Heaven and Earth

The Judge on the throne is such that from before His face the earth and the heavens are said to flee away. A passage in Peter's second Epistle is kindred (2 Peter 3. 5-13). Therein the day of judgment and perdition of ungodly men is associated with a catastrophic dissolution of heaven and earth which is followed by the coming of a new heaven and a new earth. It is stated that the present heavens and the earth 'have been stored up for fire being reserved against the day of judgment and destruction of ungodly men' (v. 7). The Revisers deemed it necessary to add in their margin an alternative translation which takes on a new meaning in the light of atomic discovery. Their margin has, 'stored with fire,' for the 'stored up for fire' of the A.V. 'Treasured up with fire, being preserved unto a day of judgment' seems to be the sense of the words.

That part of God's creation affected by an ancient watery judgment seems designedly to be contrasted with those parts affected by a coming fiery one. In the former judgment 'the world' is said to have perished. In the latter, it is predicted that the heavens and the earth will. A world (*kosmos*—system of life) may perish and the platform, the heavens and the earth, upon which it has existed, remain. The fiery catastrophe of the future goes deeper than did the ancient cataclysm. Then the heavens will pass away with a whizzing thunderous roar, the elements will be loosed with fervent heat and the earth and the works therein will be burned up.

The words, 'and by Him all things consist' (Col. 1. 17) bear upon this matter. They indicate that Christ holds the universe together (*ta panta*=all things, becomes almost a technical expression equivalent to our word 'universe'). The Revisers emphasize the meaning of the word, 'consist' (*sunistêmi*) by putting 'that is, hold together' in their margin. This much is stated in another way in the Epistle to the Hebrews (Heb. 1. 3). There it is stated that the Son 'upholds' all things by the word of His power. He keeps the heavens and the earth with the potentialities of their every atom safe from any precipitate wholesale fission until that day.

Thrice in the passage in Peter the word 'dissolve' (*luô*—literally —loose) occurs (2 Peter 3. 10, 11, 12). It seems to convey an idea precisely opposite to the 'consist' (hold together) of the Epistle to the Colossians. It seems that, in that day, He, who 'holds together' now, will release His hold and that dissolution will come with fire, perhaps with atomic fission.

Two theories of this dissolution are current. The one takes the words literally and considers that the whole substance of the heavens and the earth will be removed. The other suggests a renovation of the surface of the earth and of the immediate heavens.

Because 'make' and not 'create' is used of the new heavens and the new earth (Isa. 66. 22), W. Scott reasons for the latter sense (W. Scott, *The Revelation*). The use of 'create' for the millennial scene in a preceding chapter, however, seems to offset this proposition (Isa. 65. 17).

J. A. Seiss argues to the same end by saying that the language describing events under the sixth seal (Rev. 6. 12-17) is similar when the shaking did not mean the removal of matter (Seiss, *Apocalypse*). Though the language is in some respects similar, the considerable difference exists, that while the heaven is said to depart and the mountains and islands are said to be moved, nothing is said about the removal of the earth.

Because the yielding up of the dead is mentioned after the fleeing away of heaven and earth it has been suggested that therefore the heaven and the earth abide the fleeing away to yield up the dead afterwards. That each event results in the same judgment indicates rather that they are contemporaneous. It is the fleeing away of the the heavens and the earth that yields up the dead. Verse 13 amplifies verses 11 and 12.

Passages that speak of the waxing old of heaven and earth seem scarcely admissible, because to wax old is manifestly different from to be burnt up. The passages of this kind are millennial ones. Ere its inauguration they will have waxed old. Then sun, moon, stars and the earth will be affected. But what John saw and Peter predicted goes deeper.

The general usage of 'pass away' (2 Peter 3. 10) does not necessarily indicate removal of substance. That it cannot may not be stated unless past time can be said to exist in any way (1 Peter 4. 3).

One wonders how much of earth is likely to be left after that terrible dissolution if the sea is to be no more (Rev. 21. 1), and if, as seems fairly certain, the centre of the earth is fire.

It appears necessary to conclude that there are holes in the canvas of the 'renovation theory' and that there is much to be said for the 'removal theory.' However, though evidence might not appear adequate to assert dogmatically removal of substance of the the heavens and the earth, the evidence forbids anything that would minimize the sense of the transitoriness of material things which John indicated. It is with this that Peter designed that we should be impressed when he wrote his second Epistle to urge believers to concentrate all their powers on the development of Christian character (2 Peter 1. 5; 3. 11, 14, 18). Genuine Christian character is not transitory. It is incorruptible. Everything else will, in some way, pass away irrecoverably.

The Lake of Fire

In further explanation of the fleeing of the heavens and the earth and of the standing of great and small before the Throne, the seer distinguished between the dead from the sea and those from death and Hades. Some have thought that the former are beings of a pre-Adamite populace of earth which perished in a catastrophe implied, but not specifically stated, between the first two verses of Genesis. Others have thought that the wicked of Noah's day are meant. It must be confessed that reason for this mysterious distinction is not clearly given.

However, about Hades and the lake of fire evidence is adequate. The place or state entitled, *Sheol* in Hebrew, *Hades* in Greek, and *Hell* in English, is said to be cast into the lake of fire. This statement distinguishes it from the lake of fire itself. The man whom Christ described as being in Hades did not possess his body there. It is stated that it was in the grave (Luke 16. 22). When Christ spoke of *Gehenna*, which is the lake of fire, He said that it was such a place that in it both body and soul would be destroyed (Matt. 10. 28—hell=Gehenna, see R.V. margin). Disembodied souls exist in Hades, Sheol or Hell, between the time of death and of resurrection. Then souls are given up by Hades and bodies by the earth. The consciousness of those souls and the normal use of their several faculties is evident (Isa. 14. 9-11; Luke 16. 23-25). Following the resurrection unto judgment the bodies and souls now united and sentenced will be cast into the lake of fire (Rev. 20. 5, 12, 14), which is equivalent to the *Gehenna* of which Christ frequently spoke.

It must not be supposed that 'destroyed' (*apollumi*) means annihilation. This word, translated 'lost' is used of the son, of the sheep and of the coin of Luke 15. 6, 9 and 24. Instead of indicating cessation of their existence, a relative state was implied, a state of misery and dishonour in contrast to that of comfort and dignity.

The term *Gehenna* was upon the lips of the Lord Jesus eleven out of the twelve times it occurs in the New Testament. He warned of its dangers. He stated that bodies as well as souls would be cast therein. Interchanging it with 'eternal fire' He explained that any loss would be worth while to escape it. He showed that false teachers could make men 'sons of Gehenna' from which inheritance of flame those teachers themselves could by no means escape. To inculcate the faith which delivers from ensnaring fear He emphasized God's power to cast into Gehenna and explained that such was the duration of that torment that the worm of their corruption would be deathless and the fire of their torment unquenchable (Matt. 5. 22; 10. 28; 18. 8, 9; 23. 15, 33; Luke 12. 4, 5; Mark 9. 43-49).

Objections to the plain meaning of these quotations have been made on the ground of the origin of the term *Gehenna*. In all probability it came from the name of the valley of Hinnom, or of the son of Hinnom (Jer. 19. 2, 6). This dreadful place was the scene of frightful pagan rites in which children were burned to the gods (2 Chron. 28. 3; 33. 6; Jer. 7. 31, 32; 32. 35). Jeremiah loudly denounced the evil practice and the godly Josiah put a stop to it (2 Kings 23. 10). Later, probably in the Chaldean invasion, it was filled with the rotting corpses of the dead too numerous to bury. As time went on, it became the refuse-dump of Jerusalem, until, in the time of Christ, this horrible place was so well-known as readily to suggest itself as a figure of that obviously worse place into which death and hell will eventually be cast in the day of judgment. By no stretch of imagination could the actual geographical spot be what Christ meant when He spoke of the casting of bodies and souls into *Gehenna*. The limitations of its size and the present state of the spot forbid the idea. Rather does this dreadful figure, so vividly expressive to the Jew of that time, create that impression of the ghastly state of the ever-present corruption of the lost and the ever-burning fire of their torment.

The strongest terms implying unending existence were used by Christ (Mark 9. 48). He did not leave the idea of perpetuity and eternality to depend upon the technicalities of an ancient language, but by the clearest negatives He postulated the impossibility of cessation of being for the lost or of termination of the fire in which they will exist.

Even so, the strongest terms available in Greek are used elsewhere to establish beyond real question the perpetuity of the state of the lost. The expression, 'for ever and ever' is used to describe the state of the saved and also the state of the lost (Rev. 14. 10, 11; 22. 5). The usage of this expression in the Apocalypse is instructive. Four times it is used of God Himself. He is spoken of as the One 'who liveth for ever and ever' (chap. 4. 9, 10; 10. 6; 15. 7). It is used of Christ (chap. 1. 18). He said, 'I am alive for evermore' (Greek, *eis tous aiônas tôn aiônôn*). The duration of the sovereignty of Christ (Rev. 11. 15), of the praise, honour, wisdom and power of God and the Lamb (chap. 5. 13; 7. 12), and of the reign of the saints (chap. 22. 5) is described by the terms. In the same way, and obviously, to convey the same sense of perpetuity it is used of the torment of the 'beast,' the 'false prophet' and the devil (chap. 20. 10). Likewise does it imply the unending torments of the unsaved (chap. 14. 11; 19. 3).

Any endeavour to limit the duration implied in the meaning of the terms respecting the state of the lost involves a similar limit being implied when the terms describe the life of God and of Christ, of the reign of Christ and the blessing of His saints. If perpetuity be admitted for the life of God, perpetuity of the state of the lost is also predicted by the same terms used in the same way respecting them.

John observed that those whose names were not written in the book of life were cast into the lake of fire (chap. 20. 15). Of those not enregistered in the sacred scroll more is told later (chap. 21. 8). They are described as the fearful, unbelieving, abominable, fornicators, sorcerers, idolaters and all liars. It is scarcely difficult to appreciate the justice of the judgment of the baser kinds included in this group of types, but that of the first two might appear at first a little more difficult to appreciate. Consideration, however, serves to dispel any doubt that might suggest itself. The present world is a system of distrust of God. To doubt Him is the natural order of thought, and, doubting Him, the attempt to live independently of Him is inevitable. This system of doubt either conquers men or is conquered by men. It is possible for God to be known in actual present experience to be all-loving and all-wise, so that knowing Him means loving Him and trusting Him, first for salvation and then for every lesser need. Those who thus believe Him overcome the world, and the faith that does so is the faith that believes that Jesus is the Christ the Son of God (1 John 5. 4, 5) whom God gave for us that we might live through Him (1 John 4. 9, 10). However, the influence of the worldly system of distrust is such that many, not sunk in sins as others, fail to trust implicitly in the Saviour. They are afraid. They are the cowardly, the fearful. Others are influenced to a greater extent by the world system of doubt, and though still not of the baser kinds, they are incredulous. They do not believe the love that gave Jesus to die. These through their cowardice and incredulity do as much despite to all-sacrificing love as the others do by their gross practices. All except those who boldly trust the Saviour will have their part in the eternal lake.

New Heavens and New Earth

He that raiseth the dead and calleth those things that be not as though they were (Rom. 4. 17), who made the universe originally, can and indeed will make a new heaven and a new earth. John saw this new universe in the great vision (Rev. 21. 1). When urging upon the seer the certainty of this coming Paradise, the Lord used the perfect tense for it and said, 'It is done' (v. 6). The Person in whom the powers for it exist is present. He is now the beginning and is already in Himself the ending (v. 6). More certain this could not be, even if it were present already.

In this new kind of heaven and new kind of earth there will be no more sea (Rev. 21. 1). Its restless, troubled, tossing waters, its dark depths of unexplored mystery and foreboding, its separating effects will not be in evidence. Rather instead, will appear the city to enrich the inhabitants of the new earth and to bring to realization the desire of God to dwell with men and the true end of men simultaneously to dwell with God (v. 3).

The Eternal City

The vision of the last things seemed to reach its climax when John saw the New Jerusalem, like a magnificent jewel, descend out of heaven. Its origin is not earth. It is the product of heaven. It originated in God and emanated from Him (Rev. 21. 2). It descended indeed—to bless earth, but never to come down to earth. Rather does it make possible the approach of men to God and the Lamb, whose dwelling it becomes. So is the triumph of God enjoyed—the tabernacle of God becomes with men—He dwells with them and they shall be His people (*ibid*).

After a brief general description of this city, a detailed description of a city follows. Expositors usually take this later, fuller description back into the millennial age which precedes the Great White Throne judgment. The propriety of this is not disputed. Yet in doing so there seems to be a tendency to leave it there, and to pass over the obvious implications of the words which close the description, 'they shall reign for ever and ever' (Rev. 22. 5). The city is obviously eternal, though its first manifestation be millennial. Everything predicated of its glory and power is eternal and will abide the eternal state, or the expression 'for ever and ever' were inappropriate.

Interminable problems would confront any attempt to take the description of the city with absolute literalness. Actual letters to spell out the name of God are scarcely expected to be imprinted on human brows (Rev. 22. 4). Rather, as the name denotes character, and the face expresses it, so those conformed inwardly naturally express the character of Him to whom they are conformed. In the same way in which we take the title, the Lamb, symbolically of the One who was sacrificed, we understand that, as a 'lamp' (Rev. 21. 23, R.V.), He is the One through whom the light of the glory of God shines to illumine the city.

Rarely, if ever, is it possible to teach a spiritual lesson apart from the use of a material illustration. When God will teach us the nature of the brilliant glory, the felicity, the joyous and perfect service of the redeemed throughout the millennial age and the ages of the ages, He uses the figure of a city of transparent gold and crystal gem through which shines the glory of God to enlighten the eternal earth. It is the symbol of a throbbing organism of ordered life, the several ranks of infinitely varied and variegated types of citizens of which harmoniously blend in affectionate devotion to God and the Lamb participating with them in the rule and blessing of men.

As Jehovah, in a limited way, dwelt between the symbolic cherubim, so does He now actually dwell among those people whose ordered society is depicted by a transparent crystal city of jasper and gold. By means of them will He rule, dispensing blessings to those who people the new earth and through them will the incense of praise and worship return to the Eternal Giver (Rev. 21. 24). This is another and more expressive way of picturing that constitution of the redeemed which elsewhere is termed a kingdom—a royal constitution—in which every person is a priest (Rev. 1. 6; 5. 10).

Gold, the most valuable of metals in Bible times, indicates the character of its populace. Job mentioned it to illustrate purity of character and Jeremiah nobility (Job 23. 10; Lam. 4. 1, 2).

The wall suggests sanctity (Rev. 21. 12). Yet it does not entirely exclude. Those whose robes are washed have right to the tree of life (Rev. 22. 14, R.V.). For them gates which point every way were seen in it (Rev. 21. 12, 13). Through them they come to the tree and bring their glory and honour to God and the Lamb. Apostles have their part and Israel is represented in this symbol of sanctity and approach.

The chemical elements of the stones which bejewel the foundations are quartz, clay, silica, flint, with certain metals. These illustrate the differing types of human beings God takes up in His regenerating grace. But to become the jewels John saw them to be, these elements underwent inimitable change. So regeneration makes each type of sinner-character a jewel, and, the form, colour and position reflect the glory of God and the Lamb by whom this regeneration was wrought.

The flowing river of living water tells of the fulness of the Spirit available for all under those eternal conditions. The tree of life is Christ, whose exquisite fruit is the delight of those within and whose leaves the blessing of those who draw near (Rev. 22. 2).

The throne is there. The rule of God and the Lamb abides. Rejoicing in its stability and bowing to its sceptre, His servants shall serve Him: 'And they shall see His face; and His name shall be in their foreheads' (Rev. 22. 4).

When Paul wrote to the Philippians, he made it clear that a city-state (citizenship) was already subsisting in the heavens (Phil. 3. 20). Then it was being developed. To the redeemed it belonged and they to it. Consequently, he exhorted that as they lived in the environment of an earthly city which was imbued with the spirit of Roman Imperialism, they should do so as citizens of a higher and heavenly commonwealth (Phil. 1. 27).

The Epistle to the Hebrews informs us further of this city. To its commonwealth Abraham looked forward (Heb. 11. 10). The God of glory appeared to him. Thenceforth, he looked for the city which hath the foundations, the designer and constructor of which is God Himself. Such a city is the fitting recompense for those who take the pilgrim pathway (v. 16). Moreover, it is the 'coming city.' All others will pass and their glory fade. This one fills the future (Heb. 13. 14).

The heavenly Jerusalem is Mount Zion, the mountain of royal blessing and power and glory (Heb. 12. 22-24). It is the living God's city. He who is the fountain of life dwells amongst its peoples. They are the society amidst which He moves. Already the spirits of just men made perfect, angels in festal array and the church of firstborn ones, all of whom are enregistered as its freemen, form part of its developing fabric. This is the holy temple in the Lord unto which all that is builded of God in preceding ages groweth (Eph. 2. 21). When John saw it, it was complete—made ready, as a bride adorned for her husband. Rapt, he watched it appear from heaven and from God, and heard the words of triumph, proceeding from the throne, 'Behold, the tabernacle of God is with men, and He shall dwell with them, and they shall be His people, and God Himself shall be with them, and be their God' (Rev. 21. 3).

What must that city be which is the result of the unparalleled art, the matchless wisdom and the unique skill of Him who has ornamented a passing creation with varieties of living things which bewilder the student of their transient beauty and which defy complete exploration of even one of them?

The Eternal State

The character and the state, whether of the redeemed or of the unregenerate, will be perpetuated without deviation after the Great White Throne.

That harmony of being and of experience (Psa. 86. 11) developed at present upon the heavenly octave of Christ's beatitudes (Matt. 5. 3-9) will be the music of eternity for the godly. He that is righteous will do righteousness still. He that is holy will be made holy still (Rev. 22. 11). And, no veneer of lie will ever besmirch the reality experienced in the city, no idol rival its Monarch and nothing common sully its beauty or defile its purity (Rev. 21. 27).

But the supposed music composed on the octave, the notes of which are doubt of God, scepticism, uncleanness, murder, immorality, sorcery, idolatry and lying (Rev. 21. 8), will abide to be the unending jangle of interminable ruin. There will be no possibility of cure then for these moral and spiritual lepers. He that is unrighteous will do unrighteousness still, and he that is filthy will be made filthy still (Rev. 22. 11).

Plain statements to be understood literally, together with chosen symbols, expressive of glories hardly otherwise described, convey truth regarding the eternal state of the redeemed. Both methods are also employed to describe the state of the lost. After the city is described and the blessing of those who wash their robes and thus have right to the tree of life is commented upon, the lot of those who have no part in this blessedness is indicated, not now by means of a plain statement regarding the lake of fire, but by a figure called up from ancient Hebrew law: 'without are the dogs, and the sorcerers, and the fornicators, and the murderers, and the idolators and every one that loveth and maketh a lie' (Rev. 22. 14, 15). This is reminiscent of the law of the leper (Lev. 13. 45, 46). In ancient days, those affected by this dread disease were barred from the cities of Israel. Outside, at a distance, amidst those of their like is the perpetual existence of the uncleansed eked out in misery and exclusion from the felicity of those who have washed their robes.

With this figure the way is prepared for the God of all grace to close His book with a gospel appeal. The Spirit and the Bride join to invite the returning Redeemer. The 'hearer' of the prophecy is called to do so also. But the men of thirsty spirits and souls are called, and whosoever of them is willing is encouraged to accept gratuitously the gift of the water of life ere He comes.

God delights to save. Therefore, every means is used to urge men to accept the blessings of His salvation while there is still time (Rev. 22. 17).

CHAPTER XXV

Doctrine and the Personal Life

A. NAISMITH

IN New Testament terminology 'doctrine' is used in a twofold sense—first and chiefly, to connote the body of teaching contained in the Scriptures as authoritative in the revelation of divine truth and principles; and secondly, to signify the impartation of such instruction to an individual or company. In his *Expository Dictionary of the New Testament*, W. E. Vine distinguishes between the two Greek words commonly translated 'doctrine' in the New Testament—*Didaskalia*, which lays emphasis on the objective aspect and is essentially active, and *Didache*, which is more often subjective and implies the application of truths and principles to heart and life by the act of teaching. Here already, in the consideration of the words used, is an indication of the necessity and value of the teaching of God through His Word and by His Spirit to the individual life. The reasoned expositions of the foregoing chapters lead, therefore, to the practical usefulness of those monumental truths which Dr. A. T. Pierson has described as the leaven and lever of their adherents during the past nineteen centuries —'the leaven to pervade and the lever to uplift.' They touch the centre and circumference of our being, enlightening our minds, enlarging our hearts and enriching our lives.

Pausing for a moment, let us consider the argument so often advanced by religious and respectable folk who are content to let those constantly-changing opinions and theories which men call science interpret Scripture for them—that it does not matter so much what we believe so long as we are sincere. A writer recently has reminded us that 'sincerity co-existed with slavery and slums, with wars of oppression and unjust social systems; and to-day with plenty of sincerity we have a welter of superstition and a flood of cruelty.' Sincerity is a fine quality but no standard for living: we need doctrine. The 'doctrine of Christ' is, like the

Lord Jesus Himself, the way for our journey through the world, the truth to stabilize our minds and influence our conduct, and the life to vitalize our activities and empower us to 'live soberly, righteously and godly in this present world' (Tit. 2. 12). Men have always possessed the capacity to idealize, but only the teaching of the truth of God by His Spirit confers the power to realize the highest ideals. We can never divorce the moral and practical from the doctrinal: in denying doctrine, we proportionately lower men's moral character.

Dr. L. Gaussen, in his prefatory observations to the *Theopneustia*, observes that 'the term Religion is not always employed in its objective sense to signify the science that embraces the truths of our faith; but it is used also, with a subjective meaning, to designate rather the sentiments which those truths foster in the hearts of believers.' Then he goes on to show how absurd it is to maintain 'that one might have the religious sentiments without the religious doctrines from which alone they spring' . . . since this would imply 'that you would have a man to be moral without having any religious tenets, pious without belief, a Christian without Christ, an effect without a cause—living without a soul! Deplorable illusion!' 'This is life eternal, that they might *know* Thee, the only true God, and Jesus Christ whom Thou hast sent' (John 17. 3). The Holy Spirit communicates the principles of God to the mind, impresses their lofty character on the heart and directs the will into obedience to the instructions thus inculcated.

The inspired Scriptures are profitable for many things: but first on the list comes 'doctrine.' 'The undoubted objective of the Spirit in the Word is to build up character, enrich personality, feed the mind and satisfy the heart—in a word, to enable the Christian to function in the full vigour of spiritual manhood, whatever his environment.' (A. McD. Redwood, *Let the Bible Speak*). In order to understand the doctrines of the Bible, there must first be a willingness to obey, for it is to the willing mind that the Holy Spirit imparts the truths that can renew the mind, restore the soul and revive the heart. 'If any man willeth to do His will, he shall know of the teaching,' said the Lord Jesus (John 7. 17, R.V.).

When He promised to His disciples the gift of the Comforter, our Lord distinguished three aspects of doctrine which the Holy

Spirit would communicate to those indwelt by Him. 'He shall teach you all things' and 'bring to your remembrance all that I said unto you' (John 14. 26, R.V.). 'He shall bear witness of Me' (John 15. 26, R.V.). 'He shall take of Mine and shall declare it unto you' (John 16. 14, R.V.). The first aspect of doctrine is here indicated: it is historic, because it concerns a historic Christ, a Saviour who occupies the central place in all history. The effect of the application of such doctrine to Christ's followers must certainly be of a devotional nature, tranquillizing their hearts and deepening their affections for their Master. Loving and loyal devotion to a living Lord Who in His Person embodies grace, purity and truth, cannot but have a transforming effect on the character and tenor of the disciple's life.

Further, the Lord Jesus stated that the province of the Holy Spirit was to 'guide into all truth' (John 16. 13). His presentation of doctrine is didactic as well as historic. Precepts and principles enunciated in the Scripture of truth regulate the life of the neophyte, bringing its acts and activities into conformity with the will and purpose of God.

The mind of the disciple of Christ receiving the instruction of the Holy Spirit will also be enlightened as to prophetic teaching, for 'He shall declare unto you the things that are to come' (John 16. 13, R.V.). Such illumination from the Word of God concerning things which have not been elsewhere disclosed gives the instructed disciple an advantage over the man of the world who, in the midst of the perplexities of his age, knows nothing of eschatology, and is therefore prone to fears and worries when circumstances are adverse, because he knows nothing of the future. The hope of the imminent return of the Lord Jesus Christ has an energizing and satisfying, as well as a purifying, effect on the believer's life.

Reference to a concordance will show that the word 'doctrine' occurs more frequently in the Epistles to Timothy and to Titus, written by Paul just before his martyrdom, than in any other portion of the Bible: and in 1 Tim. there are more occurrences of the word than in any other single book. The time when the three Pastoral Epistles were written was one of peculiar difficulty and trial in the early Christian Church. In addition to the truculent Neronic persecutions which fell so heavily on the followers of

Christ, and perhaps largely because of them, there were many defections among the Christians, and grievous wolves had come in to scatter the flock of God. As the monster Error reared its many ugly heads, Gnosticism was influencing many who were satisfied with a cold intellectual grasp of theology apart from the ethical power of the truth revealed through Christ. It was clear to the apostle that departure from the truth and moral delinquency were concomitant states, so in his last letters he not only reiterates the necessity for the doctrine of Christ, but applies to it an epithet which in this particular association is found only in the Pastoral Epistles—the word 'sound.' In one instance the form in the original is adjectival, and in the other eight occurrences (once rendered wholesome) it is the translation of the present participle of the verb, 'to be healthy.' Both the adjective and the noun are applied elsewhere in the New Testament text to physical health and soundness of body. From the root of the Greek adjective and verb thus used in these letters we derive our English words, hygiene and hygienic. Sound doctrine is, therefore, teaching which is salutary and health-giving in the spiritual realm of man's being.

The two spheres in which the Christian moves bring him into spiritual associations that are both friendly and hostile. In the church, in fellowship with fellow-Christians, and for the realization of the presence of his Lord and his God, he needs to be instructed in sound doctrine. In the world, among the ungodly and subject to the assaults of Satan, he must be fortified and kept spiritually fit by sound doctrine. This is, in effect, what Paul tells his son in the faith in the two letters he addresses to him.

It may help us to an understanding of the main purport of the two epistles to Timothy if we think of each as an edifice, the first in the form of a church building, the second after the similitude of a war memorial. Over the archway into the former we read —'How men ought to behave themselves in the house of God' (1 Tim. 3. 15), and over the entrance to the latter, 'that he may please Him who enrolled him as a soldier' (2 Tim. 2. 4). On entering, we find that the Lord Jesus Christ is the central figure in both, His Incarnation as 'the mystery of godliness' (1 Tim. 3. 16) filling the first, and His Resurrection (2 Tim. 2. 8) as Man from the dead constituting the greatest record of triumph in the grand memorial. The Holy Spirit through Paul sets before us in both epistles the great ideal of loyalty to the Incarnate Son of God. In the church the loyal servant is 'a good minister of Jesus Christ' (1 Tim. 4. 6): in the memorial he goes down to posterity as 'a good soldier of Jesus Christ' (2 Tim. 2. 3). Both buildings have in common four panel pictures, a perfect portraiture of the man of God in four distinct attitudes—fleeing, following, fighting and furnished: and he rises out of the sinister, unfriendly background of 'men of corrupt minds' who will not endure sound doctrine.

Whether in association with fellow-Christians or in the world, sound doctrine is absolutely indispensable for healthy Christian living. It is embodied in the Gospel message entrusted to the individual and to the Church by the Lord (1 Tim. 1. 10). When Jesus in the synagogue of Nazareth plainly outlined His mission, it was a ministry of healing for the sin-sick soul, not a form of Communism or Socialism that He envisaged. The glorious evangel has been, down through the centuries, and still continues to be, the great healing message for the sinful soul of man. The preacher of the Gospel may well boast in the content of his message, the good deposit entrusted to him.

The wholesome words spoken by our Lord (1 Tim. 6. 3) while on earth are rightly appraised as 'the most precious literary heritage of the human race': they are the essence of sound doctrine. They produce, when received and assimilated in the life, true piety which is by all means desirable, in all respects profitable, and at all times obtainable. What a treasury of truth is contained in the words of the Lord Jesus! 'In the words of Christ all the scattered and intersecting rays of truth extant in humanity are collected and blended into the full and perfect light of day,' writes Stier. And again, 'Hear these His words to you, so shall you apprehend who He is, and what you are, and further learn to cry—Lord, to whom shall we go? Thou hast the words of eternal life; and we believe and are sure that Thou art Christ, the Son of the living God (John 6. 68, 69); that Thou art indeed Christ, the Saviour of the world' (Stier, *The Words of the Lord Jesus*). Listening to His words, His audience said, 'Never man spake like this Man' (John 7. 46), as His messages fell on their ears in the form of preaching, parable, precept and prophecy. There is balm for the weary soul, comfort for the mourning spirit, reproof for the rebellious heart, warning for the unconcerned mind, and instruction for the discerning intellect in the words of the Lord Jesus: His teaching was truly salutary. There are many people in the world to-day who, while they have never experienced the new birth and are therefore devoid of that life and power which is essential to the ethical practice of the teachings of our Lord, nevertheless admit the Sermon on the Mount to be the highest ideal ever formulated for the character and conduct of man. The late Gandhi, more highly esteemed in India during his lifetime than any other man, was largely influenced by the Sermon on the Mount in his insistence on achievement of India's national aspirations by non-violent means. It was not uncommon for him, we are told, towards the end of his life to read extracts from Matt. 5 in public meetings.

Paul further exhorts Timothy: 'Hold fast the form of sound words, which thou hast heard of me, in faith and love which is in Christ Jesus' (2 Tim. 1. 13). The healing ministry of the Holy Spirit through the lips and pen of His apostles is of the highest value, and is to be prized and treasured. It is that which constitutes 'the faith once for all delivered to the saints' (Jude 3), setting forth the great teachings concerning our Lord—His Incarnation, immaculate life, death, resurrection and glory—concerning His Church, concerning such practical issues as holiness, purity and truth, concerning human relationships and concerning the purposes of God yet to be fulfilled in the second advent of Christ and His future glory. So long as the disciples 'continued steadfastly in the apostles' doctrine' (Acts 2. 42), the Church of God flourished and the work of the Lord prospered.

Among the last charges given to Timothy by the great apostle from his prison in Rome is the mandate: 'preach the Word; be instant in season, out of season; reprove, rebuke, exhort with all longsuffering and doctrine; for the time will come when they will not endure *sound doctrine*; but after their own lusts shall they heap to themselves teachers, having itching ears; and they shall turn away their ears from the truth and shall be turned unto fables' (2 Tim. 4. 2-4). Already, with his keen discernment, Paul could detect the development of that diseased condition that refuses the only remedy, wholesome doctrine, and turns to all kinds of ruinous quackery.

In his letter to Titus, the remaining pastoral epistle, Paul continues to stress the need of the health-giving teaching of the Scriptures for the life of each and every member of the Christian community. Parallel with this throughout the epistle, emphasis is laid on good works, the expression, in church and social life, of the doctrine of Christ received and assimilated in the mind. Through this the Christian may be 'a pattern of good works' (Tit. 2. 7), 'zealous of good works' (Tit. 2. 14), 'ready to every good work' (Tit. 3. 1), and 'careful to maintain good works' (Tit. 3. 8). To the elders in the Christian church sound doctrine is indispensable for the purpose of exhorting the saints and of silencing false teachers whose doctrine is unsound and whose lives are unsavoury. The same teaching is desirable for all classes in the local church because of its powerful influence on the mind, demeanour, deportment and duties of the individual believer in the several relationships of life. The older men and women in the assembly, the younger ones too, and those members engaged in the daily performance of servile tasks for masters who exact the utmost ounce of toil and sweat, all need the truth of God to mould their minds and fashion their lives. The grand cumulative effect of such instruction will be the regulation of the individual life on lines of sobriety and self-control, of the social life in honesty and righteousness toward all men, and of the hidden life of the soul in devotion and piety toward God, as the Christian learns to live 'soberly, righteously and godly in this present world' (Tit. 2. 12).

The religion that Mohammed claimed to have received as a revelation from heaven was enforced by his zealous followers at the edge of the sword. Those who embraced the Muslim faith were not attracted to it by the excellence of its tenets, and so the teachings of the Koran have no elevating moral influence on the lives of its adherents. A similar defect is stamped on the other faiths of mankind, several of which are further debased by idolatrous or animistic systems. Christian doctrine is unique in its world-wide influence for purity, uprightness and self-denying service to God and man. In India, for example, its transformation of the individual life and of the conditions of the community, its uplift of the down-trodden and depressed, and its social service through the medium of education and hospital treatment, are readily acknowledged even by the enemies of Christianity. The experience of the missionary, in whatever land his sphere of labour may be, invariably has been that those Christian churches which receive regular teaching from the Word of God and in which New Testament principles have been inculcated, become dynamic in holy living and faithful service, while groups of Christians that for any reason are denied the privilege of such faithful ministry yield disappointing results. This furnishes concrete evidence that 'the Word of God is living and powerful' (Heb. 4. 12), and its dissemination productive of spiritual fruit.

The annals of history provide numerous examples of the power and value of sound doctrine in the personal life but let us, having followed consecutively in our Bible, through the epistles of Paul to Timothy and Titus, the development of the forceful argument he advances that sound doctrine and holy living are inseparably connected, turn for a final example to the concise little letter of the apostle to Philemon, which comes next in the order of books in the New Testament.

In the lines of this letter we make the acquaintance of three men, each unique in his own circle, who came from very different ranks of society, had followed different religious creeds, and were poles apart as far as morality is concerned. A cursory perusal of the letter leads us to the conclusion that those three men—Paul, the Jewish convert, Philemon, the wealthy Gentile slave-owner, and Onesimus, the slave on the lowest rung of the social ladder, are the closest of friends and enjoy a fellowship that is inexplicable apart from their having accepted the same elevating teaching and principles. Each of those three lives powerfully attests the value, necessity and benefits of the doctrine of Christ. Consider further the tremendous transformation the life and outlook of the runaway slave, Onesimus, had undergone. Socially he was a slave, belonging to the least respectable section of the lowest class in the Roman world: morally he was a thief, for he had misappropriated some of his master's property and absconded: and legally he was an outlaw. In Rome, where doubtless the profligate and the criminal were his daily companions and associates, he heard one day a manacled prisoner proclaim a new doctrine which attracted him, and he accepted the truth of the Gospel message thus propagated by Paul, with all its implicates, giving evidence of repentance toward God and faith toward the Lord Jesus Christ. There must have been a unique power in that doctrine, for it made the fugitive slave willing, for righteousness' sake, to renounce his self-acquired freedom and return to slave for a master he had grievously wronged, regardless of possible severe punishment. The metamorphosis went deeper still into that man's being, for Paul can truthfully describe the former delinquent as now his child in the faith, 'begotten in his bonds' (Phil. 10), as a 'brother beloved' (v. 16), and 'a partner' (v. 17) in the same great business in which both Paul and Philemon were engaged. Onesimus, with his innate slave mentality, had endeared himself to the man with the giant intellect educated at the feet of Gamaliel, one of the most scholarly Jews of his day. This poor serf had become so useful in the performance of loving ministrations that Paul feels the return of Onesimus will be like tearing out his own heart and sending it to Philemon. Further, the altogether useless servant who had occasioned such loss to his Christian master was returning, miraculously changed into a profitable helper in Philemon's household (v. 11) because of what little he had apprehended and assimilated of the truth of God.

The whole fabric of Christian living rests upon the divine foundation of Christian doctrine: therefore it is well continually to remind ourselves, as Paul reminded Timothy, to 'take heed to ourselves and to the doctrine' (1 Tim. 4. 16). It is because, as Prof. James Orr remarks, there is 'a great distrust of clear and systematic thinking about divine things,' and because 'men prefer to live in a region of haze and indefiniteness in regard to these matters' that there are not many more lives transformed as were the lives of Paul, Philemon and Onesimus.

APPENDIX I

HOW WE GOT OUR BIBLE

'The Bible may be treated historically or theologically. Neither treatment is complete in itself; but the treatments are separable; and here, as elsewhere, the historical foundation rightly precedes and underlies the theological interpretation.' So wrote Dr. Westcott eighty years ago. More recently Sir F. Kenyon has stated: 'The foundation of all study of the Bible with which the reader must acquaint himself if his study is to be securely based is *the knowledge of its history as a book*.' Both statements, in somewhat different aspects, reflect a profound understanding of spiritual values in regard to Bible study.

The subject, 'How we got our Bible,' involves enquiry into at least two historical questions. The first: By what process did this Book come to be recognised as Scripture, divinely authoritative for Christian life and teaching? The second, How has it been handed down to us in the past centuries? The first has to do with the Canon, the second with the Text of both Old and New Testaments. Problems there are in both, but there is also secure ground for faith to rest on.

The very names applied to the Bible from earliest times remind us that it is a composite volume. Jerome (fourth century) first called it *Bibliotheca Divina*, the Divine Library. Later in the thirteenth century the Latin plural 'The Books,' became by common consent 'The Book' (*Biblia*, singular), which has passed into the languages of modern Europe. This Library contains sixty-six books, thirty-nine in the Old Testament and twenty-seven in the New Testament, a period of four centuries separating the two divisions. The Old Testament is composed of writings collected over a period of approximately fourteen or fifteen centuries; the New Testament of the writings of one century.

In the Old Testament the process of its composition was necessarily divided into stages, and each group of records had its own history. The national Book, which eventually came to be, grew with the slow development of the divine revelation. It was indeed the *history* of this revelation, each stage adding its quota to the total. In the case of the New Testament books the process was somewhat different. Each writer wrote independently of the others, with various ends in view and without any idea of adding either to the previous Scriptures or of making a collection of writings, which subsequently would become a rule of faith. Yet in the Providence of God we now possess all these writings, together with the Old Testament writings combined into one volume and speak of it as the 'Canon of Holy Scripture.'

(1) The word 'canon' is of Christian origin, from the Greek *kanon*, meaning rule or measuring rod by which a thing is measured. From this it came to mean a standard or test of measurement, and then the area or thing measured. As applied now to the Scriptures it signifies a collection of religious writings divinely

inspired and hence authoritative, directive, and binding. It implies that these are separated off from all other religious writings—from the Apocrypha, for example, which is accepted in the Roman Catholic community but rejected by the Christian Church as being uncanonical. They did not derive authority merely by some ecumenical decree of Jews or Christians but because they already possessed a distinctive quality indicative of a supernatural origin which marked them off from all other books.

The familiar division of the Jewish Scriptures into (*a*) the Law—*Torah*; (*b*) the Prophets—*Nebiim*; and (*c*) the Holy Writings—*Kethubhim* (or, as in the Septuagint, the *Hagiographa*), probably indicated the three stages in which the Old Testament was acknowledged as authoritative by the Jews. The Law included Genesis to Deuteronomy. The Prophets were divided into two classes: (i) the *Former* Prophets (Joshua, Judges, Samuel, Kings); (ii) the *Latter* Prophets (Isaiah, Jeremiah, Ezekiel, and the twelve Minor Prophets, Hosea to Malachi, counted as one). The Kethubhim, included the remainder.

(1) The *Law*, or as it is often called the Pentateuch, was always recognised as the work of Moses the Lawgiver, and seems to have formed the Jewish Bible up to the time of the Captivity. The various laws and decrees were communicated through Moses and accepted by the people as the utterances of God. They were written down by divine command and so preserved for the future instruction of the people, to which they might always turn for guidance (Exod. 24. 3, 4; 34. 27; Deut. 31. 9-12, 24-26). That this continued to be the authoritative guide in the days of Joshua also is suggested by such references as Josh. 1. 7, 8; 1 Kings 2. 3. But the more positive evidence of the general recognition of these books is found in 2 Kings 22. 8-13 (cf. 2 Chron. 34. 14) when, in the reign of Josiah, Hilkiah found 'the book of the Law' in the house of the Lord. 'There can be no reasonable doubt,' says Dr. Westcott, 'that the book of Hilkiah was substantially the Pentateuch which we now have.' That it had been so long neglected is no evidence that it lacked authority in any sense. It had been held in pious regard by the great spiritual leaders of the past such as Samuel, David, Solomon, and Hezekiah. 'It was the *recognition* of its authority, not of the issue of a *new* authority, which provoked Josiah's distress upon finding how long it had been neglected' (2 Kings 22. 11).

(2) The recognition of the group of writings included in the *Prophets* is not so easy to follow. That other writings were in process of composition after Moses' days is hinted at in Joshua 24. 26, 27 and 1 Samuel 10. 25 (also Prov. 25. 1). The powerful ministry of the prophets during the long period of the kings became increasingly active, especially as the time of the Captivity drew nearer, A considerable amount of this ministry was committed to writing, and if not immediately yet in due time these writings were accepted as given by revelation of God (2 Kings 17. 13; Jer. 7. 25; Zech. 1. 4, 6). Jeremiah himself provides illustration of how the oral message was written down (Jer. 36; 45. 1) by divine command. Not a single prophet whose writings are preserved betrays the shadow of a doubt that he was the Lord's spokesman, and his writings bore the seal of approval in the wonderful measure of their fulfilment in subsequent history.

It is well to point out here that the Jews were actuated by a sound motive in combining both the prophetical and the historical books in this second group. 'The prophets were God's witnesses to a divine kingdom among men, and naturally became the commentators of its history, the exponents of its laws, and the heralds of its triumphs. History and prophecy jointly illustrate the principles of God's moral government and disclose His purposes of grace, the one by narrating the past, the other by linking the past and present with the future.'

The date to which probably we may assign the completion of this second group is the commencement of the third century B.C. The writer of 2 Maccabees (chap. 11. 13, 14) describes how 'Nehemiah founded a Library' of just such books as are included in this section. The reference in Daniel to 'the books' (chap. 9. 2) may conceivably have included portions of such a collection. The conquests of Alexander the Great and the influx of anti-Jewish Hellenic philosophy and literature at that time would have provided the impulse to place these records on the same footing as the Law because of their long recognition as the 'oracles of God.' Also the voice of prophecy had ceased (1 Macc. 9. 27) as foretold by Zechariah (13. 2-5). It needed no arbitrary decision to accept the books just as they were as 'the Word of the Lord.'

(3) The recognition of the books in the *Hagiographa* belongs to the last stage of the history but it is not possible to be exact as to the date of its final recognition as canonical. It is significant, however, that in the book, 'The Wisdom of Jesus the Son of Sirach' (or Ecclesiasticus), written about 200-180 B.C., reference is made in chapters 44-49 to all the books of the Law, the Prophets, and some portions of the Writings. It is known that a number of the sacred books of the Jews were destroyed in the persecution of Antiochus Epiphanes (1 Macc. 1. 56, 57), and a tradition is extant in 2 Macc. 2. 14, that Judas Maccabeus (and other loyalists) set on foot a movement 'to gather together all those things (i.e. the Writings) that were lost by reason of the war we had, and they remain with us.' Three times over in the Prologue to Ecclesiasticus, prefixed in 133 B.C. by the writer's grandson to his Greek translation, we find the mention of 'the Law and the Prophets and the *other* Writings.' This is one of the earliest evidences that 'other books' were mentioned in the same class with the Law and the Prophets. This would point to the probability that the threefold canon had been fixed by this date, though Ryle prefers to place it about 105 B.C., in the more peaceful and prosperous period before the death of John Hyrcanus.

When the Christian era opened there was already a fixed body of writings recognized as of divine origin to which the term 'Scripture' was applied. To these Christ and His disciples made constant reference, e.g. Luke 4. 21; 24. 27, 44; John 5. 39, 46; Acts 1. 20; 7. 42, etc. 'It is very important to observe,' says Ryle, 'that all the direct citations of the New Testament writers (as well as Philo) are made from the Old Testament Canon.' The individual books of Obadiah, Nahum, Ezra, Nehemiah, Esther, Song of Solomon and Ecclesiastes, though not mentioned in the New Testament were joined with other books which were recognised, which would imply equal acceptance. For example, Obadiah and Nahum indisputably belong to the Twelve Prophets; Ezra and Nehemiah were joined definitely to Chronicles.

Apart from the testimony of the New Testament writers there is the evidence of Josephus, who, writing at the close of the first century A.D. (*Contra Apion*, I. 8), speaks of twenty-two (not twenty-four) sacred books of the Jews 'containing the history of all time, books that are justly believed in. And of these, five are the books of Moses, which comprise the Laws and the earliest traditions from the creation of mankind down to Moses' death. . . . The prophets who succeeded Moses wrote the history of the events that occurred in their own time, thirteen books. The remaining four documents comprised hymns to God and practical precepts of men.' He is probably following the LXX, and classes the books by subject-matter, joining Ruth to Judges, and Lamentations to Jeremiah. He goes on to speak of other later records 'from the time of Artaxerxes to our own time,' but says, 'these recent records have not been deemed worthy of equal credit with those which have preceded, because the exact succession of the prophets ceased.' And then he significantly adds: 'But what faith we have placed in our own writings is evident . . . for though so long an interval of time has now passed (i.e. since they were written) not a soul has ventured either to add, or to remove, or to alter a syllable.' Most authorities are agreed on the value of Josephus' evidence. He reflects the popular belief of his age, and voiced the accepted tradition which was universal and undisputed.

We may sum up the accepted findings of scholarship thus: (*a*) The Law was recognised as authoritative first, about 444 B.C.; (*b*) The Prophetical group assumed equal validity probably about 200 B.C.; (*c*) The Writings were added not later than 100 B.C. It seems clear that their canonicity was recognised primarily on the grounds of the divine inspiration of the *authors*, not on any formal decision of some Jewish Council, although the Synod of Jamnia (near Jaffa) in A.D. 90, may be considered the official occasion when the Jews finally pronounced on the limits of their canon. We may not be able to trace in detail the long process which thus eventuated in the completion of the Old Testament canon, but we can judge the *results* as seen in the volume we hold in our hands. The supreme test of its validity as Scripture is the place it held in the mind of Jesus Himself. What He esteemed as being not above suspicion, but as actually possessed of divine authority in His teaching or exposition of it, we can safely accept.

The historical development of the New Testament canon follows an entirely different line from that of the Old Testament. During the first decades of the Gospel's history the need for any 'official' body of writings would scarcely be felt. There were in use the Old Testament Scriptures to which appeal was made as exemplified in our Lord's teaching (Matt. 5. 17; Luke 24. 44; John 5. 39). The apostles no doubt made use of these also in their writings and speeches to a very large extent. There would also be felt a natural shrinking from making any attempt to add to these sacred books.

At the first, oral teaching was the only means of disseminating the Christian message—the method still very extensively used in teaching the illiterate masses of many lands. As time went on oral instruction tended to assume a certain fixed 'form' or 'body of teaching' which was passed on from one to another. This 'oral tradition' was undoubtedly a most important vehicle of instruction, though possibly Biblical criticism has often over-emphasized it.

As time went on and the Gospel spread to distant regions bringing young churches into existence, whose members would need spiritual instruction, the insufficiency of merely oral teaching would become apparent. It is not surprising, therefore, that before A.D. 50, Christian writings began to appear. Some think that parts of Christ's teaching were in writing even before the crucifixion, but this is conjectural. Nevertheless before the first generation of Christians had passed away there were many narratives in circulation as may be inferred from Luke (1. 1-4), who wrote his Gospel about A.D. 57. It is acknowledged by all authorities that Paul's letters were in circulation by 66–67 A.D. Other New Testament books had emerged earlier. So that before the fall of Jerusalem the New Testament in its several parts was practically complete.

For the purpose of our present enquiry we may divide the history of the canon into four stages, using the utmost brevity.

(1) *From the Apostles to* 120 *A.D.* It is evident from the writings of the Apostolic Fathers (from 70 A.D. onwards) that the Gospels and the Epistles were well known before the end of the first century. The extant writings of Clement of Rome, Ignatius, Polycarp, and Barnabas contain numerous 'correspondences' or partial quotations from New Testament books. The Epistle of Barnabas, for example, makes free use of Philippians, and quotes from nine other of Paul's letters. The date of Polycarp's birth is placed at about 69 A.D., that is, he was thirty when the Apostle John died (*c.* 98), so that he must have known the Christian Scriptures. Evidence of this is found in his own Epistle where he makes reference to eighteen books of the New Testament, including Hebrews (Lightfoot). The free use made of the apostles' words in these writings shows that the several books of the New Testament were carefully treasured and studied. They bear distinct witness to the 'Gospels' also. Clement, Ignatius, and Barnabas draw a clear distinction between their own and the apostolic writings, attributing to the latter inspiration and divine authority (1 Clem. 1. 47; Ign. *Ad Rom.* iv). Later in date the testimony of Papias, whose chief work, *An Exposition of Oracles of the Lord*, written apparently about 126, is of exceptional importance because he was in all probability a disciple of the Apostle John. He is the first who alludes by name to the writers of the Gospels, and mentions the writings of Matthew and Mark. Eusebius records that he quoted from 1 John and 1 Peter, and acknowledged the Revelation to be divinely inspired. We may note finally how the reference in 2 Peter 3. 16 would lead us to believe that Paul's letters were well known and in circulation.

(2) *From* 120–170 *A.D.* We now reach the age of the Greek Apologists. By this time persecution by the civil government and the heretical teachings of Gnosticism had arisen to test the Church's foundations. The Christian writings were brought into great prominence being on the one hand attacked by heretical writers, and on the other defended by the leaders of the Church. From both sides they receive remarkable testimony in different ways.

Of the apologists, Justin Martyr (*c.* 148) was by far the most important. He specially mentions the 'Memoirs of the Apostles called Gospels,' which were read on Sundays interchangeably with the Prophets (*Apol.* I. 66, 67). This is possibly the first clear proof of the *beginnings* of a canon. It is of interest that Tatian, a disciple of Justin, wrote a harmony of the four Gospels, the 'Diatessaron,' of which there is extant an Armenian version and commentary dated *c.* 343. He mentions the Apocalypse by name and its author as John. But he seems to have known also the Acts, six epistles of Paul, Hebrews and I John.

On the side of the heretics the most noted was the Gnostic Marcion (*c.* 140), and later Celsus (*c.* 170), who has been called 'the chief literary opponent of Christianity in the second century.' Marcion's main activity was directed to the formation of a canon of his own, consisting of Luke's Gospel and Paul's Galatians, I and 2 Corinthians, Romans, I and 2 Thessalonians, Ephesians, Colossians, Philemon, Philippians. The importance of his work to us is that he provides the first clear evidence of the canonization of the Pauline epistles by selecting a Canon out of the books recognised by the Church of that age. At the same time it cannot be claimed that finality had yet been reached. The Epp. Hebrews, James, 2 and 3 John, Jude, were still in doubt in some quarters, and 2 Peter was almost in the same position. So that within a hundred years of the fall of Jerusalem all the remaining parts of the New Testament had been collected and received by the church as fully inspired.

(3) *From* 170-303 *A.D.* This takes us on to the time of the persecutions under the Emperor Diocletian. It was an age of rapid expansion of Christianity, which in spite of persecution spread far beyond the confines of the Roman Empire. It has been called 'the age of a voluminous theological literature tense with the great issues of church, canon and creed'. The names which stand out most prominently as leaders of the Church are Irenæus (disciple of Polycarp and pupil of St. John), Clement of Alexandria, Origen (who succeeded Clement as head of the Catechetical school in Alexandria), and Tertullian, representing the three great spheres of Christian learning respectively, Asia Minor, Egypt and North Africa. The important writings of this period, products of these great writers, mark the progress towards agreement which prevailed respecting the full canon of the New Testament.

Irenæus had a wide acquaintance with the scattered churches and with established apostolic tradition. He was an earnest defender of the truth and bases his teaching very largely on the New Testament. In his writings allusions are made to every book in the New Testament except Philemon, James, 2 Peter, 3 John, and Jude. Clement likewise makes use of all the New Testament books with the exception of James, 2 Peter, and 3 John, and by such usage acknowledges their authoritative character. Origen, who is acknowledged to be one of the greatest scholars of that age, accepted the divine authority of the same books as Clement had received. What is most important, however, is that he places the Apostolic Scriptures on the same equality as the Old Testament in his statement 'the Scriptures believed by us to be divine both of the Old and of the New Covenant' (*De Princip.* iv. I).

(4) *The Fourth Century. The Close of the Canon.* Up to this point no concerted action had been taken to establish a final canon of the New Testament. But Diocletian's persecution and the decree for the confiscation and destruction of the apostolic writings forced the issue. The Scriptures were by now 'unofficially' yet indubitably recognised by all as to their sources, their authority and their divine inspiration. It now became necessary to 'separate' them from all *other* ecclesiastical treatises including the many apocryphal works in circulation. This did not actually come to pass till near the end of the century, at the Council of Carthage 397 A.D.

Eusebius (270-340) was the one who took a leading part in this great work. He himself had witnessed the burning of the Scriptures, a tragic event which doubtless urged him to his task of securing a clearer understanding of what were authoritative and what were spurious. He was peculiarly fitted by his great learning and wide acquaintance with the prevailing thought in other Christian centres, having travelled extensively. He classes the writings which were best known and widely used into three classes, the second of which he divided into two sections:

(*a*) The 'acknowledged,' whose authenticity and apostolicity were fully accepted: the Gospel, Acts, Epistles of Paul (including Hebrews), 1 Peter, 1 John, and the Revelation (somewhat doubtfully).

(*b*) The 'disputed': (i) those admitted by the majority, including himself, were James, 2 Peter, 2 and 3 John, Jude; (ii) those not so authenticated were Shepherd of Hermas, the Didache, Epistle of Barnabas, Acts of Paul.

(*c*) The 'heretical' included the purely apocryphal and heretical works.

The somewhat later list made by Athanasius (367) representing the opinion of the Church of Alexandria contains the whole of the New Testament books as we now have them. The two master theologians of the West, Jerome and Augustine, also accepted the same Canon, which was confirmed by the Third Council of Carthage (397), decreeing that 'aside from the canonical Scriptures nothing is to be read in church as under the name of "the divine Scriptures".' This finally settled the question regarding authority and canonicity of the Bible.

How has the Text been handed down during the centuries since first written? Is our Bible an accurate representation of the originals? It will be obvious that this covers a wide field and involves more than one line of enquiry, for which the student must consult larger and specialised works. Our present treatment can only be extremely cursory. Let us begin with the Old Testament.

A remarkable fact meets us at the start: we have no manuscripts of the Old Testament in Hebrew earlier than the ninth or tenth century A.D., except one small papyrus. It can be asserted, however, that we have sufficient evidence to show that the Hebrew text has suffered no material change since the first century A.D., when it was finally fixed at the Synod of Jamnia 90 A.D. (Kenyon). The present Hebrew manuscripts contain what is known as the Massoretic text. That is, it was edited and made by schools of Jewish Rabbis and scholars who were called Massoretes (from *Massoreth*, 'to hand down'; Num. 31. 5). These men were imbued with the great ideal to preserve the purest text possible, and were noted for the meticulous care with which they copied their Scriptures. They flourished in the seventh century A.D., and with unremitting toil they produced by the help of the ancient Jewish Targums and Talmud the text of the Hebrew Bible as it was accepted at the Synod of Jamnia.

In addition to this two other forms of the text have come down to us from pre-Christian times; the Samaritan Pentateuch (which includes only the five books of Moses) and the Septuagint, a Greek version containing the whole of the Old Testament. The former is strictly not a version, as it is in Hebrew, but written in different characters from that of other manuscripts. It differs from the Hebrew in about six thousand places, but the great majority of these are said to be of very trifling importance.

The Septuagint (usually written LXX) or Greek version, is by far the most important of all the ancient translations. It was the Bible of the Greek-speaking Jews; edited in the original text by Origen. The only other version we need mention is the Old Latin or Vulgate (fourth century) containing both Old and New Testaments, which is still in use by the Roman Catholic Church, but of no great importance in questions of textual criticism.

'The general position,' remarks Kenyon, 'with regard to the text of the Old Testament is this: It may be accepted that since about the year A.D. 100 it has been handed down with no substantial variation.' Coming from such an acknowledged authority this statement is of value in connection with the transmission of the text.

The literary evidence for the text of the New Testament is vastly more abundant than that for the Old Testament—in fact, far greater than in the case of any other series of writings in the whole range of ancient literature. It is computed that there are over four thousand manuscripts available of the Greek New Testament, or parts of it. If we include all the versions in addition the total is greatly enhanced.

The fourteen hundred years between the completion of the autographs and the fifteenth century constitute the most important era in the history of the New Testament documents. It furnishes us with the great mass of Greek manuscripts, the most essential materials we possess for arriving at the true text. Three stages of development are discernible in this era: (*a*) the Papyrus, from the first to the fourth century; (*b*) the Uncials, from fourth to the ninth, during which vellum (made from skins) took the place of papyrus for writing purposes; (*c*) the Minuscules, or Cursives, from the ninth to the fifteenth century. Uncials are the large square separate letters used in early writings, minuscules being the smaller characters, usually linked together, hence also called cursives.

The discovery and significance of the New Testament papyrus writings has been well told by Sir F. Kenyon and Prof. Geo. Milligan, to whose writings the student is referred. The earliest extant papyrus manuscripts and the most important are the famous Chester Beatty Codices, which contain a considerable part of the New Testament, dating from the third century. During this early stage of the Scriptures it was natural that their circulation was greatly limited, but it is evident that the work of copying went on undaunted. Besides the

Greek manuscripts there were translations made into other languages (called versions) from the Greek, even before the end of the third century. These provide further evidence for the text of the New Testament. Of these versions there are three principal ones, the Syriac, the Egyptian or Coptic, and the Latin. The Syriac and Latin date about the middle of the second century. The Egyptian number at least five in different dialects but are not of much value in comparison.

Before the close of the third century two circumstances arose of far-reaching consequences. The Emperor Constantine accepted Christianity as the official religion of the Roman Empire (*c.* 313-25); and, secondly, vellum began to take the place of papyrus as a writing material more durable and more easily used. Constantine's first act was to order fifty copies of the Greek Scriptures, written on vellum, for the churches of his new capital. It is of interest also that to this period belong two great Codices, Sinaiticus and Vaticanus. This codex (or 'book' form) was an advance on the earlier papyrus rolls and single sheets, and made for greater permanence. It was natural that the circulation of an increasing number of copies of the Greek Bible in parts would be greatly stimulated.

From the fourth to the ninth century a standard type of *text* gradually came to be accepted, which spread over the whole Greek-speaking world. It is now known as the Byzantine type and is found in the vast majority of manuscripts that have come down to us. Of this Byzantine (or Received) Text Kenyon says, 'at least ninety-six per cent. of the extant manuscripts are later than the eighth century; and of these only a handful preserve traces of *other* types of text which were in existence before the adoption of the standard text.'

About the middle of the fifteenth century the invention of printing revolutionized everything, even the circulation of the Scriptures. The new method began to do away with the old hand-copying, and by 1516 the first Greek New Testament was printed by Erasmus, who adopted the standard text. The first complete Bible printed was the Latin Vulgate but it has had no influence on the transmission of the text. Erasmus' work fired the devout zeal of Tyndale who printed an English translation in 1525. He also published the Pentateuch from the original Hebrew, and had translated the historical books before his martyrdom in 1536. With the help of Tyndale's version and a translation of his own from German and Latin Bibles, Miles Coverdale produced the first complete English Bible in 1535, which culminated in our great English Authorised Version in 1611, 'a masterpiece of literary skill and style which embedded itself in the life and literature of the English people.'

But the question may be urged: 'Can we absolutely rely on the accuracy of the text of our English New Testament, assuming that the history of the several books has demonstrated their authenticity?' In answer to this we shall close by making two quotations from recognised authorities on the subject. The first is from Westcott and Hort,[1] whose work on the Greek text is universally known.

'With regard to the great bulk of the words of the New Testament . . . there is no variation or other ground of doubt; and, therefore, no room for textual criticism. . . . The amount of what *can*, in any sense, be called substantial variation,

[1] *The New Testament in the Original Greek*, Vol. ii, p. 2.

is but a small fraction of the residuary variation, and can hardly form more than a thousandth part of the entire text.' In other words, it is only in regard to one word in a thousand that the textual critics, by laborious comparison of manuscripts, have to determine the exact reading of the original text.

The second quotation is from Sir Frederick Kenyon's book, *The Story of the Bible*, the last page: 'It may be disturbing to some to part with the conception of a Bible handed down through the ages without alteration and in unchallenged authority; but it is a higher ideal to face the facts, to apply the best powers with which God has endowed us to the solution of the problems which they present to us; and it is reassuring at the end to find that the general result of all these discoveries and all this study is to strengthen the proof of *the authenticity of the Scriptures*, and our conviction that we have in our hands, in substantial integrity, the veritable Word of God.'

Let it be stated categorically that *all* the authorities in the field of textual criticism assure us that no single doctrine of the Gospel is affected by any of the variations still unexplained.

A. McD. Redwood

APPENDIX II

THE VIRGIN BIRTH

It was to prove 'Jesus come in the flesh' that John wrote his epistles. To deny this is to undermine His atoning work. He must partake of flesh and blood in order to die. He must be truly man to be (1) the Seed of the woman and act the Kinsman's part (Gen. 3. 15; Gal. 4. 4); (2) the Seed of Abraham to inherit the promises (Gal. 3. 16); and (3) the Son of David, to claim the throne of Israel (1 Chron. 22. 10). When King Ahaz refused to ask a sign, God gave one for all time greater than earth or heaven could afford: 'Behold a virgin shall conceive and bring forth a Son and shall call His name Immanuel' (Isa. 7. 14). This was fulfilled by the birth of Jesus as narrated by Matthew and Luke.

Gesenius, the well-known Hebraist, asserts that the word *galmah* does not mean *virgin*, but a youthful spouse recently married, and cites this passage in proof, which seems like begging the question. But it would hardly be a 'sign' for a young married woman to conceive and bear a son. Dr. Tregelles, a scholar of at least equal reputation with Gesenius, and his translator, denies his conclusions, and refers to the fact that the LXX renders the word 'virgin' by *parthenos* in this passage, which must have been a difficulty to them. *Galmah*, in Punic, does undoubtedly signify 'virgin,' as the doctor points out. Gesenius says that *b'thoolah* is the true word for virgin, but this is not always the case as a study of the references shows. *Galmah* occurs in six other places in the Old Testament: in Gen. 24. 16 of Rebecca; Exod. 2. 8 of Miriam; Psa. 68. 25; Prov. 30. 19; Cant. 1. 3; 6. 8. In not one of these occurrences is Gesenius' meaning apparent. One would suppose, as Dr. Tregelles suggests, that the use of the passage in Matt. 1. 23 would settle the dispute for any Christian.

If the Eternal Son was to become incarnate, how else but by virgin-birth could it take place? If Jesus were the son of Mary and Joseph, then there was no incarnation and those who worship Jesus are credulous idolaters. To deny the virgin birth and His divine personality, while accepting results of His life and influence, is to accept transcendent effects without adequate cause.

Wm. Hoste

APPENDIX III

THE KENOSIS THEORY

THE expression *kenosis* is taken from Phil. 2. 7, where we read of our Lord Jesus Christ: 'Who being in the form of God, thought it not robbery to be equal with God but *made Himself of no reputation.*' The words in italics are represented by one word in the Greek, *ekenosen.* It is from this verb that the noun *kenosis* is derived. In the R.V. it is translated, 'He emptied Himself,' and this is the *kenosis* fact. The Son of God 'emptied Himself' in wondrous grace and for love of us men and for our redemption.

The first thing we notice in the text is that He was *in the form of God.* Since God has no outward or physical form, this can only mean that He was Himself essentially God, of the very nature and being of God—very God of very God.

There are three words used in Scripture to denote the interrelation of the Father and the Son. In this case it is *morphe*, 'in the form of,' that is, essentially God. In Col. 1. 15 and 2 Cor. 4. 4, the word is *eikōn*, 'the image of the invisible God,' that is, as manifesting the Father to us, and later *charakter* (Heb. 1. 3), 'the express image of His person,' or (R.V.) the 'very image of His substance,' which would include both—His nature and His expression, and manifestation in time. It is this One of whom it is true that 'He emptied Himself.'

Therefore, in thinking of the *kenosis*, we must never permit ourselves to conceive of Him as any other than God, who changes not. In His humiliation, He was 'God manifest in flesh' (1 Tim. 3. 16).

In what sense did He empty Himself? The text affords us clear guidance here. We are told two things: (1) He took upon Him the form of a servant, being made in the likeness of man; and (2) He humbled Himself and became obedient. In neither of these statements is there any suggestion that He changed His essential being or divested Himself in any way of His Godhead or any of the attributes of Deity.

Two things, however, He did which He had never done before: (1) He became dependent; (2) He became obedient. So dependent as servant and man was He that He could say, 'The Son can do nothing of Himself' (John 5. 19, 30; 8. 28; 12. 49; 14. 10). For it is the very essence of a man and his servant that he is dependent. Any independent action is not for such. This, then, was the grace of the Son that He willingly submitted Himself in all things to depend on the Father. 'I live by the Father' (John 6. 5). His words were the Father's; His works were the Father's; even in His voluntary sacrifice of Himself in death He must have authority and commandment for what He was doing (John 10. 18). It was this that drew forth special love from the Father's heart (17).

And He became obedient. He whom all principalities and powers obeyed, learned in a new experience the grace of obedience (Heb. 5. 8). His was the open ear—He was the instructed One of Isa. 50. 4. Dependence and obedience constitute faith (Rom. 16. 26).

But because He thus became dependent and obedient, does it mean that He divested Himself of the powers He possessed as God? This is impossible—that He should avail Himself of them only at the will of the Father is possible, but that He should cease to be God in the full sense of the word is unthinkable.

That One should be both Man and God at the same time is the great mystery of our Faith. To deny it is to cease to be a Christian, for this truth is the rock upon which all is built (Matt. 16. 18; 1 John 5. 1; 1 Cor. 3. 11). It is, of course, easy to object thus: because He said, 'The Son can do nothing of Himself,' therefore He was not *omnipotent*; and because He said, 'I am glad I was not there' (John 11. 15), therefore He was not *omnipresent*; and because He knew not the hour (Mark 13. 32), therefore He was not *omniscient*. As well go the whole way and say: 'Because He was man, therefore He was not God,' and deny the great mystery of Godliness. As Martin Luther justly said, 'If there were no mystery, where is the work of faith?'

'Concerning the communion of the natures in this personal union, three things are to be observed,' says Dr. John Owen. '(1) Each nature doth preserve its own natural essential properties entirely unto and in itself; without mixture, without composition or confusion. . . . Unless this be granted, there will not be two natures in Christ, a Divine and a human; nor indeed either of them, but something else composed of both. (2) Each nature operates in Him according unto its essential properties. The divine nature knows all things, upholds all things, rules all things, acts by its presence everywhere; the human nature was born, yielded obedience, died and rose again. But it is the same Person, the same Christ, that acts all these things—the one nature being His no less than the other. Wherefore (3) the perfect complete work of Christ in every act of His mediatorial office—in all that He did as the King, Priest and Prophet of the Church—in all that He did and suffered; in all that He continueth to do for us in or by virtue of whether nature soever it be done or wrought, is not to be considered as the act of this or that nature in Him alone, but it is the act and work of the whole Person of Him that is both God and Man in one Person.'

'Some things in the Scriptures are spoken of the Person of Christ wherever the enunciation is verified with respect unto one nature only, as, "The Word was with God and the Word was God" (John 1. 1). "Before Abraham was I am" (John 8. 58). "Upholding all things by the word of His power" (Heb. 1. 3). These things are spoken of the Person of Christ, but belong unto Him on account of His Divine nature. So it is said of Him, "Unto us a Son is born, unto us a Child is given" (Isa. 9. 6). "A Man of sorrows and acquainted with grief" (Isa. 53. 3). They are spoken of Christ, but are verified in the human nature only and the Person on the account thereof.'

These weighty words will serve to guard us on the one hand from the danger of derogating from His perfect Deity, and on the other of avoiding His perfect Manhood, or worse still, of representing Him as a composite Being, neither perfectly God nor perfectly man, but something novel and unknown to Scripture.

George Goodman

APPENDIX IV

ATONEMENT AND RECONCILIATION

ATONEMENT is not a New Testament doctrine; its place is taken by the far deeper and more radical truth of reconciliation. Unfortunately in the seventeenth century the two words atonement and reconciliation were used practically as equivalents, but there is no possibility of confusion in the language given by the Holy Ghost.

In atonement sins are *covered* and thus hidden from sight, but in reconciliation they are *cancelled*, obliterated, and pass out of existence. In atonement the blood was carried into the sanctuary but was never put upon the sinner; in reconciliation the blood of Jesus Christ, God's Son, cleanses from all sin as well as purifying the heavenly things themselves (Heb. 9). In atonement the heart could rest for a brief period, at most one year, upon the blood of an animal sacrifice; in reconciliation the soul is brought to God in unclouded acceptance and enjoys a title without a flaw. In atonement the priest enters the presence of God, but the worshipper stands outside; in reconciliation the prodigal is brought within the Father's house and is sealed with the Father's kiss. In atonement the sin is removed but the man is unchanged; in reconciliation not only the sin has gone, but the man that did it disappears from before the eye of God and another Man takes his place.

In a sentence, we may sum the matter up by saying that the doctrine of atonement is an inspired foregleam of the forbearance of God in Old Testament times, while the truth of reconciliation is the crown and glory of the Gospel.

A list of New Testament passages in which is the Greek word used as an equivalent for 'atonement' in the Old Testament, will enable readers to verify this:

(1) *hilaskomai*, to make an atonement, occurs in Luke 18. 13, 'God be merciful to me a sinner,' and in Heb. 2. 17, 'To make propitiation for the sins of the people.'

(2) *hilasmos*, that by which atonement is made, is found in 1 John 2. 2, 'And He is the propitiation for our sins,' and in 1 John 4. 10, 'And sent His Son to be the propitiation for our sins.'

(3) *hilasterion*, the actual mercy-seat on which the blood was sprinkled, is used in Rom. 3. 25, 'Christ Jesus whom God set forth to be a propitiation,' and Heb. 9. 5, 'Cherubim of glory overshadowing the mercy-seat.'

HAROLD ST. JOHN

BIBLIOGRAPHY

Books Referred to or Relevant to the Subject

CHAPTER I

Alexander, L. - - - *System of Biblical Theology*
Berkhof, L. - - - *Systematic Theology*
Bernard, T. D. - - - *The Progress of Doctrine*
Cooper, D. L. - - - *What Men Must Believe*
English, E. S. - - - *Things Surely to be Believed*
Hammond, T. C. - - *In Understanding be Men*
Hodge, C. - - - - *Systematic Theology*
Hoste, W. - - - - *Studies in Bible Doctrine*
Moule, H. C. G. - - *Outlines of Christian Doctrine*
Murray, A. - - - *The Spirit of Christ*
Pierson, A. T. - - - *Knowing the Scriptures*
Scott, W. - - - - *Doctrinal Summaries*
Shedd, W. G. T. - - *Dogmatic Theology*
" - - - *History of Christian Doctrine*
Smith, J. P. - - - *First Lines of Christian Theology*
Torrey, R. A. - - - *What the Bible Teaches*

CHAPTER II

Allbright, W. F. - - *From the Stone Age to Christianity*
" - - *Archæology and the Religion of Israel*
Beasley-Murray, G. R. - *Christ is Alive!*
Bentley, G. B. - - - *The Resurrection of the Bible*
Bruce, F. F. - - - *Are the New Testament Documents Reliable?*
Brunner, E. - - - *Revelation and Reason*
Cable, M., and French, F. - *The Book Which Demands a Verdict*
Collett, S. - - - - *The Scripture of Truth*
Cunliffe-Jones, H. - - *The Authority of the Biblical Revelation*
Dodd, C. H. - - - *The Apostolic Preaching and its Development*
" - - - *The Authority of the Bible*
" - - - *History and the Gospel*
Duncan, J. G. - - - *New Light on Hebrew Origins*
Dugmore, C. W. - - *The Interpretation of the Bible*
Fairweather, A. - - - *The Word as Truth*
Finn, A. H. - - - *The Unity of the Pentateuch*
Gaussen, L. - - - *Theopneustia*
Guthrie, C. J. - - - *History of the Reformation in Scotland*
Hebert, A. G. - - - *The Authority of the Old Testament*
" - - - *The Throne of David*
Hunter, A. M. - - - *The Unity of the New Testament*
Jones, J. Morgan - - *The Revelation of God in the Old Testament*
Marston, C. - - - *The Bible is True*
Moule, H. C. G. - - *The Epistle to the Romans*
Ockenga, H. J. - - - *The Word of God and the Reformed Faith*

Orr, J. - - - - *Revelation and Inspiration*
Phillips, G. E. - - - *The Old Testament in the World Church*
Ramsey, A. M. - - - *The Resurrection of Christ*
Richardson, A. - - - *The Miracle Stories of the Gospels*
Robinson, H. W. - - *The Bible in its Ancient and English Versions*
Rowley, H. H. - - - *The Relevance of the Bible*
Saphir, A. - - - - *The Divine Unity of Scripture*
Short, A. R. - - - *Modern Discovery and the Bible*
Stonehouse, N. B., and Woolley, P. - - - *The Infallible Word*
Tasker, R. V. G.- - - *The Old Testament in the New Testament*
Urquhart, J. - - - *Inspiration and Accuracy of the Scriptures*
Warfield, B. B. - - - *Biblical Doctrines*
" - - - *Revelation and Inspiration*
Wright, G. E. - - - *The Challenge of Israel's Faith*
Wright, J. S. - - - *The Authority of the Bible*

CHAPTER III

Bartlett, C. N. - - - *The Triune God*
Brightman, E. S.- - - *The Problem of God*
Charnocke, S. - - - *The Existence and Attributes of God*
Clarke, W. N. - - - *The Christian Doctrine of God*
Cook, J. - - - - *The Trinity and Tritheism*
Hammond, T. C. - - *In Understanding be Men*
Hodge, C. - - - - *Systematic Theology*
Illingworth, J. R.- - - *The Doctrine of the Trinity*
Ironside, H. A. - - - *The Holy Trinity*

CHAPTER IV

Charnocke, S. - - - *The Existence and Attributes of God*
Lofthouse, W. F. - - *The Father and the Son*
Morgan, G. Campbell - *The Teaching of Christ*
Selbie, W. B. - - - *The Fatherhood of God*
Speer, R. E. - - - *God in Christ the Only Revelation of the Fatherhood of God.* ("*The Fundamentals,*" *Vol.* 3)
Westcott, B. F. - - *The Revelation of the Father*

CHAPTER V

Bellett, J. G. - - - *The Son of God*
Boettner, L. - - - *The Person of Christ*
Liddon, H. P. - - - *The Divinity of our Lord*
Mackintosh, H. R. - - *The Person of Christ*
Robinson, W. C. - - *Our Lord*
Smith, W. M. - - - *The Supernaturalness of Christ*
Vine, W. E. - - - *Christ's Eternal Sonship*
Warfield, B. B. - - - *The Lord of Glory*

CHAPTER VI

Bernard, H. N. - - - *The Mental Characteristics of the Lord Jesus Christ*
Cornwell, K. - - - *If not Virgin-Born—What Then?*

Findlay, J. A. - - - *Jesus as They Saw Him*
Gifford, E. H. - - - *The Incarnation*
Machen, J. G. - - - *The Virgin Birth of Christ*
Morgan, G. Campbell - *The Crises of the Christ*
Orr, James - - - *The Virgin Birth of Christ*
Rogers, W. H. - - - *The God-Man*
Tschudy, E. H. - - *The Virgin Birth of Our Lord*
Westcott, B. F. - - *Christus Consummator*

CHAPTER VII

Anselm - - - - *Cur Deus Homo?*
Berkhof, L. - - - *Vicarious Atonement Through Christ*
Borchert, O. - - - *The Original Jesus*
Brunner, E. - - - *The Mediator*
Bushnell, H. - - - *The Vicarious Sacrifice*
Campbell, McL. - - - *The Nature of the Atonement*
Candlish, R. S. - - - *The Atonement*
Cave, S. - - - - *The Doctrine of the Work of Christ*
" - - - - *The Scripture Doctrine of Sacrifice*
Crawford, T. J. - - - *The Doctrine of Holy Scripture Respecting the Atonement*
Dale, R. W. - - - *The Atonement*
Denney, J. - - - - *The Death of Christ*
" - - - - *The Atonement and the Modern Mind*
Fleming, J. D. - - - *Redemption*
Franks, R. S. - - - *The Atonement*
Grant, F. W. - - - *The Atonement*
Guillebaud, H. E. - - *Why the Cross?*
Hammond, T. C. - - *In Understanding be Men*
Hodge, A. A. - - - *The Atonement*
Hoste, W. - - - *Bible Doctrines*
Lamont, D. - - - *God's Word and Man's Response*
Mackintosh, H. R. - - *The Christian Experience of Forgiveness*
Moberley, R. C. - - *Atonement and Personality*
Pierson, G. P. - - - *The Cross of Christ*
Riddell, J. G. - - - *Why Did Jesus Die?*
Thomas, W. H. Griffith - *Christianity is Christ*
Weatherhead, L. - - *A Plain Man Looks at the Cross*
Vine, W. E. - - - *Expository Dictionary to the New Testament*

CHAPTER VIII

Brookes, J. H. - - - *Did Jesus Rise?*
Dobson, C. C. - - - *The Empty Tomb and the Risen Lord*
Edersheim, E. W. - - *Life and Times of Jesus the Messiah*
Hayes, D. A. - - - *The Resurrection Fact*
Johnston, R. D. - - - *Resurrection: Myth or Miracle*
Morrison, C. R. - - *The Proof of Christ's Resurrection*
Moule, H. C. G. - - *Jesus and the Resurrection*

Orr, J. - - - - *The Resurrection of Jesus*
Pierson, A. T. - - - *Many Infallible Proofs*
Ramsey, A. M. - - - *The Resurrection of Christ*
Robinson, W. C. - - *Christ: The Hope of Glory*
Westcott, B. F. - - *The Gospel of the Resurrection*

CHAPTER IX

Machen, J. G. - - - *The Origin of Paul's Religion*
Milligan, W. - - - *The Ascension and Heavenly Priesthood of Our Lord*
Owen, J. - - - - *The Person and Glory of Christ*
Perowne, T. T. - - - *Our High Priest in Heaven*
Robinson, W. C. - - *Christ: The Hope of Glory*
Sanday, W. - - - *Priesthood and Sacrifice*
Swete, H. B. - - - *The Ascended Christ*

CHAPTER X

Bickersteth, E. H. - - *The Spirit of Life*
Cummings, J. E. - - *Through the Eternal Spirit*
Dolman D. H. - - - *Simple Talks on the Holy Spirit*
Frost, H. W. - - - *Who is the Holy Spirit?*
Hammond, T. C. - - *In Understanding be Men*
Houghton, T. - - - *The Holy Spirit*
Kelly, W. - - - *Lectures on the Doctrine of the Holy Spirit*
Kuyper, A. - - - *The Work of the Holy Spirit*
Morgan, G. Campbell - *The Gospel According to John*
" - - - *The Spirit of God*
Moule, H. C. G. - - *Veni Creator*
Murray, A. - - - *The Spirit of Christ*
Pierson, A. T. - - - *The Acts of the Holy Spirit*
Ridout, S. - - - - *The Person and Work of the Holy Spirit*
Simpson, A. B. - - *The Holy Spirit*
Soltau, G. - - - *The Person and Mission of the Holy Spirit*
Thomas, W. H. Griffith - *The Work of the Holy Spirit*
Walvoord, J. F. - - - *The Doctrine of the Holy Spirit*
Wolston, W. P. - - *Another Comforter*

CHAPTER XI

Clark, R. E. D. - - - *Creation*
" - - - - *Darwin: Before and After*
" - - - - *Scientific Rationalism and the Christian Faith*
" - - - - *The Universe: Plan or Accident*
Dawson, J. W. - - - *Modern Science in Bible Lands*
Delitzsch, F. - - - *Genesis*
Dewar, D. - - - - *Difficulties of the Evolution Theory*
" - - - - *More Difficulties of the Evolution Theory*
Fleming, A. - - - *Evolution or Creation*
Graebner, T. - - - *God and the Cosmos*
Hammond, T. C. - - *Reasoning Faith*

Rimmer, H. - - - *The Theory of Evolution and the Facts of Science*
Saunders and Clark - - *Order and Chaos in the World of Atoms*
Short, A. R. - - - *Modern Discovery and the Bible*
Turton, W. H. - - - *The Truth of Christianity*
Wiseman, P. J. - - - *Creation Revealed in Six Days*
" - - - - *New Discoveries in Babylonia About Genesis*

CHAPTER XII

Bishop, T. B. - - - *Evolution Criticised*
Clark, R. E. D. - - - *Darwin: Before and After*
Cooper, D. L. - - - *Man*
Delitzsch, F. - - - *System of Biblical Psychology*
Dewar, D. - - - - *Man: A Special Creation*
Finn, A. H. - - - *Creation, Fall and Deluge*
Gore, C. - - - - *Reconstruction of Belief*
Grant, F. W. - - - *Facts and Theories as to a Future State*
Hammond, T. C. - - *In Understanding be Men*
" - - *Perfect Freedom*
Hodge, C. - - - - *Systematic Theology*
Hoste, W. - - - - *Studies in Bible Doctrine*
MacColl, D. S. - - - *Who Made Man?*
Machen, J. G. - - - *The Christian View of Man*
Mauro, P. - - - - *Evolution at the Bar*
Orr, J. - - - - *God's Image in Man*
Price, G. McC. - - - *The Predicament of Evolution*
Rimmer, H. - - - *Embryology and the Recapitulation Theory*
" - - - *The Theories of Evolution and the Facts of Palæontology*
" - - - *The Theory of Evolution and the Facts of Science*
Wright, G. F. - - - *The Origin and Antiquity of Man*

CHAPTER XIII

Bryan, W. S. P. - - *An Enquiry into our Need of the Grace of God*
Clark, R. E. D. - - - *Conscious and Unconscious Sin*
Drummond, H. - - - *Natural Law in the Spiritual World*
Gracey, D. - - - - *Sin and the Unfolding of Salvation*
Hammond, T. C. - - *In Understanding be Men*
Machen, J. G. - - - *The Christian View of Man*
Muller, J. - - - - *The Christian Doctrine of Sin*
Newman, F. W. - - *The Soul, her Sorrows and Aspirations*
Orr, J. - - - - *Sin as a Problem of To-day*
Rashdall, H. - - - *The Theory of Good and Evil*
Reynolds, E. - - - *On the Sinfulness of Sin*
Sauer, E. - - - - *The Dawn of World Redemption*
Tulloch, J. - - - - *The Christian Doctrine of Sin*
Urquhart, J. - - - *The New Biblical Guide*

CHAPTER XIV

Anderson, R. - - - *For Us Men*
Bushnell, H. - - - *The New Life*
Fleming, J. D. - - - *Redemption*
Hammond, T. C. - - *Perfect Freedom*
Law, R. - - - - *The Tests of Life*
Liddon, H. P. - - - *The Divinity of our Lord*
Machen, J. G. - - - *What is Faith?*
Mackintosh, C. H. - - *Regeneration*
Mackintosh, H. R. - - *The Christian Experience of Forgiveness*
McNicol, J.- - - - *The Christian Evangel*

CHAPTER XV

Anderson, R. - - - *The Gospel and its Ministry*
" - - - *The Way*
Ironside, H. A. - - - *The Eternal Security of the Believer*
" - - - *Full Assurance*
McNicol, J. - - - *The Christian Evangel*
Morgan, G. Campbell - *The Teaching of Christ*
Strombeck, J. F. - - - *Shall Never Perish*
Tatford, F. A. - - - *Early Steps in the Christian Life*

CHAPTER XVI

Anderson, R. - - - *The Gospel and its Ministry*
" - - - *The Silence of God*
Boettner, L. - - - *The Reformed Doctrine of Predestination*
Butler, J. - - - - *The Analogy of Religion*
Guillebaud, H. E. - - *Some Moral Difficulties of the Bible*
Hammond, T. C. - - *In Understanding be Men*
Hodge, A. - - - - *Outline of Theology*
Lamont, D.- - - - *The Anchorage of Life*
Machen, J. G. - - - *The Christian View of Man*
Moule, H. C. G. - - *Outlines of Christian Doctrine*

CHAPTER XVII

Anderson, R. - - - *The Gospel and its Ministry*
Calvin, J. - - - - *Romans*
Godet, F. - - - - *Romans*
Grant, F. W. - - - *The Two Natures and the First Resurrection*
Hodge, C. - - - - *Systematic Theology*
Illingworth, J. R. - - *Christian Character*
Ironside, H. A. - - - *Holiness: The False and the True*
Luther, M. - - - - *Galatians*
MacIlvaine, C. P. - - *Righteousness by Faith*
Moule, H. C. G. - - *Justification by Faith*
Ryle, J. C. - - - - *Holiness*
Thomas, W. H. Griffith - *Grace and Power*
Westcott, F. B. - - *St. Paul's Teaching on Justification*

CHAPTER XVIII

Bevan, Edwyn - - *Christianity*
Dale, R. W. - - - *Essays and Addresses*
Denney, J. - - - - *Studies in Theology*
Eusebius, H. E. - - *Ecclesiastical History*
Goodman, G. - - - *God's Principles of Gathering*
Henson, H. - - *The Church of England*
Hooker, J. - - - - *Ecclesiastical Polity*
Hort, F. J. A. - - - *The Christian Ecclesia*
Hoste, W. - - - - *Bishops, Priests and Deacons*
Hoste, W., and Vine, W. E. *Light for Dark Days*
Jenkins, D. T. - - - *The Nature of Catholicity*
Kelly, W. - - - *Lectures on the Church of God*
Payne, E. A. - - - *The Free Church Tradition in the Life of England*
Short, A. R. - - - *The Principles of Open Brethren*
Stibbs, A. M. - - - *The Church, Universal and Local*
Streeter, B. H. - - - *The Primitive Church*
Stuart, C. E. - - - *Simple Papers on the Church of God*
Thomas, W. H. Griffith - *Principles of Theology*
Underwood, A. C. - - *A History of the English Baptists*
Vine, W. E. - - - *The Church and the Churches*
Watson, J. B. - - - *The Church—A Symposium*
Whale, J. S. - - - *Christian Doctrine*
Whitley, W. T. - - - *A History of British Baptists*

CHAPTER XIX

Bruce, F. F. - - - *The Acts of the Apostles*
Godet, F. - - - - *A Commentary on John's Gospel*
Grimm, C. L. W. - - *Greek-English Lexicon*
Hogg, C. F. - - - *What Saith the Scriptures?*
Kelly, W. - - - *An Exposition of the Acts of the Apostles*
" - - - - *Lectures on the Church of God*
Knowling, R. J. - - - *The Expositors' Greek Testament, Vol.* 4
Machen, J. G. - - - *The Origin of Paul's Religion*
Morgan, G. Campbell - *The Acts of the Apostles*
Moule, H. C. G. - - *The Epistle to the Romans*
Plummer, A. - - - *St. Luke*
" - - - - 1 *Corinthians*
Price, A. - - - - *In the Way of His Steps*
Rackham, R. B. - - - *The Acts of the Apostles*
Ramsay, W. - - - *The Bearing of Recent Discovery on the Trustworthiness of the N.T. Research*
Robertson, A. T.- - - *A Grammar of the Greek N.T. in the Light of Historical Research*
Sanday, W., and Headlam, A. C. *The Epistle to the Romans*
Torrey, R. A. - - - *How to Pray*
Westcott, B. F. - - *St. John's Gospel*
Whyte, A. - - - *Lord, Teach us to Pray*

CHAPTER XX

Anderson, R. - - - - *The Coming Prince*
" - - - - *Daniel in the Critics' Den*
Anstey, M. - - - *The Romance of Bible Chronology*
Cooper, D. L. - - - *The God of Israel*
" - - - *Messiah, His Nature and Person*
De Burgh, W. - - - *The Early Promises of a Redeemer*
Edersheim, E. W. - - *The Laws and Polity of the Jews*
" - - *Sketches of Jewish Social Life*
Harrison, L. Sale - - *The Remarkable Jew*
Moule, H. C. G. - - *Romans*
Ritchie, J. - - - - *From Egypt to Canaan*
Samuel, E. Bendor - - *The Blessing of the Tribes*
Stanley, A. P. - - - *The Jewish Church*
Vine, W. E. - - - *Romans*
Wilkinson, S. H.- - - *The Israel Promises and their Fulfilment*
Wingate, A. - - - *Palestine, Mesopotamia and the Jews*

CHAPTER XXI

Hodge, C. - - - - *Systematic Theology*
Morgan, G. Campbell - *The Teaching of Christ*
Pember, G. A. - - - *Earth's Earliest Ages*
Smith, W. - - - - *Dictionary of the Bible*
Torrey, R. A. - - - *What the Bible Teaches*
Vine, W. E. - - - *Spiritism Unmasked*

CHAPTER XXII

Barry, A. - - - - *Article in Smith's Dictionary of the Bible*
Chafer, L. S. - - - *Satan and the Satanic System*
English, E. S. - - - *Things Surely to be Believed*
Findlay, G. G. - - - *The Epistle to the Ephesians*
Gaebelein, A. C. - - *As it Was—So Shall it Be*
Hodge, C. - - - - *Systematic Theology*
Jennings, F. C. - - - *Satan*
" - - - - *Studies in Isaiah*
Pember, G. A. - - - *Earth's Earliest Ages*
Réville, A. - - - - *The Devil, His Origin, Greatness and Decadence*
Schwarze, C. T. - - - *The Programme of Satan*
Tatford, F. A. - - - *The Person and Work of the Devil*
Torrey, R. A. - - - *What the Bible Teaches*

CHAPTER XXIII

Barth, K. - - - - *The Knowledge of God and the Service of God*
Davies, D. R. - - - *The Two Humanities*
Godet, F. - - - - *Romans*
Grant, F. W. - - - *Man and the Future State*
Hogg, C. F., and Vine, W. E. *Touching the Coming*

Ironside, H. A. - - - *The Great Parenthesis*
Jennings, F. C. - - *Studies in Revelation*
Kelly, W. - - - *Lectures on the Second Coming of our Lord Jesus Christ*
,, - - - - - *Matthew*
McNicol, J.- - - - *The Fundamentals, Vol.* 6
Newell, W. R. - - - *The Revelation*
Sauer, E. - - - - *The Triumph of the Crucified*
Scofield, C. I. - - - *Prophecy Made Plain*
Scott, W. - - - - *Exposition of the Revelation of Jesus Christ*
Tatford, F. A. - - - *Prophecy's Last Word*

CHAPTER XXIV

Anderson, R. - - - *Human Destiny*
Grant, F. W. - - - *Man and the Future State*
Hengstenberg, E. W. - - *The Revelation of St. John*
Kelly, W. - - - *Lectures on the Second Coming of our Lord Jesus Christ*
Mackintosh, H. R. - - *Immortality*
Salmond, S. D. F. - - *The Christian Doctrine of Immortality*
Seiss, J. A. - - - *The Apocalypse*
Tatford, F. A. - - - *Prophecy's Last Word*
Trotter, W. - - - *Plain Papers on Prophetic Subjects*

CHAPTER XXV

Gaussen, L. - - - *Theopneustia*
Pierson, A. T. - - - *Knowing the Scriptures*
Redwood, A. McD. - - *Let the Bible Speak*
Smith, W. M. - - - *Therefore Stand*
Stier, R. - - - - *The Words of the Lord Jesus*
Vine, W. E. - - - *Expository Dictionary of the New Testament*

APPENDICES

Barton, G. A. - - - *Archæology and the Bible*
Bruce, F. F. - - - *Are the New Testament Documents Reliable?*
,, - - - *The Books and the Parchments*
Collett, S. - - - - *The Scripture of Truth*
Deissman, G. A. - - - *Light from the Ancient East*
Hoste, W. - - - - *Studies in Bible Doctrine*
Kenyon, F. - - - *Our Bible and the Ancient Manuscripts*
,, - - - - *The Story of the Bible*
Manley, G. T. - - - *The New Bible Handbook*
Milligan, G. - - - *The New Testament and its Transmission*
Robertson, A. T.- - - *Textual Criticism of the New Testament*
Scott, W. - - - - *The Story of Our English Bible*
Tatford, F. A. - - - *Is the Bible Reliable?*

GENERAL INDEX

SCRIPTURE INDEX

Printed at the Press of the Publishers

Notes